```
HT
690
G7      The Culture of
C84        capital
1987


   $60.00         g   b
```

THE CULTURE OF CAPITAL

edited by JANET WOLFF and JOHN SEED

The culture of capital:
art, power and the nineteenth-century middle class

 MANCHESTER UNIVERSITY PRESS
Distributed exclusively in the USA and Canada by
St. Martin's Press, New York

Copyright © Manchester University Press 1988

Whilst copyright in this volume as a whole is vested in Manchester University Press, copyright in the individual chapters belongs to their respective authors, and no chapter may be reproduced wholly or in part without the express permission in writing of both author and publisher.

Published by Manchester University Press
Oxford Road, Manchester M13 9PL, UK
Distributed exclusively in the USA and Canada
by St. Martin's Press
175 Fifth Avenue, Room 400, New York, NY 10010, USA

British Library cataloguing in publication data
The Culture of capital: art, power and the
  nineteenth-century middle class.
  1. Arts and society — Great Britain —
  History 2. Arts, British 3. Arts,
  Modern — 19th century — Great Britain
  I. Wolff, Janet II. Seed, John
  700'.941 NX180.S6

Library of Congress cataloging in publication data
The Culture of capital.
  1. Middle classes — Great Britain — History — 19th
century — Congresses. 2. Art and society — Great Britain –
History — 19th century — Congresses. I. Wolff, Janet.
II. Seed, John.
HT690.G7C84   1988   305.5'5'0941   88–10982
ISBN 0 7190 2460 9 *hardback*

32872

Typeset in Linotron Ehrhardt
by Northern Phototypesetting Co, Bolton
Printed in Great Britain by
Anchor Brendon Ltd., Tiptree, Essex

CONTENTS

List of illustrations   *page* vi
Notes on contributors   viii
Preface   ix
Introduction *John Seed and Janet Wolff*   1

1. The 'failure' of the Victorian middle class: a critique
   Simon Gunn   17

2. 'Commerce and the liberal arts': the political economy of art in Manchester, 1775–1860 *John Seed*   45

3. Class, culture and control: the Sheffield Athenaeum movement and the middle class *Alan White*   83

4. The culture of separate spheres: the role of culture in nineteenth-century public and private life *Janet Wolff*   117

5. 'Without distinction of party': the Polytechnic Exhibitions in Leeds, 1839–45 *Caroline Arscott*   135

6. Employer, husband, spectator: Thomas Fairbairn's commission of *The Awakening Conscience* *Caroline Arscott*   159

7. The partial view: the visual representation of the early nineteenth-century industrial city *Caroline Arscott and Griselda Pollock with Janet Wolff*   191

Index   235

LIST OF ILLUSTRATIONS
the art section is placed between pp. 178–9

1 F. M. Brown, *Work* (1852–65), Manchester City Art Galleries.
2 W. H. Hunt, *The Awakening Conscience* (1854), Tate Gallery, London.
3 W. H. Hunt, *The Children's Holiday* (1865), from the Torre Abbey Collection, property of the Borough of Torbay.
4 P. H. Calderon, *Broken Vows* (1856), Tate Gallery, London.
5 J. C. Horsley, *Pay for Peeping* (1872), Bradford Art Galleries and Museums.
6 A. Soloman, *First Class – the Meeting: 'And at First Meeting Loved'* (1854), National Gallery of Canada, Ottawa.
7 William Wyld, *Manchester from Kersal Moor* (1851), Royal Collection. Copyright reserved. Reproduced by gracious permission of Her Majesty the Queen.
8 T. Allom, engraved J. Tingle, *Power Loom Weaving*, in E. Baines, *History of the Cotton Manufacture in Great Britain* (1835), Fisher, Son and Co., London, 1835, opp. p. 238.
9 J. Ralston, lithographed J. D. Harding, *Market Place, Manchester*, Plate 2, in *Views of The Ancient Buildings in Manchester* [1823–5], reprinted Hugh Broadbent (ed.), Oldham 1975.
10 J. Ralston, lithographed A. Aglio, *Market Street*, Plate 4 in Broadbent, *op. cit.*
11 T. Taylor, engraved Charles Heath, *The Moot Hall*, published Robinson and Hernaman, Leeds, and J. Hurst, Wakefield, 1 May 1816, and in T. Whitaker (ed.), *Ducatus Leodiensis* (by Ralph Thoresby), 2nd edn, 1816, opp. p. 24.
12 Joseph Rhodes, *The Old Moot Hall*, Leeds (n.d.), Leeds City Museums, Courtauld Institute negative.
13 N. Whittock, engraved J. Rogers, *Corn Exchange, Leeds*, published J. T. Hinton, London 1829, Thoresby Society.
14 J. Greig, *Upper Part of Briggate, formerly called Cross Parish* (1851), watercolour in W. Boyne, grangerised edition of *History of Leeds* (7 vols.) Vol. IV, pp. 2–88, Leeds City Libraries.
15 Engraved Lee, *The Corn-Exchange*, Leeds City Libraries.
16 Trade advertisement for J. W. Bean, in W. White, *Directory and Gazeteer of Leeds... and... the Clothing Districts*, Sheffield 1853.
17 W. Nelson, lithographed G. and J. F. Masser, *Commercial Buildings, Leeds*, in *The Strangers' Guide through Leeds and its Environs*, H. Cullingworth and Son, Leeds, 1842, frontispiece.
18 N. Whittock, engraved J. Rogers, *Commercial Buildings, Leeds*, published J. T. Hinton, London, 1829, Thoresby Society.
19 Harwood and M. J. Starling, *The Exchange, Manchester*, in E. Baines, *op. cit.*, opp. p. 360.
20 Engraved E. J. Roberts, *Court House, Commercial Buildings and Yorkshire*

District Bank, published J. and F. Harwood, London, 11 August, 1842, Leeds City Libraries.
21 N. Whittock, engraved W. Sims, *Court House, Leeds*, published J. T. Hinton, London, 1829, Thoresby Society.
22 N. Whittock, engraved N. Shury, *Central Market, Leeds*, published J. T. Hinton, London, 1828, Thoresby Society.
23 J. N. Rhodes, engraved S. Staers, *The Central Market &c, Leeds, from the end of Cloth Hall Street*, in J. Heaton (publ.), *Walks through Leeds*, Leeds 1835.
24 South view of the mills in Marshall Street, *c.* 1850. Reproduced in W. G. Rimmer, *Marshalls of Leeds, Flax-spinners 1788–1886*, Cambridge University Press, 1960, p. 205.
25. North view of the mills in Marshall Street, *c.* 1850. Rimmer, *op. cit.*, p. 204.
26 Harwood, engraved McGahey, *The Twist Factory, Oxford Street, Manchester*, in T. Allen, *Views in Lancashire*, 1832, opp. p. 41.
27 Austin, engraved McGahey, *Cotton Factories, Union Street, Manchester*, in *Lancashire Illustrated*, 1831, opp. p. 70.
28 N. Whittock, engraved J. Shury, *The Aire and Calder, at Leeds*, published J. T. Hinton, London, 1829, Thoresby Society.
29 T. Allom, engraved J. Tingle, *The Factory of Messrs. Swainson, Birley & Co., near Preston, Lancashire*, in *Lancashire Illustrated*, 1831, opp. p. 185.
30 William Marshall Craig, engraved John Landseer, *Manchester from Mount Pleasant* (1802), Manchester City Art Galleries.
31 Henry Burn, *View of Leeds, from near the Halifax New Road*, published by T. W. Green, Leeds, 1846, Thoresby Society.
32 Joseph Rhodes, *Leeds from the Meadows*, probably *c.* 1820–5, Leeds City Art Galleries.
33 English School, *Manchester from Chester Road*, early nineteenth century, Manchester City Art Galleries.
34 Thomas Burras, *View of Leeds* (1844), Thoresby Society.
35 *Ibid.*, detail.
36 Robert Buttery, etched J. W. Cook, engraved R. C. Reeve, *Leeds taken from Beeston Hill* (1833), Thoresby Society.
37 Alphonse Dousseau, *Leeds from Rope Hill* (1827–31), Leeds City Museums.
38 J. M. W. Turner, *Leeds* (1816), Yale Center for British Art, Paul Mellon Collection.

NOTES ON CONTRIBUTORS

CAROLINE ARSCOTT
is a Research Assistant in the Department of Fine Art and a former Research Assistant in the Department of Sociology at the University of Leeds. She is currently completing a Ph.D. thesis on modern life subjects in early Victorian painting.

SIMON GUNN
is a Fellow at the Institute of Historical Research at the University of London. He is completing a Ph.D. thesis at the University of Manchester on the middle class in mid-nineteenth-century Manchester.

GRISELDA POLLOCK
is a Senior Lecturer in the Department of Fine Art, University of Leeds. She is the author of a number of books and articles, particularly on Van Gogh, nineteenth-century French art, and women and art.

JOHN SEED
is a Senior Lecturer in Modern History at the Roehampton Institute of Higher Education in London, and Review Editor of *Social History*. He has published a number of articles on religion and the nineteenth-century middle class.

ALAN WHITE
is a Lecturer in Sociology at North-East London Polytechnic. He is currently completing a Ph.D. at the University of Leeds on the nineteenth-century middle class in Sheffield.

JANET WOLFF
is Reader in the Sociology of Culture at the University of Leeds. She is the author of a number of books and articles on the sociology of the arts, sociological theory, and gender and culture.

PREFACE

The work for the essays in this book (apart from Chapter 1) was carried out with the assistance of the Economic and Social Research Council, who provided a personal research grant for a pilot study by Janet Wolff in 1979, a project grant for the period 1982–5 and a 'linked' studentship. Janet Wolff was Director of the research, John Seed was its Research Fellow for eighteen months, Caroline Arscott its Research Assistant for twenty-one months, and Alan White held the studentship. Griselda Pollock was associated with the work of the project throughout this period, particularly through the fortnightly seminar held to discuss topics related to the research. We would like to thank all those who participated in that seminar, particularly Hilary Diaper and Paul Street, who were regular attenders.

In May 1983 a two-day seminar was held at the University of Leeds on nineteenth-century middle-class culture. We would like to thank those who participated in this event, and to acknowledge the importance of that seminar for our ideas and continuing discussions. Apart from those already associated with the project, the participants were Philip Corrigan, Leonore Davidoff, John Field, Robbie Gray, Catherine Hall, Patrick Joyce, Bob Morris and John Oakley. Simon Gunn's association with the research started somewhat later, and developed from common interests in the study of the nineteenth-century middle class and its culture.

Part of the preliminary work for this research was undertaken by Janet Wolff when she held the Simon Marks Research Fellowship at the University of Manchester in 1980, and we would like to thank the Department of Sociology there for their support. We would also like to thank the Department of Sociology at the University of Leeds, which housed the research project and provided support and assistance of various kinds. Finally, we are grateful to Margaret Gothelf and Carol Peaker, who typed most of the text for this book, and helped us with the word processor.

The editors gratefully acknowledge the financial assistance of the University of Leeds in the preparation and publication of this book.

Janet Wolff and John Seed
Leeds and London, September 1986

JOHN SEED and JANET WOLFF

Introduction

I

For Marx, the nineteenth-century bourgeoisie, whose advance guard, of course, were the British, was a revolutionary class of world-transforming character. 'The bourgeoisie, historically, has played a most revolutionary part', the *Communist Manifesto* declared in 1848:

> The bourgeoisie cannot exist without constantly revolutionising the instruments of production, and thereby the relations of production, and with them the whole relations of society... All fixed, fast-frozen relations, with their train of ancient and venerable prejudices and opinions, are swept away, all new-formed ones become antiquated before they can ossify. All that is solid melts into air, all that is holy is profaned, and man is at last compelled to face with sober senses, his real conditions of life, and his relations with his kind.[1]

Other contemporaries were no less certain of the historical significance of the bourgeoisie and the new industrial order it represented, whether they approved of it or detested it. For modern historians, nineteenth-century Britain – workshop of the world and shining beacon of Liberalism and free trade – has often provided the exemplar of the modernising, industrialising nation with which others have been compared unfavourably. While other European nations were plagued by revolution, by right-wing coup and popular uprising, by a militant working class and a recalcitrant peasantry, by retarded economic development or too precipitate an economic growth, culminating sometimes in a collapse into communism or fascism in the early twentieth century, Britain seemed to provide the very model of appropriate economic and political development. And it was the strength of the British middle class, in contrast to their continental equivalents, which was of decisive significance. There alone the middle class stamped its authority on the whole social order. Britain, by the mid-nineteenth century, was 'a middle-class nation'.[2]

Yet in recent years the *failure* of the bourgeoisie in Britain, rather than its success, has become a predominant theme. 'Somewhere in the nineteenth century (though there are earlier signs) the English middle class lost its nerve, socially, and thoroughly compromised with the class it had virtually defeated', Raymond Williams proposed in 1961.[3] In his article 'Origins of the present crisis', three years later, Perry Anderson went further and provided an historical analysis of four centuries of British development in which the failure of the industrial bourgeoisie was a central issue.[4] Anderson argued that the English revolution of the 1640s was premature, giving rise to a dynamic agrarian capitalism in which the landed aristocracy remained hegemonic. Thus the emergent bourgeoisie did not (as in France) confront feudal barriers to growth. After winning the Great Reform Act of 1832 and the repeal of the Corn Laws, the bourgeoisie became subsumed as a junior partner within the ruling class. What determined this incorporation?

> Undisturbed by a feudal state, terrified of the French Revolution and its own proletariat, mesmerised by the prestige and authority of the landed class, the bourgeoisie won two modest victories, lost its nerve and ended by losing its identity. The late Victorian era and the high noon of imperialism welded aristocracy and bourgeoisie together in a single social bloc.[5]

Three main factors in the failure of the British bourgeoisie can be adduced from this analysis. First was the lack of a feudal state, which through its parasitic appropriations of social wealth and its repressive interventions in civil affairs might have forced the bourgeoisie into direct confrontation. Secondly, the violent denouement of the revolution in France generated panic about popular mobilisation against the status quo and encouraged a degree of *rapprochement* with the landed classes in government. The kind of radical movements in which working class and middle class were allied, such as recurred in nineteenth-century France, were thus vetoed in Britain. Thirdly, there was the simple cultural dominance of the aristocracy, and the utter failure of the bourgeoisie to construct ideological alternatives which could have become hegemonic.

It is this last point which is one of our central concerns in these pages. For Anderson, the English bourgeoisie in the nineteenth century was culturally and intellectually null. Utilitarianism was, he argues, 'the one authentic, articulated ideology with universal claims' produced by the

English bourgeoisie. 'This played an extremely important role in the early decades of industrialization, as a militant, single-minded creed of capital accumulation and cultural nihilism.'

However, utilitarianism was intrinsically incapable of becoming a hegemonic ideology: 'Its fanatically bleak materialism ipso facto precluded it from creating that cultural and value system which is the mark of a hegemonic ideology.' Instead, some time around mid-century there was a fusion of aristocratic traditionalism and bourgeois empiricism. 'A comprehensive, coagulated conservatism is the result, covering the whole of society with a thick pall of simultaneous philistinism (towards ideas) and mystagogy (towards institutions) . . .'[6]

Depite a blistering reply from Edward Thompson in 'The peculiarities of the English'[7] which did extensive damage to important aspects of Anderson's analysis, these kinds of assessment of the English middle class have continued to circulate. Indeed, in many respects they have become a new intellectual orthodoxy in some – predominantly Conservative – political circles. Historians too have argued along the same lines about the inherent emptiness of bourgeois culture in nineteenth-century Britain. Thus Igor Webb sees the Gothic architecture of the new Bradford Wool Exchange of the 1860s as an index of the failure of northern industrialists to develop their own cultural styles: 'Their sense of social inferiority and political illegitimacy, their suspicion of art, their willingness to participate in an essentially aristocratic nostalgia for the past, hindered the creation of an architecture truly expressive of industrial capitalism and helped make way for the triumph of Gothic.' Mid-nineteenth-century industrial capital lacked, according to Webb, 'a coherent cultural image in which art and society reinforced one another'. The landed estate, the ethics of paternalism and traditional cultural styles of the English aristocracy, offered an alternative 'cultural image' with which industrialists were eager to identify themselves.[8]

Martin Wiener in his *English Culture and the Decline of the Industrial Spirit 1850–1980* has pushed this kind of argument further, and traced the economic decline of modern Britain to the cultural subordination of the industrial middle class to the values of land, tradition and so on. 'As a rule', he writes, 'leaders of commerce and industry in England over the past century have accommodated themselves to an elite culture blended of preindustrial aristocratic and religious values and more recent professional and bureaucratic values that inhibited their quest for expansion, productivity and profit.'[9] His argument follows that of Anderson very closely. He argues that in the late eighteenth century the explosive growth of industrial wealth disrupted the continuity of British history. There emerged a class of *nouveaux riches* who were both outside of and opposed to established social elites. This was the industrial bourgeoisie of the north and of religious dissent, the central protagonists of parliamentary reform and of the Anti-Corn Law League – two symbolic moments in the weakening of aristocratic power. But in the second half of the century, the antagonism of land and industry began to dissolve. Instead, the industrial bourgeoisie was 'gentrified': 'As capitalists became landed gentlemen, JPs, men of breeding, the radical ideal of active capital was submerged in the conservative ideal of passive property, and the urge to enterprise faded beneath the preference for stability.'[10] Instead of the active and ferocious pursuit of profit, the industrial bourgeoisie opted for the lifestyles of landed gentlemen. Industry, technology, applied science, remained low-status activities, overshadowed by the glories of tradition, the classics, Oxbridge, the professions.

Central to the accounts of bourgeois failure in the work of Anderson, Webb and Wiener is a model of industrial bourgeois culture as a thin and acrid brew of utilitarianism, religious dissent and anti-aristocratic sentiment in the years until mid-century, followed by a lapse into false consciousness, a general subordination to aristocratic culture. What are these historical judgements based on? Partly, they are based on some very crude assumptions about the ways in which particular discourses (political economy, utilitarianism) or particular architectural styles (Gothic) belong to particular classes and express their consciousness. In fact there is nothing inherently aristocratic about Gothic architecture. Bradford Wool Exchange and Manchester Town Hall are not monuments to bourgeois false consciousness or cultural subordination.[11] Nor did the industrial middle class subjectively inhabit the categories elaborated by Bentham, Malthus or Ricardo. Partly, too, these arguments are based on secondary sources of the period: the cultural criticism of writers like Pugin, Arnold and Ruskin, or the fictions of Dickens, Disraeli, Mrs Gaskell and so on. There has generally been little attempt to penetrate beyond these kinds of important but partial sources.

The received picture of the philistine, Nonconformist, Liberal, northern middle class has been reinforced by a long tradition of writings on 'the entrepreneur', from Samuel Smiles and Andrew Ure to recent meditations on Britain's impending economic demise. There the argument has been primarily concerned with the causes of the Industrial Revolution, among which, it has been held, the innovatory mentality of the entrepreneur was crucial. As Bergier puts it, 'the entrepreneur is a man with an original mental, not to say moral, make-up'.[12] He is an innovator bringing to fruition new forms of technology, new modes of organising production, new methods of managing labour. As such, the entrepreneur was a dynamic force for economic and social change. But Promethean force though he may have been, economic historians have found little to admire in his extra-economic activities. As an influential economic history text-book of the 1930s (still in print in the 1960s) commented:

> Apart from their ability as men of business they were not remarkable, as a class for general intelligence... Most of the manufacturers were ill-educated, coarse and rough, with an extremely limited range of ideas; intellectually they were in most cases not markedly distinguishable from their foremen, save in the knowledge of business method and their ruthless determination to make money quickly.[13]

For others too the entrepreneurs of the Industrial Revolution combined an immense economic energy with a profound philistinism. For Halèvy, for instance, the new industrialists were 'a class of austere men, hard-workers and greedy of gain, who considered it their twofold duty to make a fortune in business and to preach Christ crucified'.[14] Historians in recent years have been similarly negative in their assessments. The industrialists were, says Sydney Checkland, 'too often philistines or imitators, unable to develop their own cultural expression to fill the gap left by the destruction of agrarian society'.[15]

There have been, then, two separate and yet, in this instance, remarkably convergent lines of enquiry into nineteenth-century Britain: one reaching its apogee in English cultural criticism, the other in the austere prose of the *Economic History Review*. Together these have constructed an image of the industrial middle class as the apotheosis of Acquisitive Man, the embodiment of an economic rationality transcending its cultural and moral context – until about 1850. (It is a remarkable coincidence that Anderson, Wiener and others locate the moment of cultural and moral collapse of the bourgeoisie in the mid-nineteenth century. This of course is precisely the historical moment of the demise of Chartism and the incorporation of the working class within a new hegemony of industrial capital. It is a coincidence which suggests that more is involved in this mid-century restructuring of class relations than loss of middle-class 'nerve'.)[16]

The theoretical and empirical shortcomings of these accounts and approaches are manifold; some of them are discussed in Chapter 1. There are a few points worth making briefly here. First, any simplistic notion of an entrepreneurial mentality disintegrates when we actually begin to focus closely on the first generation or two of industrial capitalists. The first generation of cotton masters in Lancashire was characterised by a striking variety of social and educational backgrounds, and every kind of religious and political avocation. They were as likely to be true-blue English Tories of the old school, port-drinking, fox-hunting, Anglican traditionalists as puritanical, Nonconformist, Liberal reformists with a bent for applied science. Of the three largest cotton-spinning firms in the Manchester area in 1833, two – Houldsworth's and Birley's – were headed by Tory Anglicans. Thomas Houldsworth was a racehorse owner and Tory MP, bitterly opposed to repeal of the Corn Laws: a victim of false consciousness indeed. Success as an entrepreneur in the early textile industry clearly did not depend upon a particular kind of entrepreneurial mentality or 'enterprise culture'.[17]

A second problem has to do with the way that the figure of the entrepreneur has often been casually superimposed over the complex structure of the middle class in nineteenth-century towns. In the first place, this focus omits women; the middle class becomes defined in such a way as to include only men. Secondly, even in the classical manufacturing town of the Industrial Revolution, such as Bradford, Stockport or Oldham, the middle class was a much wider grouping than simply industrial employers; it included lawyers and doctors, merchants and agents, as well as the occasional prosperous shopkeeper. In the case of larger commercial centres like Manchester or Leeds this is even more important. As a commercial centre of international significance, Manchester had a very substantial bourgeoisie who were not industrial employers: professional groups, bankers, wholesalers and merchants of all kinds, agents and financiers. By 1851 there were 214 lawyers and barristers, 381 physicians and surgeons, sixteen bankers, and nearly 1,500 men working in the commercial sector as merchants, brokers, agents, accountants, and so on. Of course, this is not to deny the central shaping significance of industrialisation in the social formation of Manchester in this period, or the manifold ways in which even professional groups were integrated into an economic structure in which, from the 1820s, industrial capital was predominant. Notions of the professional middle class as an almost watertight social compartment, contiguous with but separate from industrialists and merchants, cannot be sustained.[18] Doctors and lawyers were often deeply imbricated in the circuits of industrial capital, investing in local business, involving themselves in the property market, interconnected with local firms by family and marriage, and so on (not to mention the role of the legal system in securing the very conditions which made trade and the accumulation of capital possible). Similarly, in the case of merchants and commercial agents of all kinds, no simple sociological division can be drawn between 'commerce' and 'industry'. The middle class in northern industrial towns was not a group of male 'entrepreneurs', but a complex and variegated social grouping, in which manufacturing, commercial and now beginning to take culture seriously.[25] This collection of essays is a contribution to that development.

The art-historical establishment has been rather more resistant to change, particularly in the English-speaking world. Writers like Hadjinicolaou[26] and T. J. Clark[27] have argued since the early 1970s against the history of art as the history of style or the history of artists, abstracted from social, political and economic conditions. Instead, they have been urging a *social* history of art, one which takes into account the social relations of patronage, art training and access to artistic production, and conditions of distribution and reception. Moreover, social historians of art now insist that discussion of the works themselves can only be in terms of ideology and representation. (Here the influence of structuralist and semiotic theories has been vital.) Paintings are analysed as the production of complex sets of social and power relations, made available through a variety of institutions and mediators, and viewed and interpreted in specific social circumstances; they are also seen as articulating ideological and other extra-aesthetic factors, through equally complex and diverse visual codes. This rejection of the notion of the total autonomy of art – the point where the social history of art meets the sociology of art – is not, however, a licence to practise a crude sociologism, in which art is nothing but the reflection of social structure or social practices. The best kind of social history of art is able to comprehend the interplay between art and social structure. It is also sensitive to the ways in which culture plays an active and constitutive role in the reproduction of social life.

Although this volume is primarily concerned with the visual arts, it is worth pointing out that many of these same arguments apply to literature, music and the other arts. (Indeed, at an early stage of the research project out of which this book has arisen, it seemed possible to study culture in nineteenth-century northern England in a far more wide-ranging way, looking for example at the Gentlemen's Concerts, and the formation of the Hallé Orchestra in 1848 in Manchester, local writers like Mrs Gaskell, popular cultural forms like choral singing and brass bands, and even the striking and impressive architecture of industrial capitalism – warehouses, factories, civic buildings. There was clearly a cultural revolution as well as an economic and social one during this period. However, although we have looked fairly closely at certain cultural institutions in Manchester, Leeds and Sheffield, it became clear that it would be too ambitious a project to look at the various arts and to do justice to them all. Despite parallels and similarities in development and theme, and despite a good deal of 'intertextuality' across forms, very different factors operated in the social relations of, say, writing and painting. Our emphasis, then, is primarily –

though not exclusively – on the visual arts.) Critical developments in art history have been matched by similar critiques in literary studies, where the 'great tradition' has been subject to interrogation, and the social, institutional and ideological processes which have produced it as 'great' have been closely and critically examined.[28] Here, too, critical literary criticism meets the sociology of literature (at least in some of its forms), as manifested in numerous interdisciplinary conferences and journals. And in the case of both art and literature the sociological or socio-historical approach for the first time enables us to consider the relationship between 'high' art and popular culture, perceiving both the interplay of theme and reference between the two and also the extra-aesthetic forces which produce this hierarchy and justify it in purely aesthetic terms. (Chapter 7, which deals with images of the city, is thus able to discuss works by Turner and other artists as well as engravings and book illustrations.)

So far, we have suggested that the study of both history and art history has been coming closer to the concerns of sociology. At the same time, sociology itself has been subject to a number of criticisms, in response to which it has begun to learn and to borrow from other disciplines. The nineteenth-century classic texts of sociology, particularly the work of Marx and Weber, were inbued with a thoroughly historical perspective. However, sociology in general has tended, during this century, to present a rather static model of society, whether on a macro- or micro-level, whether positivistic, interpretative or structural in orientation. It is now argued by some authors that sociology should rediscover the older historical tradition, and that even the sociological study of contemporary institutions and structures must be informed by the historical imagination.[29]

The sociology of the arts is a rather different case. It has tended (at least in Britain, though not in the USA) to be more interdisciplinary in practice, sociologists of art and literature working closely with literary critics and social historians of art. It has also been influenced by, or even formed in, Marxist cultural theory to an extent which has no parallel in other areas within sociology. And it has devoted a great deal of its energies to questions of theory, rather than empirical analysis. (There are of course, many exceptions to this generalisation, particularly in media studies, but also in the sociology of literature.[30]) Even where studies in the sociology of literature have produced close textual analysis, it has not been common, at least until recently, to go beyond a sociologically informed reading of those texts to an investigation of the actual relations of their production, distribution and consumption. In the last few years, sociologists of culture have begun to engage in work which examines the social processes and institutions of the arts in relation to their ideological character, getting away from the debates of the 1970s about culture and structure, base and superstructure and other more abstract issues, whose clarification was crucial, but whose resolution in *a priori* terms turned out to be impossible.[31] In this, the historical development of cultural institutions is central to any such study. We see this book as also participating in this work.

The convergence of a number of disciplines is thus the result of a history which acknowledges the social, and which also recognises the centrality of culture in social life; of an art history which is prepared to comprehend the location of visual texts in specific social and ideological relations; and of a sociology of art which operates with a historical imagination, which is sensitive to texts and their meanings, and which is able to combine conceptual clarity with theoretically-informed empirical study. The more traditional or mainstream approaches in each discipline would not only produce an impoverished or distorted account of their subject matter; they would also be constitutionally blind to certain key concepts and issues. One of the most important of these is the question of gender. We would argue that it is only by taking an interdisciplinary approach that gender inequalities in society, and the representation of women in art, can be properly understood. Sociology can describe the role and position of men and women in society, but only with a historical perspective can it grasp the origin, and hence the present tendencies, of these factors. Art history or criticism can analyse the ways in which women are depicted in art, but only with a sociological understanding can it account for this representation adequately, or in appropriate terms. Historians may notice how few women are visible in history, but it is only a social-historical perspective (informed by a sensitivity to the role of culture in social process) which will enable them to explain these absences and to begin to remedy them. Hence in this volume we address questions of gender in the context of our examination of class and culture (directly in Chapter 4, but also in Chapters 6 and 7). It is no accident that the new areas of study and research of cultural studies, social history and women's studies are fundamentally and necessarily interdisciplinary. They are founded on the clear knowledge that their subject-matter and problematic cannot be contained within one discipline, or even allocated piecemeal, for different purposes, to a number of disciplines. Our argument here has been that, as with gender, the investigation of class and culture must be conducted in a collaboration across disciplines, and must be cognisant of both theoretical debates and the need for careful empirical research.

III

The seven essays which follow, though in many ways rather disparate, have a common set of concerns which we have attempted to identify in this introduction. Specifically these can be summarised as: (1) the nature and specific identity of the urban industrial bourgeoisie in the first two-thirds of the nineteenth century, and the role of culture in the formation of that class; (2) the relationship between class and gender in this period; (3) types of visual representation and their relationship to social groups and processes. Simon Gunn's chapter examines critically the thesis that the urban industrial middle class 'failed': that it remained, or became, subservient to the landed interest and finance capital. He shows that this thesis is founded on very tenuous and misleading evidence, and he argues that the new middle class did indeed have its own identity and did achieve and retain social as well as economic dominance. John Seed challenges the common view of the bourgeois class as uncultured and philistine, providing plenty of evidence of the involvement of members of this class in the art market of Manchester, as patrons and as founders and members of important cultural institutions. He also stresses the importance of the political economy of art – particularly the constitution and operation of the art market – in tracing out the cultural formation of the middle class in a precise urban context.

Alan White's essay pursues the theme of the importance of culture to the life of the bourgeoisie. In a study of the two Athenaeums set up in Sheffield in the mid-nineteenth century, he demonstrates the political, ideological and social roles played by what were essentially cultural institutions. He shows too the complex and subtle tensions within the middle class. Caroline Arscott, in Chapter 5, also rejecting the notion of the philistinism of the bourgeoisie, examines its involvement in the Polytechnic Exhibitions in Leeds in the mid-nineteenth century, and shows how here culture is put to work in the interests of that class.

Janet Wolff considers the relationship between class and gender in the nineteenth century, addressing particularly the question of 'public' and 'private' spheres. She argues that culture and the arts were central to the process of sex segregation (itself closely related to class development in that period), and that the arts both reflect those social divisions and operate to constitute and reinforce them. In Caroline Arscott's Chapter 6 a more detailed examination of these processes is presented, in the case of Thomas Fairbairn's commission of Holman Hunt's *The Awakening Conscience*. The essay concentrates on the class location of the patron, and its connection with the commission and the work, but it also addresses the question of gender ideology and its representation in this and other paintings. Finally, Chapter 7 looks in some detail at a range of representations of the industrial city (in doing so, refuting the art-historical orthodoxy which maintains that there were very few such representations). The authors argue that these images must be read in the context of other discourses about the city, and that they are deeply enmeshed in the real relations of class and gender.

The forms and cultural practices of the middle class in the first two-thirds of the nineteenth century were immensely complex – far more so than the received picture of the dour, Nonconformist, philistine entrepreneurs suggests. What was the place of art within the institutional structure of northern towns? In what ways were some of the ideological presuppositions and social values of middle-class men and women realised in cultural practices? Is it possible to identify a class project in such institutions or in various forms of representation, or are we rather looking at a profoundly divided and fragmented class? If we reject simplistic models of middle-class culture such as inform much of the historiography of this period, is it possible to begin to construct a more viable model? The essays in this book address these questions, attempting, in doing so, to explore new issues, but always conscious of the need for caution and for continual reassessment in an area which has only just begun to be investigated.

Notes

1. K. Marx and F. Engels, *The Communist Manifesto [1848]*, in D. Fernbach (ed.), *Karl Marx: the Revolutions of 1848, Political Writings* I, 1973, p. 70.
2. The term used in both J. F. C. Harrison (ed.), *Society and Politics in England 1780–1960*, New York, 1965, p. 50, and E. Weber, *Europe since 1715: A Modern History*, New York, 1972, p. 375.
3. Raymond Williams, *The Long Revolution*, 2nd edn, 1965, p. 346.
4. Perry Anderson, 'Origins of the present crisis', *New Left Review*, 23, 1964, pp. 26–54.
5. Anderson, 'Origins', p. 29.
6. Anderson, 'Origins', pp. 31–2, 41.
7. E. P. Thompson, 'The peculiarities of the English', *Socialist Register*, 1965, pp. 311–62, reprinted with earlier editorial cuts restored in *The Poverty of Theory and Other Essays*, 1978. For two useful accounts of this exchange and its wider implications see Richard Johnson, 'Barrington Moore, Perry Anderson and English social development', *Working Papers in Cultural Studies*, 9, 1976, pp. 7–28; and K. Nield, 'A symptomatic dispute? Notes on the relation between Marxian theory and historical practice in Britain', *Social Research*, 47, 1980, pp. 479–506.
8. I. Webb, 'The Bradford Wool Exchange: industrial capitalism and the popularity of Gothic', *Victorian Studies*, 20, 1976, pp. 45, 52–5.
9. Martin J. Wiener, *English Culture and the Decline of the Industrial Spirit, 1850–1980*, Cambridge, 1981, p. 127.
10. *Ibid.*, p. 14. But for the wider debate about the structural roots of British

economic decline in the nineteenth century see the following: R. Church (ed.), *The Dynamics of Victorian Business. Problems and Perspectives to the 1870s*, 1980; D. N. McCloskey, *Enterprise and Trade in Victorian Britain, Essays in Historical Economics*, 1981, Chs. 3 and 5; B. Elbaum and W. Lazonick (eds.), *The Decline of the British Economy*, Oxford, 1986; K. Burgess, 'Did the Victorian economy fail?', in T. Gourvish (ed.), *Late Victorian Britain*, forthcoming 1987. See also C. Hampden-Turner, *Gentlemen and Tradesmen. The Values of Economic Catastrophe*, 1983, which brings 'catastrophe theory' to bear on the British economy, an approach which at least sounds appropriate to its object.

11 For an excellent study of Victorian appropriations of the past see C. Dellheim, *The Face of the Past. The Preservation of the Medieval Inheritance in Victorian England*, Cambridge, 1982, especially Chs. 4 and 5, which provide some salutary criticisms of Wiener.

12 J. F. Bergier, *The Industrial Bourgeoisie and the Rise of the Working Class 1700–1914*, trans. R. Greaves, 1971.

13 A. Redford, *The Economic History of England (1760–1860)*, 1931, p. 45.

14 E. Halèvy, *England in 1815. A History of the English People in the Nineteenth Century*, 1, trans. E. I. Watkin and D. A. Barker, 2nd revised edn, 1949, p. 284.

15 S. G. Checkland, *The Rise of Industrial Society in England 1815–85*, 1971, pp. 296, 300.

16 Of course it is notions of 'labour aristocracy' which have dominated recent accounts of working-class incorporation in the 1850s; see especially John Foster, *Class Struggle and the Industrial Revolution: Early Industrial Capitalism in Three English Towns*, 1974, and R. Q. Gray, *The Labour Aristocracy in Victorian Edinburgh*, Oxford, 1976. For an attempt at the beginnings of an explanation of shifts within the middle class, see J. Seed, 'Unitarianism, political economy and the antinomies of liberal culture in Manchester, 1830–50', *Social History*, 7, 1982, pp. 1–25.

17 The two most recent accounts of the familial, social, educational, religious and political characteristics of early industrialists are: A. Howe, *The Cotton Masters 1830–60*, Oxford, 1984; and F. Crouzet, *The First Industrialists. The Problem of Origins*, Cambridge, 1985.

18 Note that Harold Perkin, who stresses very strongly the divergence between the 'ideals' of the business class and the professional class, dates the origins of that divergence to the mid-twentieth century with the rapid growth in numbers of the latter and, beginning with the British Medical Association in 1856, the emergence of professional organisation. Prior to this, he argues, the industrial and professional middle class shared a similar economic, political and ideological position. Harold Perkin, *The Origins of Modern English Society 1780–1880*, 1969, pp. 428–9.

19 For some recent work on the social and economic formation of the middle class, see Patrick Joyce, *Work, Society and Politics. The Culture of the Factory in Later Victorian England*, 1980, Ch. 1; R. J. Morris, 'The middle class and British towns and cities of the Industrial Revolution, 1780–1850', in D. Fraser and A. Sutcliffe (eds.), *The Pursuit of Urban History*, 1983; and John Field, 'Wealth, styles of life and social tone amongst Portsmouth's middle class, 1800–75', in R. J. Morris (ed.), *Class, Power and Social Structure in British Nineteenth-Century Towns*, Leicester, 1986.

20 See J. Morley, *The Life of Richard Cobden*, 1903, pp. 892–3, and G. Saintsbury, *Manchester*, 1887, p. 109.

21 See J. Tait, *The Chetham Society: A Retrospect*, Chetham Miscellanies, new

series, 7, 1939.
22 Peter Burke, *Sociology and History,* Allen & Unwin, London, 1980, pp. 23–7.
23 Introduction to John Merriman (ed.), *Consciousness and Class Experience in Nineteenth-Century Europe,* New York, 1979, p. 8.
24 For example, Richard Johnson et al. (eds.), *Making Histories. Studies in History-Writing and Politics,* Centre for Contemporary Cultural Studies, University of Birmingham, Hutchinson, London, 1982
25 See, for example, Gareth Stedman Jones, *Languages of Class. Studies in English Working Class History 1832–1982,* Cambridge, 1983; John Clarke et al. (eds.), *Working Class Culture. Studies in History and Theory,* Centre for Contemporary Cultural Studies, University of Birmingham, Hutchinson, London, 1979.
26 Nicos Hadjinicolaou, *Art History and Class Struggle,* Pluto, London, 1978.
27 T. J. Clark, *Image of the People. Gustave Courbet and the 1848 Revolution,* Thames & Hudson, London, 1973, Ch. 1, 'On the social history of art'; also 'The conditions of artistic creation', *Times Literary Supplement,* 24 May 1974.
28 Terry Eagleton, *The Function of Criticism. From* The Spectator *to Post-Structuralism,* Verso, London, 1984; Peter Widdowson (ed.), *Re-reading English,* Methuen, London, 1982; Tony Davies, 'Education, ideology and literature', *Red Letters,* 7, 1978, reprinted in Tony Bennett et al. (eds.), *Culture, Ideology and Social Process,* Open University, 1981.
29 Peter Burke, *op. cit.;* Philip Abrams, *Historical Sociology,* Open Books, 1982.
30 See, for example, the essays in James Curran et al. (eds.), *Mass Communication and Society,* Open University, 1977. For work in the sociology of literature, see Peter H. Mann, *From Author to Reader. A Social Study of Books,* Routledge & Kegan Paul, London, 1982, and J. A. Sutherland, *Fiction and the Fiction Industry,* Athlone Press, London, 1978, two studies of literature and its institutions, though not ones informed by theoretical developments.
31 For example, Michèle Barrett et al., 'Representation and cultural production', in Michèle Barrett et al. (eds.), *Ideology and Cultural Production,* Croom Helm, London, 1979; Janet Wolff, 'The problem of ideology in the sociology of art: a case study of Manchester in the nineteenth century', *Media, Culture & Society,* Vol. 4, No. 1, 1982

The 'failure' of the Victorian middle class: a critique

The absence of a coherent social history of the British middle class has become ever more conspicuous as, with growing precision and sophistication, labour historians have reconstructed the experience and historical trajectory of the working class. This neglect has become simultaneously less and less defensible. For if at one time most history was middle-class history, as many historians have pointed out, it is no longer justifiable to equate it with the history of the middle class *per se*. As John Field has remarked, 'to write the history of working people alone, on the grounds that the history of the influential has already been written, is by implication to accept the existing histories of the influential'.[1]

The persistence of representations of the Victorian middle class as provincial Gradgrinds, locked in the dour pursuit of 'Facts' and profit margins, is one of the more striking examples of this historiographical acquiescence.[2] It is not merely that such representations are empirically defective. More important, this recourse to figurative and psychological stereotypes represents an evasion of the real problems involved in more scrupulous class analysis. It is impossible to conceive this order of caricature passing for analysis, for example, in contemporary debates in labour history or popular culture.

This is not to suggest that the nineteenth-century middle class has been entirely overlooked in the last twenty years. Important contributions have been made in political, social, and women's history, sufficient of late to indicate a minor revival of interest.[3] But the tendency has been for research to proceed discreetly, rarely seeking a more ambitious historical synthesis, while coverage remains very uneven. Significant areas are still virtual *terra incognita* in terms of research: the role of the City or the Church of England, the middle-class experience of work, bourgeois perceptions of class and society.[4] In important respects, therefore, the totalising aspiration of social history stands unfulfilled while the elementary constituents of such an enterprise, the formation and culture of the middle class and its role in power relations, remain inchoate and fragmentary.

As a result, the major impetus towards an understanding of nineteenth-century social development has come from outside the mainstream of British historiography: from, on the one hand, the now vintage 'New Left' critique of Anderson and Nairn, and on the other, from North American historians Mayer, Wiener and W. D. Rubinstein. Collectively, this unlikely assortment of academics and critics, Marxists and non-Marxists, has come to represent a common and influential standpoint on the historical role of the middle class in modern British society.[5] For despite very different aims and assumptions, their respective works are linked by a single, pervasive theme: the 'failure' of the middle class to realise its hegemonic ambitions, its consequent political and cultural subordination to the landed governing class, and the disastrous effects which have resulted from this conjunction for British economy and society.

This interpretation clearly represents a complete inversion of the classic Marxian thesis which would see the industrial bourgeoisie as the real master of British society after 1846, and the aristocracy merely as its accomplice, retaining no more than the formal trappings of power.[6] In the revised historical landscape Gradgrind and Bounderby have forsaken the imperatives of capitalist dynamism for the lures of a rentier income and gentrified lifestyle. Now the lineage of such an interpretation is lengthy and complex. Its outline can already be discerned in the charges of apostasy levelled at the northern bourgeoisie after the demise of the Anti-Corn Law League by Cobden and Bright, or in the indictment of the 'new feudalism' which middle-class radicals like John Morley saw as moulding employer behaviour in the Lancashire cotton towns by the late 1860s. Versions of the argument were subsequently appropriated and developed in diverse ways and at different points by both conservative and radical critics from Belloc to Orwell.[7] It is not altogether surprising, therefore, that while the revisionist thesis has been met with polite indifference by the majority of social historians, it has been taken up enthusiastically by politicians and commentators as an explanation of Britain's protracted economic decline. Indeed, it is not going too far to see it as an important undercurrent in contemporary Conservative party thinking, the historical rationale behind the concerted attempt to establish the conditions for the new 'enterprise culture'.[8]

The prominence of these ideas underlines the need for detailed study of the modern middle class. This chapter has two aims: to provide a critique of the work of the two most recent historical advocates of the 'failure' thesis, Martin Wiener and W. D. Rubinstein; and to suggest briefly alternative means by which the social formation and culture of the nineteenth-century middle class may be comprehended. Much of this discussion must be provisional; as yet we lack the social and geographical spread of studies to allow for the formulation of clear conclusions. This deficiency is in itself a warning of the dangers of summary judgement or over-hasty conceptualisation. The 'failure' or 'success' of the Victorian middle class is not to be concluded on appearances alone.

I

In the seminal critiques of British social development offered by Perry Anderson and Tom Nairn in the early 1960s, the middle class was accorded a pivotal, if inglorious, role. It was the inability of the bourgeoisie to fulfil its historical mission of class domination at critical moments, in the 1640s, but most especially in the first half of the nineteenth century, which enabled the aristocracy to maintain the power structure in a normatively archaic or 'feudalised' mould. After the victories of the Reform Bill and Corn Laws the middle class was seen to suffer a 'crisis of nerve', resulting in 'symbiosis' with the landed governing class, but with the former as mere subaltern partner. The characteristic ideological expression of the bourgeoisie, utilitarianism, was too inherently materialistic and abstracted to be hegemonic in the face of a patrician culture whose inherited values and practised style of leadership were given a renewed lease of life under later Victorian imperialism. The 'knock-on' effect of bourgeois capitulation was disastrously visible in the historical behaviour of the working class: 'in England, a supine bourgeoisie produced a subordinate proletariat'.[9]

Despite the important strictures on this thesis made subsequently by E. P. Thompson and others, key features of the earlier argument, notably the post-1846 construction of landed hegemony, have been incorporated into the recent work of Wiener and Rubinstein.[10] Their respective aims and perspectives, however, are substantially different. While Wiener's primary concern was to solve the vexed problem of Britain's economic decline, Rubinstein's stated ambition was to provide nothing less than 'an alternative theory of the growth and evolution of class structure' in modern Britain to that of Marx.[11] The sense of radical urgency and polemical style which marked the writing of Anderson and Nairn have here been replaced by sober academic enquiry and an altogether more conservative intellectual outlook.

The arguments of the newer critics also reveal significant conceptual modifications to the synthesis of their Marxist forebears. The idea of bourgeois/aristocratic symbiosis after 1846 has been displaced by the notion of 'rival' or 'competing elites'. Most important, the division within the middle class is stressed, between, on the one hand, the manufacturing elite of the industrial North, and on the other, the commercial and financial elite centred on London. According to this revised version it was precisely that fractured formation, within which the industrial elite became cast as 'poor relations', that constituted the fundamental weakness of the English middle class and opened the way to continued landed supremacy down to 1914. Two important contentions, then, are at issue in the current debate: the occupational/geographical segmentation of the Victorian middle class, and its ultimate acquiescence to landed politico-cultural domination. Each demands critical examination in relation to the work of its principal proponent, Rubinstein and Wiener respectively.

Rubinstein's thesis is premissed on an extensive survey of probate records and income tax statistics. These, he claims, affirm the greater individual and collective wealth of the metropolitan commercial middle class as against its northern industrial counterpart, increasingly marked after mid-century. On the basis of this differential wealth structure, Rubinstein infers broader divergences at the level of social and economic formation. Industry and commerce, he argues, represented 'distinct forms of property'; they nurtured different 'occupational ideologies', necessitated disparate 'authority structures', and fostered contrasting status priorities.[12] Above all, the two segregated 'middle classes' were distinguished by their relations to landed society, the dominant elite to 1914. Here the middle class based in London and the South held a decided advantage, both by virtue of its proximity to the centres of landed power, and in the growing interchange between land and commerce in the last quarter of the century, manifested in 'High Society', intermarriage, and City directorships. It was a movement that sealed the isolation of the northern industrial interest, and paved the way for the creation of a single elite after 1918, the familiar Southern-dominated 'Establishment'. 'In the nineteenth century', Rubinstein concludes, 'the geographical/occupational paradigms were the primary reference groups; these cut vertically instead of horizontally; "class" in the Marxist sense was not salient until after 1918.'[13]

These are weighty conceptual claims, but any proper consideration of Rubinstein's argument starts with an evaluation of his sources, especially probate, which provides the bulk of the evidence. The probate records confront the historian with a number of technical difficulties, many of which Rubinstein details.[14] However, they also hold major problems for interpretation, which if unresolved can cause the figures to be seriously misleading.

This is particularly noticeable in the case of nineteenth-century industrial wealth-holding. First, probate was intended to record unsettled personal wealth only. Real estate (realty), which would include land and freehold building, in the form of mills, workshops, warehouses, and so on, was not evaluated. Secondly, wealth was recorded at the place of death, not necessarily in the locality where the individual's wealth was made. Hence if a wealthy northern industrialist died outside the North, the valuation was assessed in the relevant court, which after 1858 was usually London. Thirdly, wealth was estimated at death, not when an individual was economically active. Yet as Rubinstein himself notes, manufacturers were probably more concerned to pass on a greater portion of business assets to younger relatives during their lifetime to preserve the continuity of the family firm than their counterparts in finance or commerce. While we have insufficient knowledge of the middle-class property cycle, the likelihood of differential employer behaviour between economic sectors with regard to capital inheritance emphasises once more the difficulty of using probate as the basis for comparative study of wealth-holding.[15]

This last point indicates the most fundamental weakness of the source as evidence. Probate estimated the wealth of the individual; the characteristic form of nineteenth-century business organisation was familial and dynastic. This was so in the great majority of leading branches of industry to 1914, as recent research has emphasised.[16] Even where limited liability had taken root by the later Victorian period, in textiles, iron, steel, and engineering, control was still commonly exercised by one or two families. As a result, capital was rarely concentrated in the hands of a single individual, but dispersed unequally through several branches of an industrial dynasty, or still more complex, through several families inter-linked by marriage. For this reason, any genuine assessment of the comparative wealth drawn from industry and commerce would need to take into account not simply that of individuals, but the collective resources of family and clan.[17]

No more immune to criticism is Rubinstein's reading of income tax records for the year 1879–80, intended to 'confirm' at a wider class level the ascendancy of commerce over industry, and of London over the provincial centres, in the accumulation of wealth. The main problem here, as Rubinstein admits, is that the records contain no *per capita* breakdown. Consequently, it is impossible to know what is being assessed, whether it be a private individual, small shop, or large limited company. This deficiency is especially acute in the case of the City, whose total tax payment for the year 1879–80 far outstripped that of any other borough, but an unspecifiable proportion of which was provided by branches or offices of firms whose operational base was in the provinces or abroad. Yet if the City is excluded from the reckoning, then it emerges on a strict mathematical basis that the inhabitants of the London boroughs actually paid less tax *per capita* in the year in question than their counterparts in Manchester, Liverpool, Glasgow and Edinburgh.[18]

Furthermore, in contrast to London where a wealthy middle class continued to reside in fashionable areas like the West End, many prosperous families of the provincial bourgeoisie no longer lived, by the mid-Victorian period, in the towns or cities in which they were economically and socially active, but in suburban mansions several miles outside the urban boundaries. As a report on the population of Manchester in the early 1880s noted, 'The merchants, manufacturers . . . and those connected with industries closely allied to the city are to be found in an area extending beyond the limits of the city, and . . . the district known to the world as "Manchester" is much more populous than it appears in any printed returns.'[19] For the same reasons the wealth of Manchester and its middle class, like that of similar provincial centres, must be considered greater than is indicated by the tax returns, based as these were solely on the population living within the urban perimeters.

Taken together these various criticisms suggest a substantial under-recording of industrial wealth, and a consequent overstatement in Rubinstein's account of the imbalance in this respect between commerce and industry. More fundamentally, it must be questionable how valid probate and income tax records may be as a guide to wealth or social structure, so hedged about are they with qualifications and unknowns. This is disappointing, but perhaps salutary. For wealth alone is not an absolute or determining category, but a dependent variable in class formation and social behaviour. What mattered in the nineteenth century was less the mere fact of wealth itself, than the way individuals and classes used it, in conjunction with other social and economic resources, to achieve and sustain power and authority.

Some of these qualitative questions are indeed taken up by Rubinstein in an attempt to put conceptual flesh on somewhat brittle empirical bones. The difficulty here is that very little historical evidence is offered to back up assertions of a broader economic, social and cultural divergence between metropolitan commerce and provincial industry. Thus we are confronted with the stark hypothesis that industrial and commercial enterprise represented 'distinct forms of property' with no more explanation than that they necessitated proportionately different forms of input. In crude economic terms, of course, this was so, but at the level of actual business organisation and practice the divergence was rather less marked. Both merchant and manufacturer required roughly similar amounts of capital to set up in business, drew on similar networks of credit, and employed the same operational form, the common law partnership. Moreover, as the industrial economy broadened its base after 1850, so the functional distinction between 'merchant' and 'manufacturer', long blurred in expanding industrial regions, became increasingly arbitrary. It was part of a more general process in the later Victorian period whereby the factory owner and overseas merchant were recast in the more anonymous mould of the 'businessman', sharing common interests in municipal utilities, insurance, banking, and shareholding, beyond those of the original economic concern.

Much of this bears equally on the contention that commerce and manufacturing engendered distinct 'occupational ideologies'. Certainly, there did exist differences of routine, business hours, and degree of supervision which need delineating as part of a broader enquiry into middle-class experiences of work. But what appears striking is the degree of consensus on attitudes to business across the range of middle-class occupations. The gospel of work was espoused as vehemently by commercial and professional men as by industrial employers; Samuel Smiles, it may be recalled, was a doctor turned journalist, never a manufacturer.[20] Time and again business handbooks and admonitory tracts stressed the same values of self-help, self-discipline and hard work for a successful career in every vocation. Much criticism was voiced in such literature against the 'speculator', the 'stockjobber', and the 'get-rich-quick' ethic. But this was identified equally with business conduct in provincial centres such as Manchester and Liverpool, as with practices existing in London and the City.[21]

The main problem with the 'geographical/occupational paradigm', however, is that it automatically reduces the essentially heterogeneous economic structure of Victorian cities to a mere caricature. Industrialism was far from synonymous with large-scale production and the mass factory work force. Nineteenth-century London shared with Birmingham and Sheffield a concentration of small workshops and craft trades, with Liverpool, Manchester, and Glasgow a swelling casual labour market.[22] Moreover, commerce was never a metropolitan preserve. As Gatrell has emphasised, Manchester by the 1840s was less a centre of manufacturing production than a 'provincial, commercial, and retailing capital'.[23] Among the substantial middle classes of the leading provincial cities commerce and distribution easily predominated over manufacturing as sources of employment. In short, far from being separate or divergent economic functions, commerce and industry were symbiotic not only within the national, but also the local and regional industrial economy. Rubinstein's paradigm only appears plausible if one deliberately selects (as he naturally does) towns like Oldham as representative of provincial industrial development – a notion of limited validity.

In the last analysis, however, it is not sufficient to assume divergent versions of 'middle-classness' without enquiring how such versions might have been constituted in Victorian experience. For following Rubinstein's rationale, there were not merely two, but a variety of 'middle classes', drawing different levels of income from a diversity of sources, and inhabiting distinct social worlds marked by disparate modes of behaviour, lifestyles, values. The middle class, by any comprehensible definition, incorporated not only Forsytes and Bounderbys, but equally the distinctive worlds of the Barsetshire clergy and 'Bohemia'.

To reject Rubinstein's thesis of middle-class dichotomy is not to reinstate an idealised notion of an immutable, monolithic bourgeoisie. The Victorian middle class was not fractured along the lines that he describes, but it was fragmented in significant ways. Differences of market situation between small and big employer, shopkeeper and large retailer, for example, could be transformed into open conflict under pressure of severe economic competition or increased municipal expenditure.[24] Even within the big bourgeoisie itself the cleavage between Liberal Dissent and Tory Anglicanism was profound and enduring in the politics and society of many urban areas.[25]

But an acknowledgement of tension and fragmentation requires to be balanced by a recognition of the potent factors serving to shore up and extend class cohesion and a sense of identity. Of these the most important derived from the development of industrial capitalism itself. It was not simply that the middle class as a whole profited from industrialisation, but that the processes of capitalist development engendered a dense web of economic networks and social relationships which bound together different geographical and occupational groupings – manufacturers, bureaucrats, financiers, professional men, *rentiers* – in ever more complex and reciprocal ways. Within this system different economic sectors and their respective 'elites' appeared less in competition with each other than increasingly enmeshed, as the national and imperial economy expanded providing fresh opportunity and outlets for capital. At the same time a whole series of linkages were developed in English civil society at the level of social, political, and business organisation, whose range has scarcely begun to be investigated by historians, but which may indicate something of the resources and scope of the nineteenth-century middle class. In the last section of this chapter I shall return to the question of these linkages to indicate some of the ways they may have acted in the process of middle-class formation and consciousness.

II

If one of the main weaknesses of Rubinstein's argument lies in the absence of evidence of cultural and ideological practice, then Martin Wiener's *English Culture and the Decline of the Industrial Spirit* might be considered to make good this deficiency. Wiener's work is a closely argued attempt to define a complex of ideas which he sees as forming a distinctive middle-class *Zeitgeist* by the later nineteenth century, and to assess its effects on economic behaviour.

The argument opens on a familiar note. British 'modernisation', of which the Industrial Revolution was the essential component, was 'incomplete'. The political victories of 1832 and 1846 did not witness the accession to power of a triumphant bourgeoisie. Far from signalling the dawn of an era of bourgeois dominance, the Great Exhibition of 1851 represented the high-water mark of industrial values, the point at which public enthusiasm for material progress began to dwindle. Reprieved from the historical death sentence, the landed class was able to reassert political and cultural hegemony after 1850, and in so doing 'to reshape the bourgeoisie in its own image'.[26]

According to Wiener, between 1850 and 1900 there occurred within middle-class ideology a 'counterrevolution of values' in which 'the urge to enterprise faded beneath a preference for stability'. Anti-industrial attitudes which had formerly been the preserve of an intellectual minority – Carlyle, Dickens, Ruskin, and others – came to represent a pervasive cultural outlook among important sections of the middle class: clergy and professional men, bureaucrats, politicians, and businessmen. Nourished in the public schools, Oxbridge, and the Civil Service, and informed by aristocratic notions of honour, duty, and antipathy to trade, this conservative 'mind-set' manifested itself in a wholesale denial of the social facts of urbanism and industrialism. Hence, the Southern counties with their intimations of an unchanging aristocratic and rural order came to stand as the idealised normative representation for the nation as a whole.

In the process of ideological revision the northern industrialist became recast as the 'poor relation' of English elite society. The effects of this social disequilibrium, Wiener argues, were soon apparent in the economic sphere. While industry was spurned as a career by those from commercial, professional, or landed backgrounds, northern industrial society itself was increasingly prone to the 'haemorrhage of talent' and the insidious processes of 'gentrification'. Even where businessmen resisted the lures of the City, the South, and the landed estate, they sought to distance themselves from the day-to-day running of their enterprises, becoming in effect 'psychological *rentiers*'. By 1914, Wiener claims, the entrepreneurial dynamism which had characterised the economy before 1850 was all but extinct. In its place stood a 'gentlemanly economy', predisposed to state intervention and restrictive practices, consistently emphasising the social obligations of industry over the economic imperatives of growth and profit.

Wiener's argument is seductive because of its apparent explicative coherence. It fits perfectly that contemporary cast of mind which, conscious of Britain's diminishing world role and irritated by corporate 'inefficiency', has begun to doubt the very liberal nostrums embodied in the construction of post-war welfare capitalism which it once held sacred. It gives historical endorsement to the demand for the removal of antiquated or bureaucratic obstacles in the way of an entrepreneurial renaissance and a second 'Industrial Revolution'.[27] Closer examination of Wiener's thesis, however, reveals significant shortcomings. These relate firstly to theoretical approach, but equally to the historical interpretation of key aspects of middle-class behaviour.

The first problem concerns Wiener's use of conceptual terminology, often seemingly functionalist in its implications, but whose precise meaning is never specified. Thus we are told that British 'modernisation' was 'incomplete', that 'pre-modern' residues lingered on in industrial society and gave legitimacy to 'anti-modern' sentiments.[28] This manner of conceptualisation implies one of two things: either it presupposes a hypothetical model of development against which the British example is being set; or it suggests a comparative treatment in which the historical experience of Britain is viewed in relation to that of other 'developed' societies. In fact, neither is explicitly the case. What is occurring, rather, is an instance of straightforward terminological euphemism. Hence, 'modern' is made to stand for 'industrial capitalist', 'pre-modern' for 'feudal', with a concomitant diminution of perceptual insight which a more historicised conceptualisation might have afforded.

Wiener's terminological deficiency is doubly unfortunate since an attempt at international comparison might have restored a proper sense of perspective to the supposed uniqueness of the British experience. For a brief consideration of recent historical debates on the Continental bourgeoisies would have revealed a similar emphasis on bourgeois 'failure', thus qualifying, at the very least, the case for English exceptionalism. French and German historians, for example, have variously lamented the inability of their respective middle classes to attain political dominance, to sustain entrepreneurial dynamism, or to conform to the social and cultural norms expected of '*le bon bourgeois*'.[29] Moreover, different historiographical traditions have sometimes engendered divergent historical conclusions. Whereas British historians, looking back over a century of economic decline, have seen in later nineteenth and early twentieth-century Germany the exemplar of mature industrial growth, their German counterparts, emphasising the weakness of an indigenous bourgeoisie as the cause of subsequent political aberrations, have looked to later Victorian and Edwardian England as the model of 'normal' social development.[30] Meanwhile, Arno Mayer has taken the argument a step further, in viewing the European bourgeoisies as collectively unassertive and deferential in the face of traditional landed elites well-versed in the exercise of political authority and cultural leadership.[31]

There is in much of this argumentation for aristocratic 'persistence' and hegemony a strong implication of bourgeois 'false consciousness'. It is as if there existed an undisclosed ideal type of bourgeois behaviour against which all such formations might be measured. It is thus possible for Wiener to ascribe certain idealist characteristics to different social groups, and to use these as the primary means of class identification. However, the anomalous status of an argument which would seek to identify class merely by reference to a pre-given set of values is revealed by the consistent discrepancy between the outward assumption of those values and actual class behaviour. Thus, 'amateurism', cited by Wiener as an archetypal aristocratic value, is not a term usually associated with aristocratic political management, agricultural 'rationalisation', or astute speculation in urban property, minerals, and railways.[32]

Clearly, it is important to separate out the meanings of terms such as 'capitalist', 'bourgeois', and 'entrepreneurial', but this is precisely the kind of conceptual confusion unwittingly generated by an over-reliance on ascriptive definitions of class. Moreover, such a mode of analysis is inherently incapable of attending to questions of change in, and appropriation of, particular forms of cultural or ideological expression. Thus, in Wiener's work, the 'traditional' and the 'aristocratic', with their associated social and moral attributes, are conceived as immutable categories, their intangible essence preserved from the disruptive impress of post-1800 socio-economic development. Similarly, there is little comprehension of how important notions such as the 'gentleman', 'culture', or 'respectability' were taken up by other social classes in Victorian society, expanding, shifting, or even inverting their meanings in the process.[33]

These conceptual limitations need to be borne in mind in considering the historical evidence for bourgeois 'gentrification' and its assumed role in blunting entrepreneurial energies. It is important, firstly, to place some of his broader contentions in historical perspective. As Stone has recently emphasised, the recruitment of wealthy members of the middle class into the landed gentry and aristocracy through judicious intermarriage had a lengthy precedent in England. But contrary to conventional wisdom, there is no evidence of a quickening of this rate of bourgeois recruitment in the nineteenth century, remaining of negligible importance by comparison with landed inter-alliance.[34] Similarly, the acquisition of a landed estate was always the exception to the rule of suburbanisation in industrial and commercial society, and in any case no more implied the wholesale withdrawal from business than it had for the eighteenth-century London merchant.[35] Likewise, only the sons of the largest industrial employers attended prestigious southern public schools before the late nineteenth century, and this was commonly followed by re-entry into the family business, as is consistently evinced by the case-histories of major industrial dynasties.[36]

The relation of industrial capital to the land and the landed class after 1850 was in fact complex, but not necessarily problematic. Even in Manchester, whose bourgeoisie has been conceived as the embodiment of urban, self-made, and anti-aristocratic values, the distance between land and industry was never great. Many of the city's leading industrial employer families – McConnel, Kennedy, Murray, Birley, Houldsworth – had landed origins and sustained connections to the gentry through kinship, the county bench and inherited or acquired landholding.[37] By the mid-Victorian period, however, the social and political privileges which landownership traditionally conferred were of diminishing consequence. Access to Parliament, the county magistracy or the higher echelons of polite society was no longer effectively contingent upon the possession of a landed estate. Thus, while estates continued to be acquired by manufacturers and merchants as a source of investment, they were also a means of resolving the vexed problem of the use of surplus capital by way of conspicuous consumption. It was noticeable that the wealthy Manchester men who chose to disburse their capital in this way after 1850 – James Watts at Abney Hall, Mark Philips at Welcombe, Henry Robertson at Pale Hall – preferred to build their own grandiose and lavishly ornamented country houses in small-scale park settings, rather than to buy up existing gentry seats with large tracts of land. In none of these cases did the purchase of a country house precipitate wholesale removal from the original sources of familial power and profit. By the 1860s the Heywoods, one of Manchester's wealthiest banking dynasties, owned houses in London and Blackpool and an estate in Staffordshire, while branches of the family were influential in four counties. But the familial domain at Claremont, in the Manchester suburbs, remained the clan's acknowledged base into the twentieth century.[38]

What needs to be emphasised in analysis of the nineteenth-century bourgeoisie is the importance of not assuming a simple correlation between social behaviour, ideology and economic practice. It was perfectly plausible for a Victorian industrialist to ride with the local hunt, build himself a castle in the country, and adopt a 'neo-feudal' pose of paternalist employer, without consciously compromising in any way the imperatives of capitalist production or class commitment. Hence many of the 'contradictions' or 'paradoxes' supposedly manifest in middle-class culture after 1850 appear rather as problems of an engrafted gentrification thesis which, by extracting behaviour from its referential context, fails to comprehend the singular adaptability of bourgeois lifestyles and ideology.

Moreover, gentrification is as inappropriate an explanation of economic as of social behaviour. The so-called 'haemorrhage of talent', the outflow of leading industrial employers in the last quarter of the nineteenth century, is itself akin to a mirage, requiring careful qualification between regions and sectors. But where something of this exodus was perceptible, as in the Lancashire cotton towns between 1880 and 1914, it appears as the product of a complex of factors, not of cultural incentives alone. Industrial amalgamation and the slow spread of limited liability, the diversification of employer capital, the growing political and industrial assertiveness of labour, and most profoundly, the myriad social changes serving to dissolve the cordoned vision of the local on which employer versions of the community of interests had rested, all these were contingent reasons for gradual withdrawal.[39]

More broadly, outflow needs to be related to the natural wastage of firms through unprofitability in the fiercely competitive conditions prevailing from the later 1870s to the mid-1890s. But if wastage was an organic part of any 'haemorrhage of talent', then the notion might be said to apply with equal validity to the 'heroic age' of the 1830s and 1840s when economic competition was scarcely less ruthless, and the turnover of firms no less rapid.[40] In sum, Wiener, like other advocates of entrepreneurial 'failure', too often appears to want the argument both ways: to lament the 'haemorrhage of talent' on the one hand, while simultaneously criticising the same industrial dynasticism for its supposed imperviousness to changes in technology, organisation and demand.

Indeed, recent research has underlined the necessity of questioning the whole teleological perception of economic decline before 1914, and in particular arguments which would identify entrepreneurial conservatism or managerial inflexibility as its primary causes. At the risk of historical commonplace it is worth reiterating two basic points often seemingly lost in the technicalities of debate. Firstly, the rationale of capitalist enterprise is profit; technical advance, the rationalisation of production, expansion of markets, or any other indicator of economic development, are contingent not necessary functions of this fundamental determinant. Entrepreneurial rationality is thus better measured by this yardstick than by retrospective or comparative models of productivity and economic performance. And certainly the evidence available suggests that in critical sectors of the industrial economy—cotton textiles, iron and steel, coal, engineering, shipbuilding – profits held up well between 1870 and 1914.[41] Secondly, it is worth recalling that the Victorian and Edwardian economy was an imperial economy, possessing vast colonial and captive markets. Despite the constantly expressed fears of external competition after 1870, therefore, the imperial character of British markets automatically minimised the practical effects of such competition in the world economy, with a consequent reduction of incentive for an organised thrust towards greater productive efficiency or export penetration.[42] Hence, if it is possible to speak of a decline of entrepreneurial dynamism before 1914, this requires to be understood as the product of a complex of factors: imperialism, organised labour, Liberal progressivism, the growing interest of the state in the economy via armaments, industrial arbitration, and so on, rather than as the simple result of the absorption of gentry values.

Ultimately, however, Wiener's thesis, like that of Rubinstein, is unsatisfactory for what is left out of historical account as much as for the inadequacy of the arguments themselves. The necessary fuller understanding of the nineteenth-century middle class cannot be conceived merely from critical refutation of existing lines of argument. Questions need to be reformulated, theoretical perspectives altered, and the empirical base broadened, if a convincing alternative account of middle-class formation and culture is to be forged. By way of conclusion, therefore, it is worth considering briefly some of the historical issues involved in a broader undertaking.

III

Within the debate on the role of the British middle class in social development little attention has been directed to the internal structuring of the middle class itself. Either that structure has been conceived as essentially homogeneous, proceeding unproblematically from economic position.[43] Or, as is the case with Wiener and Rubinstein, the concept of class has been largely displaced by that of 'elite', the assumption being that a social group thus defined represents a natural distillation of class interest.[44] Both modes of conceptualisation, however, present difficulties for an historical understanding of class formation.

From the late eighteenth century (and earlier), the 'middle ranks' were composed of a range of variegated social and occupational elements: merchant and manufacturing capitalists, small masters, tradesmen, farmers, middlemen of all kinds. Subsequent economic development witnessed the growth of other significant groups: middle-class *rentiers*, newer professions, white-collar workers, large retailers and wholesale distributors. All these groups had a claim to middle-class status, sensed themselves to be part of a larger middle class. The 'elites' of large capitalist and professional men, so often taken for the *ipso facto* middle class, were bound into this broader urban social formation in a variety of material ways: by ties of business and religion, marriage and kinship, political and economic interest. Their leadership in the local community was predicated on the support of the wider middle-class constituency.[45]

At the same time, that support was by no means automatic or unqualified. Into the later nineteenth century, urban politics was dominated by conflicts between middle-class groups under protean guises: Liberal Dissent against Tory Anglicanism, old wealth against new, 'shopocracy' against 'elite'. After 1850 these conflicts appear more evidently structural, with small and big business commonly contesting political space on a variety of important local issues: rates, docks and transport, municipal expenditure, civic improvement.[46]

This generic antagonism indicates some of the difficulties in the way of considering elites as the organic representatives of common class interest. Fundamental structural fragmentation meant that middle-class interests were always likely to be diffuse, always subject to negotiation, modification, or countermand by different sectional groupings in a given situation. If, as Cobden noted, it was the shopocracy who provided the electoral foundations for liberal hegemony in Manchester in the 1830s, then it was the withdrawal of support on the part of important sections of the city's commercial and manufacturing bourgeoisie which sealed the fate of the

Manchester School and its programme of radical reform at the 1857 election.[47] For the nineteenth-century middle class, intra-class relations were as important in determining the parameters of class action as relations with the landed order or urban working class.

The significance of the urban and local as a middle-class power base is a further dimension overlooked by Rubinstein and Wiener. However, as historians have long pointed out, local autonomy in relation to central government was a cardinal tenet of the Victorian construction of power[48]. It was for this reason that the private Bill and the non-compulsory or discretional Act remained staple instruments of the legislative process until well into the later nineteenth century. The decentralised character of the Victorian state served the interests of the middle class by placing at its disposal a significant range of executive functions: the levying of a local rate, the management of police, poor and criminal law, the implementation of parliamentary legislation, the regulation of the local labour market. These powers, and especially the financial and judicial elements, were proportionately reinforced as urban representatives moved on to the county bench after 1840.[49]

Moreover, authority derived from the economic and political determinants of class power was buttressed by the network of middle-class institutions which characterised the Victorian city: town council, church and chapel, philanthropic and voluntary association. This network lent to the local middle class both the sense of a collective identity and an organisational scope beyond that predicated simply on wealth, occupation and economic interest. Institutional pluralism facilitated the integration of a broader middle class into the dominant order, while minimising the potential for disruptive internal conflicts over ideology and objectives.[50] At the same time, it allowed the middle class to project its impress over a considerable part of urban existence from the spheres of work, leisure and education to the physical layout of the town, civic architecture and sanitary improvement. The impulses to class cohesion and to social action thus worked in congruency through the institutional agencies of the public domain. To be sure, bourgeois authority within the urban and local was not ubiquitous, and far from uncontested and unproblematic in its exercise; but it is as well not to underestimate the self-confidence of the Victorian bourgeois in his native urban habitat, symbolised most unequivocally in the ostentatious town halls, the warehouses, churches, and suburban mansions of the mid-Victorian period.[51]

Middle-class social organisation, however, did not stop at the municipal boundaries. If we lack the evidence to chart with any fullness the processes which fostered class cohesion at regional and national levels, it is clear that certain factors inexorably drew the local bourgeoisies into wider relationships of power and interest. The most visible of these was the way in which, from the mid-eighteenth century on, leading families became linked in complex and extended webs of clan and cousinhood. These familial networks, often predicated on common politico-religious allegiance and cemented by business interests, increasingly spanned cities and regions. The cotton and woollen districts of the North, in particular, were criss-crossed by such dynastic alliances, and similar linkages can be found for the Black Country, the North-East, and the Home Counties.[52] The cotton-spinning Ashtons of Hyde show clearly this growing imbrication in wider kinship networks after 1850, with connections to Manchester cotton (Greg, Tootal Broadhurst, Donner), Liverpool merchanting (Gair, Rathbone), the Leeds woollen trade (Lupton), and Oxford academia (Bryce). The marriage patterns of the banking Heywoods reveal evidence of an analogous broadening of horizons, adding to ties established with the industrial bourgeoisie (Kennedy, Barton, Peel) and Liverpool commerce (Robinson), links to the higher reaches of the Church of England (Sumner, Bishop of Winchester) and the legal profession (Foster and Howell, both wealthy county barrister families with estates in Bedfordshire and Cornwall respectively).[53] As clans proliferated and expanded, so their branches penetrated more extensively the institutional fabric of national power relations. When the family of Edward Baines gathered at his deathbed in 1848, 'politics and commerce, religion and philanthropy, the House of Commons, the *Mercury*, the *Liverpool Times*, Sheffield, London and East Parade, Leeds were swept together into the eye of eternity'.[54]

The function of these familial linkages was multiple: to provide capital, credit, and business information, to place younger sons or find marriage partners for difficult daughters, to ensure the financial maintenance of widowed or unmarried dependants. The entry of male members of commercial or manufacturing families into the law, the ministry, or colonial service, tended to strengthen rather than weaken clan structures by providing access to new sources of wealth, prestige, and connection.

Thus, if city and region remained potent sources of middle-class identity till 1914 at least, the overlap of business and family networks acted to soften these distinctions particularly among the big bourgeoisie. Links to London remained strong: from early in the nineteenth century it was common for the larger provincial firms to maintain a family member in the metropolis for the purposes of credit and business intelligence, a practice later superseded by the representative branch.[55] But there were also more powerful and impersonal forces serving to integrate the local and regional middle class into the financial life of the nation, most marked after 1850:

the spread of the joint stock bank with multiple branches, underpinned by the stabilising influence of the Bank of England; the diversification of surplus capital by industrialists and wealthy and commercial and professional men into railways, land and property, and foreign shares; the formation of business syndicates, such as those organised by David Chadwick, the company promoter, to enable Manchester businessmen to obtain large holdings in the expanding iron and steel industries; and the activities of individual brokers, or private banks such as Glyn Mills, who found outlets for the multitude of more modest middle-class and *rentier* investors, a significant proportion of whom were women – in 1856 the *Economist* reported that women composed twenty-four per cent of the shareholders of the eight largest London banks.[56] The operation of these flows of capital remains largely obscure, but the evidence suggests that their overall effect after 1850 was integrative, not, as Rubinstein would appear to maintain, divisive.

The characteristic institutional forms of middle-class life, church, chapel, and voluntary association, likewise generated their own corporate linkages beyond the merely local. The recruitment of ministers by Nonconformist congregations, for example, reveals clearly the workings of the denominational grapevine along the nodal centres of urban Dissent: London, Bristol, Birmingham, Manchester, Glasgow, and so on.[57] And despite their traditional emphasis on autarchy, the nineteenth century witnessed the organisation of dissenting churches in denominational hierarchies of regional and national associations.[58] Similarly, the movement of voluntary and political associations was inexorably outwards from the provincial strongholds in which their originating impulse lay to the wider spheres of pressure-group politics. At national level the provincial and metropolitan leadership of radical nonconformity tended to coalesce in a single political voice; thus, in the 1850s and 1860s the Liberation Society was connected to the Dissenting Deputies, the Reform Movement, the Ballot Society, and the Peace Society, in a 'system of interlocking directorships'.[59]

Examples of this integrative movement could be multiplied in the private as well as the public spheres of middle-class life, and in bourgeois self-representations as the 'productive' and 'respectable' class, or still more commandingly as 'public opinion'.[60] But the point is clear: if the development of the English middle class was marked by a significant degree of structural fragmentation, there nevertheless existed resources in social and economic organisation which served as powerful impulses to class cohesion. Such a perspective is suggestive, more generally, of the resilience and adaptability of Victorian bourgeois culture, capable of absorbing diverse ideological influences while retaining the sense of a distinct historical inheritance and identity. These complementary facets were apparent even where middle-class culture was supposedly most vulnerable to the impress of landed values: in education and ideology.

As has already been indicated, only the sons of the greater bourgeoisie attended major public schools before the later Victorian period. Much more typical as institutions of middle-class education in the first half of the century were the numerous academies, commercial colleges, and grammar schools. Here the elements of business and applied science were dispensed along with classics and the appurtenances of polite culture in greater or lesser proportions. Similarly, the demand for higher education was more usually met by the Scottish universities, University College, London (1825), or occasionally, Dutch and German universities, than by Oxbridge. If in the later period a gradual shift is perceptible in favour of the minor public school and, after the final removal of Nonconformist disabilities in 1871, the ancient universities, then this was still mainly confined to a wealthier stratum. Overall, the pattern of middle-class education was neither markedly entrepreneurial, nor gentrified. Such tone as it possessed was rather the product of a distinctive blend of rationalism, evangelicism, and classical learning, the tenacious legacy of post-Enlightenment provincial culture.[61]

Moreover, the Victorian public school has too often been interpreted as the vehicle, via its curriculum and prevailing ethic, for the insertion of 'traditional' landed values in the aspiring bourgeoisie. In fact, as an ideological medium, the public school was a far more ambiguous enterprise. Thus, the retention of classics as the cornerstone of the academic curriculum has to be comprehended alongside the Arnoldian ideal of the 'Christian gentleman', and the stress on work, competition, and educational efficiency indicated by the Clarendon Commission of 1861.[62] The fundamental project of the public schools, on the other hand, was both simple and ambitious: to instil into its pupils, whatever their background, the habit and moral certainties of leadership. Hence the fagging system, the complex hierarchies of authority structuring life in 'house' and school, the insistence on organised games. Skills and attitudes transmitted at public school were resolutely non-vocational. Instead, emphasis was laid on a more generalised conception of 'man management', the acceptance and exercise of authority.[63] Lessons learned at public school could be applied in any likely subsequent position of responsibility: on the landed estate, in Parliament or the army, but equally in the factory, the boardroom, or the colonial post. Thus, if the notion of leadership is stripped of extraneous aristocratic connotations, then it is possible to comprehend the Victorian public school for what it actually was: an educational system finely adjusted to meet the directive needs of a class society that was at once agricultural, industrial, commercial, and above all, imperial.

Public school education proved itself capable of accommodating different socio-economic interests by concentrating on the major interest they held in common, the exercise of power. 'Landed hegemony' is thus as inappropriate a description of that conjuncture as any notion of bourgeois infiltration. The function of the public schools was integrative rather than assimilative, designed to demonstrate a mutuality of experience, not the subordination of one set of values to another. It was thus comprehensible to a middle class whose own ideological outlook tended to be inclusive rather than exclusive. Liberal ideology was never reducible to a Gradgrindian admixture of classical political economy and Benthamite utilitarianism. It encompassed a whole series of discourses, these being integral categories, but which also comprised other leavening elements: romanticism, paternalism, evangelicism, domesticity. Within this polymorphic ideological framework it was possible to live out the best of all possible bourgeois existences, to plume oneself on 'pride of order' and patronage of the arts, to intersperse management of factory and warehouse with lengthy sojourns in Switzerland and Italy. As a prosperous member of the middle class, it was not necessary to sell one's soul to the aristocracy to enjoy the benefits of gentry life.[64]

But if liberal ideology contained no simple organising fulcrum, it possessed powerful ideological resources in political economy and the tradition of radical dissent. The cluster of ideas centred on the classical notion of the sovereignty of the market, and the construction of social and economic relations these demanded, represents the nearest approximation to a hegemonic explicative system perceptible in the nineteenth century. The scope and penetration of political economy is suggested equally by its early nurture within the matrix of eighteenth-century agrarian capitalism, as by the effective inability of trade unions to argue outside the terms of the capitalist marketplace after 1850. Its flexibility is indicated by the capacity to accommodate employer paternalist strategies without any noticeable reduction of its ideological utility.[65] Nor, it may be noted, did Tory sections of the middle class offer substantive resistance to its prescriptions, despite the flickerings of concern evidenced by Fielden, Oastler, and others in the Factory Reform movement of the 1840s.

Political economy, of course, spawned its own tensions and contradictions. The 'market' could prove a problematic category for capital itself, demanding of employers a range of ideological and entrepreneurial responses, from business associations to welfare provision, scarcely envisaged by Smith or Ricardo. Likewise, government was frequently forced to abandon individualist principles in favour of more active legislative intervention in factory, sanitary, and housing conditions. These assumed limitations, however, can equally be read as an indicator of the strength of political economy, its flexibility as a guide to political and economic practice. Certainly, it would be historically inapt to overlook the combined force and staying power of ideas of free trade, the operation of the 'natural' laws of the market, and minimal government intervention, as ideological expedients of both capital and the state before 1914.

For the nineteenth-century middle class the main functions of political economy were to maintain the appropriate economic and legal conditions for sustained capitalist development, and to set the limits to the power of the central state. Of equal significance in activating a sense of cultural identity among the liberal middle class was the tradition of militant Dissent. Victorian radical Nonconformity saw itself as in direct descent from sixteenth-century puritanism; it conceived itself in a profound way as both heir and representative of that tradition. Key reference points in this elaborate mythology were the Commonwealth, the Ejection of 1662, and the Glorious Revolution of 1688; its heroes were Shakespeare, Bunyan, Cromwell, and Milton. But it was also a living tradition. To this lengthy pedigree, more recent events – the successive reform campaigns, the Anti-Corn Law League – could be assimilated, acquiring in turn their own symbolic place in the collective historical memory.[66]

It was this idea of a distinct historical patrimony which gave middle-class radicalism much of its sense of mission, and charged issues like church rates, disestablishment, and educational reform with a peculiar atavistic intensity. But it was a notion that also received a wider diffusion in liberal culture: through the tightly-knit networks of chapel and its multifarious dependent associations, through the press, liberal education, and the Whig interpretation of the past, as well as through visual reproduction in painting and civic decoration. As such, it offered the liberal middle class a constant reminder of a particular inheritance, and a unique historical role. Moreover, its significance was not confined to the industrial community: together with utilitarianism, radical dissenting discourse can be seen as the ideological matrix out of which major intellectual tendencies in late Victorian and Edwardian political culture, Liberal progressivism and Fabian socialism, were forged.[67]

Liberal ideology, of course, was not synonymous with bourgeois ideology. Tory Anglicanism represented the creed of a substantial, and growing, section of the Victorian middle class. Nourished in church, grammar school, corporation, and convivial club, and fortified by the Anglican revival, Tory Democracy, and Disraelian business Conservatism, Tory Anglicanism appeared no less markedly bourgeois and urban than Liberal Nonconformity. But again, what is suggested here are the powerful cultural resources immanent in nineteenth-century provincial life, their rootedness in a specifically urban experience, and their links to national institutional networks of power: in this case, the Church of England and the ancient universities.

There are, then, not only important flaws, but crucial omissions in a reading of nineteenth-century middle class development which would emphasise structural cleavage and gentrification as fundamental tendencies. This said, we are scarcely in a position, historiographically, to substitute an unequivocal thesis of bourgeois 'success' for that of bourgeois 'failure'. Attempts to reinstall such a version of events have stressed the local dominance of the Victorian middle class and catalogued its achievements in influencing the institutions of government and state.[68] While these dimensions are not to be gainsaid, there are no less fundamental categories outstanding, some of the more important of which have been discussed here: class structure, social organisation, ideology.

It is in particular the development of linkages between local, regional and national sites of middle-class formation and interest that required both elucidation and periodisation. Some of the critical processes in this formation have been hinted at in the foregoing discussion; the insertion of the middle class in widening networks of economic and political life after 1850, the gradual coalescence of a distinctive 'business' class between 1880 and 1914, the points of cultural intersection – the public school, the ethic of the gentleman – serving to consolidate the worlds of industry, land, and commerce. This movement to class integration was slower than is often assumed: 'pride of order' and anti-aristocratic sentiment left a powerful mark on the outlook of employers to 1914, while the tardy development of a coherent local bourgeoisie in industrial areas such as the Clyde region indicates something of its uneven, non-linear nature.[69]

The social development of the mid- and late-Victorian middle class was thus shaped within a dialectic of tension and accommodation, independence and integration, played out in class and cultural relations. The complex and ambiguous character of this process marked relations of power and cultural formation down to the level of the local and particular. In May 1857, Prince Albert and his courtly retinue arrived at Abney Hall to stay with James Watts, cotton magnate and Mayor of Manchester, on the occasion of the Art Treasures Exhibition. While Life Guards paraded at the Hall gates, Watts entertained the royal company in his recently-built mansion, lavishly hung with paintings by Rubens, Holbein and

Gainsborough, and furnished with mementos of such heroes as Byron, Southey, John Wesley, and Cromwell, the Mayor's 'patron saint'.[70] If the irony of this encounter between Radical Nonconformist businessman and the representative of monarchy and aristocracy was not missed by contemporaries, no sense of incongruity was disclosed by the participants themselves: business and the state appear to have gazed back at one another with mutual approbation. Watts was duly rewarded for his services with a knighthood later the same year, while it became his lifelong pride 'to point to a motto on the ceiling of the library, "Seest thou a man diligent in business, he shall stand before kings", and say that the nearest approach to it he knew was that he had several times sat and chatted under that motto with Prince Albert'.[71] The visit, like those subsequently paid by Lord Derby, Gladstone and Disraeli, did nothing to weaken Watts's commitment to radical Liberalism, Nonconformity, or the affairs of factory and warehouse. the significance of the occasion – as of the Art Treasures Exhibition more generally – lay rather in the symbolic reconciliation of supposed antitheses: art and industry, 'high' and 'self-made' culture, metropolis and provinces, aristocratic state and industrial bourgeoisie. The terms on which this symbolic accommodation was reached were, as ever, complex and provisional, precisely because the interests and identities of the power-groups involved were not synonymous. Some twenty years after her husband's visit Queen Victoria rejected an invitation to open the newly-built Manchester Town Hall, a rebuff which was variously blamed on the radical political past of the then Mayor, Abel Heywood, and the recent erection by the Corporation of a memorial to Oliver Cromwell in the town centre. The slight was noted, but quickly passed over.[72] For was it not now manifest for all to see, what a local author was later able confidently to pronounce, that 'Portland Street, or Mosley Street or Church Street has hardly meant less to the world, and might be held to have meant more, than the High Street of Oxford'?[73]

Notes

1 J. Field, *Bourgeois Portsmouth: Social Relations in a Victorian Dockyard Town, 1815–75*, Warwick Ph.D., 1979, Introduction.
2 For further comments on the Gradgrind myth see J. Seed, 'Unitarianism, political economy and the antinomies of liberal culture in Manchester, 1830–50', *Social History*, vii, January 1982, pp. 1–2.
3 For example, J. Garrard, *Leadership and Power in Victorian Industrial Towns, 1830–80*, Manchester, 1982; G. Crossick, *The Emergence of the Lower Middle Class in Britain, 1870–1914*, London, 1978; L. Davidoff and C. Hall, 'The architecture of public and private life in English middle-class society in a provincial town, 1780–1850' in D. Fraser and A. Sutcliffe (eds.), *The Pursuit of*

Urban History, London, 1983.
4 Though important contributions are beginning to appear. See, for example, Geoffrey Ingham, *Capitalism Divided? The City and Industry in British Social Development*, London, 1984; J. Cox, The *English Churches in a Secular Society: Lambeth, 1870–1930*, London, 1982.
5 P. Anderson, 'Origins of the present crisis', *New Left Review*, 23, 1964; T. Nairn, 'The British political elite', *New Left Review*, 23, 1964; T. Nairn, *The Break-Up of Britain*, London, 1977, Ch. 1 (for a more recent restatement of these themes); M. Wiener, *English Culture and the Decline of the Industrial Spirit, 1850–1980*, Cambridge, 1981; A. Mayer, *The Persistence of the Ancien Régime*, London, 1981; W. D. Rubinstein, 'Wealth, elites and the class structure of modern Britain', *Past and Present*, 76, 1977; *Men of Property*, London, 1981.
6 See *Marx and Engels on Britain*, London, 1962; or for a more recent non-Marxist interpretation of middle-class hegemony, H. Perkin, *The Origins of Modern English Society, 1780–1880*, London, 1969, Ch. VIII.
7 See N. McCord, 'Cobden and Bright in politics, 1846–57' in R. Robson (ed.), *Ideas and Institutions of Victorian Britain*, London, 1976, pp. 87–114; J. Morley, 'The chamber of mediocrity', *Fortnightly Review*, December 1868, p. 690; H. Belloc, 'Appeal to the Squires', *New Witness* 2, October 1913; G. Orwell, *The Lion and the Unicorn: Socialism and the English Genius*, London, 1962.
8 C. Barnett, *The Collapse of British Power*, London, 1972; J. Sumption and K. Joseph, *Equality*, London, 1979; F. W. S. Craig (ed.), *Conservative and Labour Party Conference Decisions, 1945–1981*, Leicester, 1981, pp. 39–40; see also the lecture on 'The fall and rise of the entrepreneur' by Lord Young, chairman of the MSC, announced in The *Guardian*, 9 July 1985. Lord Young, we are informed, is 'a firm believer that Britain cannot cure its social and economic problems without a positive return to an enterprise culture'.
9 Anderson, 'Origins', Section 1.
10 E. P. Thompson, 'The peculiarities of the English' in *The Poverty of Theory*, London, 1978; Richard Johnson, 'Barrington Moore, Perry Anderson and English social development' in S. Hall *et al.* (eds.), *Culture, Media, Language*, London, 1980; R. Gray, 'Bourgeois hegemony in Victorian Britain' in J. Bloomfield (ed.), *Class, Hegemony, Party*, London, 1977.
11 Rubinstein, 'Wealth', p. 99. The critique which follows relates exclusively to this article, though many of the points made bear equally on the evidence and conclusions presented in *Men of Property*.
12 Rubinstein, 'Wealth', pp. 112–17.
13 Rubinstein, 'Wealth', p. 117, footnote.
14 For a more extensive review see *Men of Property*, Ch. 1.
15 Rubinstein, 'The Victorian middle classes: wealth, occupation and geography', *Economic History Review*, 1977; R. J. Morris, 'The middle class and the property cycle during the industrial revolution', in T. C. Smout (ed.), *The Search for Wealth and Stability*, London, 1979.
16 For example, R. Floud and D. McCloskey (eds.), *The Economic History of Britain since 1700*, Vol. 2, Cambridge, 1981.
17 See, for instance, the collective wealth of the Pease, Straker and other Newcastle dynasties detailed in Benwell Community Project, *The Making of a Ruling Class*, Newcastle, 1978, Appendix 2.
18 J. Field, review of 'Men of Property', *Social History*, January 1983.
19 Cited in A. Redford, *A History of Local Government in Manchester, Vol. 2: Borough and City*, Ch. 24, Manchester, 1940.

20 A. Briggs, *Victorian People*, London, 1965, p. 128.
21 A literature which has received little systematic attention from historians, but see E. Helm, 'The middleman in commerce', *Transactions of the Manchester Statistical Society*, 1900–1, pp. 55–65; R. Spencer, *The Home Trade of Manchester*, London, 1896; B. G. Orchard, *Liverpool's Legion of Honour*, Liverpool, 1893.
22 G. Stedman Jones, *Outcast London*, Oxford, 1971; C. Behagg, 'Custom, class and change: the trade societies of Birmingham', *Social History*, October 1979; A. J. Kidd, 'Charity organization and the unemployed in Manchester, c.1870–1914, *Social History*, January 1984.
23 V. A. C. Gatrell, *The Commercial Middle Class in Manchester, 1820–57*, Cambridge Ph.D., 1971, Ch. 2.
24 D. Fraser, *Urban Politics in Victorian England*, Leicester, 1976; Crossick, 'Emergence of the Lower Middle Class'; for a wider comparative perspective see F. Bechofer and B. Elliott (eds.), *The Petite Bourgeoisie*, London, 1981.
25 P. Joyce, *Work, Society and Politics*, Brighton, 1981, Ch. 1; Fraser, 'Urban Politics', *passim*.
26 Wiener, 'English Culture', Chs. 2, 3.
27 Endorsed by critics on the political left as well as the right. See Tom Nairn's call for a renewed phase of 'modernisation' in *The Break-Up of Britain*, Ch. 1.
28 Wiener, 'English Culture', p. 7 and *passim*.
29 T. Zeldin, *France 1848–1945*, Vol. 1, Oxford, 1973. For the historiographical critique see D. Blackbourn and G . Eley, *The Peculiarities of German History*, Oxford, 1984; S. Wilson, ' 'They order . . . this matter better in France': some recent books on modern French historiography', *Historical Journal*, XXI, 1978.
30 D. Blackbourn, 'The discreet charm of the bourgeoisie' in Blackbourn and Eley, 'Peculiarities', Ch. 1.
31 Mayer, 'Persistence'.
32 J. Harris and P. Thane, 'British and European bankers. 1880–1914: an "aristocratic bourgeoisie" ', in P. Thane, G. Crossick and R. Floud (eds.), *The Power of the Past*, Cambridge, 1984, pp. 215–19.
33 For comments on this see Gray in Bloomfield, 'Class, Hegemony', pp. 83–91.
34 L. and J. C. F. Stone, *An Open Elite?: England 1540–1880*, Oxford, 1984, pp. 402–7.
35 N. Rogers, 'Money, land and lineage: the big bourgeoisie of Hanoverian London', *Social History*, October 1979.
36 A. Howe, *The Lancashire Textile Masters, 1830–60*, Oxford, 1984; C. Erickson, *British Industrialists: Steel and Hosiery, 1850–1950*, Cambridge, 1959; Benwell, 'Making'.
37 E. Walford, *The County Families of the United Kingdom*, London, 1860 onwards, for a number of such families.
38 J. S. Leatherbarrow, *Victorian Period Piece: Studies Occasioned by a Lancashire Church*, London, 1954.
39 Joyce, 'Work', Epilogue.
40 See, for example, S. D. Chapman, 'Financial restraints on the growth of firms in the cotton industry, 1790–1850', *Economic History Review*, 32, 1979.
41 S. B. Saul, *The Myth of the Great Depression*, London, 1969; R. Floud and D. McCloskey, 'Economic History'; McCloskey and L. G. Sandberg, 'From damnation to redemption; judgements on the late Victorian entrepreneur', *Explorations in Economic History*, 9, 1971–2. For a comparative treatment see R. Fox, 'Britain in perspective: the European context of industrial training and

innovation, 1880–1914', *History and Technology*, 1985.
42 E. Hobsbawn, *Industry and Empire*, London, 1969, pp. 182–94.
43 The conventional view of most labour historians since Engels. See, for instance, G. D. H. Cole and Raymond Postgate, *The Common People*, London, 1938; or more recently, T. R. Tholfsen, *Working-Class Radicalism in Mid-Victorian England*, London, 1976, Chs. 4, 5. For a survey of recent historical approaches to class formation see R. J. Morris, 'Introduction', in R. J. Morris (ed.), *Class, Power and Social Structure In British Nineteenth-Century Towns*, Leicester, 1986.
44 An example of the application of the notion of 'elites' in the study of the middle class can be found in R. Trainor, 'Urban elites in Victorian Britain', *Urban History Yearbook*, 1985. For some of the sociological difficulties engendered by the use of the concept see J. Scott, *The Upper Classes: Property and Privilege in Britain*, London, 1982, Preface.
45 For a useful discussion of the 'middle ranks' and politics in the late eighteenth century see J. Brewer, 'Commercialization and politics' in N. McKendrick, J. Brewer and J. Plumb (eds.), *The Birth of a Consumer Society: The Commercialization of Eighteenth-Century England*, London, 1982.
46 Fraser, 'Urban Politics'; Crossick, 'Emergence of the Lower Middle Class'.
47 Gatrell, 'Commercial Middle Class', Ch. 10; Fraser, 'Urban Politics', pp. 203–10.
48 S. and B. Webb, *English Local Government from the Revolution to the Municipal Corporations Act*, London, 1906–29, Vol. 3; G. Best, *Mid-Victorian Britain, 1851–70*, London, 1979, pp. 53–67.
49 See, for example, D. Foster, *The Changing Social and Political Composition of the Lancashire Magistracy, 1821–51*, Lancaster Ph.D., 1971.
50 R. J. Morris, 'Voluntary societies and British urban elites, 1780–1880: an analysis', *Historical Journal*, March 1983.
51 See Garrard, 'Leadership and Power', for an important assessment of the scope of, and the limits to, middle-class authority in the urban context.
52 R. H. Trainor, *Authority and Social Structure in an Industrialized Area: A Study of Three Black Country Towns, 1840–90*, Oxford D.Phil., 1981; C. Binfield, 'Hindhead Highmindedness', *PN Review*, 48–50, 1986; Joyce, 'Work', Ch. 1; Benwell, 'Making', Appendix 1.
53 Ashton family papers, Manchester Central Reference Library; Leatherbarrow, 'Victorian Period Piece'.
54 C. Binfield, *So Down to Prayers*, London, 1977, p. 56.
55 R. J. Morris, 'The middle class and British towns and cities of the industrial revolution, 1780–1870' in D. Fraser and A. Sutcliffe (eds.), *The Pursuit of Urban History*, London, 1983.
56 For Chadwick see P. L. Cottrell, *Industrial Finance, 1830–1914*, London, 1980, Ch. 5. Figures on women shareholders cited in Field, 'Bourgeois Portsmouth', p. 131.
57 J. Seed, 'Theologies of power: Unitarianism and the social relations of religious discourse, 1800–50' in R. J. Morris, 'Class, Power'; Binfield, 'So Down'.
58 E.g. the Congregational and Baptist Unions.
59 J. Vincent, *The Formation of the Liberal Party*, Brighton, 1976, p. 69.
60 The languages of the middle class remain an under-researched domain. But see A. Briggs, 'The language of 'class' in early nineteenth-century England' in A. Briggs and J. Saville (eds.), *Essays in Labour History*, London, 1967. Also R. Gray, 'The languages of factory reform' in P. Joyce, *The Historical Meanings of Work*, Cambridge, forthcoming 1987.

61 See, for instance, J. Seed, 'Manchester College, York: an early nineteenth-century dissenting academy' in *Journal of Educational Administration and History*, 1982.
62 Indeed, Arnold was reputed to have tried to exclude sons of the aristocracy from Rugby in the 1840s. See E. Dunning, 'The origins of modern football and the public school ethos' in B. Simon and I. Bradley (eds.), *The Victorian Public School; Studies in the Development of an Educational Institution*, London, 1975, p. 171.
63 See G. Best, *Mid-Victorian Britain, 1851–70*, London, 1979, p. 185. For a more detailed treatment, R. Wilkinson, *The Prefects: British Leadership and the Public School Tradition*, London, 1964.
64 As Seed argues, 'Unitarianism and liberal culture'.
65 As suggested by the behaviour of the autocratic Ashton employer, Hugh Mason. For a vivid description of Mason's relations with the local community see W. H. Mills, *The Manchester Reform Club, 1871–1921*, Manchester, 1922, pp. 10–12.
66 For further discussion of this tradition see Vincent, 'Liberal Party', pp. xlii–xliv.
67 P. Clarke, *Liberals and Social Democrats*, Cambridge, 1978.
68 See the valuable discussions of Thompson, 'Poverty of Theory', and Gray, 'Bourgeois Hegemony'.
69 J. Melling, 'Scottish industrialists and the changing character of class relations in the Clyde region, 1880–1914', in T. Dickson (ed.), *Capital and Class in Scotland*, Edinburgh, 1982, pp. 61–142.
70 B. L. Thompson, *The Town Hall, Cheadle*, Manchester, 1972, for details of the contents of Abney Hall.
71 F. Moss, *Pilgrimages*, Vol. 2, Manchester, 1903, p. 391. Watts family papers, Manchester Central Reference Library.
72 See G. S. Messinger, *Manchester in the Victorian Age: The Half-Known City*, Manchester, 1985, pp. 154–5, for a brief description of the episode.
73 Mills, 'Manchester Reform Club', p. 4.

'Commerce and the liberal arts':
the political economy of art in Manchester, 1775–1860

'The phenomenon has absolutely astounded us!' an anonymous reviewer of a book of poems published in Manchester wrote in *Blackwood's Edinburgh Magazine* in 1821. 'There is something in the very name itself which puts to flight all poetical associations. Only couple, for instance, in your mind the ideas of Manchester and Wordsworth, and see if, by any mental process, you can introduce them into any sort of union. The genius of that great man would have been absolutely clouded for ever by one week's residence in the fogs of Manchester.' The name 'Manchester' conjured up for the littérateurs of *Blackwood*'s 'a little whey-faced man, in a brown frock coat and dirty coloured neck-cloth, smelling – not of perfumes or cassia, but of cotton and calicoes; talking – not of Shakespeare or Pope, but "Yours of the 11th ult. duly came to hand in which per advice etc. etc." ' Even the town's better off inhabitants were 'gentlemen, whose erudition, we believe, consists in the playing whist, drinking port and damning "form" . . . If five or six have the rare ability to get through a few sentences of mawkish common-place at some public meeting, we apprehend that is the extent of their powers, and the summit of their ambition.'[1]

An intended provocation by the Tory periodical and transparently overdrawn, nevertheless, this kind of caricature became an important element in the received picture of the northern industrial middle class as bluff, plain-speaking, uncultured, Nonconformist, Liberal, self-made men, concerned wholly with making money. It was a caricature rooted, of course, in the social and political antagonisms of nineteenth-century Britain: in the tensions between land and industry, between capital and labour, between Church of England and nonconformity, between old capital and new capital, between the cultivated 'centre' and the philistine provinces. But it is a picture that has a continuing resonance in the modern historiography of the period which, from quite divergent perspectives, has tended to represent the middle class of towns like Manchester or Bradford as wealthy philistines, heroes of capital accumulation, incapable of transcending a narrow and dogmatic set of categories derived from Benthamite utilitarianism, political economy and a stern puritanical religion. 'The stout main body of philistinism', Matthew Arnold called the northern Liberal middle class and few historians have subsequently dissented from this judgement.[2]

In the introduction to this book some of the sources of these kinds of judgements of 'bourgeois philistinism' have been examined. In this chapter I want to focus on art in industrialising Manchester: firstly to question unsubstantiated allegations of philistinism, but also – and more importantly – to go beyond the terms of that kind of argument. I will not be focusing on paintings or forms of representation. Rather, I want to look at the emergence of an 'art-world' deeply embedded in the town's economic and social structure. A whole network of participants, not just the artist – producers of paint and canvas and brushes, artists' models, picture framers, art dealers, organisers of exhibitions, art critics, supporters of art institutions, among others – made the production of art possible and determined the character of that art.[3] The cultural infrastructure built up by the middle class of Manchester in the nineteenth century was complex and multi-faceted and this art world was only one component of it. However, it provides a route into important questions about changes in the character of the 'cultural economy', about the new institutional structures which shaped a rapidly growing middle class, about the ways in which art was appropriated into the emerging civic culture of a major nineteenth-century city.

I

'This is a thriving place', Celia Fiennes remarked of Manchester around 1700 and was impressed by the substantial brick and stone houses, the large market, the trappings of refinement such as music and dancing and 'a very fine school for young gentlewomen, as good as any in London'.[4] In the course of the eighteenth century Manchester developed as a major business centre. It was the nexus of a network of roads and canals and had become the main co-ordinating centre of textile production in the region with a population of around 30,000 by the 1770s. Many of its merchants – controlling the 'putting out' system or the finishing trades – built up substantial fortunes. And with prosperity went a demand for all kinds of consumer goods and professional services. Jewellers, hairdressers and peruke makers, retailers of china, plate and cut glass, tobacconists, wine and brandy merchants, clock and watch makers, confectioners, and so on, sprang up in the town centre and found a buoyant market for their services, as did the medical and legal profession.

Growing prosperity and leisure among the upper strata of Manchester Society during the eighteenth century created a market also for culture. The town's first theatre was opened in 1753 and another in the 1760s. Public concerts of music were held periodically from the 1740s and in 1777 the Gentleman's Concert Hall was opened. A substantial reading public developed, catered for by a growing number of weekly newspapers and all kinds of locally printed books and pamphlets – poetry, sermons, cookery books, metaphysical disquisitions, political polemics, commercial manuals, and so on. The town's first circulating library was established in 1757. With the Literary and Philosophical Society, set up in 1781, Manchester possessed an intellectual forum which quickly established a national reputation. John Aikin could write in 1795: 'The town has now in every respect assumed the style and manners of one of the commercial capitals of Europe.'[5]

To what extent was art part of this expansion of demand for the luxuries of life among a prosperous bourgeoisie? In fact retail outlets for pictures developed slowly in eighteenth-century Manchester. In the first directory in 1772 there was a single supplier – William Newton, bookseller, stationer and printseller.[6] One or two bookshops selling prints and the occasional painting remained the only kind of retail outlet, though these varied widely in their stock and their clientele. There were, for instance, shops exploiting the popular market for simple cheap broadsides, sensational tales and chapbooks – like that of Swindells on Hanging Ditch which Samuel Bamford recalled, exhibiting in its windows 'numerous songs, ballads, tales and other publications, with horrid and awful woodcuts at the head' which fascinated him as a child.[7] On the other hand there were shops dealing at the upper end of the market, with antiquarian books and recent London publications. These often stocked a considerable quantity of prints and some paintings. William Ford, listed in the trade directory of the time as 'bookseller and stationer', had a substantial stock of prints and paintings. His printed catalogue of 1805 included in lot 53: 'Several thousands of English and foreign portraits, many of them extremely rare and curious ....'.[8] Only in the directory of 1800 does there emerge for the first time a specialist art shop, with Sillo and Co., picture frame makers and printsellers – a firm which seems to have disappeared within a few years.

There were other ways of purchasing pictures. Itinerant dealers and auctioneers passed through the town, advertising their wares in the local newspapers and often selling work of dubious provenance. In this period itinerant painters – especially portrait painters – were commonplace, setting up in a town until the supply of commissions seemed exhausted and then moving on.[9] Thus in October 1792 S. Poleck, 'Artist from London', announced an exhibition of specimens of his portraits open to the Manchester public – with what success in procuring commissions it is impossible to say.[10] Daniel Stringer, of Knutsford, much patronised by the Cheshire gentry for his landscapes and animal paintings, also spent periods in Manchester and found buyers there in the last years of the eighteenth century. The manufacturer Thomas Kershaw, the merchant Samuel Barton and the Unitarian solicitor George Duckworth each owned two pictures by Stringer in this period.[11] There were, then, painters and dealers passing in and out of the town. Indeed, one artist resident in the town for a while stated in 1809 that 'there is, generally a prejudice against a Provincial artist, who vegetates upon one spot, let his merit be what it may.'[12]

However, there was always a population of artists in Manchester from the mid-eighteenth century. Peter Romney found two artists when he passed through the town in 1767 but little scope for patronage. He complained that the Manchester people were unadventurous, 'old women in everything, except trade and manufacture.'[13] The first town directory in 1772 specified a single professional artist – Joseph Legard Jnr., 'Miniature-painter, and Musick-maker', son of a local shoemaker. Subsequently their numbers increased, but slowly, according to the trade directories:

1788	1794	1797	1800	1804	1809
3	4	3	6	4	6

Clearly a number of painters found commissions in Manchester at the end of the eighteenth century. Farington reported in July 1797 that Charles Towne was 'much employed at Manchester, has six months work bespoke.'[14] Joseph Parry was based in the town from 1790 and found a number of patrons – including the Quaker cotton manufacturer David Holt and the merchant Otho Hulme.[15] William Tate of Liverpool received several important commissions in Manchester, including portraits of Dr Charles White and James Massey.[16] And there were others – Joshua Shaw, Patrick McMoreland, John Rathbone, Richard Bonnington, W. M. Craig, among others – who made some kind of living by their art in Manchester. William Green (1761–1823) combined the careers of artist, drawing master and surveyor in late eighteenth-century Manchester. From 1783 he ran a school 'for the instruction of young gentlemen in the arts of drawing and painting' and in the early 1790s he set up an exhibition of his paintings and drawings, charging an entrance fee of one shilling. His major project, however, was a new street plan of the rapidly developing town which occupied him from 1787 until 1794 but brought him little material reward.[17] There was even a 'natural genius' in the town. Joshua Shaw was a chair painter at the fancy chair warehouse of David Bancroft on Chapel Street in Salford in the 1790s when his landscapes were brought to the notice of David Holt and several other patrons. He set up as a professional artist, appearing in the directories as such for the first time in 1800, and was soon earning between fifty and sixty guineas for his landscapes. Within a few years he departed for the more lucrative waters of Bath, where he shocked Benjamin West by his speed and facility in copying the style of other painters, and subsequently emigrated to North America.[18]

We turn now to the question of who in Manchester was purchasing art. There were two very substantial art collectors in Manchester at the end of the eighteenth century – John Leigh Philips and William Hardman. Philips belonged to an old merchant dynasty in the town and was involved in the silk trade. He was prosperous and active in Manchester affairs – he was a magistrate, a founder of the Literary and Philosophical Society and for many years, as treasurer, the key figure in the management of the Manchester Infirmary.[19] Philips was more than a casual collector. His library was extensive, numbering nearly 1,500 volumes, his private papers include all kinds of comments and reflections on the fine arts, on the success of the Royal Academy, on the techniques of painters, and he occasionally wrote for such periodicals as the *Montly Magazine.* His art collection was large and raised nearly £5,500 when it was auctioned off – in a ten-day sale of over one thousand lots – after his death in 1814.[20] Hardman too was from an old Manchester family well established in trade.[21] A prosperous drysalter, he spent considerable sums of money on his artistic tastes. He added a spacious music room to his house on Quay Street for private rehearsals of the 'Gentlemen's Concerts' – and here too came local writers, scientists, antiquarians, connoisseurs of art and music. Nowhere in or around Manchester, said the eccentric local antiquarian Thomas Barrit, himself a frequent guest, 'could cope with the studio in Quay Street, for literature, science and the arts'.[22] Hardman's collection of paintings – which ranged widely and included, reportedly, works by Titian, Canaletto, Veronese, Ruisdael, Rembrandt, Wilson, Wright and Fuseli – was said to have cost between thirty and forty thousand pounds and by 1807 numbered around seventy pictures.[23]

Clearly Philips and Hardman were unusual in Manchester in the extent of their investments in art. But both exemplify a wider point. The town's manufacturers, merchants and professional men were very mobile, frequently travelling to other towns, London especially, on business. The capital's art world – its dealers and auctions, its exhibitions at the Royal

Academy and, from 1805, the British Institution, its artists' studios – was part of the itinerary for any visitor. Philips clearly knew London's art dealers, noting their improvement over recent years in an undated notebook.[24] William Hardman was a visitor to the Royal Academy exhibitions and to the studios of such academicians as Fuseli and Farington, and he attended art sales. When Richard Potter, young Manchester merchant, Unitarian and political radical, visited London in 1807 he went to the Royal Academy exhibition at Somerset House along with visits to the theatre, the British Museum, the Houses of Parliament, and a public hanging at Newgate. Unlike Philips or Hardman, Potter was not a collector of paintings, yet he called in at Somerset House on subsequent visits to London. Thus in May 1809 he noted in his diary: 'I looked over the Paintings at Somerset House with which I was highly gratified'.[25] The Royal Academy was clearly successful in establishing its reputation as a national centre of the best art. Indeed, its members at times seemed to have been almost slavishly relied upon for advice and reassurance in purchasing pictures. When Hardman was looking for paintings to buy in London in 1795 he depended very much upon the advice of Joseph Farington, who accompanied him to several sales. Several other Manchester men at this time made a bee-line for Farington to seek guidance on the London art market.[26]

Already in the closing years of the eighteenth century, then, the prosperous middle classes of Manchester – through a few local printsellers, through the occasional itinerant auctioneer, through the London art market or even direct from the artists themselves – had access to art. 'There are many collectors of pictures at Manchester at present', Farington noted in his diary in 1808.[27] Insurance policy registers for Manchester in the 1780s and 1790s sometimes covered household contents and occasionally specify paintings and prints. These were generally insured for the modest sum of ten pounds. The largest valuation was £40 for 'prints and paintings' belonging to John Nash, a local cotton manufacturer, in 1794.[28] And in the early nineteenth century there were periodical sales of the household goods of local men who had either died or gone bankrupt, which suggests that a few paintings and some prints were – along with a reasonable number of books and periodicals, perhaps a harpischord, a few fine pieces of furniture – an essential part of the bourgeois interior. However, they seem often to have been 'old masters', and frequently were forgeries – less often the work of contemporary British painters.

Undoubtedly there were Manchester art collections which did contain genuine old masters. When the German artist Passavant travelled through the town in the early 1830s, he visited an exhibition of locally-owned old masters and noted that a number of them were of 'great interest' – among them pictures by Giorgione, Murillo and one ascribed, probably wrongly, to Raphael.[29] Edward Loyd (1790–1863), wealthy partner in a Manchester banking firm, built up a valuable collection of paintings. Like Robert Peel, he had a taste for Dutch art and his collection included pictures by Cuyp, Hobbema, Ruisdael, Steen, de Hooch and others – validated by John Smith in his *catalogue raisonné* of Dutch masters.[30] And in the 1820s William Ford, a local bookseller, publisher and art dealer, commended several local collectors for their possession of works of modest but solid value. But he also noted that fraudulent dealers – 'Picture Jockeys' as he called them – had found easy prey among some Manchester collectors, despite public warnings. The worst victim of all, in Ford's opinion, was the barrister Richard Ashworth, but it is apparent that a number of local men had possessed forgeries, or copies sold as originals.[31] Under Samuel Carter Hall, the *Art Union Journal* had engaged in something of a moral crusade against gullible buyers and fraudulent dealers from its inception in 1839. It detailed the multitude of fraudulent dealers, from those who auctioned off fifth-rate paintings as the work of leading living painters for a few pounds to the *petite-bourgeoisie* to those engaged in more elaborate forms of deceit. Fraud and deceit riddled the art market in the late eighteenth and early nineteenth century – from threadbare hawkers and back-sheet dealers to established art dealers like Christie's, peddling forgeries for anonymous clients.[32] When an exhibition of the works of 'Ancient Masters' opened at the Royal Manchester Institution in April 1847 the *Art Union Journal* took the opportunity to underline its message. Only ten out of two hundred of these pictures was worth anything at all; many of them were forgeries. 'We earnestly hope the manufacturers of Manchester – enterprising, liberal and wealthy as they are – will not be, hereafter, the victims of vagabond picture dealers, as they have been.'[33]

To summarise: an increasingly prosperous bourgeoisie in Manchester in the late eighteenth century and the opening years of the nineteenth began to provide a market for paintings and prints. However, partly under the influence of the dominant aristocratic tradition, and partly duped by unscrupulous art dealers, a significant proportion of buyers in the town were interested primarily in 'old masters'. The influence of the Royal Academy and the contemporary English school in general was becoming more marked from the end of the eighteenth century and some Manchester buyers were beginning to invest in living painters. However, Manchester lacked much of an art world in this period: there were few artists permanently based in the town, few art dealers and no public exhibitions. A local writer commented in 1828 that until recently

Manchester ranked lower in the fine arts than any other major British city.[34]

II

By the 1820s things were beginning to change. With the establishment of the Royal Manchester Institution in 1823 there were significant steps in the direction of building a public culture in Manchester in which art had an important role. At the same time, and closely linked to it, there developed a much more substantial art market with many more working painters.

With regard to the development of dealers, it is apparent that their numbers rose steadily: there were ten art dealers in 1825 and fifteen by 1836. This is an underestimate, since as well as ostensible 'picture dealers' there were other retailers of paintings and prints. Bookshops continued to play an important role in selling prints and paintings. Jacob Williamson was listed in the trade directory of 1836 merely as 'bookseller'. But Richard Proctor recalled his shop on Smithy Door in the 1830s as stocked not just with books but also with masks and wigs and all kinds of stage properties, birdcages, clocks, stationery, razors, tools, oil paintings, prints and engravings. The windows of the shop were crowded with coloured squibs and caricatures by the likes of Rowlandson, representing Fox and Pitt and the Prince Regent. Proctor used to spend hours poring over the numerous prints: 'Who that remembers Jacob can forget his portfolios of engravings, some of them containing revelations of beauty that brightened his small dark sanctuary . . .'[35]

However, a different kind of art dealer began to emerge in early nineteenth-century Manchester. A number of firms initially involved in picture-frame making developed into dealers of art and other luxury goods. Vittore Zanetti, for instance, from 1804 ran a business framing pictures but quickly diversified: his firm made frames for pictures and mirrors, published and sold prints, cleaned and restored paintings, sold coins, medals, mirrors, bronze figures, lamps, furniture, scientific instruments, barometers, artists' materials, paper and sweepstake tickets. He also began to import paintings from Europe and exhibited them for sale in his rooms, grandly termed 'The Repository of the Arts'.[36] Other firms evolved in the same way, combining the sale of paintings and prints with the cleaning, restoring and framing of pictures and/or selling all kinds of collectable items or luxury household goods and specialised scientific instruments. Thus, for instance, Grundy and Goadsby were by the 1830s an important firm publishing and selling prints, water-colours and oil paintings – yet they continued to produce their own frames, restore and frame pictures, sell all kinds of glass, lamps, bronze figures, mirrors, artists' materials, and so on.[37] Thomas Agnew took over Zanetti's business and developed it into one of the major art dealers and print publishers in Britain. Yet still in the late 1840s Agnews were dealing in all kinds of items – coins and medals, scientific instruments, chandeliers, furniture and so on.[38]

Other firms dealt in art as part of an auctioneering business. William Ford, for instance, advertised himself in 1825 as 'English and foreign book and print seller and auctioneer of literary property'.[39] Thomas Dodd, a well-known London bookdealer and print seller, bankrupted in 1817, settled in Manchester as an auctioneer.[40] His main interest was in books, prints and paintings but he auctioned any kind of property. For instance an auction in 1822 was announced – 'to the Cognoscenti of Manchester' – as a sale of 'a truly superb collection of PICTURES, and a variety of ARTICLES of TASTE and virtue'. It included Italian, Venetian, Flemish, Dutch and English paintings as well as bronzes, ivory carvings, silver, china, antique guns, a dress sword, snuff boxes set in gold and silver, a variety of medals and coins and jewellery.[41]

In early nineteenth-century Manchester, then, there developed a number of substantial firms dealing in art. Several of these – Zanetti and Agnew, D. and P. Jackson, John Clowes Grundy – had permanent exhibitions of pictures for sale and were of more than local importance. Though still generally combining art dealing with a number of other business activities, some of these firms began to develop beyond the framework of the retail shop with a workshop behind and provided a gallery for viewing the stock of paintings. The profits to be made were substantial. Zanetti and Agnew were clearing a surplus of £2,000 a year in the early 1820s on an annual turnover of around £8,000, and Zanetti retired in 1828 with enough capital to invest in a small landed estate in his native Italy. Total assets of the firm in 1847 were £16,000 and by 1851 had risen to £27,000 – from which Agnew was drawing a personal income of £1,080. Profits in the early 1850s were around £4,000 per annum and a few years later were £8,000.[42] 'Agnew's play the first fiddle in this town – their establishment here is very extensive and various', one dealer visiting Manchester commented in 1858.[43] Certainly Agnew's were the premier art dealers in the town and by 1860 had branches in Liverpool and London. But other dealers in Manchester were highly successful – notably John Clowes Grundy, who by 1851 was living in style at Cliff House in the fashionable Manchester suburb of Broughton with a large family and four servants. On his death in 1867 his stock of works numbered no less than 3,924 lots, filled a catalogue of 271 pages and took eighteen days to sell: it included paintings by

Tintoretto, Kneller, Barry, Morland, Stanfield, Haydon, Turner, Landseer and Lawrence, among many others.[44]

The emergence of a number of substantial dealers in art from around the 1820s, as well as testifying to the massive wealth circulating in Manchester, marked a significant shift in the nature of the local art market. First, several of these firms were becoming integrated into the networks of the national and even the international art market. It was increasingly unnecessary for the Manchester collector to travel to the salerooms and exhibitions of London to see the best of contemporary art. Several dealers in the 1820s and 1830s were drawing into the Manchester art market pictures from throughout Britain. Thus in August 1821 John Ford (son of William), announced that he now had 'a few Pictures of the very highest class of Art, collected during the latest sales in London, particularly at that of the late Marchioness of Thomond's (Sir Joshua Reynolds's) collection'.[45] By the end of the 1830s Grundy was buying in a number of the best known contemporary British artists and was dealing with some of them directly. In 1849 he was exhibiting in Manchester three paintings by Ary Scheffer, one of them commissioned by Grundy. This was something of a coup for the town – Scheffer was highly fashionable at this time and none of these three pictures had been exhibited in Britain before.[46] By the early 1840s Agnew's too were dealing directly with several artists and were putting up for sale in Manchester pictures by Turner, Constable, Etty, Stanfield, Frith, Martin, Landseer and many others.[47] Secondly, these dealers provided a forum in which members of the Manchester public could see and discuss the latest art. Henry Gibbs recalled an art dealer's shop on Oxford Road, Manchester, where he spent much time talking to the owner (Mr Rareworthy – clearly a pseudonym), learning about art and the art market. Here also a number of men gathered regularly to talk and sometimes argue heatedly about art: 'Mr Rareworthy must in his time have been the quiet observer of many a contest between zealous and excited art disputants'.[48] In this way art dealers were more than merely retail outlets. They became a cultural institution of sorts – a kind of art gallery, a forum for art lovers to meet and debate, and a place where the art dealer could exert a measure of influence on his clients. In this way some of these dealers – Thomas Agnew and John Clowes Grundy certainly – succeeded in shifting the interests of Manchester buyers away from shoddy and third-rate 'old masters' towards contemporary English artists. The *Art Journal* observed in 1871, on the occasion of Agnew's death:

> When we knew him and Lancashire first, it was a rare event to find a purchaser for any work of modern Art: cartloads of trash under the pretence of being ancient masters were annually sold in the north of England; works with the

names of 'Rubens' or 'Raphael' or 'Titian' found ready buyers, but pictures by British artists had little or no chance of sale: the 'old' must be worth money, the 'new' worth nothng.[49]

Agnew challenged this and succeeded in improving the status of contemporary British art and in redirecting taste away from 'old masters'.

However, though of strategic importance, art dealers were not the only means by which the art market and public tastes were reshaped. A number of public institutions played a significant role, especially the Royal Manchester Institution, set up in 1823. Originally this was intended as an organisation primarily concerned with the management of regular art exhibitions in the town.[50] In May 1827 an exhibition of living British artists was opened with entry to the 'public' on payment of a shilling. It proved a financial success with many visitors and a substantial number of paintings sold. Subsequently there was an annual exhibition of this kind as well as other occasional exhibitions of water-colours, old masters, and so on, constituting a significant marketplace for art in the town. Of course actual sales at these exhibitions fluctuated, as did the quality of the work exhibited. In the early 1840s especially the standard of the exhibitions appears to have gone into decline. The *Art Union Journal* complained that too few eminent artists were sending work and many pictures that had failed to find a buyer at the London exhibitions ended up at the Royal Manchester Institution. In 1842 it commented: 'in gone-by years, it was a famous market for works of Art of all classes. For some time past, however, its annual "shows of the season" have been gradually deteriorating; few good pictures have been sent; consequently few have been purchased . . .'.[51] In fact sales at this time were only around ten to fifteen per cent of paintings exhibited. However, these were years of economic depression, and even so, annual sales seem never to have fallen below £1,200 and were frequently much higher: £3,500 in 1845, for instance.[52] At the same time, under the auspices of the RMI, an Art Union was set up in 1840 with 780 subscribers of one guinea each, the vast bulk of which was spent on paintings from the annual exhibition.[53]

The RMI, then, from its first exhibition of 1827, constituted a significant art market in the town, generating annually several thousands of pounds' worth of business. But the institution did more than that. Its very existence and its fine building on the town's most fashionable street – built at considerable expense – declared that art was an important part of the emerging public culture of an increasingly powerful Manchester. As an institution it focused considerable public attention on art and artists. Thus the annual exhibitions were discussed at length in the local press. The work and the careers of individual artists were carefully scrutinised.

Contemporary aesthetics became a part of the vocabulary of Manchester plutocrats shopping for new pictures.[54] The RMI became – with the Assembly Room balls and the races – one of the fashionable places to be seen promenading and a topic of polite conversation. It also provided regular series of public lectures on a wide range of intellectual topics, including many on the fine arts. A permanent art collection was also established at the RMI, though it grew slowly. Finally the RMI provided a physical base for a number of new cultural groups in the 1830s and 1840s – including the choral society, the Chetham Society, the Architectural Society and the Madrigal Society. From 1838 to 1849, and again after 1853, the School of Design was based there.

In section four below, the role of the RMI will be examined in more depth. The main purpose of this section has been to sketch in the emergence of an art market in Manchester and the concomitant, if gradual and uneven, shift away from 'old masters' to contemporary art. 'We have reason to know', the *Art Union Journal* declared in 1845, 'that in Manchester the rage for paintings by 'old masters' is dying out, and that attention is already directed to the good results that cannot fail to arise from judicious patronage of the living'.[55] But were they living in Manchester? In the next section attention shifts from markets to producers.

III

how many working artists found an economic base in early nineteenth century Manchester? There was certainly a significant growth in their numbers from the 1820s. Pigot and Dean's directory of 1821 listed only six portraitists and a single landscape painter. Within a very few years their number had, apparently, trebled. Baines's directory of 1825 listed twenty-one professional artists and their number had risen to twenty-nine by 1836. Clearly these figures are a significant underestimate because the census listed a total of ninety-two professional artists in the town only a few years later in 1841. 'There is, perhaps, no Provincial Society that numbers so many excellent Artists', the *Art Union Journal* stated in 1847.[56] A few years later the 1851 census listed 156 painters in the town and a decade later the figure had risen to 181. Thus Manchester in 1851 had the third largest population of professional painters in England, behind London (of course) and Liverpool. By 1861 it had moved up to second place, way beyond such southern centres of Arnoldian 'sweetness and light' as Oxford, Bath and Brighton.[57]

Who were all these painters in Manchester? What kind of social position did they occupy? Utilising trade and street directories, obituaries, records

Table 1 *Ten provincial towns with largest population of professional painters, 1861*

		1861			1851	
Rank		Male	Female	Total	Rank	Total
1	Manchester	141	40	181	2	156
2	Liverpool	133	20	153	1	168
3	Birmingham	107	39	146	3	156
4	Brighton	48	24	72	7	40
5	Bristol	59	9	68	4	68
6	Bath	42	11	53	5	60
7	Leeds	40	7	47	6	43
8	Sheffield	46	0	46	8	38
9	Plymouth	32	12	44	9	36
10	Nottingham	30	11	41	13	24

of the RMI and other miscellaneous biographical data, it is possible to sketch in some provisional categories of working artists in the town in these years.[58]

There were firstly those who began their career in Manchester but moved on to greater things in the metropolis. Some – Frank Stone (1800–59), Thomas Armstrong (1832–1911), or Randolph Caldecott (1846–86) – moved to London at an early stage of their career before making any kind of impact in Manchester. Stone worked in the office of his father's cotton mill until he was twenty-four, abandoning business for art without any formal training. He eventually became a successful painter in London, an Associate of the Royal Academy, noted for his rather sentimental representations of lovemaking scenes.[59] Armstrong similarly abandoned a career in the Manchester cotton trade, against sharp family opposition. With a letter of introduction from the industrialist Salis Schwabe to the artist Ary Scheffer, he went off to study art in Paris. Here he fell in with Whistler, Poynter and du Maurier, served as one of the originals of the young artists in the latter's *Trilby* and established himself in a successful career in London's art world – ultimately becoming director of the South Kensington Museum (later the Victoria and Albert).[60]

Other Manchester artists, however, built up some kind of local reputation before moving into the larger market of London, or kept a foot in their home town. William Bradley (1801–57), son of a partner in Thackray and Co., cotton spinners, was already picking up small commissions in 1819 at prices ranging from one shilling to six guineas. He was also giving drawing lessons. In 1822 he was described by Butterworth as a Portraitist 'who is eminent in the art, and has practised for many years with very great success here'. In that year he moved to London and soon built up a successful practice, charging up to two hundred guineas for a full-length portrait and exhibiting regularly at the Royal Academy. His prosperity was such that he could afford to pay £300 per annum for the rent of a house in fashionable Fitzroy Square.[61]

Several other Manchester painters broke into the London art market. Daniel Orme (*c.* 1766–*c.* 1832), son of a prosperous Manchester merchant, trained at the Royal Academy schools and in the 1790s had a successful London practice as a portrait painter, exhibiting frequently at the Royal Academy. He was also involved in engraving and printselling and he ran the British Naval and Military Gallery in Cavendish Square, shrewdly exploiting the war hysteria of the 1790s.[62] Benjamin Rawlinson Faulkner (1787–1849) abandoned a business career in Manchester after a spell of poor health and in 1816 moved to London, where he built up a lucrative practice as a portraitist, exhibiting regularly at the Royal Academy.[63] Thomas Henry Illidge (1799–1851), a former pupil of Bradley, moved to London in 1842 after years of profitably representing the social elite of Manchester and its satellite towns. Exhibiting regularly at the Royal Academy, he quickly established himself as a fashionable portrait painter with a fine house in Berkeley Square.[64]

In general, success in London was precarious and such painters frequently returned to Manchester. Daniel Orme abandoned London in 1814 after a period of difficulty and settled permanently in his home town, glorying in his metropolitan prestige. Bradley and Faulkner similarly capitalised on their London success, fulfilling many lucrative commissions in industrial Lancashire and exhibiting regularly at the RMI. Bradley always maintained a house and studio in Manchester with a brass plate on the door stating simply: 'Bradley, Artist'. In fact he increasingly neglected his London practice and got entangled in debt. Embittered and largely forgotten, he spent his last years in Manchester drinking himself to an early grave with cheap brandy, leaving a wife and six children practically destitute.[65]

Conversely, painters from other parts of the country took advantage of the developing market for pictures in early nineteenth-century Manchester. Joseph Allen, for instance, a native of Birmingham (born *c.* 1769), moved to Manchester in 1810 after a number of years of relative success in London. Here he quickly built up a successful portrait practice. A contemporary recalled how at any one time thirty or forty portraits lined the walls of his studio, all in progress, each bringing in fifteen or twenty guineas. Allen eventually made enough money to retire to a small estate. A number of other successful artists came to the town for varying spells.[66] George Freeman (*c.* 1788–1868), an American with a lucrative portrait practice in London – among his sitters were William IV and Queen Victoria – worked in Manchester in 1822 and again in 1834. He also exhibited at the RMI on several occasions during the 1820s and 1830s.[67] Henry Wyatt (1795–1840), pupil and assistant of Sir Thomas Lawrence, was based in Manchester from 1819 to 1825 and returned a number of times afterwards to fulfil commissions.[68] A number of other artists with London bases – Henry Bielfeld between the 1830s and the 1850s, John Bostock in the same period, John Lamont Brodie in the 1850s and 1860s – nevertheless visited Manchester regularly, maintained an address in the town and publicised their work on the walls of the RMI. Not all of them, of course, found success. Mather Brown (1761–1831), once portrait painter to the Duke of York, son of George III, and in the 1780s described as being 'in the highest state of success' with 'a great run of business' among the nobility, tried to rescue his fading career in the north of England. In 1815 he was seeking work in Manchester but, it was reported, 'his circumstances were indifferent'. By 1817 he was settled in the town. He sold a few pictures – one for as much as thirty guineas. But he struggled to survive. In 1820 he complained that he had more than thirty unsold pictures in his studio and four years later he moved back to London.[69]

A number of artists in early and mid-nineteenth-century Manchester were visible warnings of the risks of pursuing art as a career; an embittered William Bradley sinking into bankruptcy and alcoholism and a premature grave; David Parry, son of the painter 'Old Parry', dead at the age of thirty-four in 1827 just as he began to receive some important commissions; John Ralston (1789–1833), after early success struggling for years at dubious addresses and dying in the workhouse in his forties; Henry Liverseege (1803–32), living in a cold bare studio on an inadequate diet, plagued by ill-health and struck down by consumption just as he began to establish a national reputation; James Gregory Pollitt (1805–43), labouring for years in a warehouse and painting into the night, his professional success cut short by an early death; Henry James Holding (c. 1833–1872), struggling hard against poverty and neglect, finally receiving a lucrative commission for a picture of a particular scene in Paris and dying of typhus on arrival.[70] It was not just in romantic fiction that the nineteenth-century artist seemed curiously doomed. Nevertheless a number of sons of the prosperous middle class did go into art as a career, among them W. Dyer, son of J. C. Dyer, owner of a substantial engineering firm, railway developer and prominent figure in radical/liberal politics in the town from the 1820s to the 1860s; John Broadie, whose family ran a successful silk manufacturing firm; Thomas Armstrong, son of a textile commission agent for the firm of Thomas Holmes and Co.; H. H. Hadfield, son of George Hadfield, radical Nonconformist solicitor, right-hand man of the Potters

(Richard and Thomas – key radical figures in the town in the 1830s and 1840s) and MP for Sheffield 1852–74.[71]

It is also clear that there were always a number of artists working and living in Manchester in relative comfort with a solid business. Charles Duval (1808–72) was based in the town from the 1830s and built up a good practice as a portraitist. Sitters included many leading figures in Manchester politics, including Richard Cobden and John Bright. He also did a famous portrait of Daniel O'Connell and several pictures which became popular engravings, notably 'The Ruined Gamester' which augmented his income considerably. In 1857 Nathaniel Hawthorne visited his 'very pretty house' at Greenheys, one of the new suburbs on the southern edge of the town, and was impressed by Duval's ability to raise a family of twelve children by his art: 'Now Duval is certainly not a foremost man among English artists; indeed I never remember to have heard his name before; and it speaks well for the profession that he should (be) able to live in such handsome comfort, and nourish so large a brood.' Duval indicates that an artist could make a reasonable living in a provincial town. But then he also received commissions in Liverpool and London, where he also exhibited regularly. He was a prolific writer too and in the 1860s diversified into photography.[72] Yet there were a number of other artists settled in Manchester making a good living: Charles Agar, for instance, had a studio on King Street, among offices of lawyers and insurance companies, and lived in the select suburb of Broughton. Similarly Edward Benson (1808–63) had a studio on King Street and lived among the middling classes at Ardwick. J. A. Hammersley, head of the Manchester School of Design 1849–62, made between £300 and £400 per annum from selling his paintings.[73] And Manchester street directories show a number of other artists living in respectable suburbs among lesser professionals and small capitalists – cashiers and clerks, small-scale manufacturers, shopkeepers and so on – who must have been making incomes of around this level.

Only the very successful could afford to live by their painting alone and in fact a number of Manchester painters depended upon other sources of income to maintain their social position. Many taught art, running classes in their studios or providing private tuition – always a useful way of cultivating new patrons. The theatre also provided an alternative source of income. William Roxby Beverley (1810–89), son of an actor-manager, combined landscape painting in water-colours – he exhibited sixteen pictures at the RMI in the late 1820s and early 1830s and frequently in the 1860s and 1870s – with scene-painting for travelling theatres.[74] Samuel Bough (1822–78) came to Manchester in 1842 as an assistant scene-painter at the Theatre Royal and left the town six years later to become a scene-painter at a Glasgow theatre. He was also a serious artist. He studied at the Manchester School of Design, exhibited regularly at the RMI from 1847 and in later years became a professional artist in Edinburgh, a member of the Royal Scottish Academy and an exhibitor at the Royal Academy.[75] Francis Chester (1811–81) came to Manchester to study at the School of Design and exhibited at the RMI throughout the 1830s. Subsequently he made his living as a partner in a firm of architects and at the same time as 'artistic designer' to the Manchester Theatre Royal.[76] In the 1860s and 1870s Frederick Holding, long working in the town as a professional painter and book illustrator, was also a scene painter at the Theatre Royal and the Prince's Theatre.[77]

Other artists diversified further. George Wilfred Anthony (1810–59), born in Manchester, exhibited sixty-nine pictures at the RMI between 1827 and his death, mostly water-colour landscapes. An enthusiast, he regularly wrote art criticism for local newspapers, especially the *Manchester Guardian*, and made a living from teaching art and running a stationer's shop.[78] William Gibbs combined the seemingly incompatible avocations of historical painter in the manner of Benjamin West and a preacher for the Methodists.[79] James Hardy (1797–1874), of Salford, exhibited several portraits and landscapes at the RMI in the 1830s and 1840s. He was listed in directories variously as 'Portrait and Sign Painter' and 'Beer Retailer and Portrait Painter'.[80] William Moses Fry figured in Manchester directories of the 1820s as a portrait, miniature, house, sign and furniture painter. Obviously catering for the lower end of the market, he never exhibited at the RMI.

The calico-printing industry employed many designers. 'Ingenious artists are employed in drawing patterns and engraving them on wood and copper', Aikin reported in 1795.[81] Edmund Potter, owner of an immense calico-printing firm near Manchester, pointed out, however, that from the 1830s both the numbers and the incomes of designers had declined. The vast bulk of designing was of cheap goods for the mass market. 'I know nothing more distressing, or more annoying, or more degrading to an artist of any taste than to have to bring himself down to draw the sort of designs that the calico printers want to supply their demands. There is little scope for taste in such work'.[82] Nevertheless, a number of Manchester artists did find work as designers in the calico-printing industry: Warwick Brookes, George Hayes, John, George, Frederick and Henry James Holding among them.[83] Others used their skills in trade: men like John Fothergill – artist, designer, printer and engraver, producing book plates, trade cards, invoice headings as well as paintings and book illustrations; or Lionel Fleming – painter, illustrator, engraver, printer and photographer.[84] Thus, if we categorise as 'artists' those men who were producing pictures for the art market in Manchester, it is apparent that they occupy no single social position. They ranged from the comfortable professional man with a town-centre studio and a house in the suburbs to artisans living in the terraced housing of the central zones of the city. Many artists, as we have seen, had to supplement their income from art by all kinds of other labour which similarly located them among the lower middle class or even, sometimes, the working class.

A final category of artists has to be specified: women. Professional women painters in the late eighteenth and early nineteenth centuries were few and far between in Manchester. One or two figure in the trade directories and occasionally advertise their services in the local press. Only three women appeared as 'artists' by occupation in the 1841 census, though this had risen to forty by 1861 – a surprising and, so far, unaccountable increase. At least a proportion of these were governess or schoolmistresses – like Miss Ann Burgoyne Gaskill, teacher of music and drawing, who exhibited a number of pictures (*Fruit, Cucumber, Convolvulus and Butterfly* and so on) at the RMI, or Mrs. John Herford, wife of a Unitarian liquor merchant, who ran a school for 'Young Ladies' and exhibited several landscapes at RMI in the late 1820s.[85] There was always a scattering of such women exhibiting their work at the RMI – very often fruit or flower paintings which were synonymous with a kind of trivial prettiness as well as being a less profitable genre.[86] A handful of women painters did sell their work and establish some sort of reputation. Jane Aspland (*c.* 1810–59), married to the painter Theophilus Lindsey Aspland, was based in Manchester throughout the 1830s. She exhibited her landscapes regularly at the RMI and often found purchasers – at the 1836 exhibition, for example, she sold a painting for the reasonably good price of twenty-five guineas.[87] The various Nasmyth sisters – Jane, Charlotte, Margaret, Barbara and Anne were regular exhibitors at the RMI and often sold their work.[88] The Mutrie sisters – Annie (1826–93) and Martha (1824–85) – established a local reputation before moving to London in 1854 and becoming regular exhibitors at the RA.[89]

However, women were absent, by and large, from the most lucrative sector of the Manchester art market: portraiture. They were excluded too from the town's art clubs and associations, formal and informal, which were important in furthering an artist's career. Thus the Manchester Academy of Fine Arts, an association of the leading local artists set up in 1857, excluded women from membership until 1884. Subsequently they were admitted but with limited access and no voting rights.[90]

The population of artists in Manchester in the early and mid-nineteenth century was clearly a complex and shifting group. It embraced itinerant artists passing through the town, those resident temporarily but for a longer period, those whose career began in Manchester but who moved into the wider national art market with a base in London and various artists resident permanently in the town and forced to eke out a living by teaching, illustrating, scene-painting, printing or designing – even writing art criticism. Some Manchester artists made a comfortable living and inhabited the inner suburbs among the lower middle classes. Others struggled harder. But all, whether male or female, successful or unsuccessful, who pursued art as a profession or a trade in Manchester, were quite outside the upper echelons of urban society. Here, as elsewhere, there was a strict line of social demarcation between the merchant, the manufacturer, the doctor or lawyer on the one hand, and, on the other, the mere retailer, craftsman or white-collar worker. Artists were securely located among the latter group and as such were, with few exceptions, excluded from the circles of the Manchester plutocracy. This was commented on in 1842:

> In these leading circles, as they are rather ostentatiously styled, but few, we regret to say, are to be found devoted to the glorious studies of literature and the arts, and even they are but as the ornamental fringe to the table-cloth, removable at the desire of caprice or fashion. Still there are a few enthusiastic amateurs at whose houses such men are welcome, who have courage enough to set fashion at defiance.[91]

At the end of the century, Katherine Chorley recalled, the wealthy bourgeoisie of Manchester's outer suburbs – though appreciative, even respectful of the arts – still viewed the artist with distant apprehension. 'The man who followed one of the fine arts as a profession was a specimen of humanity unknown to our circle and his natural habitat was assumed to be that untidy society known by those who are acquainted with it only at secondhand as Bohemia'.[92] The relatively low status of the artist in Manchester is indicated also by his (or her) absence from positions of power within the town's cultural institutions. Artists do not figure on the managing committees of bodies like the Literary and Philosophical Society, the Portico Library, the Mechanics' Institution or the Royal Manchester Institution. Nor do they figure in political circles or among the new town councillors in the 1840s. Thus artists had little or no direct impact on the shaping of cultural policy in the town.

IV

Art was everywhere in Manchester by the mid-nineteenth century: in the hallways and drawing rooms of spacious mansions in Broughton and Victoria Park, in the smoky billiard rooms of gentlemen's clubs, in public institutions like the Exchange or the Infirmary and even, sometimes, in the damp unhealthy houses in which many working people had to live. Manchester's art world was in no sense homogeneous. As previous sections of this essay have indicated, there were various markets for paintings and the population of working artists in the town was highly differentiated. Side by side on the walls of the RMI's annual show were family portraits, architectural drawings, water-colour landscapes, little pastel sketches, portentous historical or allegorical works, sentimental genre paintings or scenes from novels or plays: *Dutch Tulips*, *The Toilette*, *Askham Mill*, *River Lowther*, *Hero and Leander*, *Gamekeeper and Dog*, *Nymph* or *Shylock* (actual examples). Prices too varied widely. At the RMI shows in the 1840s one could pay as little as four or five pounds for a small water-colour landscape or over one hundred pounds for a picture by an artist with some kind of national reputation.[93] Similarly the town's art dealers sold all kinds of pictures – large and small, oil paintings, water-colours, sketches, prints – and in every price range. Agnews and Grundys dealt in fashionable London artists for the upper reaches of the art market, but they were also deeply involved in the much wider market for cheap prints of all kinds.

All sorts of people, then, were buying pictures. Certainly those Manchester men seriously involved in establishing weighty art collections in this period were, and needed to be, men of substance. Hardman and Leigh Philips were both wealthy. Those specified as art collectors by Ford in the 1820s included a barrister, a number of substantial merchants and a major cotton manufacturer.[94] Major collectors in the town in the early and mid-nineteenth century included one of Britain's largest cotton manufacturers, Henry McConnel, the opulent bankers Edward Lloyd and John Greaves, and the 'merchant prince' Samuel Mendel.[95] Yet involvement in the art market was not confined solely to the *haute bourgeoisie*. Butterworth in 1822 mentioned several individuals in trade who were art collectors on a humbler scale and he observed of the dentist John Faulkner: 'he seems very curious also in collecting prints, paintings and antique remains'.[96] George Gilbertson, a bookkeeper, bought a picture from Henry Liverseege in the 1820s and held on to it for the rest of his life.[97] And there must certainly have been many other tradesmen, shopkeepers, white-collar workers who occasionally spent a few pounds on a picture at the RMI or at a bookshop or art dealer's, or subscribed to an edition of a print of a local dignitary or national hero. The market for portraits especially reached into the working class. There was a demand for 'a good likeness' in all ranks of Manchester society, even the poorest. In the late 1840s the young Frederick Shields toured from pub to pub doing portrait sketches at a penny each and occasionally obtaining commissions at a few shillings.[98]

Among purchasers of art there was obviously a wide diversity of involvement. For many well-heeled bourgeois families buying the occasional picture was like buying any other commodity suitable for the domestic interior. Pictures were part of the furniture and fittings.[99] The purchase of pictures was, the Manchester calico-printer Edmund Potter told a Select Committee in 1864, generally less a matter of love of art than love of 'display': 'I believe it is a fact that whenever there is a very successful period in trade it is a good time for the sale of pictures'. Conversely, in periods of economic depression the art market, like the market for other luxury items, contracted sharply.[100] Like finely-bound books, good furniture or eighteenth-century porcelain, art was one of the luxury items of private leisure and firms like Agnew's or Grundy's thrived upon the effective and expanding demand for such items.

Such objects served a number of important social functions. They displayed the wealth and cultivation of the family and thus transmitted messages about their social status and 'cultural capital'. Portraits, the largest sector of the market, served quite specific purposes: the commemoration of family events, such as coming of age, marriage or inheritance, or the election to some kind of prestigious public office. Art, then, like other material objects of the bourgeois interior, was an element in the symbolic structuring of social relations. But, of course, pictures possessed a particular ideological potency since they penetrated far more deeply into the discursive complexities of social relations within the household – into the ordering of relations between male and female, between masters (and mistresses) and their servants, between adults and children, and so on. Limitations of space forbid pursuing this crucial question of the interplay between representations and the social relations of the middle class household – though it is a question addressed by a number of the other contributions to this book.

If in all sorts of ways, art was a constituent of middle-class private life by the middle of the nineteenth century – as a topic of conversation, a passion for accumulation, an object of fantasy, a speculative investment, a cultural marker, or whatever – it was also an element of Manchester's *public* life. Complementing the market, as we have seen, was the Royal Manchester Institution. Initiated by a group of young artists in 1823 who wanted to organise regular exhibitions of their work, it was soon appropriated by the town's governing class and developed as an institution which had little to do with furthering the careers of the town's working artists. Thus the committee of twenty-eight men established at the founding meeting on 1

October 1823 included no artists at all, and was, by and large, representative of the local 'power elite'. It included the President, Vice-President, Treasurer and several directors of the Manchester Chamber of Commerce. It included also several boroughreeves, a number of major cotton manufacturers (H. H. Birley, R. H. Greg, David Holt), prosperous merchants, bankers, doctors and lawyers. It was, importantly, representative of both the Tory and the Whig-radical leadership of the town and of both Church of England and Nonconformity.[101] This committee instituted Hereditary Governships (at forty guineas), Life Governorships (at twenty-five guineas), and Annual Governorships (at two guineas) – effectively restricting membership to the upper reaches of Manchester society. Nevertheless money flowed in. By the beginning of 1825 there were 697 Hereditary and Life Governors, subscriptions reaching £32,000. As well as strong financial support, the RMI continued to absorb into its administrative elite some of the town's leading public men, of all political colours.[102]

Why was there this kind of active support for an institution devoted to the fine arts among men already busy in local and national politics, in business activities and in all kinds of other institutions – church or chapel, Chamber of Commerce, the Assembly Rooms, the Literary and Philosophical Society, and so on? In fact the RMI was an organisation serving a number of important social and political purposes for the Manchester middle class. Firstly, the RMI, like other voluntary associations, was embedded in the town's social structure. But these institutions were not so much the creation of an already-formed and coherent class as one of the means by which that class was constructed as an active social agent. While for the working class co-operation in the workplace and daily association in the neighbourhood created multiple social ties – for the middle-class association was less 'automatic'. As a local clergyman commented, the propertied class of Manchester were very often strangers to each other: 'Habits of general intercourse have become impossible among a community so numerous and scattered as ours, and so men are driven necessarily to that intercourse to those connected with them by the ties of relationship, similarity of taste and occupation, or the contiguity of neighbourhood.'[103] Social distance was exacerbated by competition in business and bitter animosities stemming from political and religious affiliations. In this kind of situation club life, philanthrophic associations and cultural institutions were important spaces for social association, providing links outside the narrow circles of immediate business associates and family and church. This role for the RMI was stressed from its very inception. 'A Proposal for Establishing in Manchester an Institution for the Fine Arts', drafted in September 1823 by G. W. Wood – wealthy partner in the Philips' hat-making business (the largest in the town), a Unitarian and from 1832 a somewhat Whiggish MP for South Lancashire – saw the new body as encouraging more social cohesion among the scattered and disparate elements which made up the town's middle class:

> An Institution such as this, would moreover serve as a point of union for the enlightened and liberal part of this widely scattered, and in some respects, unconnected population . . . As many people who might otherwise have continued strangers to each, would thus be brought into harmonious cooperation, the Institution, besides the direct benefits which it would confer upon the community, would have the pleasing effect of removing prejudice, of softening the asperity of party feeling and of fixing the public attention upon an object, with regard to which vehement differences of opinion can hardly be expected to arise.[104]

Art then provided a sphere transcending the antagonisms of business, religion and politics, and as such an institution like the RMI could bring together and unite different elements of the town's propertied class.

But art provided more than a neutral forum. 'A place more destitute of all interesting objects than Manchester it is not easy to conceive', declared Southey in 1807 in a book which helped to stamp on the town the image of a grim collection of factories, black canals and haggard factory workers crowded together in 'narrow streets, the houses all built of brick and blackened with smoke'.[105] Public disquiet was intensified by the Peterloo massacre in August 1819. Manchester came to represent not just ugliness and poverty but a disturbed and unnatural state of society. The phrase 'Liverpool Gentleman and Manchester Man' underlined the opposing contemporary stereotypes of a traditional merchant culture, part of the established order, and the new parvenu factory master risen from the ranks of the hoi polloi. If Manchester was to achieve parliamentary representation, if its business interests were to receive a respectful hearing from central government, then the town needed to proclaim its status as a centre not just of industry and wealth but also of men of culture and refinement worthy of entry to the genteel circles of state power. There was a growing consciousness among the town's leading groups of the need to combat their boorish public image. This was stressed by Wood in his 1823 'Proposal'. He argued that an institution devoted to the fine arts would educate the future businessmen of Manchester: 'the candid and reflecting will not deny that an exclusive interest in the pursuit of gain has a very unfavourable influence on the taste and manners. . . .' An active interest in the arts was essential, he went on, because without it 'wealth only furnishes the means of voluptuous indulgence and talent itself is but an instrument of sordid aggrandizement'.[106] Art, in other words, was to become one of the means by which the youth of the town's middle class were educated for the role of cultured gentleman and prepared for the morally and intellectually improving use of their wealth and leisure.

It is important to stress that this was not merely a crude emulation of aristocratic social behaviour and leisure activities. An ostentatious aping of upper class fashions and manners was undoubtedly there in early nineteenth century Manchester society, in all kinds of spheres[107] – though there were no great aristocratic families exerting direct political and social influence over the town. But the development of the RMI was part of a significant change in the social location of culture. The emergence from the late eighteenth century, and especially from the 1820s, of all kinds of voluntary associations of the middle class devoted to music, philosophy, literature, art, science, education, and so on, marked an important shift in the cultural economy. Such associations were an expression of the growing power and autonomy of urban and industrial capital. They were also an active force in the extension of that power and autonomy. Thus, for instance, the RMI began to show that patronage of art was no longer the monopoly of landed wealth. When Passavant in 1832, Waagan in 1838 or Sarsfield Taylor in 1841 listed the most important art collections in Britain they were still, of course, almost all owned by the landed aristocracy.[108] These were generally open to respectable members of the public. When the young radical Nonconformist shopkeeper George Heywood, on a jaunt from Manchester in 1814, called at Lord Grosvenor's Cheshire seat, Heaton Hall, he was admitted on payment of a tip of two shillings to the butler. Conducted around the house, proudly signing his name in the Visitors' Book, he was overawed by 'the grand pictures' and the great rooms 'furnished and finished much grander than I ever saw or could have imagined'.[109] Such visiting of aristocratic houses in the late eighteeenth and early nineteenth centuries was very widespread.[110] And it had ideological effects, proclaiming the authority and discrimination of the landed elite. The fine houses, with their rich furnishings and fittings, their picture galleries of ancient family portraits and a scattering of old masters, the ornamental parks and gardens, peacocks, and ancient trees, carried a Burkeian message about power, about political continuity, about dominant cultural traditions. Country house-visiting was one of the forms by which aristocratic cultural values – including the pre-eminence of European 'old masters' and Italian 'painters and decorators' – were transmitted to provincial groups. But the emergence of urban cultural institutions, established and controlled by the middle class, began, slowly and unevenly, to erode these assumptions and to question the 'naturalness' of aristocratic predominance. The development of finely-housed institutions – like Charles

Barry's impressive and expensive RMI building on Manchester's most fashionable street – was one way of publicly announcing the existence of another class possessing wealth and power and a different kind of patronage of the arts.

The appropriation of art into new public institutions had another dimension: the civilising of the working class. The 1830s marked a period of particular crisis, especially in the industrial North. In Manchester the liberal and reforming middle class were now politically dominant – controlling parliamentary representation, the press, the Chamber of Commerce and the new town council. However, the cholera epidemic of 1832, in which over one thousand people died in the town, and James Kay-Shuttleworth's subsequent exposé of the appalling slums in the central zones of Manchester, provided a warning of the threat to social order. This was reinforced by the turbulent industrial relations of these years and the emergence of a powerful Chartist movement. The new oligarchy could see the urgent need to build a new institutional framework within the town which would begin to incorporate an uneducated, disorderly and politically volatile populace. The 1830s and 1840s saw a substantial investment of energy into the creation of all kinds of institutions for penetrating the closed working-class world of the slums: educational agencies of various types, town missions, churches and chapels, all kinds of visiting societies, and so on.[111] There was also a new stress on the need to 'diffuse' the benefits of high culture, including art, to the labouring poor. The radical utilitarian *Penny Magazine*, linked to the Society for the Diffusion of Useful Knowledge, had from its inception in 1832 propounded this kind of argument. It produced a popular guide to the National Gallery and campaigned for working-class access to all kinds of art exhibitions and museums. The 1835–6 Select Committee on Arts and Manufactures, packed with Liberals, similarly pushed for much wider access to 'cultural treasures'.[112] These arguments found a response among Manchester's leading liberals. James Nasmyth and Benjamin Heywood were instrumental in establishing at the Mechanics' Institution a series of exhibitions from 1837 open to the working class. These combined all kinds of exhibits – machinery, industrial products, scientific apparatus and works of art. The third exhibition, in the summer of 1840, for instance, had a gallery with paintings by Turner, West, Landseer, Leslie, Eastlake, Callcott and others – all loaned by Manchester collectors. These exhibitions attracted considerable numbers. Around fifty thousand people visited the first in the winter of 1837–8 and subsequent exhibitions were attended by around one hundred thousand people – and to widespread surprise among the upper orders, without any disorder or vandalism. From 1839 the Mechanics'

Institution began to form a permanent museum in which works of art were included alongside scientific and technological exhibits.[113] The same group launched a School of Design in Manchester in 1838 – the first outside London.[114] The RMI was rather more conservative and remained exclusive and inward-looking. For this it was sharply criticised by the more radical younger generation who were beginning to find a voice through bodies like the Anti-Corn Law League and journals like *The North of England Magazine*. Thus one writer in the latter in 1842 sardonically described the achievements of the RMI: 'In the midst of a population thirsting for knowledge, its results have been an annual exhibition of the unsold pictures from the London galleries, and periodical lectures to ladies and gentlemen, (being governors) in the middle of the day, a time when few, in this commercial district, but the fair ones can attend.'[115] These criticisms of the RMI's exclusiveness eventually got a response and it too began to show a new concern with the broader population. In 1845 its annual exhibition was opened to the populace on Saturday evenings for sixpence and in 1849 this was reduced to twopence and extended over the whole of the last four weeks.

This attempt to bring art and the working class together had a utilitarian dimension. For designers in the calico-printing trade especially but also for other kinds of skilled workpeople a sense of design was thought to be important. Thus Nasmyth, an engineering employer in Manchester, told the Select Committee on Arts and Manufactures in 1836 that efficiency and economy in machinery generally coincided with beauty of design. Exposure to art would develop taste in the mechanic and would thus enhance his design skills. There was an urgent need therefore for art exhibitions open to the working class, perhaps even within the workplace itself.[116] Others made the same connection between art and industrial design and pushed the utilitarian benefits of art for the working class. However, and more importantly, this use of art exhibitions was part of a wider social project to integrate the lower orders into the cultural hegemony of capital. The provision of popular art exhibitions, argued George Jackson in 1838, provided a worthwhile alternative to the corrupting influence of the public house: 'We have society on society to induce men to go to church or chapel on Sunday, and leave them to seek their own amusement in the week, during which there is only one source of relaxation a working man can get, and which it would be the greatest blessing that could be conferred on him, if he could be induced to avoid'.[117] This appeal for the provision of alternative leisure facilities to the public house was part of the wider and many-sided movement reconstructing the cultural framework of the town.[118] Art had a particular role to play, according to its devotees, because of its connection with the feelings. For Jackson, contemplation of a work of art produced feelings with ethical and religious implications: 'They tend to elevate the soul beyond the mere pursuits of time, and lead us to admire and adore the works of the Creator'.[119] Finally the financing of cultural facilities for the working class enabled Manchester's employers to point to their own munificence. The profits generated by industry were not merely for their own private gratification but were utilised to create a civilisation which benefited all social classes. Such institutions as the RMI, the School of Design, the Mechanics' Institution, and so on, were of course financed out of capital which might otherwise have been reinvested in production so that these facilities did constitute a kind of indirect wage, and this was not lost on the Manchester plutocracy who knew their political economy. Thus a local employer rebutted charges that industry benefitted only the masters, who accumulated large fortunes: 'out of these large fortunes come the funds for many of those great undertakings and benevolent institutions which tend to increase the prosperity and happiness, of the country, and in which the working man is more or less a sharer.'[120]

Many of these different facets of the appropriation of art into an emergent civic culture in early nineteenth-century Manchester converge together in the Art-Treasures Exhibition of 1857.[121] It was a collective project of the town's middle class, absorbing thousands of pounds and thousands of man-hours of organisational work. It attracted nearly a million and a half visitors – among them the intellectual and political elite of Europe. Some employers gave their workpeople the day off work to visit the exhibition and there were special trains to bring factory workers from further afield. Local charities paid for pauper children to attend, and there were specially printed guides to help the skilled workmen to profit from it.[122] The Art-Treasures Exhibition brought art out of the private interior of the aristocrat and into the public sphere. As the *Athenaeum* commented of the exhibition, patronage was replaced by the egalitarianism of the market place.[123] It also exposed the paltry extent of the National Gallery. The exhibition even made an overall profit – vindicating Manchester's grasp of *laissez-faire* even in so unpromising a venture as an art exhibition. Finally it was an assertion of the town's refusal to be condescended to any longer. According to *The Times*, Manchester had been the rival, for a season, of London.[124] No longer, argued a local journalist, could the town be represented as being dedicated only to getting rich and a vulgar leisure passed in 'abundant feasts, copious potations, rough pleasures and brutal sports': 'Manchester manufacturers are the best patrons of living artists'.[125] And the *Illustrated London News* stated that now Manchester was of equal standing to other major cultural centres in Europe and America – 'and the new-made city hurls back upon her detractors that she is too deeply absorbed in the pursuit of material wealth to devote her energies to the finer arts!'[126]

V

In 1851 Richard Cobden urged Archibald Prentice, who was writing the history of the Anti-Corn Law League, to show the new 'moral power of Manchester': 'Contrast Manchester after the League had done its work, and beaten the landed aristocracy, with Manchester forty years ago, when its richest men were ready to bow down to the dust before the veriest Tony Lumpkin of a Cheshire squire.'[127] Within a generation the political and cultural infrastructure of the town – and its relations with the state – had been utterly transformed. In 1832 it had gained two parliamentary seats out of the Reform Bill. In 1838 it had obtained an Act of Parliament to establish an elected town council.[128] In the 1840s its Chamber of Commerce had led a national campaign against the British political status quo. The Anti-Corn Law League became a movement not just against agricultural protectionism but against dominant values and institutions – the landed aristocracy, the Church of England, Oxbridge. Its own counter-culture – of individualism, thrift and respectability, productive enterprise, the free market – became indelibly imprinted with the name 'Manchester'. As Saintsbury commented, 'the distinction... which it gained as designating a particular sect or school of policy and politicians is not exactly rivalled by any other English town'.[129]

As radical a shift had occurred in the sphere of culture as in politics. A whole institutional infrastructure was gradually built up in Manchester. Some of its components, notably the Literary and Philosophical Society, originated in the late eighteenth century. But its general shape becomes visible by the 1830s, marking a watershed with the *ancien régime* as decisive as, and parallel to, changes in the directly political sphere. Some aspects of this transformation have become clear in the course of this discussion of Manchester's art world: the rapid expansion of an art market no longer under the tutelage of the landed elite, whether 'the veriest Tony Lumpkin of a Cheshire Squire' or not; and the construction of a public sphere through which social networks within the middle class could be multiplied and through which leadership could be exerted. Much more needs to be said about this but perhaps the scale and the form of the transformation in terms of culture – or, to use Cobden's phrase, 'moral power' – can be suggested by a brief contrast between the town hall opened in 1825 for the old Tory oligarchy and the new one opened in 1877: the former built and fitted out at a total cost of forty thousand pounds, the latter at around one million pounds; the former built in King Street on a cramped site and in a narrow and busy eighteenth-century thoroughfare; the latter erected in a new and spacious square and in an imposing position; the former a traditional classical structure, its façade a replica of the Erechtheion at Athens, the latter built in the newly fashionable Gothic style; and finally, the former's interior decorated with murals by Augustine Aglio (Senior), an Italian, now almost forgotten, who specialised in decorating country houses and churches – a bizarre combination of allegorical, historical and mythological representations; the latter decorated with murals by Ford Madox Brown, one of the outstanding British artists of his generation, and providing – in the painter's own words – 'the most comprehensive epitome of the rise and progress of Manchester that can be compressed into twelve pictures'. If the old town hall suggests a backward-looking ruling group of limited ambition and rather conventional tastes, devoid of any coherent intellectual or political tradition, the new town hall, by contrast, suggests immense power and wealth, a remarkable sense of historical mission and a loud declaration of political sovereignty.[130]

To affirm the significance of art to a commercial-industrial capital like nineteenth-century Manchester is not simply a matter of indicating that among its prosperous businessmen were serious art collectors who exemplified learning, taste and discrimination. Nor is it to deny that among this same class there were those who were profoundly 'philistine'. There were men – and women – of both kinds among the middle class of Manchester, as there were, of course, among the gentry and landed aristocracy. Rather, it is a matter of showing that art was being produced and consumed in the town on a significant scale; that there was considerable investment of resources in organisations and events connected with art; and that, in a variety of ways, only cursorily indicated in this essay, art was being appropriated into the discourses of private and public life in Manchester. Art, in other words, was much more important than merely an exemplification of private 'taste' or 'sensibility'. It was an element of the urban economy, it was part of the private world of the propertied classes, it was an instrument of cultural aggrandisement for industrial wealth, it was one of the ways through which a new class identity was struggling to emerge and it was a crucial dimension of the new civic culture which was becoming synonymous with 'Victorian Liberalism'.

74 The culture of capital

Notes

Versions of this essay were presented to seminars at the University of Essex, Manchester Polytechnic, Newcastle Polytechnic and the University of Surrey. I would also like to thank Simon Gunn and Janet Wolff for helpful comments.

1 ('Christopher North'), 'Manchester Poetry', *Blackwood's Edinburgh Magazine*, IX, April 1821, pp. 64–6. It is interesting to note that, a few years later, North's regular articles in Blackwood's were the favourite family reading of the Ruskins: see T. Hilton, *John Ruskin. The early Years 1818–1859*, New Haven, 1985, p. 23.
2 M. Arnold, *Culture and Anarchy, An Essay in Political and Social Criticism*, in R. H. Super (ed.), *The Complete Prose Works of Matthew Arnold*, V, Ann Arbor, 1965, p. 105.
3 For a useful discussion and elaboration of the concept of an 'art-world' see H. S. Becker, *Art Worlds*, Berkeley, 1982.
4 Quoted in W. Farrar and J. Brownhill (eds.), *The Victorian County History of Lancaster*, IV, 1911, p. 179.
5 J. Aikin, *A Description of the County from Thirty to Forty Miles Round Manchester*, 1795.
6 I shall be using the Manchester trade and street directories frequently in the course of this essay. It would serve no useful purpose, I think, to cite these unwieldly texts again and again. The following are the main directories I have utilised: *Raffald's Manchester Directory*, 1772; Edmond Holme, *A directory for the towns of Manchester and Salford*, 1788; John Scholes, *Manchester and Salford Directory*, 1794 and 2nd edn 1797; Gerard Bancks, *Manchester and Salford Directory*, edns for 1800, 1802; R. & W. Dean & Co., *Manchester and Salford Directory* (edns for 1804, 1808, 1811); J. Pigot & R. W. Dean & Co., *Manchester and Salford Directory*, edns for 1815, 1817; J. Pigot & R. & W. Dean, *New Directory of Manchester and Salford*, 1821; Edward Baines, *History, Directory and Gazetteer of the County Palatine of Lancaster*, 1824, Vol. 2; J. Pigot & Son, *General Directory of Manchester & Salford*, 1829; J. Pigot & Son, *General Classified Directory of Manchester & Salford*, 1836. And see, for some salutary warnings about the dangers and limitations of directories as accurate sources, P. J. Corfield and S. Kelly, ' "Giving directions to the town": the early town directories', *Urban History Yearbook*, 1984, pp. 22–35.
7 S. Bamford, *Early Days*, 1849, p. 90.
8 Quoted in *The Palatine Notebook*, II, Manchester, 1882, p. 270. See also R. W. Proctor, *Memorials of Bygone Manchester*, 1880, p. 36 and *The Dictionary of National Biography* (hereafter cited as DNB). On the diversity of booksellers in this period see J. Feather, *The Provincial Book Trade in Eighteenth Century England*, Cambridge, 1985, Ch. 5.
9 Frith recalled how itinerant painters were commonplace in West Yorkshire in the early nineteenth century. One set himself up in Knaresborough in a studio above a linen-draper's shop and picked up a number of commissions, including one from Frith's father, an innkeeper, who paid £20 for a portrait of his wife. See W. P. Frith, *My Autobiography and other Reminiscences*, 1887, I, pp. 11–12.
10 *The Manchester Herald*, 13 October 1792.
11 W. Ford, 'The Stringers, father and sons, of Knutsford, artists'; manuscript notes from the early nineteenth century printed in *The Palatine Notebook*, I, 1881, pp. 190ff.

12 Quoted in T. Fawcett, *The Rise of English Provincial Art: Artists, Patrons & Institutions outside London 1800–30*, Oxford, 1974, pp. 175–6.
13 J. Romney, *Memoirs of the Life and Works of George Romney*, 1830, p. 298.
14 *The Farington Diary*, ed. J. Greig, I, 1923, p. 211.
15 For Parry see DNB and 'Biographical Notices of Deceased Local Artists' in *Catalogue of the First Exhibition of the Works of Local Artists (Living and Deceased): Inauguration of the New Wing of Peel Park Museum, Salford*, Manchester, 1857, p. 8. This useful source is hereafter cited as 'Biographical Notices', 1857.
16 A. Nicholson and J. H. Nodal, 'Tate, the portrait painter', *City Notes and Queries* V, 1883–4, p. 205.
17 C. Roeder, 'William Green, the lake artist', *Lancashire & Cheshire Antiquarian Society Transactions*, XIV, 1896; J. J. Bagley (ed.), *Miss Weeton's Journal of a Governess*, Newton Abbot, 1969, I, pp. 226–7, 299–300.
18 'Biographical Notices', 1857, 9; G. Reitlinger, *The Economics of Taste: The Rise and Fall of Picture Prices 1760–1960*, 1961, p. 82.
19 See Papers of John Leigh Philips in the Archives of Manchester Public Library (hereafter cited as MPL).
20 *A Catalogue of the Valuable Collection of Paintings and Drawings, Prints and Etchings, etc. The property of the late John Leigh Philips, Esq.*, Manchester, 1814; *A Catalogue of the Valuable Extensive, and Well Chosen Library of John Leigh Philips, deceased . . .*, Manchester, 1814. Copies of both of these catalogues are to be found in the Philips papers, *loc. cit.*
21 J. Croston, 'The Hardman family of Manchester', in *The Palatine Notebook*, IV, 1884, pp. 168–9.
22 'Old Manchester families and residences', in J. Harland, 'Collecteana relating to Manchester and its neighbourhood, at various periods', II, *Chetham Society*, LXXII, 1867, p. 208.
23 E. Conran, 'Art Collections', in J. H. G. Archer (ed.), *Art and Architecture in Victorian Manchester*, Manchester, 1985, p. 68; *The Farington Diary*, ed. J. Greig, V, 1925, p. 43.
24 In Papers of John Leigh Philips, *loc. cit.*
25 Ms Diary 1801–38, III, 239, 268 in Richard Potter Collection, Library of Political and Economic Science, Archives Dept., London School of Economics.
26 *The Diary of Joseph Farington*, ed. K. Garlick and A. Macintyre, New Haven, 1978, II, pp. 314, 319, 345–6, 353, 358.
27 *The Farington Diary*, ed. J. Greig, 1925, Vol. V, p. 97.
28 See the Sun Fire Insurance Company Policy Registers, New Series, in the Guildhall Library, London: Mss 11937, various volumes. I have to say that so far, I have only examined a dozen or so of these numerous, large and unindexed volumes. See also C. Trebilcock, *Phoenix Assurance and the Development of British Insurance;1 I, 1782–1870*, Cambridge, 1985, Ch. 7, for warnings about uncritical use of insurance policy registers.
29 J. D. Passavant, *Tour of a German Artist in England with Notices of Private Galleries, and Remarks on the State of Art*, 1836, II, p. 20.
30 E. Conran, *op. cit.*
31 W. Ford, 'Character of the Different Picture Collectors, in and about Manchester, faithfully and impartially delineated', *c.* 1827, ms in Archives Dept., MPL. See also F. D. Astley, *Varnishando; A Serio-Comic Poem: Addressed to Collectors of Paintings By an Admirer of the Arts*, Manchester, 1809, which had warned local collectors of fraudulent art dealers.

32 See, for examples, *Art Union Journal*, VIII, 1846, pp. 67–8; X, 1848, p. 33.
33 *Art Union Journal*, IX, 1847, p. 139. Note the elision here between Manchester's middle-class picture-buyers and its manufacturers. Manchester's barristers, merchants and bankers were at least as likely to own forgeries as its manufacturers: see W. Ford, *op. cit.*
34 (W. Rowlinson), 'Manchester exhibition of paintings, by living British artists, in *The Phoenix, or Manchester Literary Journal*, 1828, p. 6.
35 R. W. Proctor, *Memorials of Bygone Manchester, with Glimpses of the Environs*, Manchester, 1880, pp. 116–18.
36 G. Agnew, *Agnew's, 1817–1967*, 1967, pp. 1–2, 6.
37 See *Pigot & Son's General and Classified Directory of Manchester and Salford . . .*, Manchester, 1836.
38 G. Agnew, *op. cit.*, pp. 8, 11.
39 C. P. Darcy, *The Encouragement of the Fine Arts in Lancashire 1760–1860*, Chetham Society, 3rd series, XXIV, Manchester, 1976, p. 128.
40 No author, 'The Last of the Grand School of Connoisseurs', in *Memories of Thomas Dodd, William Upcott and George Stubbs R. A.*, Liverpool, 1879.
41 *Manchester Guardian*, 21 September 1822.
42 G. Agnew, *op. cit.*, pp. 5, 11.
43 Quoted in J. Maas, *Gambart, Prince of the Victorian Art World*, 1975, p. 29.
44 See DNB; 1851 Census Enumerator's Book in Public Record Office, HO 107/2222; and *Catalogue of the Very Extensive and Valuable Stock of Modern Pictures and Drawings, and Ancient and Modern Engravings . . . of that eminent connoisseur, Mr. John Clowes Grundy*, Manchester, 1867.
45 *Manchester Guardian*, 25 August, 1821.
46 *Art Journal*, new series, I, 1849, p. 289; II, 1850, p. 262.
47 G. Agnew, *op. cit.*, p. 9.
48 H. S. Gibbs, *Autobiography of a Manchester Cotton Manufacturer*, 1887, pp. 127, 190.
49 Obituary of Thomas Agnew, *Art Journal*, n.s., X, 1871, 183. Note that Agnew was a lifelong Nonconformist and political liberal; indeed in 1851 he was the Mayor of Salford – the very archetype of the Arnoldian philistine! Of course, not everyone approved of the success of such dealers. Ruskin was critical of Agnew's for corrupting taste in Manchester. They have, he said,

> covered the walls of that metropolis with 'exchangeable property' on the exchanges of which the dealer always made his commission, and of which perhaps one canvas in a hundred is of some intrinsic value, and may be hereafter put to good and permanent use. But the first of all conditions for this use, is that Manchester men should, for a little while, 'choose for themselves'! That they should buy nothing to sell it again; and that they should buy it of the artist only, face to face; with him; or from the exhibition wall by direct correspondence with him.

J. Ruskin, *Fors Clavigera*, Letter 79, July 1877, in *The Works of John Ruskin*, XXXIX, 1907, p. 154
50 For the early development of the RMI see S. D. Cleveland, *The Royal Manchester Institution, Its history from its origin until 1882 . . .*, Manchester, 1931; R. F. Bud, 'The Royal Manchester Institution', in D. S. L. Cardwell (ed.), *Artisan to Graduate*, Manchester, 1974.
51 *Art Union Journal*, IV, 1842, p. 233. See also the critical remarks about the RMI in 'Horace Heartwell', 'Characteristics of Manchester V' in *The North of*

England Magazine, I, 1842, p. 564.
52 RMI Collection: 'Minutes of the Exhibition Committee 1832–46' in Archives Dept., MPL.
53 See *Annual Report of the Committee of the Manchester Association for the Patronage of the Fine Arts*, 1842, 1843; *Art Union Journal* II, 1840, 125.
54 Aesthetics was, of course, much more than an esoteric branch of philosophy. It helped produce some kind of consensus – though always contradictory and provisional – about how to assess the value of works of art. Aesthetics provided a communicable basis on which people could make judgements about a picture and an artist. Thus it was a crucial element of the art market. In a situation where artists were competing and different styles were in play then aesthetic discourses provided a primary site of contest. As Becker observes, 'The heat in discussions of aesthetics usually exists because what is being decided is not only an abstract philosophical question but also some allocation of valuable resources.' *Op. cit.*, p. 135.
55 *Art Union Journal*, VII, 1845, p. 266. Edmund Potter told a Select Committee in 1864: 'I believe that the largest support to modern painting has really been given in Manchester. I believe the purchases made of paintings and works of Art in the last twenty or thirty years, have been larger in the Manchester district than in any district in the country.' *Report from the Select Committee of Schools of Art*, PP 1864; (446), p. 127.
56 *Art Union Journal*, IX, 1847, p. 182.
57 *Census of 1841*, 'Occupation Abstract' PP 1844, XXXVII; *Census of 1851*, PP 1852–3, LXXXV–LXXXVI; *Census of 1861;. Ages and Civil Condition of the People*, PP 1863, LIII, 1, 2.
58 I should like to thank the Director of the Manchester City Art Galleries for permission to consult the Arnold Hyde papers, which were helpful in the pages that follow. This is an incomplete biographical dictionary of artists with a Lancashire connection in manuscript form and is located in the archives of Manchester City Gallery on Mosley Street. It is hereafter cited simply as 'Hyde'. Another useful starting-place is J. H. Nodal, *Art in Lancashire and Cheshire: a list of deceased artists*, 1884.
59 W. Sandby, *The History of the Royal Academy of Arts*, 1862, II, pp. 328–30; DNB; Stone flits in and out of the correspondence of Dickens and Thackeray, his friends.
60 L. M. Lamont, *Thomas Armstrong CB, a Memoir 1832–1911*, 1912.
61 DNB; S. Redgrave, *A Dictionary of Artists of the English School*, 2nd edn. 1878, p. 51; Louise Pennant-Rea, 'William Bradley 1801–57: "A Man of whom Manchester ought to be proud"; unpublished dissertation, University of Manchester, 1972; J. Johnson, 'William Bradley, the artist' in *City News Notes and Queries*, ed. J. H. Nodal, I, Manchester, 1878, p. 50.
62 DNB; 'Biographical Notices', 1857, p. 7; Swindell's *Manchester Streets and Manchester Men*, 1906–8, II, pp. 100–1.
63 DNB; 'Biographical Notices', 1857, p. 6; obituary in *Art Journal*, n.s., II, 1850, p. 94.
64 DNB: Redgrave, *op. cit.* p. 233; obit. in *Art Journal*, n.s., III, 1851, 182.
65 Bradley detailed 'the painfulness of my situation' and his anxieties about getting back into prominence in London in a letter to his friend Etty: W. Bradley to W. Etty, 16 April 1836, in Etty letters, 107, ms in York City Reference Library.
66 'Biographical Notices', 1857, p. 5; Hyde.

67 Hyde.
68 Albert Nicholson, 'Henry Wyatt', in *City News Notes and Queries*, III, 1880, p. 104, 'Biographical Notices', 1857, p. 9.
69 See Dorinda Evans, 'Mather Brown (1761–1831): A Critical Study', Courtauld Institute of Art, University of London Ph.D., 1972.
70 For David Parry see DNB and 'Biographical Notices', 1857, p. 8. For Ralston see 'Biographical Notices', 1857, pp. 8–9 and obituary in *Arnold's Magazine of the Fine Arts*, 1833–4, pp. 469–71. For Liverseege, among many others, see DNB, *Engravings from the Works of Henry Liverseege with a Memoir by George Richardson*, 1857. R. Edwards, 'The pictures of Henry Liverseege (1803–32)', in *Apollo*, XX, 115, 1934, pp. 25–8. For Pollitt see Hyde and 'Biographical Notices', 1857, p. 8. For Holding see DNB, Hyde and F. M. Ford, *Ford Madox Brown. A Record of his Life and Work*, 1896, pp. 275–6. The Principal of the Manchester School of Design warned his students against painting as a career: 'The career of the mediocre artist must be one of poverty and disappointment. No one, unfortunately, sympathises with him, – no one regards him or his works; whereas, had he pursued the occupation of the ornamental designer, he might have attained a lucrative and respectable position.' G. Wallis, *Introductory Address, delivered 15 January 1844, to the students of the Manchester School of Design*, 1844, pp. 10–11.
71 For J. C. and W. Dyer see DNB and Hyde. For Broadie see Hyde. For Hadfield, *inter alia*, see Hyde and B. Nightingale, *The Story of the Lancashire Congregational Union 1806–1906*, Manchester, 1906, pp. 128–9.
72 DNB; obit. in the *Manchester Examiner & Times*, 17 June 1872; Hawthorne quoted in Darcy, *op. cit.*, p. 77.
73 DNB; in 1851 he was living in the comfortable northern suburb of Broughton with his wife, son and two domestic servants: Census of 1851 Enumerators' Books, *loc. cit.*
74 Hyde.
75 Sidney Gilpin, *Sam Bough*, 1905.
76 Hyde.
77 DNB.
78 Hyde.
79 Nodal, *op. cit.*
80 F. L. Tavare, 'James Hardy, A Salford Artist', *City News Notes & Queries*, IV, 1881, p. 118.
81 J. Aikin, *op. cit.*, p. 268.
82 Evidence to *Select Committee*, 1864, *loc. cit.*, p. 126. See also his *Calico Printing as an Art Manufacture*, 1852.
83 For Brookes see T. Letherbrow, *In Memoriam, Warwick Brookes*, Manchester, 1882; R. W. Procter, *Memorials of Manchester Streets*, 1874, p. 249. For Hayes see Procter, 39, and obituaries in *Papers of the Manchester Literary Club*, XXII, 1896, p. 484 and in *Manchester Faces & Places*, VII, 1896, p. 80. For the Holdings see n. 70 above.
84 Hyde.
85 Hyde; for Mrs Herford see biographies of her sons: H. McLachlan, *Robert Travers Herford. A Brief Sketch of his Life and Work*, privately printed, n.d.; W. C. R. Hicks, *Lady Barn House and the Work of W. H. Herford*, Manchester, 1936. Another son was Edward Herford, Manchester coroner for many years.
86 See R. Parker and G. Pollock, *Old Mistresses: Women, Art and Ideology*, 1981, p. 54.

87 Hyde; Minutes of the Exhibition Committee 1832–46 in RMI papers, *loc. cit.*
88 Hyde; Minutes of Exhibition Committee, *loc. cit.* Thus in 1836 two Nasmyth sisters sold pictures for seventeen and eighteen guineas.
89 DNB.
90 No author, *Manchester Academy of the Fine Arts. A Short History of the Academy*, 2nd edn, Manchester, 1973, pp. 8–9.
91 'Horace Heartwell', 'Characteristics of Manchester III', *North of England Magazine*, 1, 1842, p. 274. The Manchester novelist Geraldine Jewsbury in 1848 put the same kind of views in the mouth of a wealthy coalowner:

> We naturally do not feel drawn to the society of artists; we have nothing in common with them – we do not admire them; neither do we feel disposed to introduce to the society of our wives and daughters a parcel of actors, artists, musicians, and so forth, who have no stake in society, who have little to lose, whose capital is all invested in themselves and their two hands, and who have, therefore, naturally cultivated themselves far beyond what we practical men have had a chance of doing, and are capable of throwing us into the shade in our own houses, whilst they show that they despise us!

Quoted in B. Jeffares, *The Artist in Nineteenth-Century English Fiction*, 1979, p. 14.

92 K. Chorley, *Manchester Made Them*, 1950, p. 265.
93 See Minutes of the Exhibition Committee, *loc. cit.*, for detailed breakdown of prices and purchases.
94 W. Ford, 'Character of the Different Picture Collectors . . .', ms, *loc. cit.*
95 See *A Catalogue of a Most Recherche Collection of Pictures . . . the Property of John Greaves Esq. of Irlam Hall . . .*, Manchester, 1847; *Catalogue of the Magnificent Collection of Modern Pictures . . . the Property of Samuel Mendel Esq.*, 1875; *Catalogue of the Important Collection of Modern Pictures formed by that distinguished Connoisseur Henry McConnel Deceased*, 1886.
96 Butterworth, *op. cit.*, p. 276, and see p. 181.
97 Proctor, *op. cit.*, p. 154.
98 E. Mills, *The Life and Letters of Frederick Shields*, 1912, pp. 13–15, 18, 20.
99 Consider Ruskin's argument about the 'fit' between English landscape watercolourists like Prout and the bourgeois interior:

> The great people always bought Canaletto, not Prout, and Van Huysum, not Hunt. There was indeed no quality in the bright little water-colours which could look other than pert in ghostly corridors, and petty in halls of state; but they gave an unquestionable tone of liberal-mindedness to a suburban villa, and were the cheerfulest possible decoration for a moderate-sized breakfast-parlour opening on a nicely mown lawn.

Quoted in C. P. Darcy, *op. cit.*, p. 79.

100 Select Committee, *op. cit.*, p. 135, for Potter's comments. For remarks on the effects of economic depression in the cotton trade on the art market see *Catalogue of the Exhibition of the Pictures by Modern Artists, in the Gallery of the Institution*, Manchester, 1829, p. 6, and *Annual Report of the Manchester Association for the Patronage of the Fine Arts*, Manchester, 1843, p. 3.

101 Royal Manchester Institution: Committee established at founding meeting October 1823.

	No.	% of total
Manufacturers	8	28·6
Merchants	7	25·0
Bankers	2	7·1
Professional	8	28·6
Gentlemen	3	10·7
Others	0	0
Total	28	

Source. Council Minute Book, 1823–35. RMI mss, *loc. cit.*

102 Royal Manchester Institution: Governing Council 1835–40.

	No.	% of total
Manufacturers	26	49·1
Merchants	7	13·2
Bankers	1	2·0
Professional	15	28·3
Gentlemen	4	7·5
Others	0	0
Total	53	

Source. Council Minute Book 1835–48, RMI mss, *loc. cit.*

103 Revd R. Parkinson, *On the Present Condition of the Labouring Poor in Manchester: with Hints for Improving it*, 1841, pp. 7–8.
104 'A Proposal for Establishing in Manchester an Institution for the Fine Arts', ms in Council Minute Book, 1823–35, in RMI mss, *loc. cit.* See also the report of Wood's speech at the meeting of 1 October 1823, which discussed this proposal, in the *Manchester Guardian*, 4 October 1823.
105 [R. Southey], *Letters from England: by Don Manuel Alvarez Espriella, Translated from the Spanish*, 1807, new edn, ed. Jack Simmons, Gloucester, 1984, p. 213.
106 *Loc. cit.*
107 Notably the Manchester Assembly Rooms. See, for instance, M., 'The Assembly', in *The Scrap-book. A Manchester Weekly Publication*, I, 1822, p. 75.
108 J. D. Passavant, *op. cit.*; G. F. Waagen, *Works of Art and Artists in England*, 3 vols., 1838: W. B. Sarsfield Taylor, *The Origins, Progress and Present Condition of the Fine Arts in Great Britain and Ireland*, 2 vols., 1841.
109 'Manuscript Diary of George Heywood 1812–40'; in English mss, John Rylands University Library, Manchester.
110 An American visitor in the 1840s was very surprised by the extent of such visiting and reported in 1844 that there were around 80,000 visitors a year to Chatsworth House, seat of the Duke of Devonshire in Derbyshire; H. Colman, *European Life and Manners; in Familiar Letters to Friends*, Boston, 1850, I, pp. 214–15.

111 I examined this project in more detail in 'Unitarianism, political economy and the antinomies of liberal culture in Manchester, 1830–50', *Social History*, 7, 1, 1982, especially pp. 12–20.
112 *Report from the Select Committee on Arts and their Connexion with Manufacturers* PP 1836, p. 568. See also T. Kelly, *A History of Adult Education in Great Britain*, Liverpool, 1970, pp. 177–80.
113 C. P. Darcy, *op. cit.*, pp. 108–11; *Manchester As It is: or, Notices of the Institutions, Manufactures, Commerce, Railways, etc. of the Metropolis of Manufactures . . .*, Manchester, 1839, pp. 102–5.
114 See C. Stewart, *A Short History of the Manchester College of Art*, Manchester, 1953.
115 'H. Heartwell', 'Characteristics of Manchester V', *North of England Magazine*, 1842, p. 564.
116 J. Nasmyth, evidence to Select Committee 1836, *loc. cit.*, II, pp. 28–31.
117 G. Jackson, *Two Essays on a School of Design for the Useful Arts . . . also Letters on the Advantages and Moral Effects of the Present Exhibition . . . and an Address to the Working Men of Manchester*, Manchester, 1838, p. 37.
118 See, for wider moves to reform working class leisure activities in these years, P. Bailey, *Leisure and Class in Victorian England: Rational Recreation and the contest for control, 1830–85*, 1985, esp. pp. 19–21, 38.
119 G. Jackson, *op. cit.*, p. 6. See also his *On the Means of Improving Public Taste*, Manchester, 1844.
120 S. Robinson, *Friendly Letters on the Recent Strikes, from a Manufacturer to his own Workpeople*, 1854, p. 27.
121 See U. Finke, 'The Art-Treasures Exhibition', in J. H. G. Archer, *op. cit.*, pp. 102–26.
122 E. T. Bellhouse, *What to see, and where to see it! Or, the Operative's Guide to the Art Treasures Exhibition, Manchester 1857*, Manchester, 1857.
123 Finke, p. 122.
124 *The Times*, 30 October 1857.
125 [Tom Taylor], *A Handbook to the Gallery of British Paintings in the Art Treasures Exhibition, Being a Reprint of Critical Notices Originally Published in the 'Manchester Guardian'*, 1857, pp. 4–5.
126 *Illustrated London News*, 9 October 1857, p. 432.
127 Quoted in J. Morley, *The Life of Richard Cobden*, 1879, 11th edn, 1903.
128 The best account of Manchester politics is these years is V. A. C. Gatrell, 'Incorporation and the pursuit of Liberal hegemony in Manchester 1790–1839', in D. Fraser (ed), *Municipal Reform and the Industrial City*, Leicester, 1983.
129 G. Saintsbury, *Manchester*, 1887, pp. 198–9.
130 For accounts of the old town hall see J. Wheeler, *Manchester: Its Political, Social and Commercial History, Ancient and Modern*, 1836, pp. 326–8; and J. Everett, *Panorama of Manchester and Railway Companion*, Manchester, 1834, pp. 214–61. For the new town hall see J. H. G. Archer, 'A classic of its age', and J. Treuherz, 'Ford Madox Brown and the Manchester murals' in J. H. G. Archer, *op. cit.*

Class, culture and control:
the Sheffield Athenaeum movement and the middle class 1847–64

We do not see here those immense capitals in the hands of a few individuals which are found in the factory districts. We find here capital scattered among a number of individuals – small masters, as we may call them – brought into daily contact with masses of vigorous and intelligent men, all of them earning their daily subsistence by manual labour, and to all of them it is essential to have a right understanding of their own interests. It is essential they should have an institution to bring them together, to guide, to soften, and refine all that is good and valuable, but rough in their character.

> H. G. Ward, Sheffield MP,
> speaking at the meeting in 1847
> to launch the Athenaeum movement.[1]

If the wide chasm which now utterly severs the working from the upper classes could be so far diminished as at least to admit of there being common pleasure and exercise grounds frequented by both, and in which the poor should see that the rich, at least, did not shun proximity to them in their walks, I am humbly of opinion that civilization would proceed far more rapidly, and that the road would be materially opened for higher and christianizing influences.

> J. C. Symons. Inspector
> for the Royal Commission of Inquiry
> into the Employment of Children
> in Trades and Manufactures not under
> the Factory Act, 1843.[2]

In this chapter I will be looking at how a local middle class[3] responded to the perception of a widening social gulf between the classes. This response took – in part – the form of creating Athenaeums; places of learning and of recreation. Roughly speaking, the ethos of the Athenaeum movement was originally one of social closure or fusion, in which the very act of attendance itself would be an object lesson in the mutual nature of class relationships. The content of the education provided was to be one which concurred with the strictures of political economy. It would create a sober and diligent workforce, who respected their employer at work, and who – at their leisure – reflected on the justification of a system which rewarded the thrifty and punished the wastrel. The Mechanics' Institutes had been one – failed – attempt to lead the working class into the paths of the righteous. The formation of Athenaeums in Sheffield was to be another.

However, this is, as it were, only the 'vehicle' of the chapter. Its main aim will be to make a further contribution to the literature on the fissiparous and divisive nature of the nineteenth-century middle class.[4] The very term 'middle class' – although adopted here – distracts us from a consideration of the many social and economic groups that make up this category. The ability to refer to them all with one concept belies their heterogeneous nature and interests. Nevertheless, this is not to imply that these divisions rendered the nineteenth-century middle class powerless. I am not suggesting a pluralist model of social relations, in which countervailing forces prevent any one group from gaining the upper hand. Despite the disagreements in the middle class about what we might term immediate goals (for example, whether education should be state-funded or financed by voluntary subscription), on fundamentals they tended to agree (for instance, that some form of social control through the medium of education was necessary). The 'bottom line' for this agreement was that the pursuit of profit needed to be defended. It is hoped that this short study, by focusing on how religion and social position can cut across political position, will further the understanding of the complex forces which both bound the nineteenth-century middle class together and forced it apart.

However, before we turn to the Athenaeums themselves it is necessary to look at the structure of industry in mid-nineteenth-century Sheffield.

I

The staple manufacturing trade in Sheffield – the production of cutlery, and its associated trades of hafting, case-making, smelting, and so on – had been little touched by the technological innovations of the first half of the nineteenth century. The one major change had been the introduction of steam power. This had enabled the workshops of the 'little mester' to move from their former positions on the sides of the fast-flowing streams in the hills surrounding Sheffield to the town centre. It had also – of course –

meant that the pace of production had been increased, as the cutlers were no longer dependent on the state of the water supply for their motive power. However, such a move had not brought about any change in the average size of the production unit.[5] Moreover, the 'heavy' side of Sheffield's industry had yet to receive the stimulus provided by Bessemer's – and later Siemen's – discoveries of cheap methods of large-scale steel production.[6]

The proliferation of the workshop mode of production produced a potentially amorphous set of economic relations between the 'datal worker' (e.g. in a literal sense 'paid by the day', the classic proletariat) and the 'little mester' on the one hand, and the merchant and manufacturers on the other. At one extreme the 'little mester' could be someone who owned his[7] own tools and workplace. He would take in the roughly finished piece of raw metal and would apply to it some or all of the processes needed to produce the finished product. This piece of cutlery, knife, sickle – whatever it may be – would be marked with either the corporate mark of the larger merchant or with the 'little mester's' own.[8]

At the other end of the spectrum the 'little mester' could be a worker in a building owned by a merchant or manufacturer, paying rent for the use of his workspace and motive power and working on articles provided for him by the owner. In this instance the distinction between the 'little mester' and the man he employed could be slight, whereas in the former, it was possible for the skilled artisan to act as if he were a 'free' economic agent who – with luck and abstemious habits – could one day rise to the rank of a large-scale manufacturer. Pollard is probably being over-simplistic when he describes the move from wage labour to manufacturer as 'gradual and fairly easy'.[9] Indeed, Erikson, in her study of the social origins of steel manufacturers for this period, has found that 'there were only a few examples of men from the working class in town or country who achieved leading positions in the industry'.[10]

Moreover, it is probable that even the apparently economically independent small producer was not outside the influence of the larger capitalists. Although the workshop mode of production may *appear* to be outside of, or in contradistinction to, the factory mode, it has been formally subsumed under the relations of capital which take a real form in the factory. However, because the small producers *look* free, it is possible for both contemporary and modern historians of Sheffield to point to the continued existence of the small workshop as an indicator of a continuous rather than dichotomous class structure.[11] Evidence from Birmingham, where the small workshop mode also predominated, suggests that although the number of large productive units may have been few, they played a vital role in dictating the nature of social and economic relationship within the workshops.[12] Caught within what Behagg has called an 'inverted political economy' the 'little mester' could find himself imposing the discipline of industrial capital on his men.[13]

One recent historian of Sheffield has placed the emergence of a class society in Sheffield in the period 1780–1830.[14] Support is given to this view by the comments of Sir Richard Phillips who passed through Sheffield in the late 1820s and wrote of Yorkshire as whole:

> There were the high bred *Aristocrats* who associated with none but their class, and who mingled by forced very casual condescension with certain other classes. There were the *Professions*, poor and proud, or rich and lordly, yet without being recognized by lords, however much they aped them in style and manners. Then there was the *Aristocracy of mere craft and position*, but one generation deep, and vulgar though affected; looking back with horror and contempt at the democratic base whence they had just sprung.... These classes constituted respectively 1 in 100, 15 in 100, and 10 in 100, or about 26 families in every 100 in the country. All, however, concurred in shunning, keeping under, and enslaving the other 74, who seemed to submit with docility to the bridle or the whip.[15] (Original emphasis.)

Within twelve years of this date, events were to take place which would place the docility of the 'other 74' in question. In January 1840 Samuel Holberry and a group of 'physical force' Chartists had made an unsuccessful attempt to take the town of Sheffield by force.[16] When they were arraigned before the local West Riding magistrates, Hugh Parker,[17] the senior JP on the bench, took the opportunity to address a homily to the courtroom and local reporters. In it he conjoined two favourite 'Victorian' roles: that of head of the family, and that of master of men. It was lack of correct control and good advice that was causing unrest amongst the young members of the workforce. Surveillance was the answer. The *pater familias* was urged to 'look more carefully after their inmates, and whenever they found them to be irregular in their habits, or concerned in such proceedings as these, they would very greatly contribute to the good order of the town, if they would be careful to keep them at home ....'.[18]

Such sentiments were not new. In May 1792 a meeting of 'the inhabitants of the Town and Neighbourhood of Sheffield' had met in the Town Hall following a number of disturbances between the local population and members of the 4th Dragoons from York and the 15th Dragoons from Nottingham. The troops had been stationed in Sheffield after a number of riots following the enclosure of common land. As well as swearing in a number of constables to patrol the streets after dark, the meeting recommended 'all masters who employ Journeymen and Apprentices, to advise them to attend to their work, and pass their evenings orderly'.[19]

It can be seen then that the masters were perceived as occupying a vitally important social role in terms of control of their work force. As the nineteenth century progressed two developments made this function even more important. First, the work force grew in size, and therefore grew in its potential as a threat to social stability.[20] Secondly, the social gulf mentioned earlier grew ever wider and increased the need to cast the 'little mesters' in the role of mediator between the two social groups. Jelinger C. Symons, who was in Sheffield to report on working conditions to the Royal Commission into the Employment of Children in Trades and Manufactures not under the Factory Act, was aware of this role. In the introduction to his Report he states that 'in the great bulk of the Sheffield trades, the workmen and children are wholly disconnected from the manufacturer, except in the case of the small cutlers who employ them themselves'.[21] However, the problem, as Symonds and a number of the witnesses saw it, was that the small employers were failing in their duty to provide a model for the young employees to emulate.

For other commentators the picture was bleaker. For them the 'little mesters' themselves could not be trusted. For example, the following description of the 'typical' independent master was included in the catalogue for an exhibition of paintings held at the Sheffield Cutlers Hall in 1840:

> They are too much their own masters to be under the restraint of others; they are too little so to be under the restraint of their own better principles and judgement; they feel themselves in some measure separated from the rest of the world, and opposed in self interest, and one common cause to those with whom they transact business. Accustomed to command their apprentices their children, and their wives, their unbending temper cannot brook controul [sic]. Bound together by one common interest they are continually plotting to advance their wages, or to gain additional privileges.[22]

So, to return once again to the words of H. G. Ward (one of the two local MPs), we can see why it was felt necessary to create an institution to 'refine all that is good and valuable, but rough in their character'. Like the Mechanics' Institute before it, the Athenaeum was to serve as a political instrument of the middle class. However, unlike the Institute, this time the working and the middle classes were to share the same building and some of the same facilities. The forlorn hope of its organisers, echoing the sentiments of J. C. Symons, was that the close physical intimacy of the classes would go some way to closing up the social gulf. In the rest of this chapter I will look at the setting up of this institution, the almost immediate split in the ranks of its supporters, and the reasons for, and arguments surrounding, this division.

II

The Sheffield Athenaeum has received scant attention from historians. When it has been mentioned, its role has been misread in two ways. First, the fact that there were *two* institutions with the same name has been overlooked.[23] Secondly, the eventual function of the second Athenaeum – a club for the local petty bourgeoisie – has been ascribed to the first.[24] The origin of both institutions can be traced back to an article on the Manchester Athenaeum that appeared in the *Sheffield Times* on 9 January 1847.

The Manchester Athenaeum had been established in 1835 to provide 'mental and moral improvement' for the growing numbers of young men of the 'intelligent middle classes' in the town. It was also seen as another location where the social divide between men and masters could be bridged; each 'pursuing one common object, that of rational amusement'.[25] (The Birmingham and Midland Institute was established in 1854 for the same ends.) Its first president was James Heywood who was also involved in the Manchester Literary and Philosophical Society, and the Manchester Geological Society.[26] Sir Benjamin Heywood, his brother, was also involved in the Manchester Lit. and Phil., was a member of the exclusive Manchester Union Club,[27] and – following the emergence of Chartist agitation in Manchester – used the Manchester Mechanics' Institute as a vehicle for his pronouncements of class harmony.[28]

On the same day that the article appeared in the *Sheffield Times,* the *Sheffield Independent* carried a copy of a requisition to the Mayor, asking him to call a public meeting to discuss the establishment of an institution in Sheffield along lines similar to the Manchester Athenaeum. The requisition was sign by 450 individuals, and shows that support for the venture came from both Tory and Whig/Liberal factions within the town.[29] It was intended that the local Mechanics' Institute should be reorganised into a Mechanics' Institute and an Athenaeum, with both occupying a new, purpose-built, building. The combined institutions were described as offering 'educational advantages' for the working class, and 'intellectual improvement and recreation' for the young of the middle class.[30] The *Independent* is not specific on the allocation of space within the building. However, it makes it plain that the Athenaeum (that is, the middle-class part of the institution) would have most of the space, with the Mechanics' Institute occupying 'smaller apartments'.

The educational side of its activities was to take place mainly at night, and the plan was to offer classes in reading, writing, arithmetic, geography, modern history, French and German, natural philosophy, chemistry and political economy (this latter being thought 'highly useful'). Actual membership was only to be open to men, but their 'daughters' were to be allowed to attend classes in 'domestic economy'. Emphasis was also placed on the importance of such an institution in providing 'sound moral and religious training' for the young. As we shall see later, it was on just this issue that the unity of the supporters was to founder. That such a split was always a potential development is indicated by the words of the Manager of the Mechanics' Institute, who hoped that the moral training would be on 'ground common to all good men'.

The meeting was addressed by many of the town's leading figures, including John Parker and H. G. Ward (the two Sheffield MPs), T. A. Ward, Wm. Fisher and Samuel Bailey,[31] all of whom spoke in favour of the new institution. However, there were some dissenting voices raised. Isaac Ironside and Richard Otley, leading figures in local working-class politics, spoke against the rule prohibiting discussion of political and religious topics.[32] Otley in particular spoke against the teaching of religion in schools and urged the two local MPs to support moves towards a secular system of national education.

The meeting closed with the Mayor (Henry Wilkinson)[33] announcing that a total of £1,000 had been subscribed towards the total amount needed of £4,000. A breakdown of the slightly larger figure of £1,077 appeared in the *Sheffield Independent* on the next Saturday.[34] Excluding the amount of £200 given by the Town Trustees and all amounts under £20, the money was donated by individuals or partnerships (see Table 2).

The involvement of such a large number of the Liberal/Dissenting group of Sheffield manufacturers gives a clear indication of the fractions of Sheffield society which supported this institution. For example, Thomas Dunn and William Fisher (Senior and Junior) were key figures in the organisations of the Liberal interest in Sheffield. Parker and Ward were the two Liberal MPs. All-in-all, the list would seem to suggest that whatever support for the Athenaeum may have existed amongst the Tory group had dropped away by this time.

This conclusion is given further weight by the fact that the Church Burghers gave no money towards the building fund. The political divisions between the Church and Town Burghers (Church Tory, Town Whig/Liberal) has been traced by Leader back to the late 1790s.[35]

Just over a month later the prospectus for the rival Athenaeum was published. In it the view is expressed that the original supporters of the plan were misled by the committee of the Mechanics' Institute about the nature of the relationship between the two institutions and, more specifically, the way that they would be administered. The committee of the Mechanics' Institute believed that the two institutes should share some facilities and

Table 2

	Amount	Religion	Politics
1 Henry Wilkinson	£100	Unitarian	Liberal
2 Thomas Turton & Sons	£100	Unitarian	Liberal
3 Naylor, Vickers & Co.	£100	George Naylor NK Edward Vickers Methodist	Liberal Liberal
4 John Parker	£50	NK	Whig/Lib.
5 H. G. Ward	£50	NK	Liberal
6 Samuel Bailey	£50	NK (Unitarian?)	Liberal
7 Thomas Dunn	£50	Cong./C. of E.*	Moderate Liberal
8 Michael Ellison	£50	Roman Catholic	Moderate Liberal
9 Wm. Jeffcock	£50	Cong./C. of E.*	Liberal
10 Thomas Birks	£50	NK	Liberal
11 Wm. Fisher & Sons	£50	Unitarian	Liberal
12 James Yates	£25	NK	NK
13 Weightman & Hadfield	£25	John Weightman NK Matthew Hadfield RC	Liberal Liberal
14 Wm. Smith	£20	NK	Liberal
15 Richard & James Solly	£20	James Solly NK Richard Solly Unitar.	NK Radical Liberal
16 Bramley & Gainsford	£20	Edward Bramley Unitar. R. J. Gainsford RC	Liberal Liberal

*Dunn and Jeffcock changed their religious affiliations at some point in their lives but it has not been possible to pinpoint the exact time.

Notes

[1] The political affiliation of each man has been ascertained by finding how they voted in the 1852 and 1857 Sheffield elections, and the 1841 and 1847 West Riding elections.

[2] The religious affiliations of each man is given, where possible, as it was in the late 1840s. However, it is recognised that there was a strong tendency for these to change over time, and that the religion at time of death (from which some of the designations are taken) may not have been the same as in the late 1840s.

[3] A number of the individuals listed above also gave money again as the Town Trustees; e.g. William Fisher, Samuel Bailey, Michael Ellison, and William Vickers, who was a partner in Naylor, Vickers & Co.

that each would be run by separate committees responsible to a joint executive board. The supporters of this new Athenaeum were arguing that the two should be distinct, both in facilities and management. This view was expressed in words that belie the message of 'social fusion' that the Athenaeums were meant to convey: 'They (Athenaeum and Mechanics' Institute) are essentially different institutions, possessing different offices and provisions and calculated for two classes of individuals widely removed from each other in mental attainments and pursuits.'[36]

A week later the Peelite *Sheffield Times* carried an editorial welcoming this rival Athenaeum and stressing once again the fact that Mechanics' Institutes and Athenaeums are different types of institutions directed towards different social groups.[37]

How did this split occur? One of the main reasons given by the rival groups at the time was bad faith. We have already seen that the members of the rival (Norfolk Street) Athenaeum claimed that they had been misled. The committee of the (Surrey Street) Athenaeum and Mechanics' Institute countered this by accusing the organisers of the Norfolk Street institution of going back on their word. According to this version, the arrangement was that the Athenaeum would only have sole use of the News Room. It was only the day after the original meeting (i.e. 17 March 1847) that certain 'parties' sent a Memorial to the Managing Director of the Mechanics' Institute claiming sole use of rooms, and separate and independent Committees of Management and financial arrangements.[38] Such sentiments were, it was argued, totally at odds with the original aims of the institutions, namely the paternal, but democratic, mixing of the classes. The sentiments of the rival (Norfolk Street) group were described as being those of a group who thought it 'objectionable to associate with and encourage intelligent and well-meaning working men, in the paths of literature and science.'[39]

The anonymous author of a letter to the *Sheffield Independent* took up the theme of whether the aims and objects of Mechanics' Institutes and Athenaeums were different. He (or she?) compared the stated objects and the structure of the Manchester Athenaeum and the Sheffield Mechanics' Institute and concluded that they were very similar. Both aimed to provide 'moral and intellectual improvement'; both provided lectures and literary meetings; both provided news and reading rooms and libraries. Moreover, he/she drove home once again the idea that discussion of the group for whom the Athenaeum was being created should be couched in the language of qualified equals. No class in Sheffield could claim to have the monopoly of 'mental attainments and pursuits' (and therefore the right to a separate institution). 'There are many *individuals* in the towns and neighbourhood who are justly honoured for their intellectual power, but they belong to no particular *class*.'[40] (Original emphasis.)

On the other hand, the supporters of the Norfolk Street Athenaeum argued that the success of the Mechanics' Institute in educating the working class made it imperative that the middle class had an institution of their own. Numerous speakers at the Norfolk Street Athenaeum's first general meeting voiced support for the Mechanics' Institute and its attempt to create an Athenaeum section. However, they also pointed out that that institution and their own must be separate. Using the metaphor of a pyramid, first one speaker, then another, argued that those at the apex of society (certain liberal members of the aristocracy, for example, Lord Morpeth) had 'advanced' in social and political matters. The base too, it was argued, had participated in this 'advancement'. What then would be the fate of the middle class if they did not participate? 'Those, therefore, who occupy the stratum above the lowest must attempt to improve themselves also and to advance with the body of the nation, or they would be left behind and the stratum below them would rise and push them from their place. They must advance with the great tide of social progress.'[41] The Norfolk Street Athenaeum was thus firmly marked out as being an institution in which middle-class equals would mingle. It was also characterised as a vehicle through which the Sheffield manufacturing class might be able to rid themselves of their uneducated, provincial image. (The – probably apocrophyal – example was given of a former Master Cutler who whilst visiting Cambridge had left a card stating that he was staying at the 'Blue Bore'.) And, finally, it was described as an institution for educating the 'young men . . . employed in commerce' who would become the administrators of the various colonies of the empire.

The committee elected at that meeting consisted of a President, two Vice-Presidents, a Treasurer and an Honorary Secretary. These were, respectively, Dr G. C. Holland, Revd J. F. Robinson and William Willott, A. F. Hammond, J. R. Roberts and W. Smith, Jun. Holland was the author of numerous medical works, campaigned for better conditions for the grinders and compiled the pioneering *Vital Statistics of Sheffield*.[42] Robinson was the Anglican curate of Bradfield; his fellow Vice-President was owner and editor of the *Sheffield Times*. Hammond was manager of the Sheffield Banking Co.; Roberts was an accountant cum estate agent cum sharebroker; Smith was a solicitor.

All of these men were involved in the running of the Athenaeum for the next four to five years, apart from Holland, who was replaced as President in 1848 by Dr M. M. de Bartolomé, a post which the latter held until 1879. This sudden change was probably due to Holland's bankruptcy, which occurred sometime in the 1840s.[43] Holland had been investing heavily in the railway boom which reached its peak in 1847.

Bartolomé was Spanish by birth but his family had fled the country in the early 1830s. In 1832 he met and married a daughter of Revd Frank Parker of Dore, thus establishing a link with Yorkshire. He obtained his MD in Edinburgh in 1836 and seems to have arrived in Sheffield in that or the next year. Certainly he was a member of the Britannia Lodge of Freemasons in 1839.[44] He seems to have been the key figure in establishing the Norfolk Street Athenaeum as a viable concern.[45]

Of the other six men, Smith was the most active in Sheffield society. On the professional side he was clerk to the West Riding Magistrates (1873–1901), secretary to the Sheffield Chamber of Commerce (President in 1872) and clerk to the Sheffield Improvement Commissioners before their functions were incorporated into the Sheffield Town Council. He was a Councillor (1855–58, 1862–66) and then an Alderman (1884–1901) on Sheffield City Council. At various times he was involved in the running of Sheffield Amateur Musical Society, Church of England Educational Institute, Sheffield Literary and Philosophical Society and Sheffield Press Club. He was an active Anglican, being at one time the organist of Crookes Church and later organiser of the choir at St Andrews Church, Sharrow. At the age of twenty-five (he was born in 1822) he must have been a shining example of the type of person the Athenaeum was meant to attract.

As well as the positions mentioned above, the Athenaeum was also to be under the control of twelve directors. Of the original twelve it has been possible to identify the occupations of eleven. There was a solicitor (John Chambers), a surgeon (Robert Roper, Jun.), a clerk (T. S. Naylor), and one who describes himself as a 'gent' (S. P. Moore). The other seven were all involved in manufacture of one form or another. Most were involved in the cutlery side of Sheffield trade (C. Fleming, F. J. Mercer, W. Riley, H. G. Carr, J. S. Warner, I. Lomax), but one described himself as a hatter (J. Towers). This mix of 'manufacture' and 'professions' continued over the next few years.

The premises that the Athenaeum occupied in 1847 were, as we have said, in Norfolk Street. The property was leased to the Athenaeum by the Sheffield Savings Bank. The house itself had been built by George Greaves (partner in Greaves & Woodhead, merchants) in 1781 on land which his partner had bought in 1780. Following the collapse of the Broadbent bank Greaves bought Page Hall from one of the partners and moved there in 1786.[46] The property in Norfolk Street had a succession of occupiers – mainly surgeons – until it was sold by Greaves's grandson in January 1846 to John Fawcett. Fawcett then sold the house to the Savings Bank in August 1846, a bank of which he had been elected a governor in 1843. The Athenaeum stayed in these premises until 1858, at which time it moved into premises in George Street. In 1897 work was begun on new, enlarged premises. These were completed in 1901 and the club continued to occupy them until the building was destroyed by fire bombs on the night of 13 December 1940.[47]

The report[48] of the first annual general meeting of the Athenaeum, in 1848, gives us some insight into the actual workings of the institution. The Athenaeum had roughly 530 members, each of whom paid – or had paid for them – an annual subscription of 25s. The Library contained 2,353 volumes, the vast bulk of which were, according to the 1852 catalogue,[49] either biographies or novels and romances. The Athenaeum was also well supplied with lighter reading matter. An advertisement from 1847[50] shows that it took a wide range of newspapers and journals. The titles shown come from all political positions; the Peelite *Sheffield Times, Dublin University Magazine* and *The Morning Chronicle;* the Liberal *Leeds Mercury, Sheffield Independent* and the *Manchester Guardian;* the Tory *Quarterly Review, Globe* and *Blackwood's Edinburgh Magazine.* There were also three copies a day of the ubiquitous *London Times.*

As well as newspapers that covered political literature, the Athenaeum took professional journals, such as the *Lancet.* Leisure activities were covered as well with publications like *Bell's Life* and the *Sports Review.* However, it is perhaps indicative of the position that the Athenaeum wished to adopt that the *Sheffield Times* (the owner and editor of which was Vice-President) chose to single out the Tory Anglican *Quarterly Review* for special mention. Henceforth, it said, 'instructive articles' from the *Quarterly Review* would now be open to the middle classes.[51]

The educational side of the Athenaeum had not been wholly abandoned, although now the emphasis was on activities to improve the social standing of the recipient, e.g. French and German classes. Chess and cricket clubs had also been established. Occasional lectures too were being given, although how frequently these occurred is not clear.

Quite when this Athenaeum ceased to see itself as an educational institution for 'social fusion' and began to define itself as a Club is hard to pinpoint. A similar transition was being mooted in the Manchester Athenaeum in 1866, much against the wishes of some elder members.[52] In Sheffield the change seems to have occurred some time in the early 1850s. There are a number of indications of this shift. First, if we look at the report of the Committee established in 1849 to investigate a number of different options for improving the accommodation of the institution, it can be seen that the mention of classrooms comes last in the list of facilties that the schemes should provide.[53] Secondly, the authors of a joint report from the members of both Athenaeums defined the function of such an institution as being – in part: '. . . to supply to young men, or those resident out of the town, the comforts and accommodation of a private club house in the town . . . .'[54]

Thirdly, the actual rules of the Athenaeum itself show such a change. In 1848 the object of the institution is defined as being to provide 'a News Room, Library, Reading Room, Rooms for classes, a Coffee Room . . .'.[55] By 1859, its aims have changed to being the provision of 'a News and Reading Room, Library, Club Room, Chess Room, Coffee Room, Ladies

Room ...'.[56] Moreover, the 1848 By-Laws have a clause which states explicitly that if an individual subscribes to the Athenaeum for 'not less than three Clerks or Servants in his employ', he shall have the right to transfer the membership to another if the 'Clerk or Servant' leaves his employ. This provision would seem to embody in concrete form the kind of 'social fusions' that the instigators of the institute had in mind. Certainly the original Prospectus[57] of the Athenaeum in 1847 said that it (the Athenaeum) would appeal to the masters and large merchants in whose interest it was to have workers 'intelligent, well-principled, and well-informed'. This appeal would be felt by the workers also. They, through the benefit of the facilities provided, would be able to 'take a higher grade in society'. The notion that an institution could perform such a function seems to have been defunct by 1859. Certainly, there is no by-law of the previous kind.

Finally, the compilers of local guide books and directories had taken to calling it a Club and to including it in the same sections as the prestigious Sheffield Club in Norfolk Street.[58] Having made this transition the Norfolk Street Athenaeum achieved stability and contined to exist far into the twentieth century. This was not to be the fate of its rival.

As we have already seen, the Surrey Street Athenaeum was to be run in co-operation with the Sheffield Mechanics' Institute. This latter institution had been established in 1832 by members of an earlier Mechanics' Library and by members of the Sheffield Literary and Philosophical Society.[59] The usefulness of the Mechanics' Institute to the working class has been generally dismissed.[60] Indeed, Pollard has argued that as early as 1836 the syllabus was offering courses that were more designed to attract men in 'clerical and similar occupations' than workers in the staple trades. If this is the case, it shows an early move towards the kind of institution that the Athenaeum was designed to become. However, the (contested)[61] control of the Mechanics' Institute by the middle class employers would seem to be typical of many such institutions.[62]

The decision to erect a new building for the combined Athenaeum and Mechanics' Institute meant that, unlike its rival, it was not able to offer activities and facilities immediately. As we have seen, a dissident group of supporters split off from the men associated with the Mechanics' Institute to form a rival Athenaeum. However, what they did not take with them was the money which the Mechanics' Institute had been accumulating towards the construction of its own premises. These funds had been growing since the initial meeting to establish the Mechanics' Institute in October 1832.[63] Construction on the new building began on a plot of land in Surrey Street on the 1 September 1847. The diary of Matthew Ellison[64] (Sheffield agent for the Duke of Norfolk and others) records that on the day before the event 'Mr. Fisher' and 'Mr. Taylor' came to see him about 'the arrangements'. 'Fisher' is almost certainly William Fisher Jun. – son of the William Fisher mentioned above – who was one of the two Vice-Presidents of the Mechanics' Institute. 'Taylor' is probably John Taylor, who was the Honorary Secretary of the Institute.[65]

The list of people present at the laying of the foundation stone gives some indication of both the importance and political position of the institution. They included the Earl of Arundel and Surrey (the future 14th Duke of Norfolk and a large local landowner), Whig MP for the family's 'pocket-borough' of Arundel; Lord Viscount Morpeth (the future 10th Earl of Carlisle), Whig MP for the West Riding; John Parker, Whig/Liberal MP for Sheffield; Col. Thompson, Liberal MP for Bradford and one of the original post-1832 cohort of 'philosophical radicals'; George Thompson, Radical-Liberal MP for Tower Hamlets; J. A. Smith, Liberal MP for Chichester and James Heywood, Liberal MP for North Lancaster and first President of the Manchester Athenaeum.[66] As well as these men drawn from the national political scene most of the representatives of the Liberal interest within the town were also present. Then, as now, the official function was followed by a tour of a factory, in this case the works of Rodgers & Sons.[67]

At the soirée held in the evening, the view was put once again that the combined Mechanics' Institute and Athenaeum would serve to bring about 'social fusion'. James Heywood, in his speech, drew an analogy between a field in the country and a reading room in the town. In the former, the squire and the farmer met as equals. In the latter, the master and his workpeople would do the same. William Fisher made the same point about the shared use of the reading room and added that he hoped that the 'institution would have the effect of introducing a better feeling between employer and employed'.[68]

Two years later, when the building was opened, the Earl of Carlisle was still making the same point, if with a somewhat greater sense of urgency:

> I would exhort one and all of you to remember who it is for whom these commodious coffee-rooms, libraries, and lecture rooms are intended, for the purpose of promoting their innocent recreations or useful instructions. Why, it is for the hard worked . . . sons of toil, for the artificers and architects of your own wealth . . . I have said – do this [support liberally] in gratitude. Do this in prudence also. The prosperity of Sheffield may wax or wane . . . but I may be allowed to remind you that there can be no such sure guarantee of this prosperity, the peace and the renown of your own Sheffield as to keep the bulk of its population occupied, orderly, cheerful and apt to be pleased. (Cheers)[69]

This meeting was once again attended by a number of influential men from Sheffield and the surrounding area. However, as T. A. Ward's diaries show, at least one of them, Revd Joseph Hunter, only attended at his 'urgent invitation'.[70] The need by Ward to exert pressure to get his old friend to attend is symptomatic of the general lack of interest in the Athenaeum and Mechanics' Institute that was to be displayed over the next five years. The problem that the organisers of the joint institutions faced was that in order to get the classes to mix, the middle class had to attend; and this they failed to do. Why should they, when a rival institution offered similar facilities without the social stigma of a chance meeting with a 'hard worked son of toil'?

The first published edition of the rules for the Athenaeum and Mechanics' Institute carries a list of the executive members.[71] As with the Norfolk Street Institution there were a President, four (instead of two) Vice-Presidents, a Treasurer and an Honorary Secretary. These were respectively Thomas Dunn; W. F. Dixon, William Fisher Jun., Richard Solly, G. P. Naylor; W. Brown; Thomas Marshall. Dunn was a partner in Hounsfield, Wilson, Dunn & Jeffcock (also known as the Sheffield Coal Co.) and was one of the leaders of the Liberal interest in Sheffield. Dixon was a senior partner in the family firm of James Dixon & Son, silver-platers. His inclusion in the list is something of a mystery as he was a staunch Tory.[72] However, he was also a staunch Wesleyan Methodist, which may explain why he was not a member of the largely Anglican Norfolk Street Athenaeum. Fisher was, as we have seen, the son of William Fisher, and a partner in the family firm. Solly was an iron-master with works in Sheffield and Staffordshire. Naylor was a partner in the firm of Naylor, Vickers & Co., which after his death in 1861 became the firm of Vickers & Son. Brown was manager of the Sheffield and Rotherham Bank. Marshall was a solicitor.

Again, as with the Norfolk Street institution, there were also twelve directors of whom it has been possible to identify the occupations of nine. Of these, only two were engaged in the staple trades of Sheffield; one was a stove grate manufacturer (J. G. Robson), the other a partner in Turton & Sons, steel and cutlery manufacturer (W. A. Matthews). The other eight were a tea dealer (H. Hills), an accountant (I. Ironside), a solicitor (R. J. Gainsford), a compositor (D. Walkinshaw), a 'professor' of music and dancing (G. L. Saunders), a rate collector (G. Padley) and the owner and editor of the *Sheffield Independent* (R. Leader, Jun.). There is thus a greater proportion of professional and trade occupations in this group than in the similar group for Norfolk Street.

When the combined institution opened its doors in 1849 the Mechanics'

Institute occupied the top floors and the Athenaeum had the ground floor. The copy of the rules mentioned above shows that already the educational aspect of the Athenaeum was beginning to be relaxed. They state that the Athenaeum would have a newsroom, library, coffee-room, lectures, chess club and occasional concerts. The membership cost of the Athenaeum was 25s. 'payable in advance in January of each year' and would have been roughly a weekly wage for a worker in the light trades.[73] This gave admittance to both sections. Women could subscribe to the lectures, concerts and the library of the Athenaeum for 10s. per annum. The main activity of the Mechanics' Institute was described as being to supply classes for 'reading, writing, arithmetic, geography, the English language'. Here the subscription was 12s. payable in advance, or in quarterly instalments. This did not entitle the members to use of the Athenaeum, and women were not allowed to join.

The report of the first Annual General Meeting[74] lays out the financial position of the combined institution. The building had cost a total of £7,071 to erect. The total amount raised had been £4,092, thus leaving a deficit of £2,979; £2,100 of this was held in the form of debentures on which interest at five per cent was being charged. An earlier article had stated that the working costs of the Athenaeum were £315;[75] with £105 interest this gives a total annual working cost of £420 (this is before the purchase of newspapers and periodicals). The same article that gives the running costs also shows the total number of members as 363; this generates an income of £454 (assuming no bad debts). This gave the Athenaeum an uncomfortably narrow margin of profit to operate on, even if the running costs were accurate. This is called into doubt by a figure produced in March of the previous year by an admittedly hostile authority – the Directors of the rival Athenaeum.[76] They estimated that the total working costs of the Surrey Street Athenaeum would be £438. With the debenture interest this would be £543. Certainly, if the Athenaeum could not keep up its current membership levels, it was in danger of running into great debt.

This is precisely what seems to have happened. By the time of the second Annual General Meeting in April 1851,[77] the representatives of the committee which ran the Mechanics' Institute were arguing for the total separation of the two sections. The Mechanics' Institute, they argued, on its own could cover its share of the costs for the building, whilst the Athenaeum on its own would be running at a deficit of £160 a year. Obviously the running costs were much closer to the estimates presented by the Norfolk Street directors.[78] Indeed, it is noticeable that no figures whatsoever for the financial position of the Athenaeum are presented in the report of the meeting. When put to the vote the motion for separation was defeated.

However, by September of that year the financial position of the Athenaeum sections had reached such a position (they owed £117 in rent for their rooms) that the separation was forced through.[79] In return for the Athenaeum section giving up all claim to the building, the Trustees would rent back to them their current rooms at £30 per annum for fifteen years.

In December 1851 the Athenaeum was relaunched under the name of the Lyceum Club.[80] As with the Norfolk Street Athenaeum, the emphasis was now more on the running of the institution as a club. At the dinner held to celebrate the occasion, John Carr – the then Mayor – listed the usual advantages and facilities which the Club would offer. However, there is no hint in his speech of the Lyceum being an avenue for 'social fusion'. Indeed, he specifically refers to 'another institution' under the same roof which offered similar amenities to the artisans of the town. It was, however, still an 'open' institution in that there was no ballot for membership. Anyone who had the money could become a member. Unfortunately for the directors of the Lyceum, not many wished to.

A directory of 1852[81] speaks of the Lyceum as having 'several hundred members'. The annual reports reproduced in the local newspapers[82] show that the actual number of members was falling, from 354 in November 1852 to 335 (twenty-three of whom were ladies) in November 1853. In addition the Club was organising balls and concerts which were losing them money – £60 in 1853. The 1853 report argued that the Lyceum was only being used by 'gentlemen who frequented the club for convenience of the newsrooms; and consequently it did not hold out the attractions for young men which were afforded by a kindred institution' (presumably the Norfolk Street Athenaeum). If this was the case, the lack of use of the Club's facilities presented a serious financial problem. Moreover, the lack of interest in the institution evidenced by Hunter in 1849 would seem to have become more widespread. The 1853 report also mentions that the rule governing the quorate number at the monthly meeting of directors had been altered to reduce the number needed from five to three.

The various reports continued to talk in confident terms of the financial security of the Club. Despite this, in October 1854[83] the committee of the Lyceum had decided to turn it into a 'closed' club in a last attempt to pay off mounting debts (£600–£700). It was planned to limit the number of members to 200 (which would indicate that the actual number of members over the past two years had always been lower than claimed) and to charge a three-guinea entrance fee, and a two-guinea annual subscription. In order to secure control over membership, they proposed to admit people only by ballot. The Trustees of the building, however, could not, they said, accept the exclusive nature of such an institution. Furthermore, any club that occupied the rooms must be open to anyone who could afford the 25s. entrance fee. This was, of course, the sum that the directors of the Lyceum had found would not support it. The directors had no option but to pass a motion winding up the Club and selling off its effects to pay its debts. A call was also made to members to contribute to this fund, a call which not all accepted without question. Michael Ellison wrote in his diary:

> *Saturday 25th November 1854*
> *Lyceum* The collector called upon me for payment of £2.5s. to liquidate the deficiency in the funds to liquidate all claims against it. I would not pay without making further enquiries.[84]

Once the club had vacated, the rooms were let to the Sheffield Council to house the Free Library.[85] In 1864 the Council bought the entire building for £4,600. The middle floor was converted into a Council Hall, whilst the Mechanics' Institute kept the use of the top floor. The Sheffield Central Library now covers the site.

III

In the rest of this chapter I would like to turn again to the factors influencing the split in support for the Athenaeum. As we have already seen, the immediate reason given by the two groups concerned arguments over the exact amount of space that would be devoted to the use of the Athenaeum. As we have also seen when discussing the Surrey Street Athenaeum, there was a tendency for the men running the institution to come from a certain political grouping, in this case the Liberal/Radical. It is this dimension that I wish to pursue further.

If we take the executive committees for both institutions in April 1850 and analyse them for voting behaviour and religion, we can see that some interesting differences emerge[86] (see Table 3).

Obviously, with such high missing values we need to exercise care in any interpretation we place on this table. However, as a provisional statement, we can say that the Surrey Street Athenaeum would seem to be under the control of a Liberal-dissenting group, and the Norfolk Street under a Tory-Anglican one. Can a study of the contemporary debates support this interpretation?

Certainly the newspaper reports of the long-running attempts to get the two Athenaeums to join forces[87] (mainly instigated by the Surrey Street

Table 3

Religion	Surrey Street	Norfolk Street
Congregationalist	3	
Methodist	2	
Unitarian	3	
Roman Catholic	1	
Quaker		1
Anglican	2	5
Not known	10	12
Voting		
Radical-Liberal	5	1
Moderate-Liberal	8	3
Tory	2	7
Not known, or did not vote	6	7

Notes The political identification is taken from the way people voted in the 1852 election. 'Radical-Liberal' are those who voted for Hadfield and Roebuck. 'Moderate-Liberal' are those who voted for Roebuck and Parker. 'Tory' are those who voted for Overend. The only exception to this rule is the vote of William Waterfall in the Surrey Street Athenaeum, who voted for Parker and Overend and who has been counted as a 'Tory'.

members) occasionally supply some evidence. For example, on 8 May 1847 the first soirée of the Norfolk Street Athenaeum took place in Sheffield Music Hall. In the course of his speech, the Mayor commented that in his view the Athenaeum was a place where they should not 'discuss whether the Government grant for education was just such a one as they ought to accept'.[88] He is here referring to the voluntarist reaction to the adoption of the '1840 Minutes'. In the West Riding this movement had its centre in Leeds, and in the activities of Edward Baines Jun.[89] In essence the voluntarist argument was that any attempt to provide state funding for educational and religious institutions would lead to a domination of the Anglican interest over the dissenting. Education, Baines argued, should be left to local voluntary activity. As Foster has pointed out, the voluntarist movement was not to take as great a hold in Sheffield as in other parts of the Riding.[90] However, the question of religion and education was to play a part in the differing perceptions of the role of the Athenaeum.

In March 1849 the Revd J. Robinson, curate of Bradfield and Vice-President of the Norfolk Street Athenaeum, was speaking at a meeting called to discuss the amalgamation of the two institutions.[91] He was totally opposed to such a move and said that he 'could not see how any original members could, as men of principle, join an institution which had a colour cast over it'. In response to many calls to explain what he meant he would only say that the Surrey Street Athenaeum had a 'bias'.

In a letter published the next week,[92] he went on to develop his argument. The 'great principle' of an Athenaeum was, he argued, association, and, more importantly, association of educated equals, since 'the institution incurs no responsibility on the grave point of formation of character'. The 'great principle' of Mechanics' Institutes was 'the instruction of youth' and it was precisely on the question of what kind of eduction the youth should receive that a body previously united 'would very probably split up into sections . . .'.

> Many members of the Athenaeum, with myself, would be very unwilling for instance, to share the responsibility of imposing a mere secular education to youth at the most critical time of life. We cannot sympathize . . . with efforts to foster the intellectual faculties of young minds, whilst religious and moral training is comparatively, if not wholly neglected.

Another speaker at the previous meeting went further than Robinson, and attacked Mechanics' Institutes outright. They were, he said, 'rickety-rockety hobbies of Lord Brougham' which those in Sheffield associated with his position had used as a *'cheval de bataille'*.[93]

How true were these two charges of secular education and political bias? On the first count at least two of the executive members of the Surrey Street Athenaeum (Fisher and Solly) had attended the first meeting of the General Committee of the National Public School Association.[94] This association,[95] which drew much of its initial support in Manchester from veterans of the Anti-Corn Law League, argued for non-sectarian education in schools maintained from local, not central, rates. Control of the schools was to be in the hands of democratically elected local committees. Such sentiments brought the association into conflict with not only diehard Anglicans, but also voluntarists, of whom Robert Leader (a cousin of Baines) was a local leader. Thus it is possible to say that some of the leading figures in the Athenaeum were involved in secular and voluntarist educational activities.

Indeed we can go further than this. G. C. Holland, in his *Vital Statistics of Sheffield*, notes that the Sheffield Church of England Instruction Society was established in 1839 as a *direct* response to the secular education being provided by the Mechanics' Institute.[96] The involvement of Isaac Ironside – who was an ardent supporter of the Lancashire system of education[97] – in both Mechanics' Institute and Athenaeum must be taken as a clear indication of its position on this issue. As we have seen, at least one member of the Church of England Educational Institute (as the Instruction Society became) was actively involved in the Norfolk Street Athenaeum.

On the political accusation, we have seen that a number of the executive committee were involved in Liberal reform activity. Indeed, when in 1849 the Sheffield Reform Freehold Land Society was established to enable 'every workman in regular employment' to secure the vote, its first meeting was held at the Surrey Street Athenaeum. Once again the familiar names appear on its management committee: Dunn, Fisher and Leader.[98] The function of clubs as organising centres for political activity is graphically illustrated in Trollope's 'political' novels in the Palliser series, particularly *The Prime Minister*. The London Reform and Carlton Clubs had indeed evolved to perform such a function for the Liberal/Whig and Tory interests in the post-1832 Westminster.

The plebeian end of radical politics was also represented on the executive committee of 1850. Two of the Vice-Presidents (Fisher and Solly) and one of the Directors (Ironside) were sitting as Democrat (sometimes called Chartist) councillors on the local council. (The degree of commitment of Fisher and Solly, however, must be open to question.) Ironside was joined on the Council by G. L. Saunders in 1851.[99]

Finally, as an indicator of the political alliance of both Athenaeums, there is the membership of Leader in one and Willott in the other. They were editors and owners of the newspapers which served as the organs of the Liberal and Tory interest in Sheffield.

Thus, it seems we can be confident in saying that the Athenaeum movement began in Sheffield as a collective attempt by factions of the middle class to provide education and recreation for the working class that would be 'improving' and 'healing': Improving in that it would seek to 'guide, to soften, and refine all that is good and valuable but rough in their character . . .', and healing in that it would produce an identification of mutual interests in the minds of the working-class men who used it. However, once this movement was established, support for it split into two groups, one which was associated with the already established Mechanics' Institute, and another which formed a new institution. The reasons for the split were many: for example, allocation of resources, political inclination of the organisers, and attitude towards the kind of education provided. Once these differences had emerged, they solidified and made any attempt at union impossible. In 1850, one of the local newspapers reported a speaker at one of the many meetings held to discuss amalgamation of the two Athenaeums: 'He believed that many parties who could not afford to subscribe to both, were prevented joining either for fear of giving offence to friends connected with one or the other, as the matter was made a personal one.'[100]

It was then simply a question of which Athenaeum would be able to survive, since both could not. In the event it was the Norfolk Street Athenaeum which did, and perhaps that outcome was inevitable. The problem which the Surrey Street Athenaeum had to overcome was that it is one thing to argue for the sharing of facilities by the classes; it is quite another to expect it to take place. As Thomas Dunn unhappily pointed out at the 1851 General Meeting,[101] many people had been influenced against joining the Athenaeum because of its connection with the Mechanics' Institute. This negative association was exacerbated by the fact that members of the Athenaeum had to use the same entrance to the building as the members of the Mechanics' Institute. Coupled with this, in an age dominated by the Smilesian ethos of self-help, was the view expressed by William Smith jun. in 1849 that the Surrey Street Athenaeum was 'in some measure a charitable institution', whilst the Norfolk Street one was 'self-supporting'.[102] The rapid emergence of this feeling of social stigma may go some way towards explaining the move towards defining the institutions as clubs.

We can then agree with Fraser when he says 'The mid-nineteenth century activist pitched his tent in whatever battlefield was open to him. Urban politics ran through many channels.'[103] But our support must be qualified. As we have seen, the 'Liberal' Surrey Street Athenaeum had a Tory Vice-President in the person of W. F. Dixion. Likewise, the 'Tory' Norfolk Street Athenaeum had a Liberal Honorary Secretary, namely William Smith jun. The explanation for this apparent anomaly would seem to lie in the fact that on this occasion *religion* was overriding politics. Dixion was a Methodist and Smith an Anglican.

One further factor to be taken into consideration is the joint membership of both Dixion and Smith in yet another club which has received scant attention from historians, namely the Sheffield Club. This club, itself an institution worthy of study, was formed in 1843 and was a meeting place for the elite[104] of Sheffield's political and economic circles. Also located in Norfolk Street, its entrance fees of six guineas and annual subscription of three guineas placed it out of the range of all but the wealthiest. More importantly, the Club operated a ballot system, so that any aspirant had also to be accepted into the status group of its members.

In addition to Dixion, Solly, Naylor and Waterfall from Surrey Street were members, and Fisher, Leader, Gainsford and Matthews had become members by 1859. Similarly, Smith from Norfolk Street was joined as a member by Robinson and Willott, and in 1868 by Roberts. The smaller number of men from Norfolk Street who were members of the Sheffield Club is an indication of the role that this Athenaeum would come to perform: namely a club for the lesser bourgeoisie of Sheffield. It is an interesting and revealing fact that when the Athenaeum was bombed in 1940 (taking with it all its archives) the Sheffield Club refused to admit its members to the use of its facilties.[105]

The Sheffield Club itself acted as a space where the conflicting factions of the 'bigger' bourgeoisie could meet together on a neutral terrain outside the political and religious divisions that manifest themselves in so many other institutions in the Victorian city. It was also a social space which, by the nature of its existence, helped the 'rival' groups to articulate a shared sense of social status and prestige. In this sense we could say that the function of the Sheffield Club was to act as an organiser for 'closure' whereby the status, as opposed to political determination, of its members could be established.

What the working class thought of these Athenaeums is not recorded; indeed virtually the only evidence for the existence of the institutions is the pages of the local press. What is clear is that, by and large, they failed to support the Athenaeum and Mechanics' Institute, as they had failed to support its precursor. The other Athenaeum drew its membership from the *petit-bourgeoisie* of clerks and shopkeepers, a social group that grew with the century. This enabled it to survive and grow, although performing a function far removed from its original one.

The *petit-bourgeois* nature of the Norfolk Street Athenaeum can be gleaned from a number of sources. First, in an advertisement that appeared in 1847 to announce the papers and periodicals available, the comment was made that this service would mean that articles would be accessible to those who were unable to 'subscribe to the somewhat aristocratic repository in Surrey Street'.[106] This is a reference to the Sheffield Library[107] which had been established as a subscription library in George Street in 1771. It was now located in the Music Hall in Surrey Street. Its 'aristocratic' nature is attested to by the composition of the 1843 committee,[108] which included Michael Ellison, two members of the Newbould family, two of the Creswick family and Benjamin Huntsman. Furthermore, there was the high cost of membership (from 1805–79 the cost of admission was five guineas) which would have placed it beyond the reach of the emerging group of clerks, managers and shopkeepers. Lastly, there was the association of the Library with the group of 'liberal' intellectuals centred on the Unitarian Upper Chapel, in particular Thomas Asline Ward (although this connection with dissent was diluted as the century progressed).

Secondly, there is the position of the president of the Norfolk Street Athenaeum: Bartolomé. Smith, in his study of class formation, has drawn on the work of Inkster[109] to argue that the majority of the 'well-born' medical men in Sheffield were new to the city, and therefore occupied something of a socially marginal position. Leaving aside for the moment any questions concerning the value of this concept of 'marginal men', let us follow Smith's argument further. Smith names three such men – Corden Thompson, Bartolomé and Ferguson Branson. Bartolomé, Smith argues, was the most obviously foreign and would therefore find it most difficult to be granted entrance to established West Riding society. Smith sees this 'outsider' role as determining Bartolomé's role as founder of the Provincial Medical and Surgical Association and as 'the mainstay of the Sheffield Medical School for eighteen years after 1848'. As we have seen, Bartolomé has also been described as the main activist of the Norfolk Street Athenaeum. Could it be that his 'marginal' position also led him into putting energy into a club which would bestow some status on groups denied access to the highest levels of Sheffield society?

Bartolomé himself never was a member of the Sheffield Club, although Branson was from 1849 onwards. Smith's inclusion of Branson in the group of 'outsiders' is almost certainly a mistake. It is true that Branson, like Bartolomé and Thompson, was a stranger to Sheffield itself. However, his father (who was a doctor in Doncaster) appears to have had contacts in the highest levels of West Riding society. For example, in 1835 at the request of Lord Fitzwilliam he (the father) entertained the Duchess of Kent and Princess Victoria (the future Queen) at his 'private house'.[110] This fact may explain why Branson was admitted to the Sheffield Club. His pre-existing social contacts enabled him to mix in the upper social strata within a short time of arriving in the city.

One final piece of evidence for the function of the Norfolk Street Athenaeum comes from the *Memorandum of Association of the Sheffield Athenaeum Ltd* of 1881.[111] This shows that the club had a capital of £10,000 divided into 2,000 shares of £5 each. The directors are shown as Edward Birks (bank manager), George Bailey Cocking (chemist), Edward Saville Foster, George Franklin and Joseph Beckett Wostinholm (all chartered accountants), George William Hawksley (boiler-maker), Richard Churchill Kitching (commercial manager) and Robert Styring (solicitor). The Athenaeum was described as comprising a 'News Room, Library, Dining Room, and all other necessary conveniences in connection therewith . . .'. This is not quite the institution that Charles Knight had in mind when, almost forty years earlier, he said that the aim of the Athenaeum should be to extend the benefits of its membership to 'all who have a desire to emerge from the slough of demoralising habits, and of ignorance which is dangerous to themselves and to others . . .'.[112]

IV

What then has this short study shown? We have seen that a group of middle-class industrialists and professionals launched themselves on a course of action over which they soon openly and publicly disagreed. We have seen that two vital elements in this dispute were the political and religious beliefs of the sub-groups or fractions within the middle class. In this concluding section, I would like to broaden the discussion to see what this incident can tell us about the process of class formation in Sheffield in particular, and England in general.

Let us take first the relationship between the working class and the middle class. The twenty or so years leading up to the establishment of the Sheffield Athenaeum had been a period of intense social and political struggle. The various strands of this struggle coalesced around the issue of industrial capitalism. In many ways, the continued existence and expansion of this new mode of production were being brought into question. In the period after 1850, this precarious state no longer existed. Economic and political relationships between the classes became more stable, and less prone to outbreaks of violence. In a real sense, then, many of the social and political conditions that created pressure for institutions such as the Sheffield Athenaeums were falling away at the very time that the institution itself was being brought into existence. Pollard, in his history of the Sheffield trades, calls this change in the behaviour of the working class 'the growth of respectability'.[113] Although this term, with its connotation of passive acceptance of norms imposed from above, may not be very helpful in an understanding of the processes at work, it does signal that some kind of change was taking place, if only in the perception of working-class behaviour by the middle class. That being the case, it is easy to see why the middle-class support for such an institution should decline. What need was there to invest energy in institutions for social fusion if that social fusion was already taking place? What need was there to devote evenings to teaching the members of the working class that they must not be misled by political radicals, if they were failing to give radical policies significant support anyway? What need was there to worry about the rights of property over the rights of labour if, when given a vote in local elections, labour still elected the representatives of property?[114] It would seem there was no need. Of course, this is an oversimplification; however, it does help us understand why the support for the original aims of the Athenaeum was so weak, and why the surviving Athenaeum was able to transform its social function.

This change in function is intimately linked to the relationship between the middle class and the emerging *petit-bourgeoisie*, which was being created as a class by the continued expansion of capitalist forms of production. This group was an amalgam of new occupations, specifically related to industrial capitalism (accountants, managers) and other more traditional occupations, which predated it (teachers, doctors). Earlier we saw how Inkster and Smith characterised certain of these men as 'marginal' – that is, lacking in power and social identity. A more helpful way of characterising them would be to see them as a social class, or a fraction of a social class, who possessed power and social identity, but who lacked the institutions through which power and social identity could be made concrete and autonomous. Thus, prior to the establishment of the Norfolk Street Athenaeum, virtually every public institution in Sheffield had been for the use of, and/or under the control of, the middle class itself. This had happened for two reasons. First, the middle class had to create its own autonomous social spheres, through which its power could be deployed and be seen to be deployed (clubs, libraries, Mechanics' Institutes, town councils). Secondly, in the period prior to the accumulation of large amounts of wealth, collective ventures were the only way that, for example, the benefit of a large library could be enjoyed.

With the physical movement of the upper strata of the middle class away from the city centres, and the weakening of their commitment to support certain public institutions, the way was open for the 'subaltern' strata to do two things. First, they were able to take over the control of institutions which the middle class was abandoning. For example, in Sheffield the library in Surrey Street, which the Norfolk Street Athenaeum was referring to in 1847 as an 'aristocratic repository' (note the appeal to democratic and radical sentiments) was by 1853 in severe difficulties. Its historian, Sara E. Joynes, notes that from the early 1840s attendance at its committee meetings was very low.[115] This state of affairs was in stark contrast to its early days, when T. A. Ward had been its President. Its fortunes were reversed by the election in 1853 of Dr Bartolomé as President. He swiftly introduced a number of reforms to make the Library a more attractive institution to potential members (for example, allowing the taking out of reference material). This seems to have had a qualified impact on the actual number of new members of the Library. Joynes quotes the following figures for new names appearing on the Library membership list:

1837	104
1846	124
1857	139
1866	108
1888	172

The actual membership figures are:

1837	261
1846	266
1857	265
1866	267
1888	218

Obviously there were large outflows of members that were balancing the inflows. However, it is the change in the social composition of the membership that is most interesting. Joynes shows that the 1857 list indicates that it was the 'clerical grade' which was expanding fastest.[116] Moreover, the involvement of the members of the Library in other powerful local institutions (local and West Riding magistrates, the Town Trust, aldermen on the Sheffield Council) was decreasing at precisely the same time.[117] So the Library was becoming an institute for the 'clerical grades' who were seeking for their class fraction the social recognition that they were still being denied in the most important local institutions. The upper strata of the middle class were abandoning institutions such as the Sheffield Library, since they were now, by and large, in a position to supply the facilities that it provided themselves. But they were not yet abandoning the real centres of power within the local community.

Secondly, this *petit-bourgeois* group could come to construct unique institutions of its own: in this case, the Athenaeum. Therefore, we should not see the Norfolk Street Athenaeum's change of function as a failure. Rather, it is in indication of the power of a class who are only just beginning to emerge on to the local social terrain. The *petit-bourgeoisie* was becoming an important economic and political force, which the bourgeoisie proper would have to take into account. It is precisely the relationship between these two groups that is now in need of historical investigation. A detailed analysis of local social institutions – of their shifting social constituencies and their changing, and often conflicting, policies – is one place to begin that investigation.

Notes

I would like to express my thanks to Catherine Hall, Michael Rustin, John Seed and Janet Wolff, who commented on an earlier version of this chapter. I would also like to thank Janet Walsh, who as well as commenting on an earlier version typed part of it, and gave me hugs during moments of authorial crisis.

1 *Sheffield and Rotherham Independent* (SI), 16 January 1847.
2 J. C. Symonds, *Report on the Trades of Sheffield, and on the Moral and Physical Conditions of the Young Persons employed in them . . .*, Sheffield, 1843.
3 In this chapter, I will follow the useful comments of A. J. Kidd on the use of

this terminology. That is, that the term 'middle class' is taken to stand for the most powerful economic grouping within the nineteenth-century city: the industrial and commercial bourgeoisie and their associated professionals. See A. J. Kidd, 'Introduction: The Middle Class in Nineteenth Century Manchester', ref. 4, p. 18, in A. J. Kidd and K. W. Roberts, *City, Class and Culture: Studies of Cultural Production and Social Policy in Victorian Manchester*, Manchester University Press, 1985.

4 Patrick Joyce, *Work, Society and Politics*, Methuen, London, 1982, esp. Ch. 1; John Seed, 'Unitarianism, political economy and the antinomies of liberal culture in Manchester, 1830–1850', *Social History*, VII, 1982, pp. 1–25; John Seed and Janet Wolff, 'Class and culture in nineteenth-century Manchester', *Theory, Culture and Society*, Vol. 2, No. 2, 1984, pp. 38–53; A. J. Kidd and K. W. Roberts (eds.), *op. cit.*, 1985.

5 Sidney Pollard, *A History of Labour in Sheffield*, Liverpool University Press, 1959, p. 54.

6 *Ibid.*, p. 56.

7 As far as can be ascertained, almost all of the people who occupied the position of 'little mester' were men; in addition, many of the unions in the Sheffield trades did not allow women to train apprentices.

8 For the history of the use of corporate marks (i.e. trade marks) see R. E. Leader, *The History of the Company of Cutlers in Hallamshire*, 2 vols., Sheffield, 1906.

9 Pollard, *op. cit.*, p. 56.

10 Charlotte Erickson, *British Industrialists: Steel and Hosiery 1850–1950*, Cambridge University Press, 1959, p. 13.

11 On the distinction between the formal and real subsumption of labour to capital see Karl Marx, *Capital*, Vol. 1, Penguin Books, Harmondsworth, 1976, pp. 1019–38, *passim*. For an example of the contemporary use of the 'continuous' class model see John Parker, *A Statement of the Population . . . of the Town of Sheffield*, Sheffield, 1830. For a modern example see Pollard, *op cit.*, p. 3.

12 Clive Behagg, 'Custom, class and change: the trade societies of Birmingham', *Social History*, Vol. 4, No. 3, 1979, pp. 455–80; and 'An Alliance with the Middle Class: the Birmingham Political Union and Early Chartism', in James Epstein and Dorothy Thompson (eds.), *The Chartist Experience: Studies in Working-Class Radicalism and Culture, 1830–60*, Macmillan, London, 1982, pp. 59–86.

13 Behagg, *op. cit.*, p. 465.

14 Caroline Reid, *Middle-Class Values and Working-Class Culture in Nineteenth-Century Sheffield*, unpublished Sheffield Ph.D., 1976, pp. 26–7.

15 The extract is taken from a work contained in Box 10 of a series of boxes containing pamphlets on Sheffield in the Freemantle Collection, which is part of the Brotherton Collection in Leeds University Library. It would seem to be a 'proof' copy of the third part of a projected multi-volume series of tours through the United Kingdom, which Phillips planned to publish. In actual fact only the first two volumes appeared. The piece in question starts at p. 221 (this runs on in sequence from the last page of Vol. 2) and has had added in hand on the first page 'Excursion through Chesterfield, Dronfield and Sheffield etc. by Sir ——————— Phillips', and the date '1828 or 9'. Phillips was an early nineteenth-century radical and a friend of Priestley and Orator Hunt. See *The Dictionary of National Biography*, Vol. XLV, pp. 210–11.

16 John Baxter, 'Early Chartism and Labour Class Struggle: South Yorkshire 1837–1840', in Sidney Pollard and Colin Holmes (eds.), *Essays in the Economic and Social History of South Yorkshire*, South Yorkshire County Council, Barnsley, 1976, pp. 135–58.
17 Hugh Parker was a prominent local Whig, and a partner in the family bank of Parker, Shore. His son John Parker (1799–1881) was MP for Sheffield 1832–52, and held various offices in the Admiralty and Treasury.
18 SI, 18 January 1840.
19 Printed notice of resolutions passed at a meeting in the Town Hall of 'the inhabitants of the Town and Neighbourhood', 1792. Home Office Class 42, Box 20, fo. 245.
20 Symonds, *op. cit.*, p. 7, evidence of witness No. 10, Hugh Parker.
21 *Ibid.*, p. 3.
22 The quotation accompanies a description of a painting of 'little mesters' at work. The painting was one of a series of genre works by Reuben Turner, a local cutler turned artist. The unknown author of the catalogue states that the description is from 'Tom and Charles'. See *Descriptive Catalogue of Reuben Turner's Pictures now Exhibiting at the Cutler's Hall . . .*, Sheffield, 1840.
23 'Thus it will be seen that the Athenaeum of to-day has always been a distinct entity, never having any connection with the vanished Surrey Street institution.' Letter from R. E. Leader (local antiquarian, 1839–1922) in Newspaper Cuttings Relating to Sheffield (NCRS), Vol. 1S, p. 32, in Sheffield City Library, Local History Department. See also another letter from Leader along the same lines in NCRS, Vol. 42SQ, p. 69.
24 'In 1847 the Mechanics' Institute . . . was persuaded to throw in its lot with the newly-founded Athenaeum, a recreational club for the well-to-do.' Dennis Smith, *Conflict and Compromise: Class Formation in English Society 1830–1914*, Routledge & Kegan Paul, London, 1982, p. 141. See also, D. E. Fletcher, *Aspects of Liberalism in Sheffield 1849–1886*, unpublished Sheffield Ph.D., 1972, p. 10.
25 *Sheffield Times* (ST), 9 January 1847.
26 Arnold Thackray, 'Natural knowledge in cultural context: the Manchester model', *American Historical Review*, Vol. 79, 1974, p. 704.
27 The Manchester Union Club was established in 1825 in Norfolk Street. It merged with the Brasenose Club in 1933, and with the Clarendon Club in 1961. It is now known as the St James's Club. See *Minutes of the Manchester Union Club* (M 17/2 1) in Manchester City Library, Archives Department.
28 Peter Bailey, *Leisure and Class in Victorian England: Rational Recreation and the Contest for Control, 1830–1885*, Routledge & Kegan Paul, London 1978, p. 36; Hugh Cunningham, *Leisure in the Industrial Revolution, 1780–1880*, St Martin's Press, New York, 1980, p. 99.
29 The Tories include Samuel Butcher (merchant and manufacturer), William Overend (surgeon), Gabriel Reedal (surgeon) and William Willott (editor and owner of the Peelite Sheffield Times). The Whig/Liberals include William Jeffcock (partner in the Sheffield Coal Co.), Thomas Jessop (steel smelter), Thomas Asline Ward (whose family fortune came from the merchant side of the cutlery trade and who, after James Montgomery, was regarded as the 'father of the town') and Robert Leader (editor and owner of the Liberal *Sheffield Independent*).
30 ST, 16 January 1847.
31 William Fisher sen. (1780–1861) was an 'Ivory, Bone etc. cutter and presser'.

He was a leading Unitarian and Whig/Liberal. He had been an active member of the Political Union of the late 1830s. He proposed Samuel Bailey as an unsuccessful candidate at the 1835 election and J. A. Roebuck as a successful one at the 1849 election. Samuel Bailey (1791–1870) was a 'philosophical radical' and may have been a Unitarian at some point in his life. His large fortune (he left £100,000 to the Sheffield Town Trustees in his will, plus large sums to local institutions) came from the family firm of Eadon, Bailey & Co., steel converters. He wrote a large number of tracts covering a number of topics, perhaps the best known being *Money and its Vicissitues in Value*, London, 1837, which Marx attacks in *Capital*, Vol. 1. Henry George Ward (later Sir) (1797–1860) was a 'progressive Liberal'. He was owner and editor of the *Weekly Chronicle* and played an active part in the early days of railway construction. In 1835 he had declared himself in favour of the ballot, triennial Parliaments and household suffrage. He served as MP for St Albans 1832–7 and then for Sheffield 1837–49. In May 1849 he was appointed Lord High Commissioner of the Ionian Islands.

32 Isaac Ironside (1808–70) was leader of the Democratic (also known as Chartist) grouping on the Town Council. He had been secretary to the Mechanics' Institute, but had been removed from his post in 1839 for allowing 'socialist' books into the library of the Institute. Richard Otley had been one of the Sheffield delegates at the 1842 Chartist conference in Manchester.

33 Henry Wilkinson (1788–1873), electroplater and silversmith, was a Unitarian and moderate Liberal, and fourth Mayor of Sheffield.

34 SI, 16 January 1847.

35 The Town Burghers held lands and investments that dated back to an original gift from Lord Furnival in the fourteenth century. Edward VI confiscated the part of the holdings that were devoted to religious use. This was returned by Mary Tudor and a group of twelve Church Burghers (or Trustees) elected to administer it. The land left by Edward was administered by twelve Town Burghers (or Trustees). The income from the trust was designed to be spent on the upkeep of the various roads and bridges. In 1865 the annual income of the Town Trust was £1,870. See John Taylor (ed.), *The Illustrated Guide to Sheffield*, Pawson & Brailsford, Sheffield, 1879 edn, p. 51; R. E. Leader, *Sheffield in the Eighteenth Century*, Sheffield, 1901, p. 226.

36 SI, 27 February 1847.

37 ST, 6, 13 and 20 March 1847.

38 SI, 6 March 1847.

39 SI, *ibid*.

40 SI, 13 March 1847.

41 ST, 10 April 1847.

42 G. C. Holland, *The Vital Statistics of Sheffield*, London and Sheffield, 1843.

43 J. D. Leader and S. Snell, *Sheffield General Infirmary*, Sheffield, 1897, pp. 102–3.

44 J. D. Leader and S. Snell, *op. cit.*, pp. 71, 73, 75, 155; see also Bartolomé's obituary in SI, 3 June 1890.

45 This is the view expressed by J. H. Stainton, *The Making of Sheffield, 1865–1914*, F. Weston & Sons, Sheffield, 1924, p. 285.

46 On the Broadbent bank see R. E. Leader, *The Sheffield Banking Co. Ltd.*, Sheffield, 1916, p. 5.

47 R. E. Leader, *A Century of Thrift: A Historical Sketch of the Sheffield Savings Bank, 1819–1919*, Sheffield, 1920; Stephen Walsh, *A Brief History of the Firm*

of Architects founded in Sheffield by William Flockton, typed manuscript in the Archives Department, Sheffield Central Library.
48 SI, 29 April 1848.
49 *Catalogue of Books, in the Sheffield Athenaeum Library*, Sheffield, 1852.
50 SI, 17 April 1847.
51 ST, 24 April 1847.
52 Michael E. Rose, 'Culture, Philanthropy and the Manchester Middle Classes', in A. J. Kidd & K. W. Roberts, *op. cit.*, 1985, p. 112.
53 SI, 10 May 1849.
54 SI, 30 May 1850.
55 *Rules and Bye-Laws of the Sheffield Athenaeum with the Report and Resolutions adopted at the Annual General Meeting, held in the Town Hall on Wednesday the 26th April 1848*, Sheffield, 1848.
56 *Rules and Bye-Laws of the Sheffield Athenaeum, adopted at the Annual General Meeting held in the Council Hall, on Monday, the 31st January 1859*, Sheffield, 1859.
57 Reproduced in the *Rules and Bye-Laws . . .*, 1848.
58 See, for example, John Taylor (ed.), 1879; also John Taylor (ed.), *Guide to the Town of Sheffield: Prepared for the Sheffield meeting of the B.A.A.S.*, Sheffield, 1879; plus the numerous local directories.
59 Dennis Smith, 1982, p. 139; A. E. Marshall, *The Sheffield Mechanics' Institute. A Study of Educational History and Interpretation*, unpublished Sheffield Polytechnic M.A., 1981, p. 197.
60 Sidney Pollard, 1959, p. 35; G. C. Holland, 1843, pp. 232–5.
61 Working-class activists did attempt to influence the policy of the Institute. See Caroline Reid, 'Middle Class Values and Working Class Culture in Nineteenth Century Sheffield – The Pursuit of Respectability', in Sidney Pollard and Colin Holmes, *op. cit.*, 1976, p. 288; Vernon Thornes, *Chartists and Reformers in Sheffield, 1846–1870; Their Impact on Municipal Politics*, Sheffield City Libraries, Sheffield, 1981, p. 7.
62 For examples from Ashton and Blackburn see Patrick Joyce, *op. cit.*, 1982, p. 187. For Leeds see Robert Morris, 'Middle Class Culture 1700–1914', in Derek Fraser (ed.), *A History of Modern Leeds*, Manchester University Press, 1980, p. 213. For Manchester see Anthony Howe, *The Cotton Masters 1830–1860*, Oxford University Press, 1984, p. 284.
63 *Proceedings of a Public Meeting held at the Town Hall on Wednesday, October 17th, 1832 for the purpose of establishing a Mechanics' Institute*, Sheffield, 1832.
64 *Diaries of Matthew Ellison*, Archives Department, Sheffield Central Library, ACMS 532 (1847).
65 A list of the officers of the Mechanics' Institute in 1847 was placed in the foundation stone of the building. This was recovered when the premises were demolished, and is located at 374.8 S in the Local History Department, Sheffield Central Library.
66 The names are taken from the report of the event in SI, 4 September 1847. The political information is taken from Michael Stenton, *Who's Who of British Members of Parliament Vol. 1 1832–1885*, Harvester Press, Brighton, 1976.
67 *Diaries of Matthew Ellison, loc. cit.*
68 ST, 4 September 1847.
69 London *Times*, 8 November 1849.
70 A. B. Bell (ed.), *Peeps into the Past: Passages from the Diary of Thomas Asline Ward*, Sheffield, 1909, p. 313.

71 *Rules of the Sheffield Athenaeum and Mechanics' Institute, Est. 1849*, Sheffield, 1850.
72 In 1852 Dixion was chairman of the election committee for the local Tory candidate, William Overend. At a dinner held after losing the election, Overend described Dixion as the leader of the conservative cause in Sheffield; see ST, 28 August 1852.
73 Sidney Pollard, *op. cit.*, 1959, p. 60.
74 SI, 13 April 1850.
75 SI, 23 February 1850.
76 SI, 31 March 1849.
77 SI, 19 April 1851.
78 The report in SI, 27 September 1851, shows that there were 350 members. At 25s. per member that would produce an income of £437.
79 SI, 27 September 1851.
80 SI, 8 November, 13 December 1851.
81 White's *General Directory of Sheffield*, Sheffield, 1852.
82 SI, 6 November 1852: 12 November 1853.
83 SI, 21 October 1854.
84 *Diaries of Matthew Ellison*, ACMS 523 (1854).
85 John Taylor, 1879, pp. 62–3.
86 For the Surrey Street Athenaeum the men are: Thomas Dunn, W. F. Dixion, W. Fisher jun., Richard Solly, G. P. Naylor, W. Brown, William Waterfall, Edward Liddell, Thomas Marshall, Robert Leader jun., John Fowler, H. Hills, Isaac Ironside, David Mitchell, R. J. Gainsford, D. Walkinshaw, J. G. Robson, G. L. Saunders, G. Padley, W. A. Matthews and George Wilkinson. For Norfolk Street they are: Dr Martin de Bartolomé, Revd J. F. Robinson, William Willott, J. H. Barber, J. B. Roberts, W. Smith jun., George Parker, J. H. Greaves, Richard Bowling, James Woolley, Charles Fleming, Edward Tozer, John Chambers, John Lennard, William Riley, F. J. Mercer, T. S. Naylor and Edward Harrison.
87 ST, 17 April 1847; SI, 8 May 1847; 31 March, 7, 14 and 21 April 1849; 16 and 23 February, 30 March 1850.
88 SI, 8 May 1847.
89 See F. M. L. Thompson, 'Whigs and Liberals in the West Riding, 1830–1860', *English Historical Review*, April 1959, pp. 214–39; Derek Fraser, 'Voluntarism and West Riding politics in the mid-nineteenth century', *Northern History*, Vol. 13, 1977, pp. 199–231; Derek Fraser, 'Politics and Society in the Nineteenth Century', pp. 270–300, and W. B. Stephens, 'Elementary Education and Literacy, 1770–1870', pp. 223–40, in Derek Fraser, *op. cit.*, 1980.
90 Derek Fraser, 'Voluntarism and . . .', p. 208.
91 SI, 31 March 1849.
92 SI, 7 April 1849.
93 At the opening of the London Institute, Brougham had said: 'Some will tell us that it is dangerous to teach too much to the working classes, for, say they, it will enable them to tread on the heels of their superiors. Now this is just the sort of treading on the heel that I long to see.' Quoted in Harold Perkins, *The Origins of Modern English Society, 1780–1880*, London, 1969, p. 305.
94 D. E. Fletcher, 1972, p. 236.
95 This account of the Association is drawn from the section in Anthony Howe, 1984, pp. 215–29.

96 G. C. Holland, 1843, pp. 230–1. See also E. R. Wickham, *Church and People in an Industrial City*, London, 1957, p. 155.
97 D. K. Jones, 'Isaac Ironside, democracy and the education of the poor', *Transactions of the Hunter Archaeological Society*, Vol. 11, 1981, pp. 28–37.
98 SI, 10 May 1849.
99 Vernon Thornes, *op. cit.*, 1981, p. 10.
100 SI, 23 February 1850.
101 SI, 19 April 1851.
102 SI, 13 March 1849.
103 Derek Fraser, *Urban Politics in Victorian England*, Liverpool, 1976, p. 9.
104 So John Taylor describes its members. *Illustrated Guide . . .*, 1879, p. 118.
105 The author has conducted a lengthy study of the Sheffield Club. This is a verbal anecdote collected during that study.
106 ST, 24 April 1847.
107 Thomas Asline Ward, *A Short Account of the Sheffield Library, its Founders, Presidents and Librarians*, Sheffield, 1825; Sara E. Joynes, 'The Sheffield Library 1771–1907', *Library History*, Vol. 2, 1971, pp. 91–116.
108 SI, 30 December 1843.
109 Dennis Smith, *op. cit.*, 1982, p. 158; Ian Inkster, 'Marginal Men: Aspects of the Social Role of the Medical Community in Sheffield 1790–1850' in J. Woodward and D. Richards (eds.), *Health Care and Popular Medicine in Nineteenth-Century England*, London, 1977, pp. 128–63.
110 See J. D. Leader and S. Snell, *op. cit.*, 1897, p. 106; the Sorby Record, Vol. 2, No. 2, 1965, 39–40, 42, shelved at 506 SQ in the Local History Department, Sheffield Central Library.
111 *Memorandum of Association of the Sheffield Athenaeum Ltd.*, Sheffield, 1881.
112 *Rules and Bye-Laws of the Sheffield Athenaeum: . . .*, Sheffield, 1848.
113 Pollard, *op. cit.*, 1959, pp. 122–4.
114 In Sheffield by 1869 the majority of voters in municipal elections were working class. See Pollard, *op. cit.*, 1959, p. 120.
115 Joynes, *op. cit.*, 1971, pp. 104–5.
116 Joynes, *op. cit.*, 1971, p. 114.
117 Joynes, *op. cit.*, 1971, p. 115.

The culture of separate spheres:
the role of culture in nineteenth-century public and private life

Writing in 1851, J. W. Hudson describes the 'liberal and comprehensive scheme of female education' introduced at the Manchester Mechanics' Institute in 1841: 'For less than thirty shillings per quarter, a young lady may receive the elements of what is termed an English education, and be taught the accomplishments now considered necessary to her position, including the French language, drawing, vocal and instrumental music, dancing, modelling, with the useful arts of millinery and dress-making.'[1] The intention of the directors of the Institute was explicitly that of teaching women 'what would make them better wives, sisters, mothers' as well as better 'members of society'.[2] It would be inappropriate and misleading to consider this a simple case of sex discrimination, for we also find that in the girls' school opened there in 1835 the subjects taught were more or less the same as those taught at the boys' school, namely reading, writing, arithmetic, geography, history and grammar. The boys also learned algebra and geometry, and the girls sewing and knitting.[3] The access of girls and women to culture and to knowledge in the first half of the nineteenth century in England was complex and often contradictory. Nevertheless, my main argument in this chapter will be that the continuing process of the 'separation of spheres' of male and female, public and private, was on the whole reinforced and maintained by cultural ideologies, practices and institutions. This applies both to women's place in *cultural production* (as artists, authors, patrons and members of cultural institutions) and to the dominant modes of *cultural representation*, particularly in literature and the visual arts, and their construction of notions of gender. Interwoven with both of these is that nineteenth-century morality which determined which books or paintings would be publicly available (I shall consider a few examples of such extra-aesthetic influence later on), and which spheres of activity were appropriate for men and women. But although my starting point is the separation of spheres, it is important to stress that any implication of a simple determinism must be rejected. The particular focus of this chapter on the role of culture does not presuppose either a ready-formed or static 'middle class', or a straightforward economic and ideological 'separation of spheres'. Indeed, this separation was constantly and multiply produced (and counteracted) in a variety of sites, including culture and the arts. So, for example, women's exclusion from various areas of productive work did not *entail* their exclusion from painting; rather, the latter was the product of the specific ideologies and practices *of* art and of 'the artist'.[4] My argument that cultural institutions and ideologies contributed to the separation of spheres should not, therefore, be read as either an idealist account (culture as producing social divisions) or a reductionist one (culture as epiphenomenal, merely reflecting existing divisions).

The separation of public and private life

Leonore Davidoff and Catherine Hall have documented the 'separation of spheres' into the public world of work and politics and the private world of the home, as well as the concomitant development of the domestic ideology which relegated women to the private sphere.[5] The material separation of work and home, which was the result of both the Industrial Revolution and the growth of suburbs, was clearly the precondition of the general process, though, as Catherine Hall has pointed out, for many families and many occupations this separation did not always occur (for example, in the case of doctors' practices).[6] The cult of domesticity was strong among the middle class by the 1830s, emphasising the sanctity and purity of family life, and the moral task of women as mothers and wives. Women who did continue to work outside the home were increasingly restricted to particular kinds of occupation – servicing rather than productive, and 'women's trades' of teaching, dressmaking and retail – and excluded from the new financial institutions associated with business.[7] At the same time, the 'public world' expanded, providing for men a multitude of additional activities and institutions – banks, political organisations, voluntary societies and cultural institutions. Women's involvement in these organisations, where it existed at all, was indirect or informal – for example, as visitors, but not officers, of philanthropic societies.[8]

Physically, the separation of spheres was marked, as well as constructed, by both geography and architecture. From the 1830s, the more prosperous members of the middle class in the major manufacturing cities began to move out of the town centre, and to build houses in the suburbs. The development of Victoria Park, Manchester, illustrates this move well.

> During the early and middle 1830s, the out-of-town villa residence was just beginning to become fashionable. There remain, even today, many examples of this type of property that were put up between about 1835 and 1850. The broad band of country from Greenheys, Chorlton-on-Medlock, the northern parts of Rusholme (i.e. Victoria Park), Plymouth Grove and parts of Longsight and Ardwick contain examples of late Georgian terraces and villa residences. These houses were all occupied by the emerging mercantile class of the city.[9]

Thirty-five such large houses were constructed in Victoria Park between 1837 and 1845.[10] Maurice Spiers describes James Kershaw, one of the earliest residents of Victoria Park (he lived there from 1838 to 1859) as typical of those setting up their homes there. He was a partner in the calico-painting firm of Leese, Callender and Co., having started life as a warehouse lad. He was a member of the Council of the League, an Alderman from 1838 to 1850, Mayor in 1842–3, and MP for Stockport from 1847 to 1859. Interestingly, Spiers also notes that before moving out of the centre of Manchester, Kershaw had lived in Great Ancoats Street, where his wife carried on a business as a linen draper.[11] He does not record whether she was able to continue her occupation after the move to the suburbs, but she certainly did not do so from the new address, and it is most unlikely that she travelled into town. Although the extent of suburbanisation should not be overestimated (many middle-class families remaining in the more central urban areas), where it did occur, the move to the suburbs entailed a clear separation of home and work, and a firm basis for the domestic ideology of the home as haven, and of women as identified with this private sphere. Davidoff and Hall trace the similar development of Birmingham in this period, in the growth of the suburb of Edgbaston.[12]

The design of the new houses themselves usually accorded well with the ideology of separate spheres. With regard to the middle-class elite, Mark Girouard argues that agreement by 1850 about what a 'gentleman's house' should be like included the requirements that 'it should provide decent quarters for servants. It should protect the womanliness of women and encourage the manliness of men.'[13] As well as an extremely complex and often impractical arrangement of rooms, so that children, servants, mothers and fathers should only coincide at approved times and in approved places,[14] Victorian houses also contained 'an increasingly large and sacrosanct male domain', whose nucleus was the billiard room. The domain often expanded to include the smoking room and the gun room, and sometimes adjoining dressing room and study.[15] Girouard is writing about Victorian country houses. The suburban dwellings of other sections of the middle class were not, of course, built on the same scale; but the same physical separation of domains was apparent, with the increase in the number of servants, and the concern to keep them separate from the family, with the nineteenth-century emphasis on the distinctness of childhood, and with the underlying ideology of the appropriate sensibilities and areas of operation of men and women.[16]

The effects of the clear distinction of 'public' and 'private' spheres, and in particular the limitation of women's existence to the latter, went beyond the lives of the middle classes who first produced it. As Girouard shows, members of the gentry redesigned their houses in accordance with the new social arrangements.[17] More generally, the Victorian domestic ideology, which Catherine Hall has analysed in relation to Evangelical Christianity, extended both 'upward', to the older ruling classes, and 'downward', to the lower middle and working classes.[18] Although women did continue to work – in factories, in some trades, in certain family businesses – the increasingly dominant ethic of woman's domestic, and subservient, role ignored this fact. Ruskin's well-known catalogue of the disasters wrought throughout the history of literature by the fallibility and corruptibility of men, redeemed only by the purity and wisdom of women, asserts women's 'guiding function' (which, he insists, is quite reconcilable with a 'true wifely subjection').[19] All this is explained by the different male and female characters. The man is 'active, progressive, defensive'; he is

> eminently the doer, the creator, the discoverer, the defender. His intellect is for speculation and invention; his energy for adventure, for war, and for conquest ... But the woman's power is for rule, not for battle, – and her intellect is not for invention or creation, but for sweet ordering, arrangement, and decision. She sees the qualities of things, their claims, and their places. Her great function is Praise: she enters into no contest, but infallibly adjudges the crown of contest. By her office, and place, she is protected from all danger and temptation. The man, in his rough work in the open world, must encounter all peril and trial: – to him, therefore, must be the failure, the offence, the inevitable error: often he must be wounded, or subdued; often misled; and *always* hardened. But he guards the woman from all this; within his house, as ruled by her, unless she herself has sought it, need enter no danger, no temptation, no cause of error or offence. This is the true nature of home – it is the place of Peace.[20]

There were certainly alternative opinions expressed in the mid-nineteenth century about 'women's proper place' and their appropriate education – for instance, by John Stuart Mill. But the strength of the Ruskinian ideal was enormous, and it was an ideal also upheld by other influential writers of the period, like Thomas Carlyle. Geraldine Jewsbury, author and a friend of the Carlyles, was outraged by his opinion that 'a woman's natural object in the world is to *go out* and find herself some sort of *man her superior* – and obey him loyally and lovingly and make herself as much as possible into *a beautiful reflex* of him!'[21] The persistence of this domestic ideal, in Ruskin's own formulation, is still evident much later in the century. Katherine Chorley, daughter of Edward Hopkins, the managing director of the engineering firm, Mather and Platt, describes her early years in Alderley Edge, just outside Manchester, in the last decades of the century. (By then, those moving into the suburbs had to go rather further afield than Victoria Park.) She writes, somewhat ruefully, about the influences of Ruskin on her own upbringing. Her father, from a Manchester Nonconformist background, had the complete Ruskin 'bound in blue calf', and Katherine Chorley believes 'he must have dipped a good bit' into these texts: 'his ideal of womanhood – a little unfortunately for me as I grew older – was obviously founded on *Sesame and Lilies*.'[22] Her mother, an Ulster Irishwoman, though from a quite different background, shared his views on the education of young women. Chorley writes of her parents:

> They very much disliked any sort of day school which approximated to the high school type. In their opinion, education at an establishment of this kind involved a 'roughening' process, a physical and intellectual scramble combined with contacts whose suitability they would not be able to control. In short, they affirmed the ideals for young women set out in Ruskin's *Sesame and Lilies* and felt that these were not likely to be nourished in a high school.[23]

Domestic life certainly reinforced these ideals:

> Mother was very particular about anything which symbolized decorous behaviour as between males and females. The downstairs lavatory, for instance, was sacrosanct to the men of the family and their guests, the upstairs was reserved with equal exclusiveness to the females. Woe betide me if I was ever found slinking into the downstairs to save time. Conversely, the good breeding and social knowledge of any male guest who was suspected of having used the upstairs while dressing for dinner was immediately called in question.[24]

Relations between husband and wife also conformed to the Ruskinian ideal. 'Throughout their married life (mother) had laid upon herself the plain first duty as she conceived it of carrying father through his troubles and difficulties.' Nevertheless, 'Father might be outwardly masterful, but mother was inwardly the mistress of her own being.'[25]

Domestic ideology and the role of culture

The fact that Geraldine Jewsbury objected to Carlyle's views about women reminds us that Victorian domestic ideology was by no means a monolithic or all-pervasive one. The separation of public and private spheres was not always a clear one. Many women did work outside the home. And many people, of both sexes, subscribed to some sort of equality of men and women, in education and more generally. For example, Tylecote points out that the propagandists of the Mechanics' Institutes had stressed the importance of female education.[26] Nevertheless, the kind of feminine ideal described by Carlyle and Ruskin was powerful and widespread by the mid-nineteenth century. The practices and the institutions of culture and the arts played a considerable part in this, and numerous cases testify to the role of culture in supporting the ideology of separate spheres.

Ruskin's views on society and morality were inseparable from his art criticism. He objected to the nudes of William Mulready (1786–1863) as 'more degraded and bestial than the worst grotesques of the Byzantine or even Indian image makers', and as 'most vulgar, and in the solemn sense of the word, most abominable'.[27] Moreover, although he was an artist himself, he never attended a life-class.[28] Ruskin's influence as an art critic was enormous (although Jeremy Maas certainly overstates the case when he claims of Ruskin that 'he had only to wonder why no-one ever painted apple-trees in blossom for the Academy walls a year later to be covered with orchards full of apple-trees in blossom').[29] Aesthetic judgments were, of course, not always or even primarily posed in moral terms. But in 1855, despite finding Leighton's painting, *Cimabue's Celebrated Madonna*, 'a very important and very beautiful picture' (an opinion shared by many other reviewers and artists), Ruskin thought Millais's *The Rescue*, shown at the same Royal Academy exhibition in 1855, a greater picture. Leighton thought that this judgment was based on the belief that 'the joy of a mother over her rescued children is a higher order of emotion than any expressed in my picture'.[30] Whether this tells us the actual basis of Ruskin's judgment, or more about his known views and reputation, the point is the same.

In literature, the moral guardians had equally tight control over cultural production – perhaps a greater power in so far as they were often in a position to determine which books were published. In particular, Mudie's circulating library and W. H. Smith's bookstands, central to the success of both authors and publishers, operated on a severe moral code. As J. A. Sutherland writes, 'The two greatest entrepreneurs of fiction in mid-Victorian England, Mudie and W. H. Smith, set themselves to impose middle-class decencies on the English novel.'[31] Mudie's influence, he goes on, was 'frequently a trespass on artistic freedom'. For fear of offending him, Trollope's *Barchester Towers*, whose success depended on a substantial sale to the circulating library, was censored by the publisher's adviser, who wanted it purged of its 'vulgarity' and 'exaggeration'; an example given by Sutherland of the changes required was the alteration of the phrase 'fat stomach' to 'deep chest'.[32] With somewhat less influence, and coming, in any case, after the event, reviewers of Geraldine Jewsbury's rather turgid romantic novel, *Zoe* (1845), expressed their shock at a heroine in love with two men (as well as at a critical attitude to religion). Her publisher, Mr Chapman of Chapman and Hall, receiving a letter of complaint from one of Geraldine Jewsbury's own friends, Mrs S. C. Hall, began to worry about the effect the publication would have on him, until reassured by Jane Carlyle.[33] But Jane Carlyle herself, who had obtained the reading of the manuscript by Chapman in the first place, had already persuaded the author, as her biographer puts it, 'into the application of "spotted muslin" to some of the more flagrantly indecorous parts'.[34] Whether because of publishers' fears of disapproval from Mudie's, from Smith's, or from other major buyers, or because of their judgement of readers' moral sensibilities, the assessment of manuscripts was clearly very much in terms of acceptable religious and moral values. The reaction to Mrs Gaskell's *Ruth*, published in 1853, was even more violent, and upset its author enough to make her ill for some days, and to cause her to think 'I must be an improper woman, without knowing it, I do so manage to shock people'.[35] As far as sexuality was concerned, these debates and editorial checks illustrate not so much a straightforward form of censorship, but rather a careful negotiation of the area, and the formulation in very specific ways of the particular, appropriate, visibility of sexuality at that time.

The direct influence of patrons on the work of painters was surprisingly common in a century when the ideology of the free, creative artist was developing. Although the relationship was not one in which, as in the early Renaissance and before, the patron might list the detail of content and use of colour pigment to appear in a commissioned work, it was not unusual for the prospective buyer to specify what he wanted in the work. Henry McConnel, of the Manchester cotton-spinning firm, McConnel and Kennedy, commissioned Turner to paint *Keelmen Heaving in Coals by Night*. Darcy suggests that McConnel 'most likely wished the artist to contrast the timeless calm of Venice with the industrial bustle of the River Tyne', since he already owned a painting of Venice.[36] Thomas Plint, a Leeds stockbroker, asked Mulready to paint him a work on a theme from *The Vicar of Wakefield* or from Sir Walter Scott's writings; both were popular sources of paintings in the mid-nineteenth century, and indeed Mulready had already illustrated Scott's novels and the Goldsmith novel, and exhibited and sold paintings on themes from them.[37] It appears that Mulready did not accept this commission, nor one from Prince Albert to paint a copy of one of his *Vicar of Wakefield* paintings, *Choosing the Wedding Gown* (1845).[38] Other artists complied with their patrons' requests, and to that extent the interests and values of buyers came to be represented in some works, although the general effect of this on Victorian paintings cannot be easily summarised. According to Maas, the nude in painting only survived the prudery of the Victorian era because of the more liberal attitudes of the 'new' patrons – the merchants and industrialists of the North and the Midlands, who, he argued, were 'uninhibited by the pruderies of the capital'.[39] But since to a large extent these 'pruderies' were the product of the new middle class itself, another explanation for the persistence and acceptance (sometimes limited, as I have already suggested) of the nude in painting must be found. This is something I shall return to later. Contrary to Maas's view, the evidence seems to suggest the more puritanical influence of the new patrons. (However, as Caroline Arscott argues elsewhere in this volume, it is entirely misleading to assume a unitary meaning for a picture, and to ignore, for example, the effects of different contexts or locations of display.)

On the rather different issue of religious evangelism (not necessarily coincident with moral prudery) another recorded instance of Thomas Plint's interest in painting documents his success in getting Ford Madox Brown to change his famous painting, *Work* (Figure 1). Having seen the sketches for this painting in 1856, he agreed to buy it, but asked for two changes. On the right of the work, the two standing figures represented are Thomas Carlyle and F. D. Maurice. Plint had requested representations of Carlyle and Charles Kingsley. In his other request, he appears to have been entirely successful in his intercession with the artist. On the left of the painting are depicted four well-dressed women, walking past the labouring men. Brown has responded to Plint's request in a letter written after seeing the preliminary sketches, in which he wrote 'Could you change one of the four *fashionable* young ladies into a *quiet, earnest, holy*-looking one, with a book or two and *tracts*? I want *this* put in, for I am much interested in *this* work myself, and know those who are.'[40]

Most paintings were not conceived or modified by their patrons. Many works were painted without a commission, for exhibition and later sale. Many buyers were not Nonconformists or Evangelical Christians, and, among those who were, this was not necessarily reflected in a strict application of their moral and religious code to the arts. So I am not suggesting that the production of culture in nineteenth-century England was dominated and overseen by an elite group of rich and powerful middle-class reformers, who ensured that painting and literature reinforced domestic ideology, bourgeois morality, and the notion of the protected place of women in society. But it is worth identifying the influence of that ideology where it clearly did operate in the production and distribution of culture. To a considerable extent, patrons, critics, reviewers, publishers and others colluded in the dissemination of a culture which was sanitised and shaped in accordance with the middle-class ideology of separate spheres. A final example of this, more explicit than most, though from a slightly later period, is discussed in Frances Borzello's article on the origins of the Whitechapel Art Gallery in the East End of London.[41] The Gallery, which was opened in 1901, had begun with a series of annual fine art exhibitions organised for the poor of the area from 1881 to 1898. The paintings shown at these exhibitions, even though the premises (a school) were temporary and unsatisfactory, were an impressive selection. The first exhibition, in 1881, included works by Watts, Leighton, and Burne-Jones, and paintings first exhibited at the Royal Academy were often lent to the Whitechapel exhibitions. Artists and lenders were extremely generous in their support of these exhibitions. Queen Victoria herself lent three paintings in 1887 and two in 1889.[42] Audiences were large; 10,000 visited the exhibition in 1881, 47,000 in 1885, 55,000 in 1890, and 76,000 in 1892. Sales of catalogues were also high: 4,600 in 1882 and 16,000 in 1885, for example.[43] Although, as Borzello says, we do not really know what audiences thought of the works shown, apart from the interpretation of their success by the organisers of the exhibition, the availability of two or three hundred paintings in the East End each year was remarkable, and the clear popularity of certain works, shown by an annual vote for the favourite painting, tells us something about popular taste. (It seems that 'pathetic' subjects were popular, but landscapes were not.) Most important, however, was the motivation of the principal organisers, and the mediation of their views through captions to the paintings, catalogue entries and commentaries, and gallery talks. The exhibitions were the inspiration and production of the Reverend Samuel A. Barnett, Vicar of St Jude's, Whitechapel, and his wife, Henrietta Barnett, social reformers who had faith in the role of art in 'de-brutalising' the poor, and educating them into Christian values. Hence, Borzello quotes the caption to a replica of Raphael's *Madonna del Cardellino*, exhibited in 1886, which read: 'In this woman there are the nobleness, and the self-forgetting, ever-watchful care of a true mother. In the children there are the friendship and the tenderness which are ever found in a true home.' A catalogue entry in the same year linked the Holy Family implicitly with the families of Whitechapel. 'The great masters painted the Virgin and Child in likeness of the people they knew; in their eyes every home had the possibility of the highest.'[44] Even the popularity vote each year may well, Borzello suggests, have been affected by the hanging policy of the organisers, giving prominence to particularly uplifting works.

Women and the institutions of culture

So far, I have considered the role of culture in producing and maintaining the social divisions of gender. But culture does not simply reflect social life, responding to transformations in ideology by producing different images and texts. Nineteenth-century culture was itself changed by those same processes which produced the middle class and its ethic. With regard to gender divisions, there were two related important processes: the increasing privatisation of leisure, and the virtual exclusion of women from 'public' cultural institutions of various types. In these ways, too, nineteenth-century culture reinforced the separation of spheres.

The increasing class segregation of leisure which began in the late eighteenth century was accompanied by a trend to private leisure – either centred on the home (reading, playing music, gardening) or based on the family (holidays, for example).[45] Those entertainments or cultural activities which did take place in the more public arena, like sports, were almost exclusively male. Women's leisure was confined to the home, particularly among the middle class. As Cunningham says, 'the general rule was that any woman in a public place of leisure, and unaccompanied by husband or other suitable male, was a prostitute.'[46] Women were not able to frequent pubs, coffee houses, or eating places other than pastry-cooks' and confectioners' shops.[47] When accompanied by men, however, women might attend the theatre, particularly in the second half of the century when theatres, having excluded the working class by a variety of measures, including the price of tickets, became 'respectable'.[48] With the rise of musical and concert life in many large cities, too, another respectable public arena for mixed audiences opened up, although a good deal of musical activity and performance occurred in the more private location of people's homes. In mid-century Leeds, for example,

> There was no sharp dividing line between the worlds of family, amateur and professional music. The Leeds Musical Soirées, started in 1848, were organised by a select society which included Heatons, Marshalls, Kitsons and Heys among it members. They met in members' houses and occupied the intervals between selections from Handel, Mendelssohn and Wesley with refreshments, including sherry and port.[49]

But many of the major new cultural institutions of the nineteenth century were men's institutions: the literary and philosophical societies, the various scientific societies,[50] statistical societies, gentlemen's clubs and societies. In Birmingham, women were

> virtually excluded... from many of the meetings of the new clubs and societies, social and scientific as well as political, which were springing up in this period. Examples would be the earliest known Birmingham Book Club probably established around 1750, the Brotherly Society (1776), the Philosophical Institution (1800), the Mechanics' Institute (1825), the Chamber of Manufacturers which grew out of the Commercial Committee of the late 1770s. A similar pattern was followed by the numerous philanthropic societies organized around the provision of medical care and education for the poor.[51]

Women were generally not allowed places as members of committees, or as book borrowers; they might, as in the case of the Birmingham Athenaeum (1839), be able to attend public lectures, but not the weekly meetings or classes; nor were they permitted to go into the reading rooms.[52] Ashton's centenary history of the Manchester Statistical Society (founded in 1833), appends a list of all the Reports and Papers produced by the Society. In the first fifty years of its existence, only two papers out of over three hundred were written by women, both in 1868–9, and one of these was a criticism of another paper.[53] In Kargon's account of science in Victorian Manchester, the only references to women's involvement are to gifts received by institutions from a Miss Brackenbury and from Lady Whitworth as one of the Whitworth legatees.[54]

Indeed, women's traditional role as patron and supporter of intellectual and cultural development continued in the Victorian era. Rich women could give donations to scientific and philanthropic enterprises, or help in the setting up and running of cultural activities. But women's access to cultural production continued to be extremely limited. Only in 1860 was the first female admitted to the Royal Academy Schools.[55] In other schools of art, provision was made for girls and women – for example, at the Glasgow School of Design, opened in 1844.[56] Where art education was mainly intended for male artisans, female pupils were more likely to be middle-class, and the reasons given for the provision of this education were usually in terms of helping them to acquire 'an honourable occupation'.[57] On the whole, the art education of ladies remained the province of the private drawing masters, and here the chief purpose was 'to occupy maidens' minds with a harmless pursuit'.[58] The majority of Mulready's private pupils were women, and their education was much in line with this ideology. Mulready himself, however, encouraged his female pupils and took their work very seriously, perhaps, as Heleniak suggests, as a result of his early marriage to an artist, Elizabeth Varley.[59]

From the information available about women painters in Manchester in the first half of the nineteenth century, it appears that although many women did paint, they did not set themselves up as artists. Those who did paint, and even exhibit work, tended to restrict their subject-matter to themes of still life and flowers. (See Chapter 2.) This confirms the general trend identified by Parker and Pollock as the marginalisation of women artists into certain kinds of paintings, which were accordingly downgraded in status, flower painting being a particularly common genre for women artists.[60] There were exceptions – women who attempted classical or historical subjects, despite the severe limitation of access imposed by, amongst other things, exclusion from the life-class.[61] But the majority of women painters limited themselves to 'women's subjects' and exhibited as amateurs, or as teachers and governesses, rather than as artists.

The separation of public and private spheres also operated to the disadvantage of women writers, although the novel was much less problematically a woman's occupation. Exclusion from public life limited the area of experience from which female authors might write, as well as placing practical constraints on their lives as authors. When Mrs Gaskell wanted to visit London in 1849 to see her publisher and to meet people in the literary world, she had to find another woman to travel with her as chaperone, since her husband could not leave his work in Manchester, and 'it was unthinkable for a married lady to go up to London alone'.[62] Geraldine Jewsbury, another Manchester writer, who was a contemporary and neighbour of the Gaskells, and unmarried, appears to have moved with more freedom; but she, as her biographer records, was a more spirited and 'masculine' woman, who smoked cigarettes and proposed to men.[63] Ellen Moers has summed up the situation of the nineteenth-century woman writer:

> Male writers have always been able to study their craft in university or coffeehouse, group themselves into movements or coteries, search out predecessors for guidance or patronage, collaborate or fight with their contemporaries. But women through most of the nineteenth century were barred from the universities, isolated in their own homes, chaperoned in travel, painfully restricted in friendship. The personal give-and-take of the literary life was closed to them.[64]

Cultural representation and the separation of spheres

The institutions of culture in the nineteenth century confirmed and reinforced the separation of male and female worlds and the ideology of femininity and domesticity. At the same time, the forms of cultural representation reproduced that ideology, though often, as Tony Davies and others have pointed out, in ambiguous (and sometimes subversive) ways.[65] (As I have already stressed, there is not a pre-given 'ideology of gender', which culture represents. As Lynda Nead had argued, the ideology of gender is also produced in artistic representation.)[66] Patricia Stubbs argues that the novel, by its very nature, enshrines women in the 'private':

> The novel... is inherently bound up with the notion of a private life, which has its own autonomous moral standards and values... This is peculiarly damaging to women. For within bourgeois society women are confined to this private, largely domestic world, and have become the focus of a powerful ideology which celebrates private experience and relationships as potent sources of human satisfaction... Richardson's *Pamela* then, initiated what has always been a fundamental association in the novel between women and private life. It is from this association that all the familiar images of women in fiction are derived – the virgin heroine, the wife and mother, the prostitute, the spinster, the mistress, the redundant middle-aged woman, the single mother. Though we may deplore this narrow range of 'types' of women represented in fiction, it is important to recognize that they are rooted in the very origins of the form and that they are part of a very strong tradition.[67]

In painting too it is not difficult to make the association between domestic ideology and its representation in art. The public world is inhabited by men; woman's place is in the home. The limits of women's social role are emphasised by dire warnings of the wages of sin. The 'fallen woman' painted by Egg, Hunt and Redgrave (see Figure 2) was a 'Victorian preoccupation', treated also (though without enthusiasm) by Mulready,[68] and particularly popular in Victorian theatre, where the 'woman with a past' also appears with great frequency.[69] Egg's painting of *Past and Present* (a set of three shown together at the Royal Academy in 1858, considering the fate of the unfaithful wife, who ends her days as a homeless prostitute sheltering under Waterloo Bridge) drew 'crowds of sensation-seekers eager to be outraged', as well as (or perhaps because of) the shocked reaction of the *Athenaeum*: 'There must be a line drawn as to where the horrors that should not be painted for public and innocent sight begin, and we think Mr. Egg has put one foot at least beyond this line.'[70]

This is not the place to attempt an archaeology or psychoanalysis of meanings in representation. However, it is important to stress the problematic nature of the apparent association of domestic ideology with cultural forms or images. In Raymond Williams's view, the 'bourgeois fiction' of the 1840s is also the locus of alternative cultural values of subordinate classes and of elements repressed by the dominant bourgeois ideology; it is only in the second-rate fiction of family-magazine serials and religious or temperance tracts that the 'explicit, conscious bourgeois values' appeared in their purity.[71] The fascination of the 'fallen woman', then, is not only explained in terms of the reassurances afforded to those who conform to the domestic and sexual ideology of the period. Even in the dominant culture, the alternative is expressed in a variety of ways. I conclude this chapter by very briefly suggesting how this operated in the case of sexuality – a central theme of domestic ideology.

In the first place, as the *Athenaeum* review itself hints, a more private showing might be considered appropriate. The paintings hung in billiard rooms or in gentlemen's clubs were more risqué than those hung in family rooms and public exhibitions. Mulready produced private drawings of couples embracing, dressed and undressed. 'The restrictions which governed his exhibited courtship scenes contrast with the sensual abandonment expressed in the poses of his private lovers – not, by the way, an unusual dichotomy in the work of artists.'[72]

Secondly, the art and literature of explicit sexuality is transferred more radically to the secret and illicit underworld of pornography, documented in the case of Victorian literature by Steven Marcus,[73] just as the actual sexuality of young middle-class men found an outlet through meetings and casual liaisons at music halls and fairs, barred to 'respectable' women.[74] Thirdly, sexuality appears legitimately, though displaced, through the device of representing the exotic. For example, in high Victorian painting the nude which would have shocked in contemporary scenes is somehow acceptable when set in Ancient Greece or Rome. As Jeremy Maas says, 'the neo-classical painters were able to paint nudes freely by placing them in varying degrees of deshabille in the *tepidarium, frigidarium* or *apodyterium*.'[75] The work of Alma-Tadema, Lord Leighton, Poynter, Edwin Long and Albert Moore provides the major examples of this neo-classical painting, which was enormously successful. Long's *Babylonian Marriage Market* (1875) was commissioned for 1,700 guineas by Edward Hermon of Henley-on-Thames, and it was sold at Christie's in 1882 for £6,615, a saleroom record until 1892. The work depicts a number of lightly-clad young women, being sold off in order of beauty to potential husbands. Taking it as an exotic subject, Ruskin was able to find it 'of great merit', commenting that it was worthy of purchase by the Anthropological Society. The critical notices in all the journals, including the *Athenaeum*, which had objected so strongly to Egg's moral tale, were highly favourable.[76]

Fourthly, and lastly, repressed sexuality appears in the spaces and ambiguities of the text or work itself. There is already a large literature on the availability of feminist readings of classic texts of nineteenth-century fiction.[77] Since it is likely that works which refuse closure in this way, inviting interpretations in opposition to the dominant domestic ideology, would be produced by women, perhaps we should expect to find fewer examples in the visual than in the literary arts. Certainly it would be interesting to consider paintings produced by women in nineteenth-century England from this point of view, for they were not all representations of flowers and fruit. Deborah Cherry, for example, has provided the beginning of such an analysis of paintings by Victorian women artists.[78]

I have argued that the institutions and discourses of culture in the nineteenth century operated in such a way as to aid in the construction and maintenance of the separation of public and private spheres and of the ideology of women's domestic role. Although by no means uniform or complete, this separation was to set the terms of existence for men and for women of all classes up to the present day. But at the same time, Victorian culture, its institutions and ideologies, provided the possibility of a critique of this separation, in the contradictions of representation, the limited access of women to education and cultural production, and the alliances produced between women in their enforced domesticity.

Notes

Thanks to James Donald, Caroline Arscott and Griselda Pollock for comments on this essay at an earlier stage.

1 J. W. Hudson, *The History of Adult Education*, The Woburn Press, 1969, p. 135.
2 Mabel Tylecote, *The Mechanics' Institutes of Lancashire and Yorkshire before 1851*, Manchester University Press, 1957, p. 186. The quotation is from a speech made in 1846 by Daniel Stone, managing director of the Institute, and printed in the 1847 Annual Report.
3 *Ibid.*, p. 184.
4 See Griselda Pollock's article, 'Vision, voice and power: feminist art history and Marxism', *Block*, No. 6, 1982.
5 Leonore Davidoff *et al.*, 'Landscape with Figures: Home and Community in English Society', in Juliet Mitchell and Ann Oakley (eds.), *The Rights and Wrongs of Women*, Penguin, 1976; Catherine Hall, 'The Early Formation of Victorian Domestic Ideology', in Sandra Burman (ed.), *Fit Work for Women*, Croom Helm, 1979; Catherine Hall, 'The Butcher, the Baker, the Candlestickmaker: the Shop and the Family in the Industrial Revolution', in Elizabeth Whitelegg *et al.* (eds.), *The Changing Experience of Women*, Martin Robertson, 1982; Catherine Hall, 'Gender Divisions and Class Formation in the Birmingham Middle Class, 1780–1850', in Raphael Samuel (ed.), *People's History and Socialist Theory*, Routledge & Kegan Paul, 1981. The public/private division has also been developed in feminist history in the United States during the 1970s.
6 In Raphael Samuel (ed.), *op. cit.*, p. 169.
7 *Ibid.*, pp. 168–9.
8 *Ibid.*, p. 171.
9 Maurice Spiers, *Victoria Park Manchester: A Nineteenth-Century Suburb in its Social and Administrative Context*, Manchester University Press, 1976, p. 2.
10 *Ibid.*, p. 12.
11 *Ibid.*, p. 6.
12 Leonore Davidoff and Catherine Hall, 'The Architecture of Public and Private

Life: English Middle-Class Society in a Provincial Town 1780–1850', in D. Fraser and A. Sutcliffe (eds.), *The Pursuit of Urban History*, Edward Arnold, 1983.
13 Mark Girouard, *The Victorian Country House*, Yale University Press, 1979, p. 16.
14 *Ibid.*, p. 28.
15 *Ibid.*, pp. 34–6.
16 See Davidoff and Hall, *op. cit.*
17 Girouard, *op. cit.*, pp. 5–8.
18 In Sandra Burman (ed.), *op. cit.*, and in Elizabeth Whitelegg *et al.* (eds.), *op. cit.*
19 John Ruskin, 'Of Queen's Gardens', *Sesame and Lilies*, George Allen & Sons, 1913, p. 135.
20 *Ibid.*, pp. 135–7. (Italics in original.)
21 Susanne Howe, *Geraldine Jewsbury, Her Life and Errors*, George Allen & Unwin, 1935, p. 105. (Italics in original.)
22 Katherine Chorley, *Manchester Made Them*, Faber & Faber, 1950, pp. 178–9. (It is worth noting, however, that Katherine Chorley wrote her account in her sixties, publishing the book in the mid-twentieth century, so that her regret at the strictness of her upbringing may well be coloured in retrospect by the more liberal views of this century.)
23 *Ibid.*, pp. 186–7.
24 *Ibid.*, pp. 101–2.
25 *Ibid.*, pp. 110, 111.
26 Mabel Tylecote, *op. cit.*, p. 263.
27 Kathryn Moore Heleniak, *William Mulready*, Yale University Press, 1980, p. 158.
28 Jeremy Maas, *Victorian Painters*, Barrie & Rockliff, The Cresset Press, 1969, p. 164.
29 *Ibid.*, pp. 16–17.
30 Quoted by Maas, *op. cit.*, p. 180.
31 J. A. Sutherland, *Victorian Novelists and Publishers*, University of Chicago Press, 1976, p. 25.
32 *Ibid.*, p. 27.
33 Susanne Howe, *op. cit.*, pp. 78–80.
34 *Ibid.*, p. 71.
35 Letter to Tottie Fox, quoted in Winifred Gerin, *Elizabeth Gaskell, A Biography*, Oxford University Press, 1980, pp. 138–9.
36 C. P. Darcy, *The Encouragement of the Fine Arts in Lancashire 1760–1860*, The Chetham Society, Manchester, 1976, p. 163.
37 Heleniak, *op. cit.*, pp. 168, 137, 138.
38 *Ibid.*, p. 168, and n. 58, pp. 260–1.
39 Maas *op. cit.*, p. 164.
40 E. D. H. Johnson, 'The Making of Ford Madox Brown's "Work" ', in Ira Bruce Nadel and F. S. Schwarzbach (eds.), *Victorian Artists and the City*, Pergamon Press, 1980, p. 146. (Italics in original.) This example is also discussed by Caroline Arscott in this volume (p. 160).
41 Frances Borzello, 'Pictures for the People', in Nadel and Schwarzbach (eds.), *op. cit.*
42 *Ibid.*, p. 31.
43 *Ibid.*, pp. 36, 37.
44 *Ibid.*, pp. 35–6.
45 Hugh Cunningham, *Leisure in the Industrial Revolution c. 1780–c. 1880*, Croom

Helm, 1980, Ch. 3; Peter Bailey, *Leisure and Class in Victorian England: Rational Recreation and the Contest for Control 1830–1885*, Routledge & Kegan Paul, 1978, pp. 59–60.
46 Cunningham, *op. cit.*, p. 130.
47 Robert Thorne, 'Places of Refreshment in the Nineteenth-Century City', in Anthony D. King (ed.), *Buildings and Society, Essays on the Social Development of the Built Environment*, Routledge & Kegan Paul, 1980, p. 235. However, some later restaurants, such as the Criterion Theatre and Restaurant in London, which opened in 1874, did make provision for ladies, offering a place 'where even the most timid of women could eat while visiting the West End'. *Ibid.*, p. 243.
48 Cunningham, *op. cit.*, p. 135. See also George Rowell, *The Victorian Theatre 1792–1914*, Cambridge University Press, 1978 edn., pp. 82–4. But even in 1843 Geraldine Jewsbury, an a visit to London, went to the theatre, to see Clara Novello in *Soppho* at Drury Lane; Susanne Howe, *op. cit.*, pp. 49–50.
49 R. J. Morris, 'Middle-Class Culture, 1700–1914', in Derek Fraser (ed.), *A History of Modern Leeds*, Manchester University Press, 1980, p. 217.
50 T. W. Heyck, *The Transformation of Intellectual Life in Victorian England*, Croom Helm, 1982, pp. 58–9.
51 Davidoff and Hall, *op. cit.*, pp. 341–2.
52 *Loc. cit.*
53 Thomas S. Ashton, *Economic and Social Investigations in Manchester, 1833–1933*, Harvester Press, 1977 edn., p. 150. The papers were: 'On the prevention of excessive infant mortality' by Mrs. M. A. Baines, and 'A criticism on the paper read by Dr. Pankhurst "On the exemption of private property at sea from capture during war" ' by Mrs. M. Hamlin.
54 Robert H. Kargon, *Science in Victorian Manchester: Enterprise and Expertise*, Manchester University Press, 1977, pp. 194, 209.
55 Stuart Macdonald, *The History and Philosophy of Art Education*, University of London Press, 1970, p. 30.
56 *Ibid.*, p. 108.
57 *Ibid.*, p. 146. As Macdonald says, the Schools 'promised a career as a governess or freelance designer to the less fortunate "reduced gentlewomen" or "daughters of decayed tradesmen" '. *Ibid.*, p. 148.
58 *Ibid.*, p. 147.
59 Heleniak, *op. cit.*, pp. 163–4.
60 Rozsika Paker and Griselda Pollock, *Old Mistresses: Women, Art and Ideology*, Routledge & Kegan Paul, 1981, p. 54.
61 *Ibid.*, pp. 35, 87–90. See also Macdonald, *op. cit.*, p. 30.
62 Winifred Gerin, *op. cit.*, p. 96.
63 Howe, *op. cit.*, pp. 54, 81, 86, 152.
64 Ellen Moers, *Literary Women*, Doubleday Anchor Press, 1977, p. 64. See also my article, 'The invisible *flâneuse*: women and the literature of modernity', *Theory, Culture and Society*, Vol. 2, No. 3, 1985.
65 Tony Davies, 'Transports of Pleasure', *Formations of Pleasure*, Routledge & Kegan Paul, 1983, p. 55.
66 Lynda Nead, 'Women as temptress: the siren and the mermaid in Victorian painting', *Leeds Arts Calendar*, no. 91, 1982; Lynda Nead, 'Representation, sexuality and female nude', *Art History*, Vol. 6, No. 2, June 1983.
67 Patricia Stubbs, *Women and Fiction, Feminism and the Novel 1880–1920*, Harvester Press, 1979, pp. xi–xii.

68 Heleniak, *op. cit.*, p. 147.
69 Rowell, *op. cit.*, p. 109. For a discussion of the painting by Hunt, see Ch. 6 of this volume. See also Linda Nochlin, '*Lost and Found*: Once More the Fallen Woman', in Norma Broude and Mary D. Garrard (eds.), *Feminism and Art History: Questioning the Litany*, Harper & Row, 1982. For a rather different, more carefully social-historical, interpretation of the same theme, see Lynda Nead, 'Seduction, prostitution, suicide: *On The Brink* by Alfred Elmore', *Art History*, vol. 5, No. 3, September 1982. For a discussion of 'happy mothers' in the rather different context of French eighteenth-century paintings, see Carol Duncan, 'Happy Mothers and Other New Ideas in Eighteenth-Century French Art', also in Broude and Garrard (eds.), *op. cit.*
70 Rosemary Treble, Introduction to *Great Victorian Pictures*, Arts Council of Great Britain, 1978, p. 32.
71 Raymond Williams, 'Forms of English fiction in 1848', in *Writing in Society*, Verso, n.d., pp. 152–3. (Originally published in Francis Barker *et al.* (eds.), *1848: The Sociology of Literature*, University of Essex, 1978.)
72 Heleniak, *op. cit.*, pp. 48–50.
73 Steven Marcus, *The Other Victorians: A Study of Sexuality and Pornography in Mid-Nineteenth-Century England*, Weidenfeld & Nicolson, 1966.
74 Cunningham, *op. cit.*, pp. 130–1; Robert W. Malcolmson, *Popular Recreations in English Society 1700–1850*, Cambridge University Press, 1973, pp. 76–9.
75 Maas, *op. cit.*, p. 169.
76 Jeannie Chapel, *Victorian Taste: The Complete Catalogue of Paintings at the Royal Holloway College*, A Zwemmer, 1982, pp. 108–9.
77 For example, Marxist-Feminist Literature Collective, 'Women's writing: Jane Eyre, Shirley, Villette, Aurora Leigh', *Ideology & Consciousness*, No. 3, Spring 1978. (Also published in Barker *et al.* (eds.), *op. cit.*) Also Sandra M. Gilbert and Susan Gubar, *The Madwoman in the Attic: The Woman Writer and the Nineteenth-Century Literary Imagination*, Yale Unversity Press, 1979; Annette Kolodny, 'Dancing through the minefield: some observations on the theory, practice and politics of a feminist literary criticism', *Feminist Studies*, Vol. 6, No. 1, spring 1980.
78 See Deborah Cherry, 'Picturing the private sphere', *Feminist Art News*, No. 5, 1981.

'Without distinction of party':
the
Polytechnic Exhibitions in Leeds 1839–45

There is a common assumption that members of the bourgeoisie in northern industrial towns were ignorant of cultural matters and inactive in cultural pursuits. Consideration of three major exhibitions mounted in Leeds in the years 1839, 1843 and 1845 gives the lie to this view. Studies of Pre-Raphaelitism have registered the fact that a number of the patrons of Pre-Raphaelite painting were from industrial cities. The assumption has been that uncultured northern industrialists took a particular liking to Pre-Raphaelite pictures, blind to their failings. Quentin Bell, in his recent book, *A New and Noble School*, exemplifies this attitude.

> From the very first these painters found their market among those whom contemporaries would have considered an ignorant and philistine clientele, the 'self-made' men and manufacturers of the North . . . Ruskin was no doubt a powerful advocate but not, one would have imagined with this class of person. The advantage from the Pre-Raphaelite point of view, of this kind of client, was that he would have been relatively uneducated. He would not have known enough to know that for a cultivated public, Pre-Raphaelite painting was full of faults. He saw what he liked – a poetic feeling which took him from the mills and mines of the North together with a technique which was exemplary in its industry – and he purchased (we are of course speaking of a very small minority).[1]

Of course the single category posited by Bell of the mill or mine-owning northerner is inaccurate. Northern patrons of the Pre-Raphaelites came from a range of social and economic positions. Even if we substitute the broader category of northern urban bourgeoisie, which would include the major Leeds purchaser of Pre-Raphaelite paintings, Thomas Plint, and others such as Ellen Heaton and Edmund Bates, there is no evidence of an ignorance of art generally, nor a low level of education or culture. Both Thomas Plint and his father took part in the Leeds Literary Institution, later the Mechanics' Institution and Literary Society, lecturing on political economy, history and literature. In May 1845 Plint senior lectured 'on the value and importance of statistics' while Plint junior read a paper later in the month on the 'early history of some of the states of antiquity'. Mr Plint (probably senior) took part in a formal debate on the influence of Charles Dickens in February 1843. Ellen Heaton, far from being immune to the influence of Ruskin, had an extensive correspondence with him and relied heavily on him for advice on picture buying. She was also on visiting terms with Elizabeth Barrett Browning and a great friend of George Richmond, the London-based portraitist.[2] Edmund Bates, the champion of Atkinson Grimshaw, published pamphlets on art, quoting Schlegel and Mrs Jameson to support his views.[3] Tom Taylor, writing in *The Times*, is nearer the mark on the Leeds patrons of Pre-Raphaelitism when he describes Plint, far from being a philistine, as being unusually imaginative and adventurous in his patronage, though as he says this, the fictional northern patron who, thoroughly philistine, just wanted an investment as safe as consols or cotton bales, creeps in as the point of comparison.[4] This chapter focuses on the decade preceding the emergence of Pre-Raphaelitism and demonstrates that patronage of painting was not a new or a strange phenomenon for the bourgeois citizens of a town like Leeds. The Polytechnic Exhibitions of that decade provide us with evidence of purposeful and energetic cultural activity which involved a large number of individuals. Many of the figures involved can be identified, and consequently the political and economic character of the exhibitions can be established.

The challenge of the manufacturing bourgeoisie to the position of the merchant elite was a crucial element of the history of Leeds in the first half of the nineteenth century. The rivalry and manoeuvring of different social groups, permanent and temporary alliances or associations (including those for social and cultural purposes such as the temporary association formed for the duration of an art exhibition) have to be seen against the background of this shift of power. The wealthy merchant families had, throughout the previous century, constituted Leeds's urban gentry: a group equivalent in income and status to what Stone calls the 'parish gentry', the localised country-dwelling gentlemen, esquires and Knights, but not mixing on equal terms with the big landowning, nationally influential 'county gentry'.[5] Accepted by and operating with this merchant elite were their Tory bankers, doctors, lawyers, clergy and other professionals. Excluded from the group were an array of other potential members of the ruling class. Small masters were not included. Before factory production became widespread most manufacturing was controlled by small masters in domestic units or small workshops. Even by 1842, when factory production had been expanding in Leeds for fifty years, only one in six of the town's workers was employed in a factory. Out of 7,000 Leeds firms in 1842, only between 150 and 200 were factories. Craft production continued alongside the factory system, playing a supplementary role in textiles and engineering, and accounting for most production in the growing number of other industries such as leather, pottery, shoemaking, tailoring, and brickmaking.[6] In the 1810s, a small master such as Joseph Rogerson ran a scribbling mill, which performed the preliminary functions of wooley milling (breaking and cleaning lumps of wool), scribbling (teasing out and straightening the fibres of the wool), carding (further straightening of fibres) and slubbing (twisting the cardings and drawing them out) before the wool was passed on to the clothiers who would send it out to journeymen weavers for spinning and weaving. It would then be passed on to a cloth dresser or finisher and then finally might return to the scribbling mill for the process of fulling.[7] Rogerson's diaries (1809–13) give us an insight into the cultural and social life of such a small master.[8] His mill takes up most of his time. He has an occasional outing to the theatre or circus in Leeds, and visits Pontefract races in 1809. A Feast (local fair) day in May 1812 is celebrated with a picnic with the family of one of his brother's partners, John Waddington of the Bramley Fall Quarries. The duties of churchwarden, activities at his local Bramley Chapel and branch Bible Society are regular items in his diary. The main social event of the year, however, is the annual training session as an officer for the local militia. He and eleven other of the officers lodge in Pontefract, at Miss Morley's, Star Yard. He lays out £6 12*s* 9*d* for a uniform. He plays cricket in the Park with the Major and several more of the officers, and, exceptionally for him, stays up drinking till 10p.m., 11p.m., or even 1a.m. He has sufficient status to be an officer and mix with his social superiors on such an occasion. His captain is a member of the Bischoff family, a wealthy and long-established Leeds merchant family, but as Unitarians not integrated in the elite group. He records a couple of occasions when he dines with the two Mr Bischoffs in Leeds and on another George Bischoff, their father, calls to see the new houses he is building, but he hardly has an intimate friendship with these people. He has slight social contact with them rather than any degree of social integration. The next layer of small masters in the textile business, the clothiers, would have had even less social standing. The gulf between the clothiers and the merchants was dramatised by the election contests of 1807 where the clothiers successfully backed the Whig Fawkes and Lord Milton against the merchants' backing of the Tory Lascelles.[9]

The dissenting families who had started up as merchants relatively recently, often making significant gains only in the last years of the eighteenth century, were excluded from the elite merchant circles of Leeds.[10] So too were manufacturers who had successfully broken into factory production. Certainly dissenting manufacturers or Liberal manufacturers would be excluded. The monopoly of the Tory merchants on power, position and polite social life was eroded gradually in the nineteenth century. Their political sway was apparently ended at a blow with the reform of the Corporation in 1835 but in fact changes had been taking place long before that. Dissenting merchants and manufacturers had been working together to gain political influence and standing in the fiercely contested sphere of the vestry and improvement commission from before 1810.[11] The merchant ranks had opened slightly to admit wealthy Tory manufacturers. As a result the occupational profile of the old Corporation of 1835 was virtually identical to that of the reformed new Corporation.[12] The Tory Anglican interest was by no means extinguished; it was a powerful opposition in the Corporation and in Leeds politics generally. The key role of the old merchant families did diminish, however, and the families gradually moved out of Leeds to take up the lives of country gentlemen.

The religious and political differences on which these changes were focused dominated Leeds society in the nineteenth century. The sectarianism of Leeds shocked Londoners. Haydon noted down his first impressions of Leeds when he came to lecture in 1838: 'Lectured last night. They seem high Church and bigotted. I was asked after if I meant to attack the Church because I said the Reformation had ruined 'High Art'!!! Hamilton has given me a letter to Hook's brother, Dr Hook – what a joke!'[13] He later became friendly with Dr Hook, undertook to paint his portrait and discussed theology with him. But his initial reaction to the tone of Leeds society is closely echoed by the combination of amusement and horror felt by Elizabeth Barrett Browning at Ellen Heaton's bald statement of sectarianism: '. . . manners provincial enough for the rest, and talking as if the world were equally divided between the "Congregationalists" and the "Church people" . . . "and really" she said "it seems to me you have as many admirers among churchmen as among dissenters"! There's glory! – and I kept my countenance!'[14] Party political differences as well as religious ones divided Leeds society into separate groups with strict demarcations. The Polytechnic Exhibitions are of special interest because they provided opportunities, over a number of months during the planning, opening and dismantling of each exhibition, for those separate groups to work together.

As the name 'polytechnic' suggests, the exhibitions were not exclusively art exhibitions. Paintings were shown as one of 'many crafts', and so they were exhibited alongside such attractions as mineral samples, stuffed birds and working models of machinery. These miscellaneous exhibitions were in vogue in the 1830s and 1840s. Similar exhibitions, mounted for the purpose of raising money for Mechanics' Institutes, had already been held in Manchester in 1837 and 1838, and in the Potteries and in Newcastle-on-Tyne in 1838. The organisers of the first Leeds exhibition referred to similar ventures in Manchester, Sheffield, Rochdale and other towns. In 1840, nineteen towns outside London had followed suit and were putting on exhibitions.[15] In Leeds the fine art displays formed an unusually large feature of the exhibitions. In each exhibition Leeds citizens were able to view over 300 paintings, and to read about them in the local papers, in the 1839 official handbook or in the 1845 journal of the Exhibition. There were some paintings contributed by the artists and for sale as in a standard exhibiting society, but the bulk of paintings were on loan from their owners, not just old master paintings lent by the country gentry, but modern British paintings too, lent by merchants, industrialists, professionals and tradespeople living in Leeds. A few of the paintings were lent by non-Leeds patrons. On at least one occasion a member of the organising committee made a special trip to London to solicit contributions, and met with some success. Among others, Queen Victoria, Sir Robert Peel, Alderman Brooks of Manchester, and Sir William Pilkington lent paintings. The exhibitions were open at the low admission charge of sixpence rather than at the normal art exhibition charge of one shilling. The organisers hoped in this way to encourage the attendance of mechanics and operatives.

The format of a loan exhibition was obviously ideal for demonstrating the collective cultural level achieved by the town. The contributor of each picture was marked in the catalogue and so they publicly demonstrated their patronage of fine art. The identity of the pictures on show was not that of a cohesive society of artists, nor of an enterprising dealer, promoter or auctioneer. Their identity came from the bourgeois citizens of Leeds and its neighbourhood who had the pictures on the walls of their dining rooms and sitting rooms. The same citizens were involved in the organisation of the exhibitions, which was carried out by committees and subcommittees on a voluntary basis. The polytechnic exhibitions in Leeds were distinguished from those in other towns by the prominence of fine art. Another distinctive feature, noted by Toshio Kusamitsu in an article on the exhibition movement, was the large number of exhibits in Leeds provided by local industrialists, demonstrating the principles and stages of different kinds of manufacturing processes.[16] The conclusion can be drawn that in Leeds there was a more marked self-presentation of the town's bourgeoisie than in other places. The Leeds exhibitions were less a venue for travelling attractions that toured the various exhibitions, or a showcase for the achievements of members of the Mechanics' Institution, and more a showcase for the local bourgeoisie itself. The same individuals can be picked out lending works of art to the exhibitions, contributing exhibits relating to their own manufacturing process, and serving on the exhibition committees, though of course not everyone was involved in all these aspects. This raises an important point, which is the way in which culture and industry were brought together in the exhibitions. R. J. Morris argues, in an article on middle-class culture in Leeds, that in their cultural activities, the middle classes 'turned their backs on the mills, forges and workshops from which their wealth came'. He cites the absence of items relating to manufacture in the collection of the Philosophical and Literary Society, which later became the basis of the City Museum, and refers to a lack of interaction between the technical and artistic sides of the Polytechnic Exhibitions.[17] On the contrary, I would argue that there were close links betwen the two sides of the exhibitions, both in publicly acknowledged contributions from the same set of people in both departments, and in the reciprocal function that an appreciation of art and an understanding of science and technical questions were thought to have. As for the collection of the Philosophical and Literary Society, comprising geological specimens, archaeological finds, and so on, a decision was taken to move it in its entirety to the exhibition hall for the duration of the 1839 exhibition. The items were dispersed among the other exhibits, and took their place, in the same rooms, alongside the examples of silk manufacture, the looms and models of warping machinery from the woollen industry, the examples of leather manufacture, steam engines, flax-spinning machinery and the printing press contributed by local businesses.

The involvement of figures from different factions within Leeds was remarked on as a major feature of these exhibitions. In this respect, once again, Leeds offers a contrast to the character of similar fund-raising exhibitions held elsewhere in the country. There were accusations by the Tories in Nottingham in 1840 of 'niggardly illiberalism' on the part of the organisers in excluding them from participating in the exhibition, and similar accusations in Leicester in 1840 of the domination of the Exhibition there by Radicals. 'Two thirds of the Exhibition Committee are Radicals, the Treasurer is a Radical, the Secretary is a Radical, the subordinate officers are Radicals – nay, the very catalogue finds its way to the office of a Radical printer.'[18]

The contrast is evident in a report given of the public dinner marking the close of the first Polytechnic Exhibition in Leeds. The company present was described in the *Leeds Mercury* as 'a respectable party of about a hundred and fifty gentlemen, including all parties and denominations ... we have seldom attended a meeting where a finer or more harmonious feeling prevailed. It included the Elite of the scientific and literary gentlemen of the town.'[19] And Edward Baines, in his speech, referred to the same unusual phenomenon of cross party co-operation: 'the delightful harmony which prevailed amongst gentlemen of all parties and denominations throughout five months of unceasing labour and engagements of a perfectly novel kind'. When the committee for the 1843 Exhibition was formed the same principle was followed. 'It will be seen that the list of the committee comprises the names of many of the principal inhabitants of the town without distinction of party – men of all parties feeling anxious to promote an object which cannot fail to be attended by great public advantage.'[20] The 'elite' present at the dinner consisted of 150 men, each with a ticket for a lady. The 1843 committee consisted of as many as 93 individuals. The picture-lenders at the 1839 exhibition amounted to 77, in 1843 to 101 and in 1845 to 66 individuals.[21] There is some overlap between these groups, but by no means a total overlap. The elite therefore, organising and contributing to these cultural events, is not just a handful of experts agreeing to forget their sectarian differences for once in the interests of science and art. It is rather an entire layer of Leeds society brought together in a grouping that begins to have a coherent class identity. Not all the picture-owners listed in the catalogue can be identified. There are many possible candidates for the commoner names, or none at all for some others. But a substantial number can be identified, their occupations and addresses traced through town directories, and their political affiliations through poll books. Few women were listed as owning pictures in the exhibitions. Female members of households may have been just as interested as the men in pictures, and as involved in the purchase of pictures, but it was the male head of the household in general who was credited as owner. Where women's names do occur they are even more difficult to identify than men's. Since they were not enfranchised, they did not appear in the poll books. Nor, very often, did they appear in their own right in the town directories. Some widows and spinsters living alone were listed, and women who were proprietors of their own businesses. Otherwise the town that is described in the directories is a men's town.

The partial identification of picture owners that can be made confirms the contemporary comments about the non-sectarian character of the exhibitions. There were Whigs exhibiting beside radicals and beside

Tories. Anglicans lent pictures as well as dissenters. Tory merchants included Henry Jennins, George Matthewman and Isaiah Dixon. Liberal merchants were represented by Thomas Benson Pease, the Quaker stuff merchant, along with George Goodman and his brother John Goodman, Baptist wool merchants, and Henry Rawson and William Smith Dickinson, cloth merchants. The decidedly Whig politics of John Hillary Hebblethwaite, cloth merchant, can be contrasted with the radical politics of Hamer Stansfeld, stuff merchant. There were picture-owners who occupied the economic position of combined merchant and manufacturer, which was a serious threat to the long-term position of the merchant elite. Edward Schmidt Swaine was a liberal woollen cloth merchant and manufacturer; James Holdforth a Roman Catholic Liberal merchant and silk spinner. A number of manufacturers can be identified. Among the Tories are John Cawood, iron and brass founder, engine-maker and flax and tow spinner, Samuel Petty, earthenware manufacturer, and Thomas Eagland, surgical instrument-maker. Among the Liberals are the members of the Marshall family, who ran the largest flax-spinning company in Europe, and Peter Fairbairn, machine-maker. William Milthorpe Maude was a Tory timber merchant, William France a Liberal wharfinger and shipping agent. Of these merchants and industrialists, four held the position of Mayor between 1836 and 1857 – George Goodman four times.

A similar picture emerges from a study of other occupational groups among the picture-owners. Of ten doctors and medical men lending pictures to the exhibitions, roughly half were Tory voters and half Liberals. Henry Chorley, William Hey senior, surgeon for twenty years at the Leeds General Infirmary, and his son, William Hey junior, were consistent Tory voters. William Hey senior had been an alderman and mayor in the unreformed Corporation. Samuel Hare, William Hey and Thomas Nunneley were consistent Liberals. Others registered cross-votes to keep out the radical candidate Molesworth in 1837, voting for both the Tory Beckett and the Liberal Baines, but then reverted to solidly Tory votes in 1841, as did the surgeon Obadiah Brooke, or to a Liberal position, as did William Braithwaite, surgeon to the Leeds Eye and Ear Infirmary. Bankers, sharebrokers, barristers, solicitors, newspaper proprietors, professors of music, school-masters, booksellers, engravers, pawnbrokers, jewellers, gun dealers, suppliers of floor coverings and wallpaper, wine and spirit merchants, flour dealers and tea merchants were all included in the catalogue, regardless of shades of social standing and differences in politics or religion.

While the Exhibitions can be seen as the occasions of a remarkable crossing of boundaries and the emergence of a coherent class identity for the bourgeoisie of Leeds, the homogenisation was not instant, and nor was it permanent. The exhibitions were one site of a process that took place in many places and repeatedly over a period of time. An interesting parallel example is that of the Leeds Conversation Club, which had the clearly stated intention of engineering social cohesion. It is described in the memoirs of John Heaton as having originated in 1849 as a discussion group that brought together a dozen prominent local figures of differing religious and political views. It was said to benefit the members because they had the opportunity to understand each other's opinions. Ten years later, in 1859, an attempt was made to use the Club as the seed for a much larger experiment in social cohesion. Regular teas were to be held at members' houses to bring together different 'coteries' – sections that otherwise would have no social contact.

> The club had been for some time discussing whether any means could be adopted for bringing together the society of Leeds so as to make acquainted with each other the different little coteries into which it was divided. It was at length decided that such members of the club as were willing should from time to time open their houses for a reception of the visiting acquaintances of all the members and other residents distinguished either officially by position or in the literary or scientific world. The invitations being given in the name of the Club would obviate all appearance of intrusion or undue familiarity on the part of the member who received the club at his house. Mr Sykes Ward offered his house for the first experiment, and from that time two receptions have been held by the Club each season. The refreshments are limited to tea and coffee with cakes etc. and the entertainment consists of any objects of scientific or artistic interest which can be provided for the occasion. The number of visitors is generally between two and three hundred.[22]

The numbers involved are particularly striking. If ladies were invited, the numbers tally exactly with the numbers of the 'elite' at the Exhibition dinner of 1839.

A need was felt for a forum where members of the Leeds bourgeoisie could come together across party boundaries. When in 1845 the Philosophical and Literary Society was encumbered by debts, and unable to run any paid lectures, a proposal was made to merge it with the more successful Mechanics' Institution and Literary Society. More than half the members of the Phil. and Lit. were already members of the Mechanics' Institution, it was urged.[23] However, a merger would have been one between an elite group of 116 members and forty-nine subscribers[24] and a broader-based group which had 872 subscribers at the AGM in January 1845 and rose to 1,000 during the year. The membership of the Mechanics' Institution was not confined to working men but it did include them and was actively recruiting among them in 1845 as the following extract from the *Leeds Mercury* shows:

> one excellent friend to the Institution has canvassed the persons in his employ with so much effect that no less than 25 of them have put down their names . . . let other employers imitate the above example and this excellent Institution might soon number its thousands instead of its hundreds of members. No employer who does so will be likely ever to repent having introduced his clerks, assistants or workmen to an institution so well calculated to draw them from all that is evil and to engage them in virtuous and honourable pursuits.[25]

The President of the Phil. and Lit. opposed the idea of terminating its existence as a separate society. The Mechanics' Institution was a good thing for the working classes but a great and influential town like Leeds needed an institution like the Phil and Lit.

> He should regret also if those diversities of opinion on political and religious questions which unhappily exist in a free country, should cause any break in almost the last link which binds them together as members of the same community. Party spirit and sectarian antipathies but too readily prevail. Here in this room they had at least one neutral ground on which they could meet and remember they were men.[26]

Reading between the lines, it seems that one particular party was mounting the campaign for amalgamation with the Mechanics' Institution – hence the (party) definition and defence of the Phil. and Lit. as beyond party differences. But the definition, which is a two-way one (the greatness and influence of the town transfers its sense to its leading citizens, excluding the working class but including men of all parties and denominations), is familiar from the efforts of the Conversation Club in the late 1840s and 1850s and from the workings of the Polytechnic Exhibitions from the late 1830s to the mid-1840s.

Art, literature and science are the meeting ground for this emergent group. There is no inherent reason why art should be politically or religiously neutral. The suspicious questions of Haydon's audience were not as absurd as he thought. An 1835 guide book to Leeds lists a dozen works of art, paintings, sculpture and stained glass that could be seen in the town. These include works in the General Infirmary, in the Parish Church, in the Roman Catholic Chapel and Christ Church, Meadow Lane. What could be a more Tory Anglican artwork than the subscription monument to Roger Holt Leigh by R. Westmacott junior in the Parish Church? 'The design consists of a figure in Statuary marble highly relieved from a white veined marble slab, seated in a cureal chair, supporting a book on which are the figures 1688 in reference to the landing of King William 3rd. Under the chair and partly concealed by the civic robes in which the figure is clothed appears a box in which are books etc.'[27] The inscription gives the story of Roger Holt Leigh, twenty-seven years a members of Leeds Corporation, and fatally injured by an excited populace when casting his vote in the 1831 General Election.

> He was a warm advocate of the established Church, an uncompromising defender of the glorious constitution of 1688 a consistent patriot and a faithful friend.

It is a Tory civic monument, taking its place in the church alongside an example of Tory military statutary, adorned with a flag and weeping soldiers. The monument by Joseph Gott to Colonel Lloyd speaks of his military career, protecting his country against foreign invasion, and equally, as commander of the Leeds Volunteer Infantry, of his service to the inhabitants of the borough in 1794:

> for the protection of their property endangered by the spread of anti-social and revolutionary principles.

It is interesting that the Parish Church also housed the monument by Flaxman to Captain Beckett and Walker in which a figure of Victory is seated on a cannon. This was far from being a Tory monument. It was erected by subscription, organised and largely supported by the dissenting friends of the Walker family. Their success in gaining permission for the erection of the monument was something of a coup. By linking the names and the heroic credentials of the Tory Beckett and the Liberal Walker, the excluded Nonconformist reformers claimed to be just as patriotic and just as respectable as the Tories.[28] A further example is the portrait of Mr Charles Cummins, to be seen in the offices of the Liberal paper the *Leeds Mercury* in January 1843. The portrait, by a local artist, B. Topham, was commissioned by Leeds reformers as a parting gift to Cummins and his wife who were leaving to live in Bristol. It was an image designed only for the eyes of a particular section of the Leeds population. The notice in the paper announced: 'friends of Mr. Cummins will have an opportunity of inspecting the portrait'.[29] The existing venue, combined with the subject of the work, made the picture as politically and religiously specific as the Westmacott monument in the Parish Church.

Some artists built up a clientele among a particular political or religious group. Marshall Claxton is described as having been in Leeds, taking portraits among a small Methodist connection, in 1840.[30] He was a London-based artist, a pupil of the Academician John Jackson, and studied at the Royal Academy School. His later career included an attempt to emigrate to Australia and set up an Australian School of Painting. Not all his work was specifically aimed at a Methodist audience. Historical subjects painted by him include *Alfred in the Camp of the Danes*, a prize-winner in 1843 in the Cartoon Competition at Westminster Hall, and *Lady Godiva*,[31] which shows Lady Godiva holding on to a last flimsy drape and about to mount her horse. But a sober family group remaining from his Australian venture and the heavily emotional *In the Sepulchre* give an idea of the kind of work that did gain him Methodist patronage. A particularly solemn atmosphere is created in *In the Sepulchre* by the contrast of serenity and excitement. A weeping angel is comforted by a calmer companion angel who gazes at the dead body of Christ. He lies as if sleeping, his wounds appear very slight, but a vicious-looking pile of instruments of his Passion appear in the left foreground. In 1843 Marshall Claxton's large painting of *The Death of the Reverend John Wesley* was exhibited in Leeds in the top Steward's Room of the Brunswick Chapel. The painting was not for sale. Claxton was reported to have turned down £1,000 for it, but was gathering subscribers for an engraving due to appear in 1844.[32]

When a picture was engraved, its circulation was extended but not necessarily beyond a limited political or religious audience. A new portrait of an Anti-Corn Law activist was announced in the *Leeds Mercury* in 1845: 'An engraving is of course in preparation.'[33] But that engraving would not have been bought by protectionists. The supporters of the Oxford Movement could subscribe to four views of St Saviour's Church. A set of tinted lithographs was mounted in a folio for £2 12s 6d. The original drawings, by the architect J. M. Derick, could be viewed at the Anglican religious booksellers, T. W. Green's, at 34 Commercial Street, Leeds.[34] These were not just topographical views of a handsome new building. The new church was the subject of fierce controversy. Exceptionally tall and cruciform, its very shape expressed its ritualistic intentions. Pusey was behind its foundation and a quasi-monastic church life was proposed for its priests. By 1845 the drift to Roman Catholicism seemed a real danger. The defection of Newman to the Roman Catholic Church took place just a fortnight before the consecration of St Saviour's, and soon after consecration even the high church Dr Hook began to voice doubts about the forms of service practised at the church.[35] Neither Dissenters nor mainstream Anglicans were likely to want a set of prints to commemorate such a scandalous building.

These examples show that many artistic images available to the Leeds public were clearly demarcated in terms of the audience addressed. There was no question that the artistic sphere was automatically removed from sectarian differences. Nonetheless the Polytechnic Exhibitions were the occasion of a remarkable cross-party collaboration, and see the mobilisation of a rhetoric of art and science which fits with it. When the Philosophical Hall acquired a statue of Michael Thomas Sadler, the celebration of this evangelical, paternalist Tory was acceptable to the members of the Philosophical and Literary Society, not, as might be thought, on the grounds of the statue's artistic value, but on the basis of Sadler's services to literature and science. On these grounds his memory was respected, 'not only by those who agreed but by those who most widely differed from him on religious and political questions'.[36] In the critical accounts of the Polytechnic Exhibitions, the keynote is the congruence of the functions of art and science to improve and instruct. At this date, in Leeds, insistent claims were not being made for an art as a sacrosanct sphere, the realm of a special kind of experience. By 1863 Edmund Bates, commenting on the exhibition of paintings at the Philosophical Hall, claims that art is 'that which cannot be out-weighed by untold wealth; – the deepest yearnings of a human heart – the loftiest reachings of a human soul – the noblest work of "tendrest human hands" '.[37] The approach twenty years earlier was more prosaic. Art and science together could 'charm the eye, instruct the mind and improve the taste' and provide relaxation from the drudgery of daily toil.[38] It was an overall effect of civilisation that had been remarked on repeatedly at the 1839 Exhibition dinner. The expectation that manufacturing districts would be uncultured is not simply a false position held by London-based art critics, either in the nineteenth century or today. It was also an element in the self-estimate of the northern bourgeoisie. The idea found a resonance so that it was present as an issue whether being asserted or opposed. So the handbook of the Manchester Art Treasures Exhibition of 1857 opened with the words 'What in the world do you want with Art in Manchester? Why can't you stick to your cotton spinning?'[39] The 'two hundred influential gentlemen' of Leeds and its neighbourhood who met to celebrate the success of the first Leeds Public Exhibition in 1839 congratulated themselves on the fact that it proved what a high degree of civilisation Leeds possessed. One of the curators of the Exhibition for the fine arts, the surgeon Mr Thomas Nunneley, made a closing address at the Exhibition and his speech harked constantly on the theme of how civilised Leeds was; Leeds could be proud of what civilised place it was, the appreciation shown by exhibitiongoers did too, and the large attendance showed that Leeds equalled or bettered others towns such as Manchester, Sheffield and Derby which had held similar exhibitions. Comparisons were made with the earlier Northern Society Exhibitions and it was concluded that even that high cultural level had been surpassed: 'Gentlemen who have taken an active part in the Exhibitions of the Northern Society admit that the collection of paintings *alone* is superior to any ever before exhibited in this town.'[40] When the paintings were viewed alongside the scientific exhibits the effect was thought to be one of overall improvement for the viewer. In 1839 these general remarks were made about the Exhibition:

> The effect of the rooms is dazzling. But it is not merely the eye that is charmed. Much solid information may be obtained here in various departments of knowledge. The useful arts are illustrated and light is thrown on practical chemistry and mechanics. The intelligent spectator may here have his mind enlarged with the new views, and furnished with valuable knowledge. He may receive hints of great utility, to be followed out in after years. His tastes may be refined, his prejudices shamed; new and better aspirations may kindle within him; and he may feel a profound reverence for the great Author of nature, whose works are so manifold, so wonderful, and all very good.[41]

It should not be thought that the art was pleasant or dazzling while the science provided the instruction. Science was presented in as spectacular a way as possible. The Chromatrope was a feature of the 1845 Exhibition, demonstrated in the intervals of the evening concerts: 'that beautiful optical Display, the Chromatrope, continues to elicit the most enthusiastic applause every time it is repeated, in fact, such a gorgeous display of colour was never before witnessed'.[42] Laughing gas was demonstrated, hilarity rivalling the shrieks produced by hydroelectric shocks. The steam gun shot lead pellets into an iron target, frightening some people with its speed and deadliness. One report comfortingly said: 'for our part we look upon them as the harbingers of peace; for who would go to fight if death were certain?'[43] The principle of the diving bell was shown by letting down live mice in 1839. By 1843, there was a diving bell that held four people. For 6*s* people could go down in it and receive a certificate to prove their courage. The experiments and displays were so lively that it is hardly surprising that an explosion was caused on one occasion by a youth applying a light to a portion of hydrogen gas.[44] He was later said to be recovering favourably. The dazzle and excitement of the whole was augmented by the literal dazzle of the lighting, provided free of charge by the New Gas Company.

In this context, the descriptions of the paintings in terms of riches and splendour, of power and brilliancy, of radiant and dazzling richness and beauty, wild and glowing imagination, of the rooms of paintings as striking or as brilliant gems, indicate that the paintings were felt to operate in a similarly exciting way. It was said that the paintings could not fail to evoke interest or arouse admiration. So much anticipation was felt over the promised portrait of Queen Victoria by Hayter that when the painting did eventually arrive, after a delay for engraving, a certain amount of disappointment was expressed:

Her Majesty's portrait by Hayter, has also arrived and was on Wednesday for the first time on view in the Cabinet. Very many persons have been to see it; the scale of the painting is not nearly so large as had been expected, but we believe a second and third visit to the Cabinet reconcile persons at first disappointed to the difference between their anticipations and the reality.[45]

No such error in presentation was made with a star exhibit of the second Polytechnic Exhibition. *Cain* by Lee was lent by Alderman Brooks of Manchester and placed prominently with a spotlight over it, eliciting an enthusiastic response.

> The walls are hung round with many excellent paintings, and amongst them is one of the most striking and wonderful that the genius of the painter ever produced. It represents Cain meditating over his deed of blood; and never was the guilty conscience depicted with more force and truthfulness.[46] This is a very powerful and extraordinary production of the artist's pencil. The expression of brooding horror and despair are given with a wonderful power . . . the main figure stands out finely from the canvas, and though the subject is one that must leave a painful impression on the beholder, he will at the same time feel that he is looking upon the production of a master spirit.[47]

The Turner watercolours lent to the Exhibitions by the local landowner Walter Fawkes were similarly described in terms of their power and spirit. Fawkes lent forty-two paintings in 1839 and six were shown in 1843. They were recommended as being in his early style, before he unaccountably fell 'into an unnatural and meretricious gaudiness of colouring'. His subjects are listed out in Baines's handbook as 'glorious view . . . savage gorge . . . roaring cascade . . . rainbow of exquisite beauty . . . magnificent lake . . . placid and cerulean lake . . . sublime scenery . . . vast ruin . . . rich palaces and bridges . . . a fearful scene'.[48] In the *Leeds Mercury* they are summed up as 'interesting and splendid scenes', unequalled in their 'truth, power and brilliancy'.[49] In the second Polytechnic Exhibition the reviewer says 'The power or spirit of these pictures, so difficult in this style of painting, are truly wonderful'[50] and immediately goes on to compare Nicholson's *Wreck on Scarborough Coast* unfavourably as wanting in the 'force' shown by Turner.

If there is a congruence between the excitement and distraction offered by art and science at the Exhibitions, then there is equally one between the didactic functions. The 'new views' and 'valuable knowledge' offered by the scientific displays and exhibits are clear. But similarly the paintings were thought to convey definite information to the viewers. The partner of Turner's 'power and brilliancy' was his 'truth'. Truth to nature was one of the most frequent critical categories used in describing the pictures, and a true picture was not only admirable in its success in imitation, but in the knowledge about the world that it transmitted. Lee's scriptural subject could tell a truth about an emotional state. Turner's landscapes could give information about different geographical locations. Even a simple genre subject by a local artist, J. N. Rhodes, could convey a truth. *Going to the Hayfield* is praised for its verisimilitude. 'Every part of this picture is true to nature, and one would almost expect to scent the fresh mown hay.'[51] The picture tells the viewer about the simple pleasures of the countryside. Such information about the world was ultimately information about God's work, and so the effect was to teach reverence for God. The literalness with which this information was extracted is sometimes surprising. So a fifteenth-century German painting of the *Murder of the Innocents* was 'interesting as illustrating the customs of that period'.[52] An article in 1845 suggested that parents, guardians and teachers take children to the Exhibition to learn history from history paintings. 'The group of Ancient Britons will awaken a desire to become acquainted with the first conquest of our Island: the fine painting of their Council will point to the manners and customs of that primitive race.'[53] From a picture of a dying man they could learn sympathy, from portraits of philanthropists, what to do about it.

This rhetoric of the civilising virtues of art and science was the common ground on which churchman and dissenter, Tory and Liberal, came together. Some items in the Exhibition were of special interest to particular groups, such as the bust of a Wesleyan minister which was advertised in 1845 specifically to attract to the Exhibition delegates at a Wesleyan Conference which took place in Leeds during the running of the Exhibition.[54] But, broadly speaking, the exhibits were thought to be universally appealing and improving. This was asserted despite a noticeable uncertainty about having the expertise required to discuss artistic questions. A London artist, J. F. Bird, was brought in to supervise the hanging of pictures in 1839, and it was left to him to write the criticism of modern pictures in the handbook published by Baines. Among Leeds writers and speakers a disclaimer frequently prefaced their remarks. Even the lengthy and detailed reviews of the 1843 *Leeds Mercury* start in this way: 'We disclaim all familiarity with what are termed artistical effects, and we shall therefore only speak of such points of the pictures would strike an ordinary observer.'[55] At other times a similar disclaimer was followed by a highly selective review: 'We must therefore be careful in the subjects we select for this paper and for that reason we shall at present refer to one or two pictures that are by "all" confessed to be splendid Works of Art'[56] or else the responsibility was left to each man to review the paintings for himself,[57] but nowhere was the fundamental function of art questioned. The lessons of art were there for all to benefit from. Nervous viewers could make sure the right lessons were drawn, and passed on to those in their care, by buying Baines's handbook.

> To the principals of Educational Establishments and to the Heads of Families, who may be presumed to seek for their youthful charge something beyond mere recreation and indeed to all who wish to obtain real instruction we earnestly recommend a perusal of the DESCRIPTION of Paintings, Models, etc. now on sale at the ROOMS as an excellent preparation for a deliberate study of such of the contributions as may be deemed especially worthy of notice.[58]

If the audience was split it was not in terms of party but of class. One of the ways in which the Leeds bourgeoisie experienced cohesion was in their role as parents and teachers, not just to children but to workers. The Polytechnic Exhibitions gave them excellent opportunities to exercise this role.

Working people did attend the Exhibitions in large numbers. Daily figures were published during the course of the 1843 Exhibition, giving the number of admissions by season ticket and the amount taken of 6*d* admissions. A total of 166,243 admissions is registered.[59] It was noted with pride that some working men had taken out season tickets for themselves and their families,[60] and some employers presented their workers with season tickets.[61] On the whole, though, most working people would not have been able to afford any more than 6*d* admission and so the comparative figures for season and single admissions give a (very) rough guide to the proportion of working-class visitors. The 49,720 6*d* visitors in 1843 constitutes almost thirty per cent of total admissions. A comparison of tickets sold (rather than admissions) gives a comparative figure six weeks into the Exhibition of 22,997 single 6*d* entries, compared to 6,200 season tickets, which is nearly seventy-nine per cent of tickets sold. In 1845 vague assertions of great attendance and interest give way eventually to acknowledgement of disappointing turnouts and poor receipts. In 1839 the total admissions were even greater than in 1843, at 183,913. This figure is broken down into 87,908 6*d* entries and 96,005 visits by 6,200 season ticket holders.[62] The cheap visits formed nearly forty-eight per cent of entries and just over ninety-three per cent of tickets.[63] Obviously workers did attend in their tens of thousands. The population of Leeds in 1841 was 152,054 and in 1851 172,270,[64] and so, assuming that most visitors to the Exhibitions came from Leeds, the figures show a huge proportion of the population visiting the Exhibitions. This gives some justification for conjecturing that when reports spoke of all ranks mingling at the Exhibition it really did mean all ranks, not just such non-members of the elite as small shopkeepers and clerks, but also domestic servants, artisans and various levels of industrial workers from higher-waged overlookers and workers with special skills to lower paid hands. Sixpence was not a negligible amount for a low-paid worker to find and the treats by employers may have boosted attendance considerably among such workers as the young women employed by William Smith the Mayor, a wool merchant. 'On Thursday a large party of young women who were employed by the Mayor of Leeds, and whose appearance was very respectable, visited the Exhibition, a holiday and tickets having been given them by the gentleman.'[65] The same applies to the children in Messrs Ripley and Ogles Mill.[66] When tickets were made available at several outlets, so that they could easily be bought in advance, this was welcomed in the press. 'We direct the attention of manufacturers and others employing large numbers to this subject. This will enable them to present their work people with tickets instead of money, for the proper spending of which they have no security.'[67] The real attendance figures would certainly have been increased by the free entry arranged at certain times for the soldiers from the barracks, the children from the charity schools and the inmates of the workhouse.[68] At other times provision was made for 'all schools of the working classes' to be admitted on Fridays at the reduced rate of 1d each.[69] Where figures are recorded for these concessionary tickets they are as high as 1,200 for a single Friday.[70]

Some apprehension was felt at the large working-class presence at the Exhibitions. They were asked not to attend in working dress in case they dirtied other exhibitiongoers, and were even turned away if they did not comply.[71] It was feared that they might be noisy and disruptive or damage the exhibits, but the fears proved unfounded. 'We are happy to perceive the utmost propriety of conduct on the part of the working classes who visit the rooms, and a strict compliance with the request not to touch any of the objects.'[72] The only incident of disruption recorded, other than a few attempts to get in without valid tickets, was when 'a number of well dressed "young gentlemen"(?) were behaving in a most disorderly and riotous manner . . . in future such parties will be in danger of having their names exposed, as well as their tickets being forfeited.'[73] By the way these are described we can suppose them to be examples of the much criticised 'gents' -- shop-boys or clerks who dressed ostentatiously and adopted fashionable airs above their station, rather than manual workers. The combination of nervousness at, and satisfaction with, the working-class visitors was a reflection of the attitude of the propertied classes in a time of disturbances. In fact the first Exhibition was proposed partly as a sort of reward for the workers of Leeds, and no doubt as a sop. This was specifically mentioned in the preliminary meetings: 'it was well observed by a gentleman who has filled a high station in the borough, that the working classes of Leeds deserve all the encouragement that can be given them, for the exemplary propriety of their conduct.'[74] The connection with Chartist activities can be read off from the pages of the newspapers. 'Our readers, disgusted with the detail which our present number supplies of the violence and outrage committed by the Chartists in several parts of Lancashire, will turn with high gratification to the honourable exception furnished by the town of Leeds, and indeed the West Riding to these most disgraceful proceedings.'[75] The confidence expressed here was partly bravado. There was no guarantee that Leeds, despite being 'proverbially peaceful' would remain so, that the exhortation of militants at mass meetings for Leeds workers to stop being so lukewarm would not take effect. Special constables were enrolled in early May 1839. August 1839 saw the arrest of White, Secretary of the Chartist organisation, the Leeds Northern Union. It was a period of extreme tension. It was shown in 1842 that Leeds was not immune to Chartist action and in late August of that year, the special constables, local yeomanry, police and troops were used to quell the rolling strike action of the so-called Plug Plot Riots. Nonetheless, apart from the spontaneous action of this year, Leeds did remain markedly less militant in the 1840s than other areas and there was never a very large working-class base for Chartism in Leeds.[76] Its major newspaper was produced in Leeds, and Chartists won control over the churchwardens and improvement commissions, but its base has been aptly characterised as 'decidedly non-proletarian'.[77] The elite of the Leeds bourgeoisie who set up the Polytechnic Exhibitions intended them to promote harmony between classes and were relieved at the lack of friction during the Exhibition. 'The rooms have been filled day after day, by respectably dressed persons of all ranks who in this delightful scene mingle together most cordially and enjoy all that it presents in common.'[78] The intellectual and moral improvement offered by the Exhibition was thought to benefit all classes, but to be especially needed by the working class, and it was the duty of the bourgeoisie to provide it for them. The political advantages of maintaining an exemplary quiet and respectable working class are a minor theme alongside the stated functions of the Exhibitions as a lure from the public houses, and as an example of how workers could spend their leisure time improvingly rather than in dissipation. Equally importantly, they were seen as schools of applied art and science where workers could learn skills of direct relevance to their trades.[79]

The proceeds of the Exhibitions were to go to schemes intended for the benefit of the working class: to the Mechanics' Institute in 1839 and 1843 and for public walks and baths in 1845. The Exhibitions were prototypes for these more permanent methods of instruction, improvement and inducement to sobriety. The mingling of classes at the Exhibitions was paralleled with the variety of classes who would take the air in the public walks. The Exhibitions displayed views of nature and natural principles. The walks would offer nature itself. The walk which in France 'encircles every town' is invoked: 'Hither every class and age resort. In the presence of each other, a gentle and refined restraint, keeps boisterous pleasure within bounds; and teaches the graceful art of being gay without coarseness and observing the limits which separate sport from riot.'[80] At the Exhibitions this ideal situation was acted out. They were exhibitions of objects, but still more, exhibitions of spectators. A spoof version of Mrs Caudle's 'curtain lectures' ran in the Exhibition Journal in 1845. The Leeds version of Jerrold's Mrs Caudle nags and bullies her husband to provide her with a new silk gown and bonnet to go to the Exhibition. 'Did you see how Mrs Briggs looked at Mrs Brown and then at Mrs Pugsley, and what glances they gave at me, and then how they eyed me from head to foot, and then how they all began smiling?'[81] Hyam the tailor advertises his business with his usual ingenious verses during the 1845 Exhibition:

> ... There's music and paintings
> Old armour and sculpture
> There's skeletons too
> From the fly to the vulture ...

and he ends up: 'Now it is a singular fact, that perhaps the most interesting part of the Exhibition is the beautiful clothing worn by the Gentlemen, and Hyam being the most popular Tailor in Leeds, it is only an act of justice to give him credit for all his splendid Improvements in Dress.'[82] In each case it is an obvious joke to make, that the bourgeois public were on show at the Exhibitions in their fashionable attire. But the workers in their respectable clothes were on show too. An article describing the visitors to the 1845 Exhibition claims that they can be learnt from as well as the exhibits 'without label or number – you need no catalogue to read them off'.[83] A group from the country in 'go to meeting clothes', a gentleman in black and a mechanic in his Saturday-night suit are identified. There is no evidence of any anxiety as to mistaking someone's social standing. The classes mixed at the Exhibitions but were not confused. Indeed the presence of all classes enabled the leading members of the urban bourgeoisie to act together and associate socially. It gave them a common paternalist role to play, and it was a field in which they could display to each other their own cultural and scientific credentials, and assert their collective level of civilisation. The Leeds Polytechnic Exhibitions put picture-owning into a context. They tell us who owned pictures and show us those pictures being put into action.

A study of the Leeds Polytechnic Exhibitions establishes that Leeds was not a cultural desert, peopled by philistines, in the mid-nineteenth century.

The many names proudly displayed in the exhibition catalogues demonstrate that the picture-owning public was far wider than the three or four notable local patrons usually mentioned, such as John Sheepshanks, Benjamin Gott and Thomas Plint. The picture-owning public was both large in numbers and broadly spread in terms of economic position. The existence, with some breaks, of an annual exhibiting society in the town, the Northern Society, from 1809 until the early 1830s was evidently one source from which Leeds citizens could acquire pictures. Pictures were also sold by booksellers such as Thomas Fenteman, included in auctions, purchased directly from artists or from travelling exhibitions. Another article would be needed to fully describe the structure of the art world in a provincial town such as Leeds, and to examine the relationship between the provincial art world and the dominant metropolitan art world. We can, however, go beyond the simple demonstration of the numbers of people involved to an understanding of the political role of culture. What the Polytechnic Exhibitions show is that art could be put to work for the bourgeoisie of the town to achieve specific aims. The emphasis, at the time of the exhibitions, on the crossing of sectarian divides within the middle class reveals a conscious effort to set up mechanisms to provide class cohesion for the bourgeoisie. The background of working-class unrest and the efforts made to promote an image of the Exhibitions as the place where classes mingled harmoniously indicate the reason why it was imperative for the bourgeoisie to close ranks and define itself, and to exert its control over the working class. The establishment of the hegemony of the bourgeoisie in nineteenth-century Britain was not achieved at one stroke with the passing of the 1832 Reform Act or the abolition of the old Corporations. It was established piecemeal over many different sites and through many institutions. This chapter attempts to show how a series of art exhibitions in Leeds could contribute to establishing that hegemony.

Notes

I would like to thank Mr P. S. Morrish of the University of Leeds Library Brotherton Special Collections, and the staff of Leeds City Reference Library, for the help they have given me in researching this article.

1 Quentin Bell, *A New and Noble School: The Pre Raphaelites*, Macdonald, London, 1982.
2 V. Surtees (ed.), *Sublime and Instructive: Letters from John Ruskin to Louisa Marchioness of Waterford, Anna Blunden and Ellen Heaton*, Michael Joseph, London, 1972; Brian and Dorothy Payne (eds.), 'Extracts from the Journals of John Deakin Heaton of Claremont, Leeds', *Publications of the Thoresby Society*, Vol. LIII, Pt. 2, No. 117.
3 Edmund Bates, *Observations on Art Proper*, Leeds, 1863; *Fine Art Versus Local*

156 The culture of capital

Journalism; Leeds First Public Library Exhibition, Leeds, winter 1884.
4 Quoted G. Reitlinger, *The Economics of Taste*, Barrie & Rockliff, London, 1961, p. 146.
5 L. Stone, *An Open Elite: England 1540–1880*, Clarendon Press, Oxford, 1984, pp. 6–8, 212–14; G. E. Mingay, *The Gentry: The Rise and Fall of a Ruling Class*, Longman, London & New York, 1976; R. G. Wilson, *Gentlemen Merchants: The Merchant Community in Leeds 1700–1830*, Manchester University Press, and Augustus McKellrey, New York, 1971.
6 W. G. Rimmer, 'The Industrial Profile of Leeds', *Publications of the Thoresby Society*, Vol. 50, 1966–8, pp. 130–58.
7 W. B. Crump, 'The Leeds Woollen Industry 1780–1820', *Publications of the Thoresby Society*, Vol. 26, 1931.
8 'Diary of Joseph Rogerson', *Ibid*.
9 R. G. Wilson, *op. cit.*
10 *Ibid*.
11 G. Fraser, 'Areas of Urban Politics – Leeds 1830–80', in Dyos & Wolff, *The Victorian City. Images and Realities*, Vol. II, Routledge & Kegan Paul, London, 1973.
12 E. P. Hennock, 'The Social Composition of Borough Councils in Two Large Cities 1835–1914', in *The Study of Urban History*, ed. H. J. Dyos, Edward Arnold, London, 1968.
13 B. R. Haydon, *Diaries*, ed. Pope, Harvard University Press, Cambridge, Mass., 1963, Vol. IV, entry for 6 February 1838, p. 457.
14 Letter, E. B. Browning to R. Browning, 6 May 1846, quoted V. Surtees, *op. cit.*, p. 258.
15 T. Kusamitsu, 'Great Exhibitions before 1851', *History Workshop*, 9, Spring 1980, pp. 70–89.
16 T. Kusamitsu, *ibid*.
17 R. J. Morris, 'Middle-Class Culture, 1700–1914', in D. Fraser (ed.), *A History of Modern Leeds*, Manchester University Press, 1980, pp. 211, 215.
18 Quoted T. Kusamitsu, *op. cit.*, from the *Nottingham Journal*, 12 June 1840 and *Leicester Journal*, 4 September 1840.
19 *Leeds Mercury*, 19 October 1839.
20 *Leeds Mercury*, 1 April 1843.
21 These figures are necessarily approximate. They exclude artists exhibiting their own work, and patrons lending works who were marked as not being from Leeds, or who are well known enough to be readily identified as from elsewhere. Some uncertainty arises from patrons exhibiting several works and being styled differently in the different entries. These are grouped as one patron where there seems grounds for doing so. For example, Mr Longbottom is identified with A. Longbottom in 1845, on the grounds of the paintings exhibited being of a similar character, and Thos. Brown with T. Brown, all his pictures being old masters. Obviously a certain amount of guesswork is involved but the exact figures are less important than the overall indication of the order of magnitude of the picture-exhibiting public.
22 *Memoir of J. D. Heaton M.D.*, ed. T. Wemyss Reid, Longmans Green & Co., London, 1883, pp. 107, 157.
23 *Leeds Mercury*, 10 May 1845, letter from FIAT LUX, a member of both Societies.
24 *Leeds Mercury*, 18 October 1845.
25 *Leeds Mercury*, 22 February 1845.

26 *Leeds Mercury*, 18 October 1845, and *Leeds Intelligencer*, 25 October 1845.
27 J. Heaton (publ.), *Walks Through Leeds*, 1835.
28 Lecture by J. Douglas, 'War, Heroism and Patronage', History Workshop Conference, Leeds, 1985.
29 *Leeds Mercury*, 21 January 1843.
30 V. Surtees, 1972, p. 148. At this date he painted Ellen Heaton's portrait.
31 *Lady Godiva*, Witt Library, London.
32 *Leeds Mercury*, 26 August 1843.
33 *Leeds Mercury*, 13 December 1845.
34 *Leeds Intelligencer*, 4 October, 1 November 1845.
35 See Nigel Yates, 'Leeds and the Oxford Movement', *Publications of the Thoresby Society*, Vol. LV, 1975, and 'A History of St. Saviours', *Yorkshire Post*, October 1872.
36 *Leeds Mercury*, 29 April 1843, statue by Parker. Exhibited at RA 1842.
37 Edmund Bates, *Observations on Art Proper*, Leeds, 1863.
38 *Leeds Mercury*, 29 July 1843.
39 *A Handbook to the Gallery of British Paintings in the Art Treasures Exhibition. Being a reprint of critical notices originally published in the 'Manchester Guardian'*, Bradbury & Evans, London, 1857. A remark attributed to a nobleman approached for pictures. This remark is parallel to the *Art Union*, January 1846 (Supplement) remarks on the Exposition of British Industrial Art at Manchester: 'Amid throstles and spindles, surrounded by power looms and jacquards, where iron gives arms and steam supplies animation it may be pardoned the man of artistic mind if he feels disposed to ask with the prophet Ezekiel – "can these dry bones live?" '.
40 *Leeds Mercury*, 19 October 1839, 12 October 1839 and 13 July 1839.
41 *Leeds Mercury*, 13 July 1839.
42 *Journal of the Leeds Polytechnic Exhibition*.
43 *Ibid*.
44 *Leeds Mercury*, 3 August 1839.
45 *Leeds Mercury*, 24 August 1839.
46 *Leeds Mercury*, 29 July 1843.
47 *Leeds Mercury*, 2 September 1843.
48 Edward Baines, William West & Others, *A Description of Some of the Principal Paintings*, etc., Leeds, 1839.
49 *Leeds Mercury*, 22 June 1839.
   Leeds Mercury, 13 July 1839.
50 *Leeds Mercury*, 2 September 1843.
51 *Leeds Mercury*, 2 September 1843.
52 *Ibid*.
53 'A Word For the Young', *The Journal of the Leeds Polytechnic Exhibition*, 1845, p. 52.
54 'The Committee have great pleasure in informing the Public that Mrs. Galland has been induced to forward to the exhibition the BUST of her late lamented Husband, the Rev. T. GALLAND MA which it is hoped will be an object of some interest to the Ministers and Members of the Wesleyan Methodist Connexion generally.' *Leeds Intelligencer*, 9 August 1845.
55 *Leeds Mercury*, 26 August 1843.
56 *JLPE*, 1845, p. 20.
57 *Leeds Mercury*, 14 June 1845.
58 *Leeds Mercury*, 21 September 1839.

59 Figures published weekly in *Leeds Mercury*, 12 August to 21 October 1843. Receipts were not published for two weeks; they were resumed between 11 and 25 November 1843.
60 *Leeds Mercury*, 20 July 1839. 'No small number of season tickets have been purchased by working men, not only for themselves but ... for various members of their families.'
61 *Ibid.* 'Some mercantile firms have also presented season tickets to all the persons in their employment', and *Leeds Mercury*, 10 August 1839, 'The principal men and mechanics employed in Mr. Holdforth's silk mills have been presented with season tickets.'
62 *Art Union*, February 1840.
63 Obviously the second percentage is higher (based on final totals) since season ticket sales would tend to fall over a long period compared to single entry tickets.
64 C. J. Morgan, 'Demographic Change, 1771–1911', in *A History of Modern Leeds*, ed. Derek Fraser, Manchester, 1980.
65 *Leeds Mercury*, 10 August 1839.
66 *Leeds Mercury*, 7 September 1839.
67 *Leeds Mercury*, 12 August 1843.
68 *Leeds Mercury*, 14 September 1837.
69 *Leeds Intelligencer*, 26 July 1845.
70 *Leeds Intelligencer*, 16 August 1845.
71 *Leeds Mercury*, 20 July, 24 August 1839.
72 *Leeds Mercury*, 13 July 1839.
73 *Journal of the Leeds Polytechnic Exhibition*, 1845.
74 *Leeds Mercury*, 20 April 1839.
75 *Leeds Mercury*, 17 August 1839.
76 'Chartism in Leeds', by J. F. C. Harrison, in A. Briggs (ed.), *Chartist Studies*, Macmillan, London, 1959.
77 Derek Fraser, 'Politics & Society in the Nineteenth Century', in Derek Fraser (ed.), *A History of Modern Leeds*, p. 285, Manchester, 1980.
78 *Leeds Mercury*, 20 July 1839.
79 *Leeds Mercury*, 28 September 1839.
80 *Journal of the Leeds Polytechnic Exhibition*, 1845, p. 18. See T. J. Clark's remarks on the ideological function of such public resorts and the mingling of classes in *The Painting of Modern Life*, Thames & Hudson, London, 1985.
81 *Journal of the Leeds Polytechnic Exhibition*, 1845, p. 23.
82 *Leeds Mercury*, 23 June 1845.
83 *Journal of the Leeds Polytechnic Exhibition*, 1845, p. 25.

Employer, husband, spectator:
Thomas Fairbairn's commission of The Awakening Conscience

When a nineteenth-century patron bought or commissioned a painting he (usually) or she did not simply exchange *x* guineas for a coloured piece of canvas *y* feet square. There was more to it than that because the object purchased was charged with meaning. It functioned ideologically. Studies of patronage and ideology such as Hadjinicolaou's *Art History and Class Struggle* have attempted to establish a one-to-one equivalence between the class position of the patron and the ideological content of the painting.[1] Whatever the degree of precision with which the patron's class position is defined, it is too limiting to read a picture exclusively in terms of its owner's assumptions, views and interests. One result of this method of analysis is to see pictures as invariably confirmatory. It does not allow for any differentiation in the role of the picture. There are shifting relationships between patron and painting when, in one case, a painting is simply aligned with the patron's viewpoint, in another it actively confirms the position of the patron, or, in a third case, it reformulates a position. But the problem with Hadjinicolaou's method is more fundamental than this. It allows neither for a multiple meaning in the picture nor for a varying context for the reception and understanding of the picture.

To posit a unitary meaning which the picture, or any text, has, is to impose from outside a coherence which takes no account of different strands, breaks and contradictions which the work may encompass. It can lead to a position which ascribes a notional 'real' meaning to the work, which is given more credence and attention than the actual material of the text.[2] If, instead, the art work is seen as an assemblage of signs which derive their meaning not just from the particular combination in which they are found, but from a variety of sign systems which extend beyond the limits of the work, then it is possible to see the work as offering many readings, as being polyvalent. The conditions of reception also play a part in extending the range of meanings borne by the picture. A picture was not just seen by the individual who purchased it but by many people, in a variety of contexts. Its ideological import would vary according to the viewer and the situation in which the picture was viewed. In the space of twelve months a picture could be moved from an artist's studio, to an academy exhibition, to a dealer's showroom, to a private house and then back to an exhibition hall as part of a loan exhibition. Within a private house it could be hung in a gallery specially for paintings, in a public reception room, or in a private apartment. It could be kept in a male preserve within the house or in an area primarily for women's use. Any change in location could affect the way in which the picture was viewed. The passing of time, also could fundamentally alter the way in which a picture was understood.

In the discussion of a painting by Holman Hunt in this chapter I intend to identify some of the available meanings of the picture, rather than to demonstrate the congruence of the world-views of picture and patron. However, the purchaser of a painting did have a special connection to the picture. The patron cannot be reduced to just one viewer among many. Patrons could, and did, intervene in the production of paintings from an early stage. The example of Thomas Plint's instructions to Ford Madox Brown shows this. Plint, a Leeds stockbroker, saw preliminary sketches for Brown's major painting *Work* (1852–65) (Figure 1) in 1856 and commissioned Brown to paint the picture for him. He specified the inclusion of 'a quiet, earnest *holy*-looking' lady with tracts to distribute because he was interested in such work, and the inclusion of the figures of Carlyle and Kingsley.[3] Here the patron was influencing the content of the picture so that it related to his own concerns and enthusiasms. Even if there were no special instructions or requirements, the very act of selecting a particular genre, artist or work put the patron in the position of influencing the market for paintings and therefore, indirectly, the production of particular works. Nothing could be more self-effacing than the commission from another Leeds collector which so delighted Haydon in June 1840. With discretion Peter Fairbairn left the details of the picture entirely up to the artist and generously urged him not to hurry it.[4] His major motive was evidently charity towards Haydon, who was continually in financial difficulties, but that is not the whole explanation. A patron's motives for buying a picture were often mingled. Ruskin spelt out a possible mix of charity on one hand and personal gratification and connoisseur's satisfaction on the other two decades later, when he urged Ellen Heaton to buy a picture by

Burne-Jones. 'He has been very ill – is depressed about Rossetti – and much about his own work. If you would buy something of him you would be doing a kindness and a service, and you would not get a first rate work by any means, but a work of the highest order, quite unique and unapproachable in a most pure and lovely way of their own.'[5] Of course there could be elements in motivation which, like that of charity to the artist, were unconnected with the substance of the picture. Pictures in general were on one level a straightforward investment. The likelihood of a picture maintaining or increasing its value was a major consideration. In some cases art was attractive because capital sunk in an art collection would not have to be passed on to a disliked or distant heir as expenditure on bricks and mortar or on improving land might have to be under the rules of entailed estates. Pictures could be willed to a relative in the female line or other non-heir.[6] The dealer Buchanan (1777–1864) studied his potential patrons with great care and pointed out to his agent that some people bought pictures because they could be used as bribes where money might be unacceptable.[7] Others chose a particular picture because it had an impressive frame, or one that matched in dimensions a picture that they already had.[8] All these reasons for buying pictures could be fused with positive reactions to the particular picture's subject.

Buchanan picked out many collectors who would buy anything with female nudes – as he said about the Earl of Wemyss at Gossford who had 'a particular rage for naked beauties'. 'I have no doubt he will take them both the moment he sees them, as he had been looking out these some years past for a Claude – and the lecherous old Dog is not likely to send a Venus and Cupid begging.'[9] Buchanan was dealing in Old Master paintings, but his observations could equally be applied to modern British paintings. William Bell Scott mentions how the Newcastle painter Carmichael mass-produced his shipping subjects for athletic young undergraduates. They were taken 'a dozen at a time to the universities and elsewhere, and at this time boating men had a tendency to indulge their taste in pictures as well as boats'.[10] Thomas Plint of Leeds stated that his interest in tract distribution governed his wish for a certain element in the picture he was buying. In all these cases we see patrons with hobbies, enthusiasms or obsessions which they wished to gratify or represent.

The interesting thing about the Plint/Brown case, however, is the mismatch between commission and product. The features specified by Plint were included but within the overall scheme of the picture they took on a meaning which perhaps Plint did not intend and would not have endorsed. Carlyle is given a strange sneering, savage expression. There is a gently critical attitude within *Work* to the well-meaning lady. She is paired with a fashionable lady who does nothing useful. Her tract, 'The Hodmen's Haven or Drink for Thirsty Souls', flutters down towards a navvy but he takes no notice of it. Meanwhile, more practical help arrives as a lad brings a tray of beer for the thirsty workmen. Certainly in his descriptive commentary on *Work*, written after Plint's death, Brown is critical of the tract distributor. He suggests that the navvy, who has a mind of his own, probably feels that the tables should be turned and that he should be giving tracts to the lady, expounding the views of navvies.[11] But it is not a case of the meaning of the picture having been altered after the death of the patron. Brown might not have pointed out that dimension of the picture in his pamphlet had Plint still been alive in 1865, but there is nothing to suggest that the scheme of the picture was altered after July 1861, when Plint died. The strange expression on Carlyle's face was commented on by William Holman Hunt in a letter quoted by Hueffer in his biography of Brown. The date of the letter is not given but it makes it clear that Brown had devised Carlyle's sardonic expression before he persuaded Carlyle to sit for a photograph. A letter from Dante Gabriel Rossetti dated 22 June 1859 refers to the reworking of the Carlyle figure.[12] It is quite possible that Plint would have been satisfied with the finished picture. For him the presence of the woman with tracts and of Carlyle and Maurice could have meant one thing in representing activities and writers whose opinions he supported, while the picture had the potential of being read in a radically different way.

It is helpful to bear in mind the possibility of such a mismatch between the patron's interpretation and other readings offered by the picture when looking at Thomas Fairbairn's commission of *The Awakening Conscience* (Figure 2). Thomas Fairbairn, the nephew of Peter Fairbairn of Leeds, was involved in the Manchester engineering firm founded by his father, William Fairbairn. Thomas Fairbairn, as eldest son, was made a partner in 1841, and became senior partner in 1853 when his father retired, leaving his two sons to run the business. By 1859 he was the sole proprietor, when his brother withdrew from the business. In his early years with the firm he was based in London and had responsibility for the shipbuilding yard at Millwall.[13] This branch of the firm proved unprofitable and when it was wound up he moved back to Manchester. So in the year 1853, when Thomas Fairbairn saw and admired William Holman Hunt's paintings at the Royal Academy, he was in a position of rising power and status. The losses at Millwall were estimated at over £100,000, but the fault was not Thomas Fairbairn's. His father had taken the decision in 1835 to set up the works there and it rapidly became clear that it was a mistaken decision and that Liverpool might have been a better venue. The crisis was partly one of credit and again it was William Fairbairn's credit that was shaken rather than just his son's. Thomas Fairbairn had to forego a university education to take over at the Millwall works but he was given the opportunity of ten months to travel in Italy in 1841–2, and the eight years spent in the metropolis must have been of considerable social advantage to him. He married his wife Allison in an Anglican church in Greenwich in 1848, at the end of his period in London.[14] When he moved back to Manchester he was therefore a married man, a full partner of the business and had experience of managing a large-scale works, undertaking prestigious Admiralty jobs such as the building of the 600 horsepower ship, Megaera, and experimental testing on pioneering tubular iron structures for bridge-building. Moreover, he was returning to a provincial northern city with all the manners, habits, and social contacts acquired during his eight years in London. The difference between London and provincial society was considerable, and particularly evident in terms of social life and etiquette. In such matters as the time of dining and the manner of serving dinner the provinces could be twenty years behind the fashion of London.[15] Of course there was no hermetic division between the two. Thomas Fairbairn's visit to the Royal Academy in 1853 was by no means unusual for a member of the northern bourgeoisie. Business or politics might take a Leeds or Manchester manufacturer to London fairly regularly, especially with the advent of railways, and the trip would give the opportunity for sampling the social and cultural events offered by the metropolis.

The key feature of Thomas Fairbairn's position in 1853 was his triumphant leadership of the combination of Manchester engineering employers in the 1852 lock-out. Strike action by the engineers seemed imminent as the powerful union, the Amalgamated Society of Engineers, sought to consolidate its position within the industry. Wages and conditions were negotiated separately in each individual workplace. The union had sought to exclude unskilled non-union labour from working on boring, planing, shaping and slotting machines in certain Manchester workshops. This step towards a closed-shop system was reinforced by a general policy to limit the number of apprentices per skilled engineer who could be taken on. The union also sought to achieve minimum wage rates for engineers, to refuse to work on piece-work wages, and to refuse to work systematic overtime, in an effort to achieve maximum employment for their members.[16] The employers, outraged at the conditions achieved by the union and the threat of strike action where these conditions were flouted, decided to take the initiative and organise a lock-out. A four-month struggle ensued from January 1852 and Thomas Fairbairn was a leading figure on the employers' side.

Not all the engineering employers in Manchester and district took part in the lock-out. *The Times* noted that in Manchester thirty-four establishments stayed open, while only thirteen took the step of closing the works entirely, suspending production and locking out union members and other workers alike. However, those thirteen firms were the largest factories, employing an average of 323 men, while the smaller firms employed on average only sixty-four men.[17] The larger employers were better able to bear the short-term loss. The benefits they stood to gain in the long term were considerable. They were operating on a large enough scale to enable them to install new machinery and benefit from employing unskilled labour at lower wage rates. The smaller companies did not have the resources to participate in the struggle or the capital to invest in the future if the union was smashed. The example of a mill fitter in Leeds was cited in *The Times* to demonstrate the advantages of beating the union. Thomas Fairbairn's uncle, Peter Fairbairn of Leeds, is not specifically named, but he fits the description of the large mill fitter who has achieved entirely non-union labour, with a high proportion of apprentices, four to one journeyman (the ASE were demanding one apprentice to four journeymen), and many unskilled machine tenders. His wage rates, averaging 14s, are contrasted with the prevailing average rate of 24s in Manchester.[18] Peter Fairbairn's struggle with the union had taken place in his early days at Leeds, when the 1833 strikes at the Wellington Foundry and his employment of scab labour led to attacks on his house and gunshots into his dining room, narrowly missing his young son and daughter.[19] One may reasonably speculate that Thomas Fairbairn had support and advice from this branch of the family. There was some co-ordination between the lock-out organised in Manchester and parallel action in London, and Thomas Fairbairn's London contacts may have been useful here.

The press was used in the campaign against the engineers' union. Fairbairn wrote a series of letters to *The Times* under the name of AMICUS. At first he seemed simply the friend of the employers, stating the facts of the lock-out and explaining their motives. Later, however, he tried to justify himself as a true friend to the workers, professing to expose the lies of the union organisers, and their communist or Blanquist leanings, and advising the workers as to their best interests. When the factory gates reopened it was only to admit workers who would sign a non-union agreement. As Amicus, Fairbairn had been spokesman for the immediate local group of large engineering firms and, in a sense, for his class. One of his letters put the struggle in a wide perspective: 'On the high ground of public duty, we will try to check a movement which, if allowed to proceed, would hurry on the most terrible social revolution which either this or any country ever witnessed.'[20] He exaggerated the situation. The engineering lock-out occurred at a low point of working-class activity. Chartism collapsed after 1848, and it would be a mistake to see the engineers' struggle as a mass working-class movement. The union was highly sectional; indeed the very demands that precipitated the conflict were sectional demands for limitation of apprenticeships and exclusion of unskilled labour. It was not generalised working-class support that enabled the union to stay out for so long, but financial contributions from other skilled unions, and, mainly, levies from their own members who were still working, amounting to £12,000.[21] The conflict rapidly moved to a defensive struggle. From the early days of the lock-out, the union was prepared to abandon its demands concerning unskilled labour, and gradually to make concessions over piece-work and overtime. By the beginning of April it was offering to abandon all demands if the employers would withdraw the compulsory signing of the non-union declaration. This was hardly a revolutionary situation. However, Fairbairn was not alone in exaggerating the importance of the struggle. A letter from Lord Shaftesbury to his father congratulated him on his 'bold, manly and righteous course of resistance to the Louis Blanc conspiracy of the mechanics and engineers'.[22] The role of the letters in *The Times* was perceived as crucial, both by the union leader Newton, and by the employers' lawyer Sidney Smith.[23] The employers' victory in 1852 must have added to Thomas Fairbairn's personal power and prestige in Manchester and to some extent nationally.

It was in the following year that Fairbairn contacted William Holman Hunt, and offered him 'an unlimited commission for some work to be undertaken at my convenience'.[24] This open-ended commission eventually became the commission for Hunt to complete *The Awakening Conscience* which he had started in 1853. It was not a straightforward commission. Despite the initial offer from Fairbairn, it was not an open commission, like Peter Fairbairn's to Haydon in 1840, nor was it the case of a patron ordering nudes or ships wholesale to suit his taste. At many stages it seemed unlikely that the purchase would go ahead. Both Hunt and Fairbairn had moments of doubt and hesitation. Several times the painter Augustus Egg interceded to help Hunt to sell the picture. At first Hunt did not imagine that the subject of *The Awakening Conscience* might suit Fairbairn. When he did decide to offer it to Fairbairn, Fairbairn needed to be persuaded by Egg to adopt the picture. When it was completed, he needed to be persuaded to accept the price of 350 guineas that Hunt set. In the months between its completion, in January 1854, and its exhibition, in May of that year, the picture was at the house of Augustus Egg, since Hunt had left for the Middle East. Hunt was hesitant about sending the picture into the Royal Academy that year, in his absence: '. . . it might perhaps be better not to risk a mistake and therefore well to keep it back from exhibition until my return when I know there would be no danger'.[25] His presence in the country would make possible an appearance at the private view and give him opportunities to speak to critics and avert or soften the hostility that the picture seemed likely to provoke. The reaction of those who went to see the picture at Egg's house gave some indication of the reception that could be expected. Egg wrote: 'All sorts of abuse have been heaped upon it by many, I may say by the majority to whom I have shown it, in a most unfeeling and uncharitable manner.'[26] In the event Hunt decided to exhibit the picture, and the deal was settled with Fairbairn. Even at this stage, however, when the Royal Academy Exhibition was open, Hunt was afraid that Fairbairn might withdraw because of the adverse criticism that the picture attracted. Fairbairn did pay his money in July 1854, and was initially pleased with the picture, but later he requested Hunt to repaint the expression on the girl's face.

If we look at the commission from Fairbairn's point of view and ask why he should have agreed to take the picture, we can make various suggestions. One of the Hunt paintings he saw and admired at the 1853 Royal Academy was *Claudio and Isabella* (completed in 1853). He would not have been able to buy this because it had been painted for Egg to fulfil a commission given by the older artist some years before, when Hunt had been badly in need of money and encouragement. Hunt insisted that Egg take the picture, although Egg urged him to sell it for a higher price, which he was by then able to command.[27] In fact, Fairbairn may have been one of the people making offers for this picture, offers which Hunt refused. If this picture is the first in a series of Hunt's pictures associated with Fairbairn, then *The Awakening Conscience* (1854) is the second, and *Valentine Rescuing Sylvia from Proteus* (1851) is the third. This third picture was bought by Fairbairn in 1855. A fourth picture by Hunt can be added to the series. Commissioned by Fairbairn in 1864 and completed in 1865, it was a group portrait of Fairbairn's wife Allison and their younger children, called *The Children's Holiday* (1865) (Figure 3). It was not until the 1870s that Fairbairn commissioned a portrait of himself from Hunt (commissioned in 1873, completed in 1874, Fairbairn family collection) and purchased the Hunt painting *The Scapegoat* (painted 1854–5, purchased by Fairbairn 1878).

The theme of *Claudio and Isabella* is taken from *Measure for Measure* and that of *Valentine Rescuing Sylvia* from *Two Gentlemen of Verona*, and so two Shakespearean subjects flank a modern-life picture at the beginning of this series. However, all three have in common themes of illicit sexual union. In the subject taken from *Measure for Measure*, Claudio is languishing in prison for fornication. His sister Isabella has it in her power to avert his death sentence if she agrees to sleep with the Duke's deputy, Angelo. Her brother's life is in balance against her chastity. In *The Awakening Conscience*, the girl is a kept mistress who starts up from her lover's lap, realising her sin. Her chastity has been lost for ever and she feels the pain of regret and repentance. In the picture based on *Two Gentlemen of Verona*, Valentine has just rescued Silvia from attempted rape by Proteus. Her chastity is defended from his lust. Julia, in disguise, toys with the ring Proteus had given her as a pledge of his love. Their union has been threatened by his attempt on Silvia. What interest can Amicus have had in these subjects? His letters to *The Times* about the engineering lock-out describe a situation where the union agitators are pitted against the sacred ties of home. He urges the workers not to attend meetings and listen to 'the turbulent and dangerous knot of demagogues', but instead to stay at home. 'Let them discuss quietly at home with their wives, parents and friends their prospects and what ought to be their conduct.'[28] He accuses the union journal, *The Operative*, of blasphemy in its reference to Christ's not owning property. '. . . page after page of such miserable perversion as this disgraces the recognised organ of the Amalgamated Society . . . such are the efforts made to excite discontent, hatred and envy, and destroy the affectionate reverence with which the moral beauties of our religion ought to be regarded'.[29] He recommends the workers to abandon the union and think of the misery and hardship a protracted struggle will bring on their wives and children: 'those whom they are bound by the ties of nature and the obligations of religion to nourish and protect'.[30] What he saw as his struggle against communist tendencies threatening the social fabric rested upon the double basis of home and religion, the sacrament of marriage, the sacred hearth. In the passages quoted from his letters to *The Times*, he is appealing to these sanctities. They are part of his ammunition in denouncing the activities of the union. He uses them as moral certainties to prove that he is right and to reinforce the recommendations he is making. He was, as we have seen, involved in a campaign to cut wages, deskill the workforce and improve the profitability of his firm. The notion of the sacred ties of home is one part of the ideological framework of that campaign. Simultaneously the campaign was to establish his position as a leading figure in the manufacturing community, and no doubt to strenthen his credit. Fairbairn could have interpreted the three Hunt pictures as moral pictures dramatising the dangers besetting sexual virtue and the need to defend it and value it. This was one element in a more extensive ideological construction of the pure woman as the dispenser of a benign moral influence within the unsullied sphere of the home. Her children received not just physical care and nourishment from her but spiritual benefits too. The industrialist husband could come home from the morally ambivalent influences of the business world, the factory, and the city or town, to the restorative virtue of the woman at home. Equally, in this construct (and we have seen Fairbairn using it) the worker could be cleansed in his home from the evil influence of union meetings at the factory gate. We can begin to see an ideological position from which the three pictures would make coherent sense. They all deal with illicit sexual union, or the threat of it. The importance of marriage and the home was a key element of Fairbairn's presentation of the employers' case. The three Hunt pictures make an issue of the threat to marriage. Fairbairn needed not only a sense of the ideal but the disturbing image of its destruction to galvanise his moralising. Similarly, he needed not only the vision of employers' freedom to dictate conditions of employment, but also its polar opposite, a threat of communism, which was, at that date, an imaginary threat. These were the demands of his rhetoric, but also the axes of his world-view. One extreme took its definition from its opposite.

This way of seeing the three pictures is supported by a consideration of the fourth Hunt picture to concern Fairbairn: *The Children's Holiday* (Figure 3). A direct comparison between this painting of 1865 and *The Awakening Conscience* of 1854 (Figure 2) can be used to demonstrate the framework of Fairbairn's attitudes to the function of women in society. Retrospectively, we can perceive a symmetrical opposition in these two pictures from Fairbairn's collection, though such a comparison would have been unthinkable at the time. It would have been an insult to Fairbairn's wife to consider her portrait in conjunction with a picture of a kept woman. In fact they were two different kinds of picture. Over ten years separated their acquisition. The family portrait was a very large picture, probably hung in the staircase of the country seat Fairbairn had bought in 1861.[31] *The Awakening Conscience* was relatively small, designed to be hung at eye-level and viewed at close quarters. It may have been moved to the country seat or may have been kept in a town residence, but at any rate it would not have been shown in the same area of the house as *The Children's Holiday*. The pictures belonged to different genres and a viewer would approach a portrait in a different way from that in which he or she would approach a subject picture.

Despite these cautions, we are able to do the unthinkable and point out the similarities between the two pictures. Harlot and wife both stand surrounded by their domestic trappings. Parted hair, earrings, lace at the collar, pink bow at the neck of their dresses, and richly patterned shawls over grey striped garments appear in both. The tea table takes the place of the piano but an oriental carpet and red–upholstered mahogany chair remain in the same place. Adding to the echo is the slightly bent posture: an effect produced by the rising motion of the woman in *The Awakening Conscience*, and in the later picture by the large bustle of Mrs Fairbairn's dress and her action in reaching over to take the teapot. There is a further slight similarity in the position of the arms, both hands clasped in front in *The Awakening Conscience*, one hand reaching across to hold the shawl in place in the portrait group. The second image is of course reversed as a mirror image would be, and that sums up the relationship between the two, the same but opposite. In every pair of parallel details the opposites are seen. The hair loose and dishevelled in the kept woman is neatly drawn back and arranged in braids in the virtuous wife. The glittering gold or gilt earrings are matched and opposed by coral earrings set in gold that do not primarily connote ostentatious wealth, as diamonds or precious material, but rather stand for the value of artistic workmanship. The earrings and brooch have been identified as a prizewinning set shown in 1862 at the International Exhibition,[32] and their public recognition as exemplary pieces of applied art identify them with the absent husband, since Fairbairn was well known for his activities in connection with art and applied art.[33] The large and lopsided floppy pink bow on the dress in *The Awakening Conscience* is opposed to the discreet points of pink ribbon that emerge from beneath the brooch and the rows of fine lace in *The Children's Holiday*. The shawl of the mistress is casually tied round her waist in a thick knot in place of an outer skirt over her white petticoat. It functions as an item of undress, like a dressing-gown. The shawl of the wife is symmetrically arranged over her shoulders and gathered in neatly at the waist, completing her dress suitably for an outdoor summer setting. The coarse and dull grey stripes of a shapeless upper garment, suggesting an uncorseted body, contrast with Mrs Fairbairn's fine striped shining silk dress which marks the tight waistline, the high buttoned neckline, and the narrow cuffs with emphasis of black appliqué and buttons. It is a dress of expensive materials but not showy, since its colours are so quiet, and it is modest in its slightly severe lines. The parallel position of their hands displays the array of rings on the hand of the kept mistress, where every finger has a ring except the ring finger, while the wife limits herself to one ring, her wedding ring.

Apart from the dress and the stance of the major figure in each picture there are a number of other aspects of the pictures that play on the parallel, but diametrically opposed, situations of the women. The room in *The Awakening Conscience* is a home that is not a home. It has all the fittings and furnishings of a comfortable parlour but it is not home. The man does not live there but comes visiting, as hat and gloves show. It is not really home for her either: she has no past connection or future stake in the setting. It is a temporary arrangement. The comfort is not a result of her homemaking. The items are newly purchased and installed as she is. Her lack of housewifely skills is evident in the neglected tapestry, wools scattered over the floor, and in his dropped glove which is not tidily put away. The incongruity between her undress, which might be natural in a bedroom, and the elaborate furnishings and decorations of the room which mark it as a formal room emphasises that she does not belong there. In *The Children's Holiday* the paradox of a home that is not a home is repeated but inverted. In so far as it has an outside setting it does not show a home, but all the signs of home, absent in *The Awakening Conscience,* are there. The woman is tending to her family, dispensing tea and cakes. The children are pledges of the future, the old oaks of the estate in the background signs of a past, and rootedness. The husband is not included in the picture, but he belongs there more than the present lover in *The Awakening Conscience.* The jewellery is a sign of him as are the other applied art objects, the silver tea pot and urn and the china, their classical motifs in tune with the jewellery. These may also have been wedding presents which would further include him in the picture, as do of course the wedding ring, and the children. The group of mother, son and spaniel shows a series of relationships. The spaniel positioned at right angles to the eldest boy signifies fidelity, a quality associated with dogs, but also submission, specifically associated with spaniels. The boy, in turn at right angles to his mother, looks at her, evincing the same qualities, her faithful supporter, but under her guidance and control. She looks out of the picture, surely gazing at her husband with the same steady submissive look. So in this way too the husband is included in the picture.

This suggests some ways in which the pictures could have made sense to Fairbairn, reading them against each other in the context of his personal Hunt collection. That is not to say that these are personal meanings. The double image of woman as either pure wife and mother or debased whore, and the idea that she took on her rightful function in a private domestic sphere, were so widespread as to be common sense. (See Chapter 4.) But it only became common sense by constant formulation and reformation in various sites, one of which was painting. Another site was that of political journalism, and the letters of Amicus show him mobilising these assumptions in a situation where he clearly had a personal stake. For Fairbairn, *The Awakening Conscience* was a picture that showed the converse of virtuous womanhood. It showed the fallen woman as the antithesis of home, virtue and stability. Her guilty relationship with the man was seen to threaten the institution of marriage and the home. This was perceived the more readily as the scene in the picture was not far removed from a happy domestic interior. It is not a scene of a prostitute in a gutter, nor of a kept mistress in a public place, but was almost a parody of a virtuous ménage. We can conjecture that Fairbairn read the picture in this way. Such a reading would be consistent with the ideas articulated by Amicus. Nonetheless the doubts and hesitations involved in the commission of *The Awakening Conscience* indicate that the picture did not slot easily into a clear ideological position. Fairbairn did not refuse or repudiate the commission in the end, but he did seem in danger of doing so. His decision to have the woman's face repainted is evidence of his uneasiness with some aspects of the picture. The subject of the picture, the fallen woman, was a problematic one in the mid-nineteenth century. Prostitution and the associated problems of female sexuality and gender identity were the subject of discussion in medical and legal literature and in social commentary and social reportage, as well as in literature and art.[34] We have seen that it was possible for Ford Madox Brown's *Work* to satisfy the demands of the patron for a 'quiet, earnest holy-looking lady' and, simultaneously, to present meanings that could not be aligned with Plint's position. Similarly, it is possible that *The Awakening Conscience* could convey contradictory meanings. By pairing the painting with *The Children's Holiday*, a way of reading the picture has been suggested that was consonant with, and supportive of, Fairbairn's economic and political position. Other readings can be posited. It is not the case that Fairbairn was duped and that the reading we can attribute to Amicus is wrong. If this interpretation were not allowed by the picture then it is unlikely that Fairbairn would have gone ahead with the purchase. Rather, the Amicus reading is one viable approach to the picture among others. It is a case where the inadequacy of reducing the ideological work of the picture to the class position of the patron becomes evident.

Other interpretations of *The Awakening Conscience* can be found in the critical notices that were published when the painting was first exhibited at the Royal Academy in 1854. The best known of these is an account of the picture by the art critic John Ruskin which appeared in a letter from him to *The Times*. In some respects Ruskin's account of the picture concurred with the response we have posited for Amicus. Ruskin's letter fixes on the woman as the key figure in the picture. It identifies her as a fallen woman and identifies the scene as one stage in a career that it takes to be an inevitable result of the woman's guilty lapse from virtue. In common with the Amicus response, it welcomes the depiction of the fallen woman as morally beneficial. For Amicus, the image of sin confirmed or bolstered a moral category of its opposite, female virtue. This is also the case in Ruskin's account, but he goes further, suggesting a way in which the attitude of the viewer can be developed beyond an initial impulse of punishing condemnation to one of pity. The punishing impulse is in any case carried forward by the fate he imagines to await the woman, while the exercise of compassion ensures that the viewing of the picture is, doubly, a morally uplifting experience.

Ruskin's letter to *The Times* was the second of a pair of letters dealing with Hunt's paintings. The first letter addressed itself to Hunt's principal picture at the Royal Academy Exhibition, *The Light of the World.* Three weeks later, the letter on *The Awakening Conscience* was published.[35] This letter occupied several column inches in the paper, but it is necessary to reprint it in full in order to examine the view of the picture that it invites.

TO THE EDITOR OF THE "TIMES"
SIR
Your kind insertion of my notes on Mr. Hunt's principal picture encourages me to hope that you may yet allow me room in your columns for a few words respecting his second work in the Royal Academy, 'The Awakening Conscience.' Not that this picture is obscure, or its story feebly told. I am at a loss to know how its meaning could be rendered more distinctly, but assuredly it is not understood. People gaze at it in blank wonder, and leave it hopelessly; so that, though it is almost an insult to the painter to explain his thoughts in this instance, I cannot persuade myself to leave it thus misunderstood. The poor girl has been sitting singing with her seducer; some chance words of the song. 'Oft in the stilly night,' have struck upon the numbed places of her heart; she has started up in agony; he, not seeing her face, goes on singing, striking the keys carelessly with his gloved hand. I suppose that no one possessing the slightest knowledge of expression could remain untouched by the countenance of the lost girl, rent from its beauty into sudden horror; the lips half open, indistinct in their purple quivering, the teeth set hard, the eyes filled with the fearful light of futurity, and with tears of ancient days. But I can easily understand that, to many persons, the careful rendering of the inferior details in this picture cannot but be, at first, offensive, as calling their attention away from the principal subject. It is true that detail of this kind has long been so carelessly rendered, that the perfect finishing of it becomes matter of curiosity, and, therefore, an interruption to serious thought. But, without entering into the question of the general propriety of such treatment, I would only observe that, at least in this instance, it is based on a truer principle of the pathetic than any of the common artistical expedients of the schools. Nothing is more notable than the way in which even the most trivial objects force themselves upon the attention of a mind which has been fevered by violent and distressful excitement. They thrust themselves forward with a ghastly and unendurable distinctness, as if they would compel the sufferer to count, or measure, or learn them by heart.

Even to the mere spectator a strange interest exalts the accessories of a scene in which he bears witness to human sorrow. There is not a single object in all that room, common, modern, vulgar (in the vulgar sense, as it may be), but it becomes tragical if rightly read. That furniture, so carefully painted, even to the last vein of the rosewood, – is there nothing to be learned from that terrible lustre of it, from its fatal newness; nothing there that has the old thoughts of home upon it, or that is ever to become a part of home? Those embossed books, vain and useless – they also new – marked with no happy wearing of beloved leaves; the torn and dying bird upon the floor; the gilded tapestry, with the fowls of the air feeding on the ripened corn; the picture above the fireplace, with its single drooping figure – the woman taken in adultery; nay, the very hem of the poor girl's dress, – at which the painter has laboured so closely, thread by thread, – has story in it if we think how soon its pure whiteness may be soiled with dust and rain; her outcast feet falling in the street; and the fair garden flowers, seen in the reflected sunshine of the mirror – these also have their language—

Hope not to find delight in us, they say,
For we are spotless, Jessy – we are pure.

I surely need not go on. Examine the whole range of the walls of the Academy; nay, examine those of all our public and private galleries, and, while pictures will be met with by the thousand which literally tempt to evil, by the thousand which are devoted to the meanest trivialities of incident or emotion, by the thousand to the delicate fancies of inactive religion, there will not be found one powerful as this to meet full in the front the moral evil of the age in which it is painted, to awaken into mercy the cruel thoughtlessness of youth, and subdue the severities of judgment into the sanctity of compassion.

I have the honor to be, Sir,
   Your obedient Servant,
      THE AUTHOR OF 'MODERN PAINTERS'

The standard art historical version of events is that the Press received *The Awakening Conscience* badly, with bewilderment and disapproval, that Ruskin went to its defence in this letter, and that the letter gives a correct account of the subject, the treatment and the moral implications of the picture. Accordingly Ruskin's account has by and large been allowed to stand as the definitive gloss. Hunt, in his autobiography, reprinted Ruskin's letter, and this has been taken as sufficient validation, despite the fact that the book was not written until fifty years later.[36] In fact the 'bewilderment' of the critics bears further investigation, as this chapter will go on to show. The rightness of Ruskin's reading should not be uncritically assumed. Its rightness or wrongness could conceivably be debated, but a more fundamental question is what the letter reveals about one particular way in which *The Awakening Conscience* could be understood and appropriated within mid-nineteenth century debates, both about sin and sexual deviancy, and about representation.

In Ruskin's account of the painting, an attitude of pity is taken towards the girl. It is pity that is exercised from a safe moral distance. Ruskin's text does not treat the woman in the picture as a psychological subject to be empathised with, like the heroine of a novel. Her state of mind is, it is true, summoned up by Ruskin, where he links it to the detailed representation of the room and its trappings, but the very next sentence of his account moves on to the parallel, but separate, heightened interest an outside observer feels. Ruskin pleads for that interest to be channelled into pity rather than disgust. The emphasis in many modern accounts is on the positive elements in the picture pointing to redemption – the leaves and flowers reflected in the mirror, the star on the frame, the ray of sunlight and, from the pairing with *The Light of the World,* the presence of Christ knocking at the woman's heart.[37] This slides easily into a notion that the girl has the freedom to choose to turn away from her captivity to the purity of nature outside, and to a happy virtuous life – possibly a twentieth-century confusion between salvation and earthly redemption.[38] For Ruskin, the emphasis was very definitely on the inexorable fate awaiting the woman in this world. His 'right reading' of the details of the picture consisted partly in imagining their past and future. He does not hesitate in reading off a sequence of events in looking at the hem of the woman's dress. '. . . nay the very hem of the poor girl's dress – at which the painter has laboured so closely, thread by thread – has story in it, if we think how soon its pure whiteness may be soiled with dust and rain; her outcast feet falling in the street'. He refers to a fictional sequence of events which was commonly associated with the fallen woman. She starts as innocent; she is seduced and loses her virtue; she tears herself away from the false protection of the man who is keeping her, or he casts her off; she has no home or means of support except prostitution; she walks the streets and finally commits suicide by drowning herself.[39] It is a horrifying future and in the expression on the woman's face he sees 'the fearful light of futurity'. As Ruskin describes the original expression on the girl's face (before the repainting) it could almost be a death's head, lips drawn back showing clenched teeth, staring eyes and a look of horror. For Ruskin she is a 'lost girl'. The natural elements, 'fair garden flowers', he sees reflected in the mirror are, in his account, unable to call the girl towards them. She is cut off from anything pure by her fall. She may escape the man but, like the bird in the picture, she is 'torn and dying'. It escapes the cat but is irreparably damaged.

One aspect of Ruskin's letter is that of footnote to his previous letter on *The Light of the World.* That painting was the real subject of controversy in May 1854. As Hunt's principal picture, it was mentioned in *The Times's* Royal Academy review, whereas *The Awakening Conscience* was not. It was the picture that drew the (scornful) attention of the prestigious German art critic, Dr Waagen. Ruskin's laudatory letter offered an explanation of the symbolism in *The Light of the World* and commented on the handling of colour, detail and recession in the picture. He maintained that the degree of detail was not microscopic as in spurious imitations of Pre-Raphaelite painting, but that things were represented as they would appear to the eye at their true distance from the viewer. He mentioned the example of the ivy on the door where individual leaves were not distinguished with sharp outlines. '. . . all is the most exquisite mystery of colour; becoming reality at its due distance'. Having taken this position, he laid himself open to the response that, in that case, he ought to denounce *The Awakening Conscience*, with its microscopic detail, as just such a spurious imitation of Pre-Raphaelitism. It was perhaps to answer or forestall this response that he published the second letter in *The Times*. Here, as we have seen, he found an ingenious way of justifying the exact delineation of every detail by referring it to the topic of the picture. Ruskin's letter on *The Awakening Conscience* can therefore be seen as much as an elaboration on his first letter as a response to a hostile critical reception of the picture.

Interest in and hostility to the painting seem to have been stimulated by Ruskin's letter. Despite the 'abuse' emanating from those who saw the picture at Augustus Egg's house before the Royal Academy Exhibition, and despite Hunt's absence and consequent inability to engage in the diplomacy of the art world, the initial press notices of the picture were not exaggeratedly hostile. They either ignored the painting or expressed relatively mild disapproval. *The Times* did not mention the picture. *The Sun* bracketed *The Awakened Conscience* (sic) with the *The Light of the World* and summed them up as 'each in its way astonishingly clever, but both wonderfully extravagant'.[40] The critics' charges of bad taste, vulgarity, ugliness and incompetence were really developed after the publication, at the end of May, of Ruskin's letter. The most sustained attack came in the September issue of the *Art Journal*. This is one reason for taking issue with a version of events which sees critical outrage and incomprehension followed by Ruskin's revelatory defence.

A second reason is that the alleged incomprehension of the critics needs examining more closely. Incomprehension was an element of the earliest reactions to the picture. J. E. Millais had written to Hunt 'I hear flocks of people are going to see your modern subject at Egg's who are mystified by the subject.'[41] Egg was anxious about this and favoured the title which was ultimately adopted, when it was suggested. 'I think the title "The Awakening Conscience" is a very admirable one, and very much assists the telling of the story.'[42] When the published criticism appeared, the critics spoke of the painting being misunderstood, but most often it was to claim that ordinary viewers failed to grasp its meaning, rather than that they themselves were baffled. This is an important distinction, because there is a big difference between actually failing to grasp the meaning of the scenario and incident portrayed, and the use of the concept of incomprehensibility to criticise the picture for dealing with the scenario in a particular way. The *Athenaeum* said: 'Innocent and unenlightened spectators suppose it to represent a quarrel between a brother and a sister.'[43] The *Illustrated London News* mentions the picture in the context of comments on the general low standard of appreciation and understanding of pictures at the Royal Academy:

> If we call to mind overheard opinions expressed in the Exhibition itself they will be found of a very mixed character . . . Mr Hunt's cold allegory of our Saviour is viewed with a devotional feeling by some, by others with a gaze of ill stifled wonderment, and by too many as a piece of Mediaeval barbarity. Nor does his smaller picture far much better, though the attempt to discover its actual meaning has too often proved abortive, for the Awakening Conscience of this clever painter is now familiarly known as 'the loose lodging'.[44]

These remarks probably rely on Ruskin's first letter to locate the 'actual meaning' of *The Light of the World* in its allegorical aspect. The tag 'loose lodging' would seem to be an accurate description of the scene in *The Awakening Conscience* but the review here implies that it is not, as if its real meaning lies elsewhere, and as if it would be as absurd to see the picture as representing a wicked ménage as to see *The Light of the World* as representing a man with a lamp and a door with ivy growing on it. The theme of incomprehensibility occurs too in the *Art Journal* review. According to the critic in this journal, the subject of the painting would be unintelligible were it not for the title, but, he claims, confusion is restored by the Biblical quotations that accompanied the title.[45] This is a way of describing the meaning as being obscure, then establishing that the reviewer knows what the meaning is, and finally re-establishing its status as obscure. The review published in the *Morning Chronicle* refers to the unintelligibility of the painting: 'This is an absolutely disagreeable picture, and it fails to express its own meaning, either in its general composition or through the agency of its details. The complicated compound shadow in the mirror is also a mere piece of intricacy without any good or valuable effort.'[46]

In the reviews of *The Awakening Conscience* in all these newspapers and journals, from the *Athenaeum* to the *Morning Chronicle,* there is a common vacillation. The approach to the picture varies, as does the degree of disapproval, but they have in common a vacillation between saying that they know what the picture means and saying that it is, through some structural defect, illegible. There is a tantalising suggestion in the *Athenaeum* reference to 'innocent spectators' – that the viewer who admits to being able to read the picture is not innocent, but is implicated in the sin of the scene. This diametrical opposite of Ruskin's morally aloof, compassionate spectatorship is a position that can be further explored in the interpretations of the picture offered by *Punch,* and F. G. Stephens, in a pamphlet on Hunt, which will be discussed later.

The basis of the *Morning Chronicle* review is the failure of the picture in compositional and formal terms. The full-scale attack on the picture in the September issue of the *Art Journal* was on the same theme.[47] The article takes on the reading of details, or, as it puts it, 'the narrative of the properties and incidents', and says that Ruskin's praise of these was absurd, since the use of accessories in the picture to tell the story was nothing new or exceptional. It was standard practice, and the job of the critic was to gauge the degree of vulgarity with which the accessories were used. The vulgarity, in the case of *The Awakening Conscience,* extended to the subject chosen. The article admits that such a subject could be treated in a way that avoided vulgarity, but here it did not. 'The subject has been dictated by the very worst taste; in similar cases we sometimes see the point made out without vulgarity of sentiment.'

The substantive fault-making is reserved then not for the failure of the picture to tell its story through its details, nor even for the substance of the story itself, but for another kind of illegibility: a formal incompetence. Defective drawing, clumsy contours, mistakes in the lighting and shadows, and inconsistencies in the size of the figures and their reflections are cited. Grouped with these criticisms is the exaggerated expression and agonised stance of the woman. This too is perceived as a formal error since 'when the profound emotions of the soul are painted, the body is passive'. Hunt, the article concludes, does not have the technical ability to paint the subject he has attempted.

We have posited a meaning that *The Awakening Conscience* may have held, if not for the individual, Fairbairn, for the member of a particular class fraction, Amicus. The meaning suggested by Ruskin's letter on the painting is not identical with that which can be drawn from a pairing with *The Children's Holiday,* that of whore versus wife, of claustrophic interior non-home versus airy exterior home, of degradation and sin versus wifely virtues. But Ruskin's reading is not in conflict with what we might call the Amicus reading. It develops the past circumstances and future consequences of the girl's fall, and constructs a position for the viewer of moralising condemnation, tempered with pity for her doom. It too gives the picture a place in the range of statements and representations that were in currency and were jointly establishing a consensus on the limitations of power and the appropriate role of women. But the other newspaper reviews of the picture that we have looked at opposed Ruskin, not simply, as modern commentators have thought, by registering incomprehension where he offered explanation. They raised objections to the technique of the picture (*Morning Chronicle, Art Journal*), and to the 'mystical, irrelevant', confusing, Biblical quotations (*Athenaeum, Art Journal*). They noticed the 'studious exactitude' with which details were made out (*Art Journal*) or even praised them as 'wonderfully true' (*Athenaeum*), but considered the work put in to achieve this closely worked, detailed surface wasted (*Art Journal, Morning Chronicle*). These apparently incoherent objections do have a unifying theme in that they all relate to features of the picture that prevent the viewer from taking the kind of superior, detached moral position that Ruskin devised.

The Biblical quotations which accompanied the picture did not lend themselves to the secure and superior position taken by Ruskin. One was inscribed on the frame:

> As he that taketh away a garment in cold weather, so is he that singeth songs to a heavy heart.

Two accompanied the title in the Royal Academy Catalogue.

> As of the green leaves on a thick tree, some fall and some grow; so is the generation of flesh and blood.
>
> Ecclesiastes, xiv, 18

> strengthen ye the feeble hands, and confirm ye the tottering knees; say ye to the faint hearted: Be ye strong; fear ye not; behold your God.
>
> Isaiah – Bishop Lowth's translation

They were not quotations referring to penance, expiation or punishment. There was no intimation in them of the fearful earthly doom Ruskin took to await the woman, but instead, in the Isaiah passage, exhortation to fearlessness, an identification of the woman as weak and tottering rather than lost and culpable. The notion of falling in the Ecclesiastes passage is not of guilty falling but of random survival or failure in nature.

When critics objected to the faulty technique in *The Awakening Conscience* – to the intricacy of the complicated compound shadows and the wasted effort on details – they were pointing to features in the picture which offended against accepted rules of painting. The objections that were raised cannot be fully understood unless they are put in the context of critical categories that were available and current in the 1840s and 1850s. Many paintings throughout this period were criticised for departing from a compositional norm that centred the viewer's attention on the main

facing 1 F. M. Brown, *Work* (1852–65)

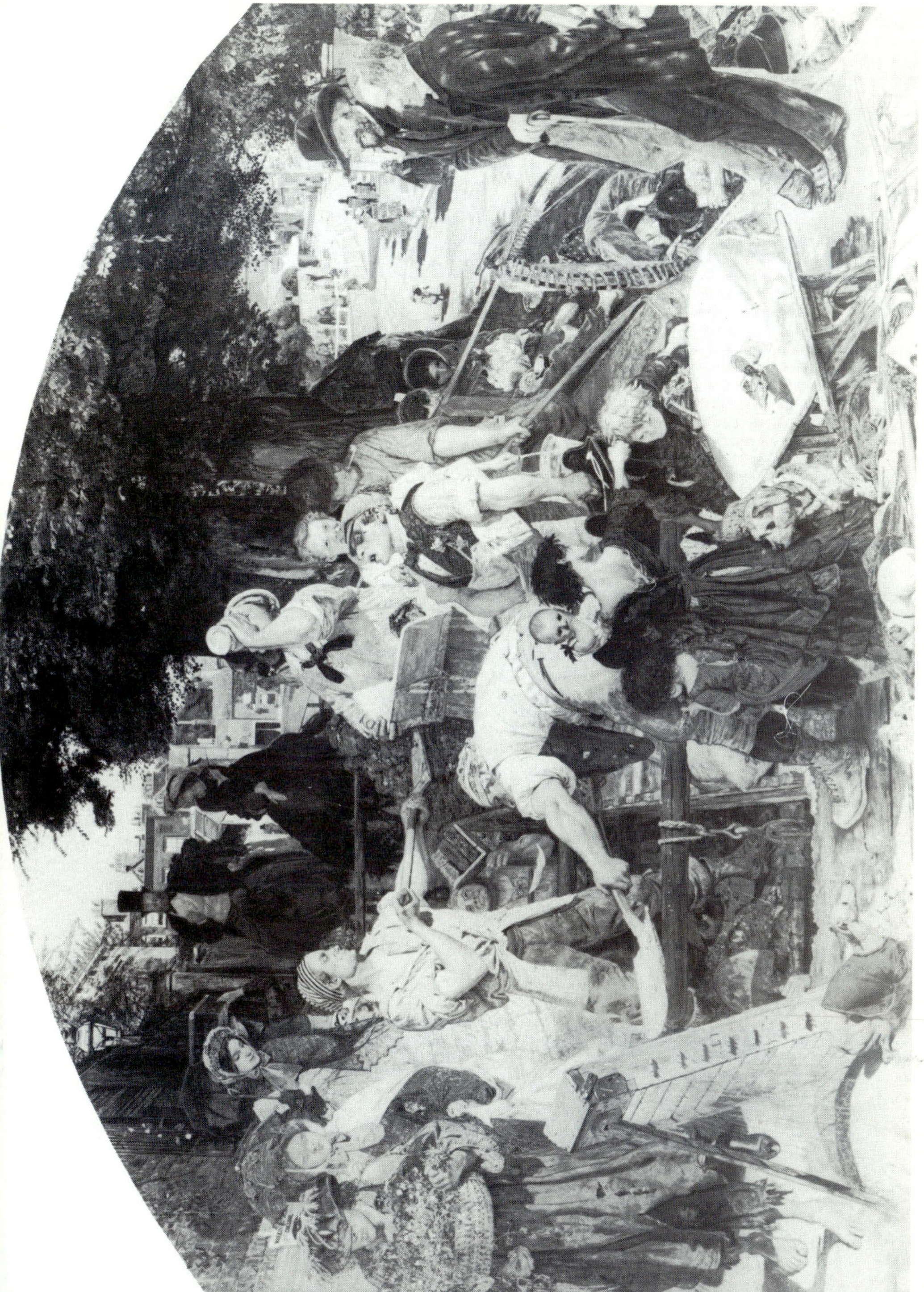

2 W. H. Hunt, *The Awakening Conscience* (1854)

facing, lower 3 W. H. Hunt, *The Children's Holiday* (1865)
upper 4 P. H. Calderon, *Broken Vows* (1856)

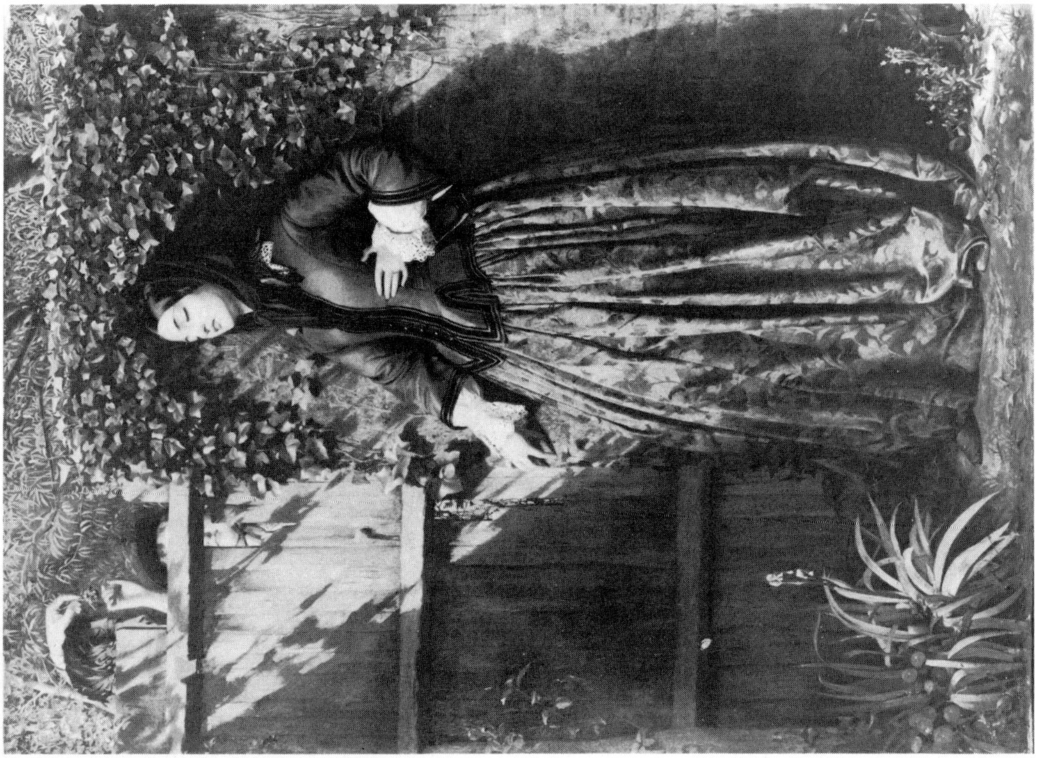

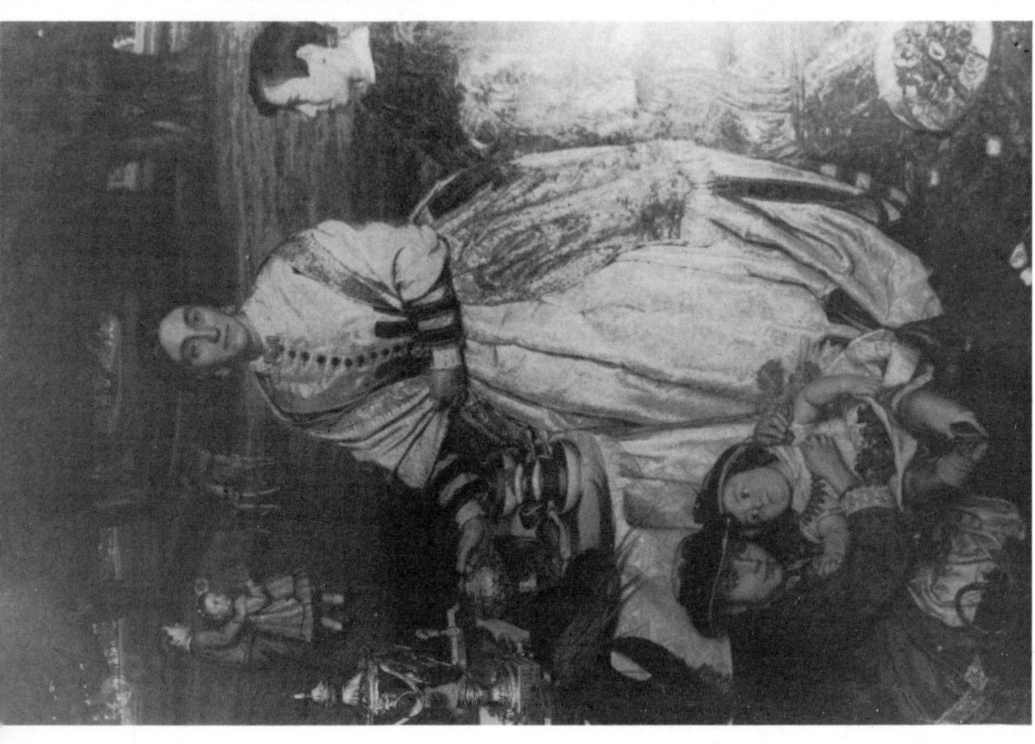

5 J. C. Horsley, *Pay for Peeping* (1872)

facing 6 A. Soloman, *First Class – the Meeting: 'And at First Meeting Loved'* (1854)

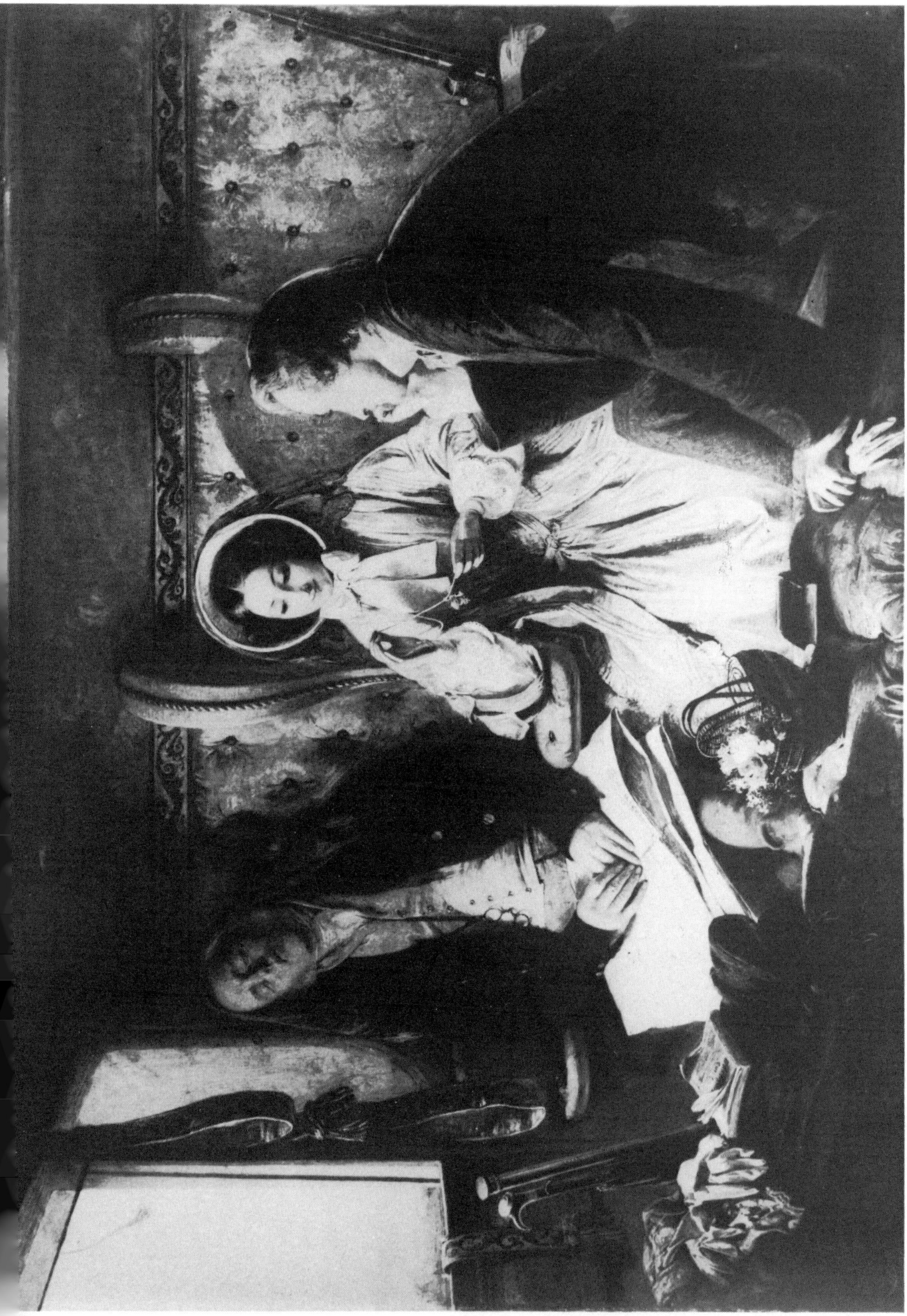

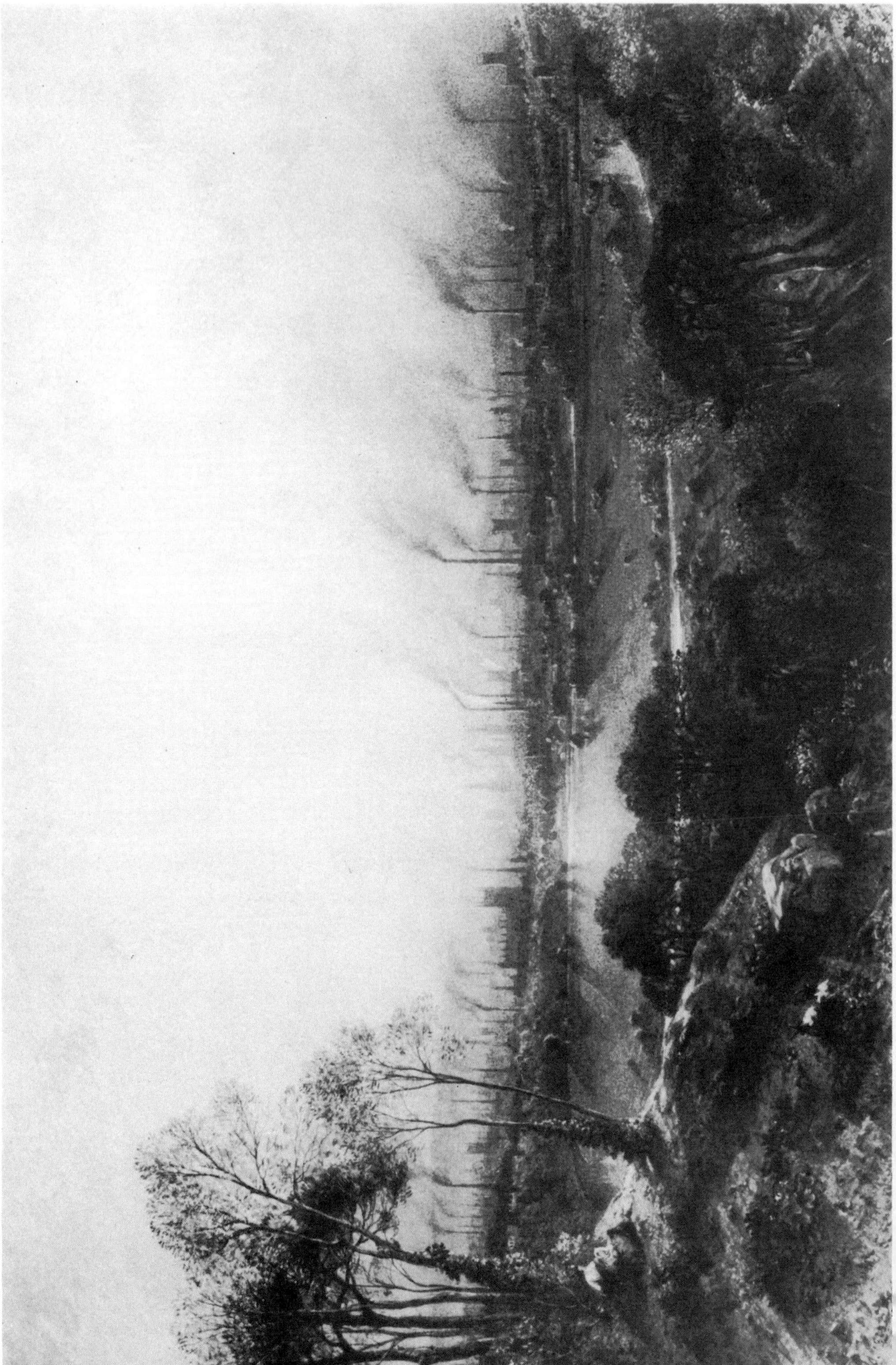

facing 7 William Wyld, *Manchester from Kersal Moor* (1851)

this page, upper 8 T. Allom, engraved J. Tingle, *Power Loom Weaving* (1835)

lower 9 J. Ralston, lithographed J. D. Harding, *Market Place, Manchester* (1823–25)

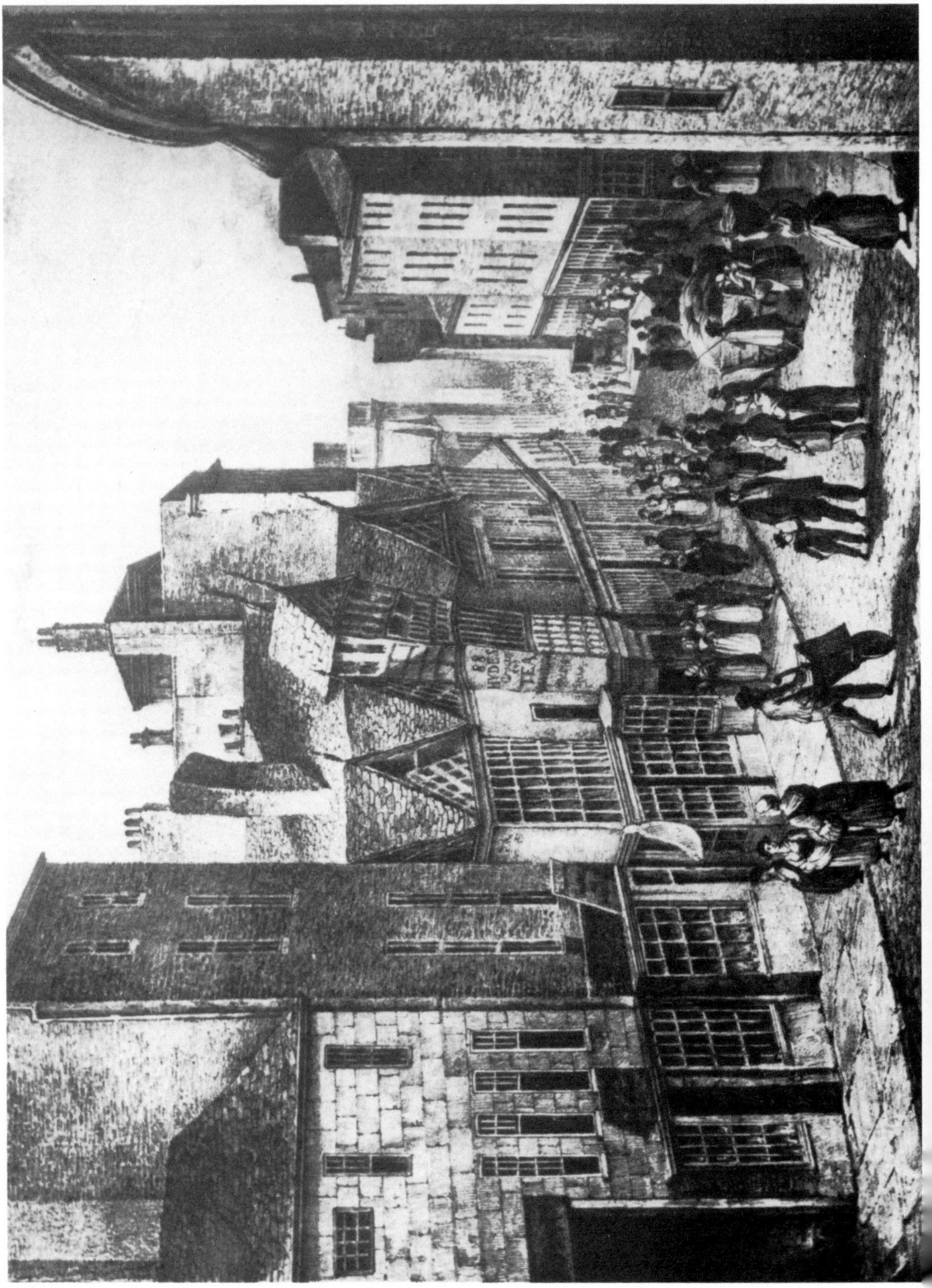

facing **10** J. Ralston, lithographed A. Aglio, *Market Street* (1823–25)

this page, upper **11** T. Taylor, engraved Charles Heath, *The Moot Hall* (1816)
lower **12** Joseph Rhodes, *The Old Moot Hall*, Leeds (n.d.)

13 N. Whittock, engraved J. Rogers, *Corn Exchange, Leeds* (1829)

14 J. Greig, *Upper Part of Briggate, formerly called Cross Parish* (1851)

15 Engraved Lee, *The Corn-Exchange* (n.d.)

16 Trade advertisement for J. W. Bean (1853)

17 W. Nelson, lithographed G. and J. F. Masser, *Commercial Buildings, Leeds* (1842)

18 N. Whittock, engraved J. Rogers, *Commercial Buildings, Leeds* (1829)

19 Harwood and M. J. Starling, *The Exchange, Manchester* (1835)

20 Engraved E. J. Roberts, *Court House, Commercial Buildings and Yorkshire District Bank* (1842)

upper 21 N. Whittock, engraved W. Sims, *Court House, Leeds* (1829)
lower 22 N. Whittock, engraved N. Shury, *Central Market, Leeds* (1828)

facing 23 J. N. Rhodes, engraved S. Staers, *The Central Market &c, Leeds, from the end of Cloth Hall Street* (1835)

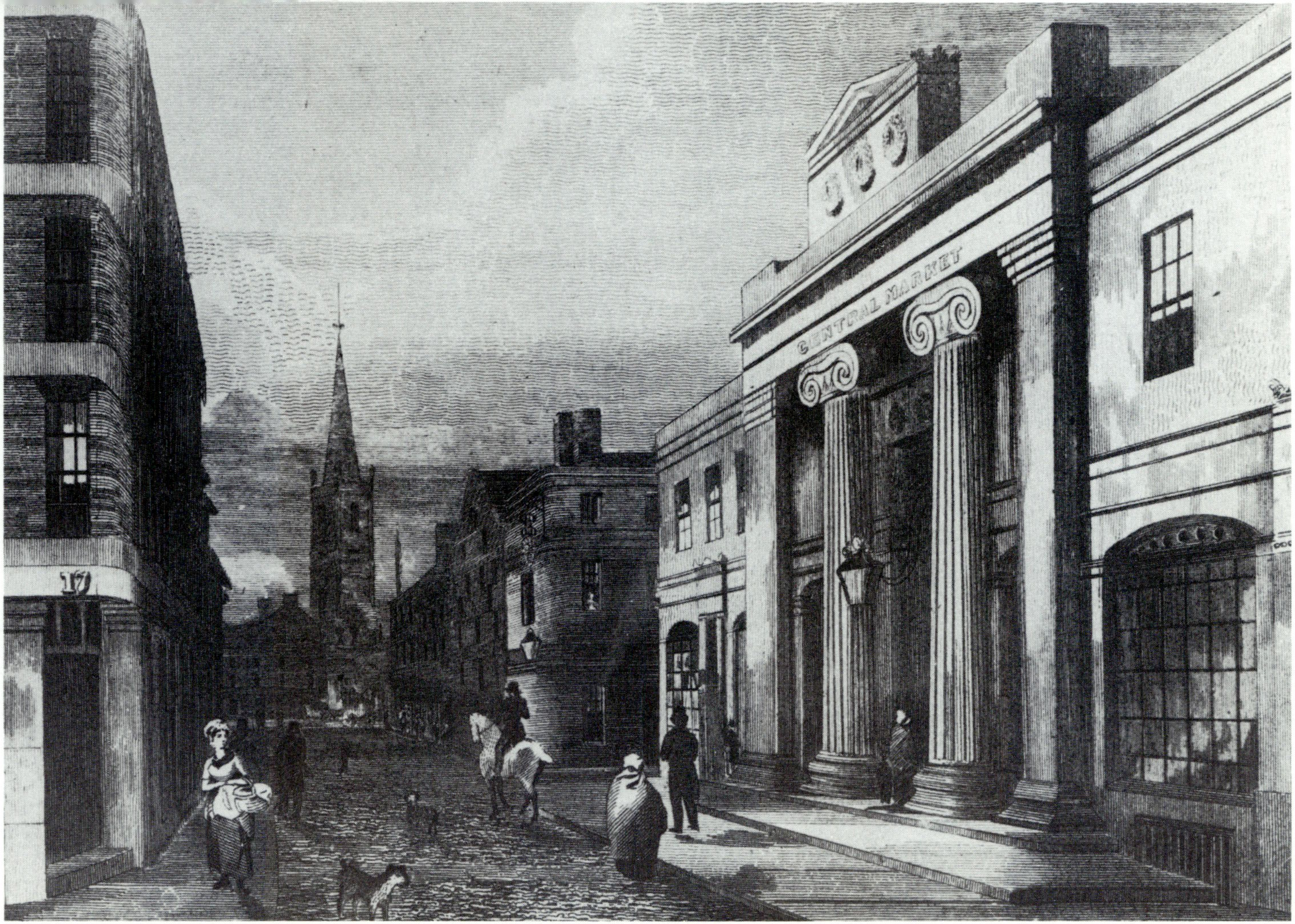
CENTRAL MARKET
17

24 South view of the mills in Marshall Street (*c.* 1850)

25 North view of the mills in Marshall Street (*c.* 1850)

26 Harwood, engraved McGahey, *The Twist Factory, Oxford Street, Manchester* (1832)

27 Austin, engraved McGahey, *Cotton Factories, Union Street, Manchester* (1831)

upper **28** N. Whittock, engraved J. Shury, *The Aire and Calder, at Leeds* (1829)
lower **29** T. Allom, engraved J. Tingle, *The Factory of Messrs. Swainson, Birley & Co., near Preston, Lancashire* (1830)

facing **30** William Marshall Craig, engraved by John Landseer, *Manchester from Mount Pleasant* (1802)

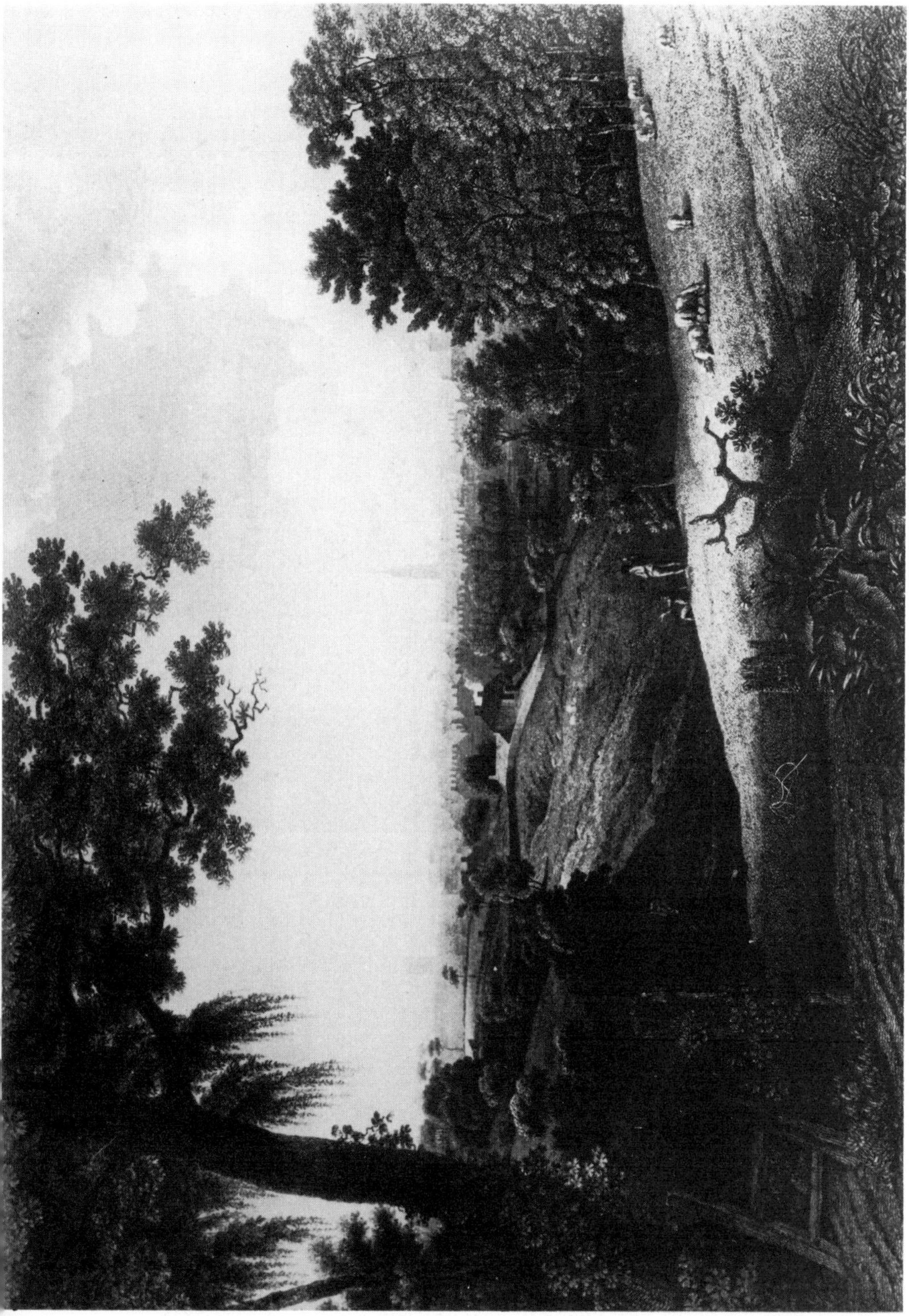

upper 31 Henry Burn, *View of Leeds, from near the Halifax New Road* (1846)
lower 32 Joseph Rhodes, *Leeds from the Meadows* (c. 1820–25)

facing 33 English School, *Manchester from Chester Road* (early 19th c.)

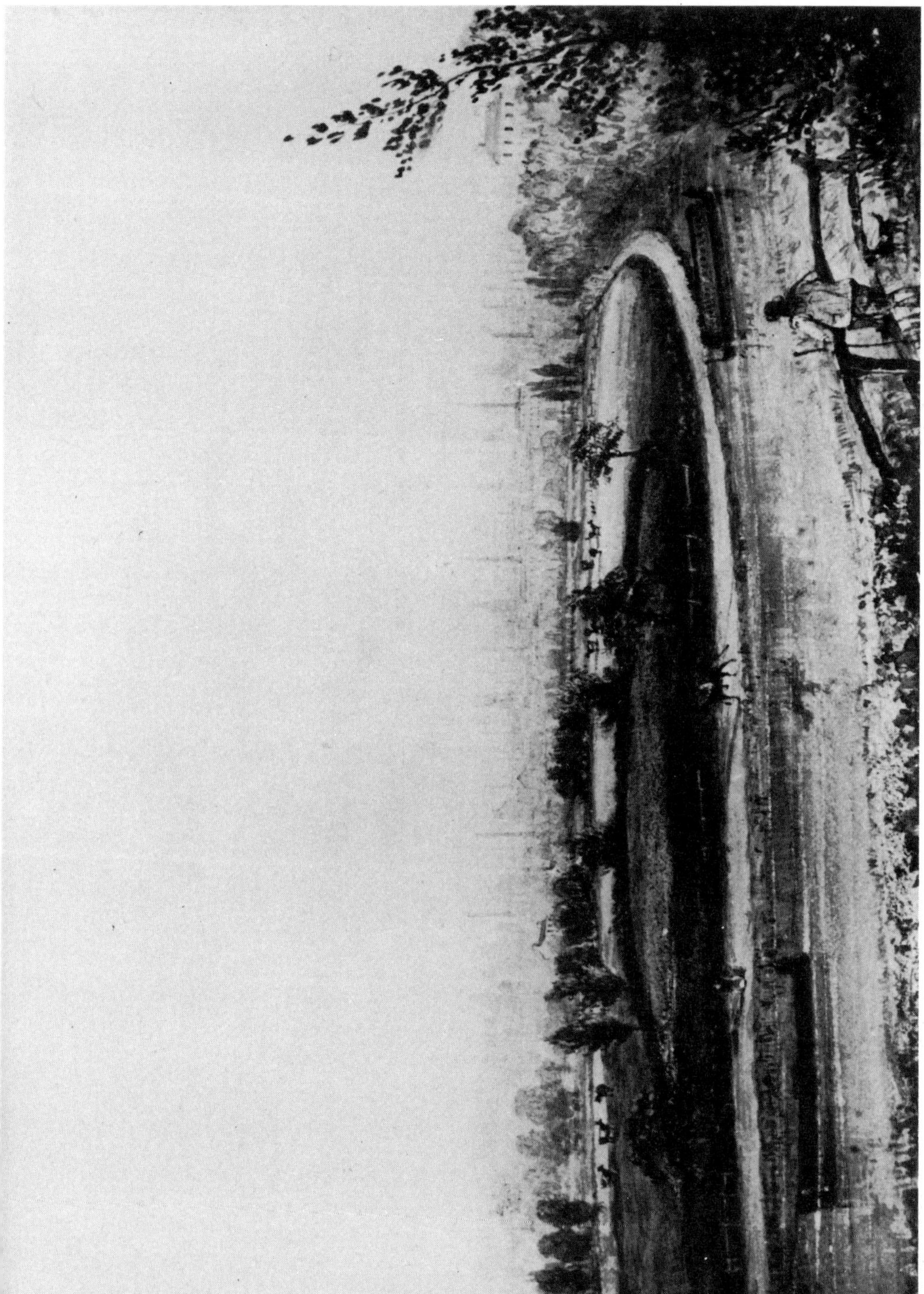

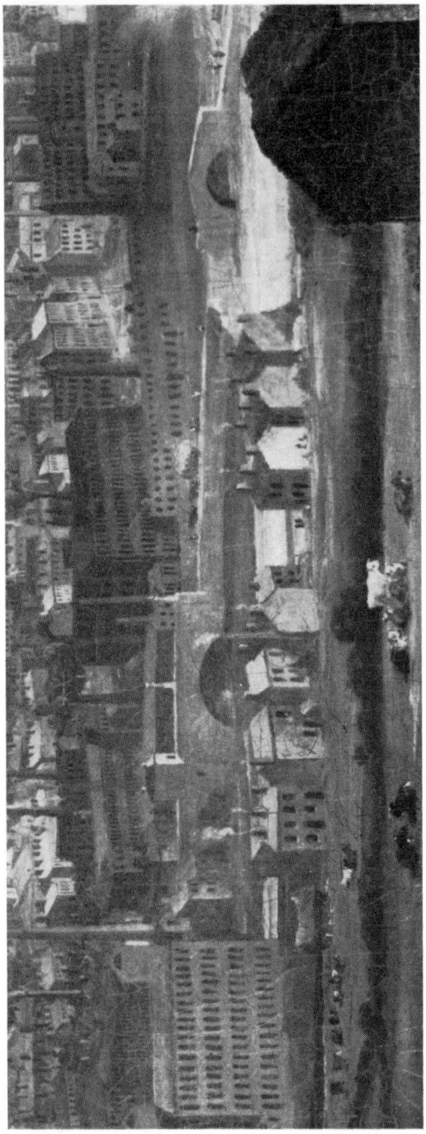

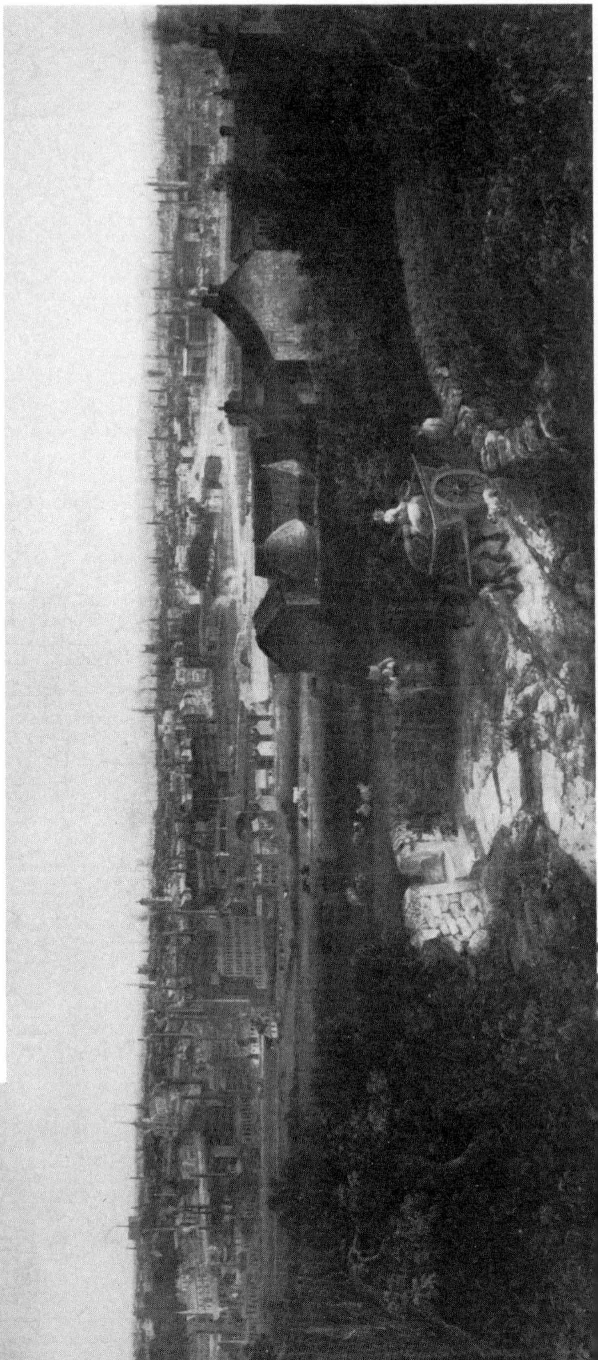

facing 34 Thomas Burras, *View of Leeds* (1844) 35 detail

36 Robert Buttery, etched J. W. Cook, engraved R. C. Reeve, *Leeds taken from Beeston Hill* (1833)

37 Alphonse Dousseau, *Leeds from Rope Hill* (*c.* 1840)

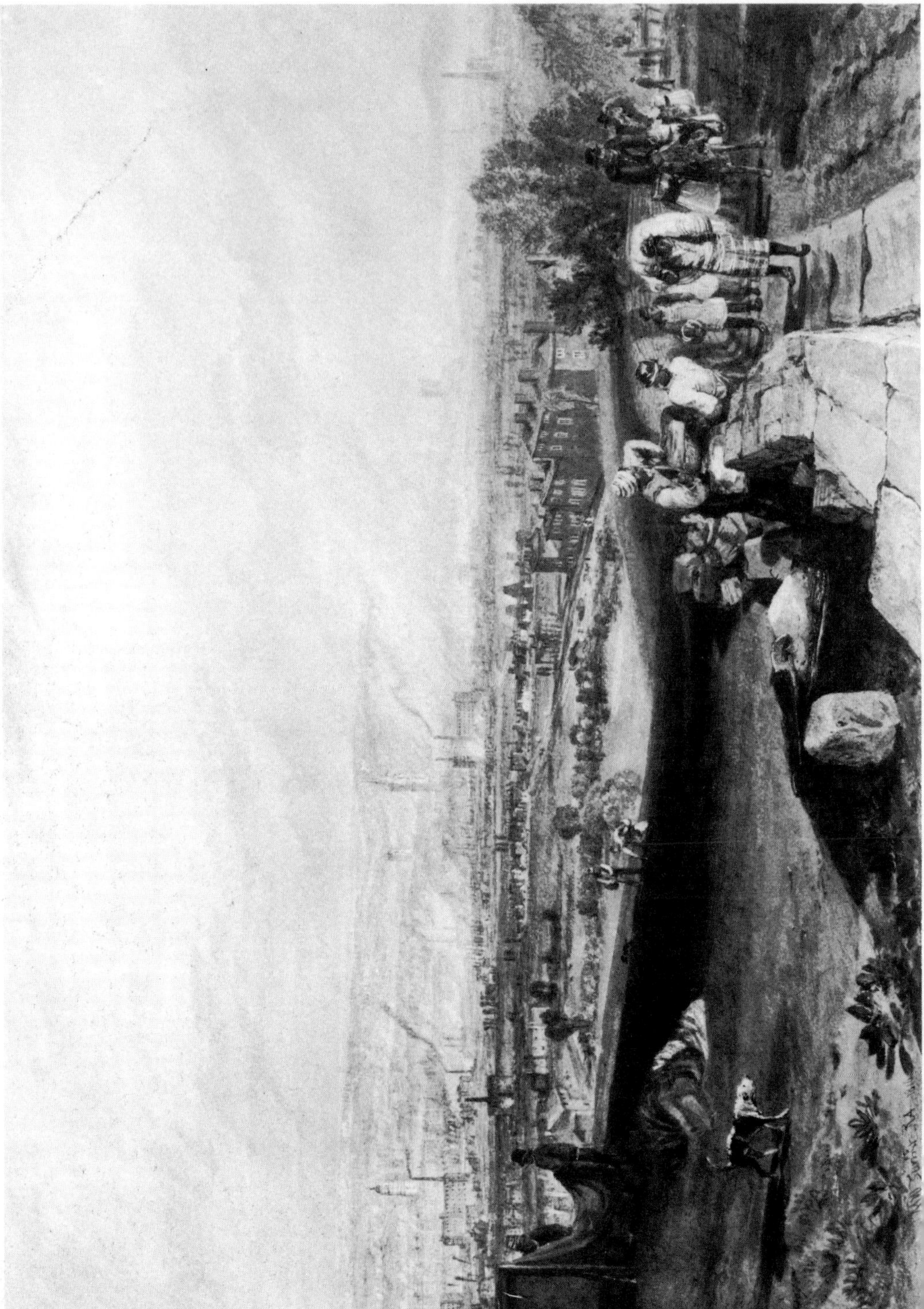

incident in the picture. Following criteria devised from Reynolds, it was thought that the subordinate parts of the picture should be kept from competing with the main incident by being made less distinct. The disposition of areas of light and shade, the emphasis gained from colour contrasts, and the compositional grouping were all expected to articulate the picture surface so that it was legible. We can see that *The Awakening Conscience* deviated from these rules of painting and this helps us to understand the response of many critics to the painting. When reviews referred to the unintelligibility of the picture, they were often indicating that the picture surface was not made legible in the way they expected. We can see that *The Awakening Conscience* does not have distinct patches of light and shade but even, indirect lighting all over the picture, except for a small pool of sunshine in the bottom right corner. The room is crowded with objects claiming our attention. Even the flat surfaces of carpet, wall and piano are richly coloured and patterned. The mirror especially tires the eye because what we see in it are not merely the reflections of objects in front of it in the picture – the side of the man's head and shoulder, the back of the girl – but of things beyond the picture space – the opened French windows and the garden setting beyond them, and the reflection of a mirrored wall beside the French window, parallel to the mirror behind the couple, which reflects in turn the wall which would be to the left of the couple, and the fireplace on that wall surmounted by yet another gold-framed mirror or picture. There is so much information contained in the mirror that our ability to interpret it is exhausted and all our eye is able to do is move restlessly from one apparent perspective to another.

A comparison of two reviews from the 1840s illustrates clearly the prevailing critical attitude as to the correct and incorrect portrayal of detail in narrative painting. J. C. Horsley's *Winning Gloves* was considered to have obeyed the rules of painting in its use of light and shade, but to have transgressed in its over-elaboration of detail:

> A lady sleeping in a chair, and a cavalier about to 'win gloves' by kissing her. In this picture there is much that is beautiful: but brilliancy in the lights and depth in the shadows are counteracted by a finish of parts which breaks the unity of these qualities. A care even zu Hollandisch has been lavished on unimportant matters in the composition, while some of the same would have advantaged the female who sits uneasily.[48]

The failure of a picture to differentiate between details and to guide the viewer's eye was particularly disturbing to mid-nineteenth century critics because it meant not just that a picture failed artistically but that it was demoted in the notional hierarchy that ranged from spiritually uplifting high art to the degraded physical stimulation of low art. At this date, and

facing 38 J. M. W. Turner, *Leeds* (1816)

throughout the first half of the nineteenth century, Dutch painting was considered to be very low in its meticulous attention to fine detail. Excess detail could block the narrative and lead to misinterpretation or render the picture unintelligible. A review of Richard Redgrave's *Going to Service*, exhibited in 1843, judged it a highly successful picture. It was said to balance a proliferation of detail, or, within the narrative context, of allusions, with a proper structure to the picture.

> Great ingenuity has been exerted to render the story perfect; every part of the canvas contains some allusion to the main incident, thrown in so judiciously as to appear in the proper place. A girl is about to leave her home in the country.... Effective narrative and delineative truth have been the artist's principal view here, and his purpose is perfectly answered. Each of the figures sustains perfectly the part allotted to it, without the slightest impertinence to interrupt the smooth currency of the history.[49]

The picture was thought successful because there was no competition for attention between the main figures and the surroundings.

Using categories current in the mid-nineteenth century, *The Awakening Conscience* can be seen as a picture that fails to balance the composition, and one where the viewer is reduced to a mere eye, a sensory organ without discrimination. Such a viewer does not have a secure narrative entry into the picture. He or she can no longer be as certain as Ruskin about the past and future of the woman in the painting. This viewer is not a judge who can choose to summon up compassion, but merely an observer. Moreover the stimulation of the eye was not, at that period, considered to be a neutral experience but had associations of guilt and excitement. Gratification of the visual sense was certainly considered low. It was associated, through the picturesque, with low subjects, despite pleas that the picturesque should not be limited to showing indigence.

> The low and the mean, the decayed and poverty-striken [sic] are often thought to be the only picturesque, as if *picture* must indulge vile associations. Let not art take habitat in 'rotten rows', nor vainly imagine that the eye should seek delight where the foot would not willingly tread – the purlieus of misery and vice.[50]

The delight of the eye, when unconnected with spiritual or intellectual considerations, was in the illusion that what was painted was real. Handsome faces and perfect buildings were thought to offer uniform lines and general truths. They evoked not just pleasure in looking but admiration and abstract reflection. In the picturesque the viewer was shown things, not told about them. With its ragged jumble of items it insisted on the specificity and actuality of every element. With every separate element, whether it were broken earthenware pitcher, uneven roof or grimy urchin face, the specificity was insisted on and the pleasure of the illusion renewed. The picture was not a unitary experience but a series of shocks of recognition. The excitement associated with the purely visual was the excitement of these ever-recurring *frissons*. Since the experience was not such that it allowed the viewer to draw any conclusions, the effect was to generate demand for more and more doses of the scopic. The parallel with a sexual appetite is one that strikes a modern commentator, but it is not simply a reading back of modern concerns, as Ruskin's discussion of ideas of imitation in *Modern Painters* shows: 'All high or noble emotion or thought is thus rendered physically impossible, while the mind exults in what is very like a strictly sensual pleasure.'[51] The excitement was a physical thrill akin to sexual excitation.

In the case of *The Awakening Conscience*, there is another kind of excitement involved, again one that is linked to the extremely distinct rendering of detail. Ruskin's letter to *The Times* identified a feverish excitement of the girl's state of mind and the viewer's consequent interest, both of which, he claims, warrant the clarity of the details. This idea that the mind becomes more aware of trivial objects when in a state of excitement or distress was not original. It is cited as a common literary device used by Dickens and Scott, and as a justification for the detail of Lauder's *The Trial of Effie Deans*, shown at the Royal Academy of 1841.

> [It] may possibly meet with censure from many who think historic art ought to have no such aim – that it should not descend to such particular and strongly defined representation of detail – that there is too much actual truth. . . . Whoever has been present at such harrowing scenes as the Trial of Effie Deans, has borne away with him, fixed upon his memory, and connected with the event in no other way than accidentally, some visual object or objects which he can never after separate. There is an effort in the mind, under the most trying circumstances, to find relief from the external senses – and the organs of the eye do their part with wonderful fidelity.[52]

A psychological mechanism is being described whereby the visual sense is exaggerated to provide relief from stress.

Pictorial characteristics of *The Awakening Conscience* can then be identified which, using critical categories available in the 1850s, would have implicated the viewer in a state of visual excitement, analogous to sexual excitement, and would have made the viewer undergo a visual experience associated with terror or distress. The art critics who objected to the painting were objecting to being put through this experience. Above all, they did not want to be thrown into a pleasurable but terrifying state of excited looking by a scene of unmistakable impropriety, a scene with no distancing mythological overlay, but one which was, on the contrary, startlingly modern. The subject matter of *The Awakening Conscience*, a private interior, and a couple, one half-undressed and intimately seated on the other's knee, put the viewer into the position of voyeur, as if he or she were peeping through a keyhole. In psychoanalytic writing the pleasure taken in looking is described as scopophilia. In Freud's description of the different instincts that operate in the sadistic-anal phase of the development of the libido, scopophilia is described as a component instinct, along with epistemophilia: the instinct for gaining knowledge.[53] He does not suggest that this instinct disappears completely as the libido moves on to later stages of development. In his analysis of the dream of a woman, about buying theatre tickets, he talks of 'a sexual desire to look [scopophilia], directed towards sexual happenings and especially on to the girl's parents'. Later he amplifies this:

> The desire to look... curiosity to discover at long last what really happens when one is married. This curiosity is, as we know, regularly directed by children towards their parents' sexual life; it is an infantile curiosity, and, so far as it still persists later, an instinctual impulse with roots reaching back into infancy.[54]

If we were to describe the effect of *The Awakening Conscience* in psychoanalytic terms, it would be to say, precisely, that it appeals to a sexual desire to look, and offers what has the appearance of a sexual happening for the viewer. But the psychoanalytic gloss can be taken further and can incorporate the effect of terror or distress that we have associated with the painting. Freud discusses children's observation of sexual intercourse by their parents, either in reality or in fantasy. This is what he calls the primal scene, and the child, led to stare fascinatedly at the scene by his or her scopophilic urge and curiosity, experiences sexual excitation. But at the same time the child commonly experiences terror, first because the scene is misconstrued as a violent struggle,[55] and secondly because it gives him or her the opportunity to see that the mother has no penis, and so confirms the existence of castration. It was in the case history known as that of the Wolf Man that Freud went most carefully into the implications of the primal scene. The primal scene, actually observed, developed as a phantasy, or recalled in a dream, has different effects on the boy at different stages in his psychological development. At the age of four he has a dream of wolves sitting in a tree, which recalls the viewing of the primal scene at the age of one-and-half, and it is in the dream that the terrifying aspect of the scene, the danger of castration, becomes apparent to him. In the primal scene recalled by the dream the rear-entry position adopted by his parents in sexual intercourse gives him the opportunity to see that his mother has no penis. '... a scene which was able to show him what sexual satisfaction from his father was like; and the result was terror . . . a conviction of the reality of the existence of castration'.[56] The primal scene can, in a case like this, allow the exercise of scopophilic pleasure in looking and simultaneously overlay it with the terror produced by the fear of castration. I would suggest that *The Awakening Conscience* produced in its mid-nineteenth century viewers a comparable combination of sensual pleasure in looking and distressful anxiety, while casting the viewer in the role of voyeur by presenting such a private and intimate scene. In following through an analysis of the picture in these terms I will refer to the viewer as 'he', not because all viewers were men but because the picture can be thought of as constructing a masculine position for its viewer.

We can identify parallel primal scene elements in a range of other paintings of this period, both by Hunt and by other artists. *The Awakening Conscience* was not alone in making the viewer witness a fearful secret event. In Hunt's early work, two paintings deal with such themes. *The Flight of Madeline and Porphyro during the Drunkenness Attending the Revelry* (1848) shows two lovers escaping secretly. *A Converted British Family Sheltering a Christian Missionary from the Persecution of the Druids* (1850) similarly presents a secret activity conducted in an atmosphere of fear. In each case the viewer is shown something that is hidden from others in the picture. The revellers in the hall cannot see the lovers escaping, and the mob chasing the Christian outside the hut cannot see the missionary being sheltered. Such paintings as *The Proscribed Royalist, 1651* (1853) by J. E. Millais and *Broken Vows* (1856) (Figure 4) by P. H. Calderon show us lovers meeting in secret. In the latter we are given the woman in the foreground to identify with. Her unfaithful lover is with another woman behind the fence. The distressful fascination characteristic of the primal scene is built up in this picture through the woman's grief at being betrayed. She leans back with closed eyes, trying to shut out what she has seen through the chink in the fence but we, as viewers of the picture, are allowed to go on looking. The theme of R. Redgrave's *The Fortune Hunter* (1843) has a comparable theme. The woman behind the screen witnesses the lovemaking of the couple entering the room. She is neglected because she is not rich and finely dressed like the other woman. The same theme runs through many of J. C. Horsley's humorous subjects. In *Showing a Preference* (1860) the man walks out with two young women but one is ignored. Her humiliation and embarrassment are the comic equivalent of the anguish in *Broken Vows*. The fearful looking is acted out in his later *Pay For Peeping* (1872) (Figure 5) where a boy who spies through a hole in the curtain on a young couple courting in the bay window is about to be punished by an older woman, who approaches him, her hand raised to slap him. In the same year that *The*

Awakening Concience was exhibited, Abraham Soloman's modern life scenes, *First Class – The Meeting* and *Second Class – The Parting* (1854), were shown at the Royal Academy. The first of these (Figure 6) is yet another voyeuristic scene, where the young couple, making eyes at each other in the railway carriage, do so stealthily while the old gentleman is asleep. A certain amount of disquiet was expressed at the impropriety of this subject, and the criticisms echo the criticisms of *The Awakening Conscience*: 'As a picture it is executed with great knowledge and power, but it is we think to be regretted that so much facility should be lavished on so bald – or vulgar – a subject.'[57] In a second version of the picture Soloman removed the objectionable *frisson* by showing the old gentleman awake. These samples indicate the wider artistic context in which the themes we have identified in *The Awakening Conscience* were being explored.

In their hostile reaction to *The Awakening Conscience* the critics we have examined registered and rejected the voyeuristic thrill and the scopophilic appeal of the painting. It offered them pleasure in looking, but only pleasure mingled with unpleasure in the castration anxiety associated with the primal scene of which they were made voyeurs The fear could be made bearable in a strategy like Ruskin's. His reading of the picture denied the aimless decentred act of looking by constructing a firm narrative. It further fended off the threat of castration with the controlling, punishing attitude it took towards the woman. The condition of his power to recommend pity and forgiveness was his power to condemn and punish. Ruskin's reading converts the dangerous scopophilia offered by the picture into a safe sadistic voyeurism. Another way in which the anxiety could be allayed is through an iconic strategy in which the beauty of the object represented is asserted, and the gaze fixes on this beautified image. In psychoanalytic terms, this is the strategy of fetishism, where the contemplation of an apparently castrated woman is replaced by the contemplation of an object, or a part or aspect of the woman that is rendered or considered phallic. By means of this substitution, the woman can once again be imagined as complete. Castration anxiety is subdued and the pleasurable component of scopophilia is allowed to predominate.[58] Notions of beauty as plenitude that were current in the mid-nineteenth century suggest how this fetishisation of the female figure operated. A clear example is given by some remarks made by William Holman Hunt on some female figures in the Elgin room of the British Museum. He described female beauty as swelling. '. . . look . . . how it has pushed forward the brow, enlarged the nose, extended the nostrils, pouted the lips, protruded the full chin, made heavy the rich hair, swollen the erect throat, and rounded the massive limbs'.[59] In the vision he presents, the female figure is very much like a penis erecting.

Later on in the same article, with the prospect of an imperfect or asymmetrically swollen figure there is the suggestion of a failing erection, as the beam of justice's balance drops: 'Beauty is justice in form. Justice is not poor in acts – beauty is rich in matter. Raphael's outlines are proud and ample – the equipoise not of empty scales, but of paired weighty fulness and variety, that single and unmatched would turn the beam to a very unequal angle.' The problem with *The Awakening Conscience* was that it failed to offer female beauty for the viewer to fix on, and so blocked off this strategy of fetishistic scopophilia. Critics repeatedly complained about the ugliness of the woman in the picture. Fairbairn eventually requested Hunt to repaint the woman's expression. A review from 1856, when the picture was shown at the Birmingham Society of Artists, typifies the complaints about her ugliness: 'Conscience does not always attest its workings by a grin, and there was no need to have made his example of its force so preternaturally ugly ... an ugly woman in the incipient stage of a hysterical attack.'[60] This review then moves on to the hideous deformity of Hunt's 'syren': Pre-Raphaelitism. '... fast bound to the Pre-Raphaelite syren [Mr Hunt] remained her votary, to find some day or other the lady's mask will fall off, and disclose to him a very deformed face'. The ugliness of the woman represented in the picture has been transferred to a notional figure, Pre-Raphaelitism, and in dubbing this figure a 'syren' the review conveys the shock and fear experienced when the beguiling and reassuring beauty is no longer there. All that is left is a threat of death, since sirens lured sailors to their death.[61] Through a siren-prostitute-fallen woman association these remarks can be taken as an indication of the castration fear aroused by the picture. In this framework the viewer is being seduced by the siren-prostitute, just as he is being seduced by the pleasure in looking at the picture surface. The metaphor chosen by the critic suggests the unconscious fear and threat of castration experienced by the viewer. An unnerving involvement at this level militated against a calm and disengaged critical discourse.

The mirror in the picture adds to the elements of *The Awakening Conscience* which put the viewer into this uncomfortable position. Logically, since the mirror reflects the space outside the room, it ought to reflect the viewer peeping at the intimate scene. It threatens to expose the voyeur. The complication of the reflection in the mirror with its frames within frames, and mirrors within mirrors, opens the possibility that the frame round the picture as a whole is yet another mirror frame. In that case, it is as if the mirror on the back wall had moved forward to take the whole pictue space. The guilty voyeur then finds that he is indeed exposed in the picture. He is present in the picture as the young man, the lover of the kept woman. By this process, the viewer is not just included in the sexual event as voyeur, but in a psychoanalytically distinct, but simultaneous role, as an actor. The modernity of the dress and accessories in the picture was unusual in the context of the Academy Exhibition at this date, except in portraiture, where the subject was a named individual. This modernity, combined with the unusual accuracy with which every detail in the picture was represented, combined to confirm the impression that the picture as a whole was a mirror. The viewer, already experiencing the fearful pleasure of looking, was invited to identify that fearful pleasure with the guilty pleasure of sinful behaviour.

There are very few reviews of the picture where critics pay any attention to the male figure in the painting. One instance is the pamphlet of 1860 on William Holman Hunt by F. G. Stephens. He gives as much space to the man as to the woman. The man is described as 'a showy handsome tiger of the human species, heartless and indifferent as death . . . insolent shamelessness . . . false, pitiless and cruel'.[62] The woman is described as 'the victim of his passions'. Despite this, there is still no identification of the writer with the man. F. G. Stephens speaks for the bourgeois (male) viewer and reader of his pamphlet, and provides him with a way to avoid identifying with the man in the picture, by describing that man at one point as 'patrician', suggesting that he is an aristocrat, and at another point as 'the double distilled essence of vulgarity . . . the true specimen of "the gent" '. In either case he does not qualify as a member of the bourgeoisie proper, and so the viewer/reader is allowed to keep at a comfortable distance from him. Only *Punch* offers us a review where these defensive tactics are dropped. The elements in *The Awakening Conscience* that tend to include the viewer in the painting and implicate him in the illicit situation are acknowledged in some measure.

> I see a courageous determination to face one of the rifest evils of our time, and to read all of us youth a terrible lesson . . . the painter preaching us a sermon . . . knocking at our hearts and awakening our consciences. Knock on Henry Holman Hunt [sic] for all that. Tell us more home truths. Set us face to face with our great sins again and again. Still paint our Magdalenes, scared by the still small voice amid their bitter splendours, mocked in their misery by the careless smiles and gay voices of their undoers.[63]

This review is very far from Ruskin in its reading of the picture. According to Ruskin, the picture encourages the viewer to exercise a judge's compassion. According to the *Punch* critic, the picture encourages the viewer to acknowledge his own guilt.

The Awakening Conscience was evidently a problematic image in the 1850s. On one hand it lent itself to the standard narrative attached to it by

Ruskin, and to a compatible position we can construct for Amicus. On the other hand, features of the picture were felt – by a large number of critics – to obstruct a secure narrative extrapolation. The tendency of the scene to position the viewer as voyeur, coupled with its refusal to provide a beautified image, made it hard to accept as a pleasing visual experience where narrative was minimised. The picture seemed to offer a threat to a secure narrative therefore, or else a threat to the pleasure of the viewer. The reaction of the *Punch* critic seems to move beyond an insistent assertion of, or demand for, one or the other. By acknowledging the possibility of the viewer/male seducer's guilt, the review suggests a radical revision of the commonly repeated narrative construct that was associated with the fallen woman. The guilt of the man in the picture raises the possibility of the innocence of, or at least a modification of the guilt attributed to, the woman. The sequence of the woman's guilty action, her inevitable earthly degradation and the distant possibility of divine forgiveness is upset at the outset. Consequently, it seems conceivable that the path Ruskin lays out for the woman in the picture might not be the one that she will follow. Some parallel examples of a questioning of the consensus myth of the fallen woman can be found in literary explorations of the theme in the late 1840s and early 1850s.[64]

Neither Ruskin's reading nor a reading we can attribute to Amicus exhausts the meaning of the *The Awakening Conscience*. It is impossible to ascribe a single unified ideological function to the picture. The vicissitudes of the commission, and Fairbairn's ultimate dissatisfaction with the expression of the woman in the painting, give some indication of the painting's failure to match exactly the requirements and expectations of its patron. We can begin to understand the reason for this when we look at the reviews of the picture that were published in the 1850s. The complications and contradictions in the picture made it very difficult for the critics to deal with. The critical positions that were developed were, as we have seen, widely divergent. *The Awakening Conscience* is a painting that deepens our understanding of the relationship between patron and painting, and of the possible incoherencies of an art work.

Notes

1 Nicos Hadjinicolaou, *Art History and Class Struggle*, trans. Louise Asmal, Pluto Press, London, 1979.
2 Pierre Macherey, *A Theory of Literary Production*, trans. Geoffrey Wall, Routledge & Kegan Paul, London, 1978.
3 Letter, Thomas Plint to Ford Madox Brown, 24 November 1856: 'Could you introduce *both* Carlyle and *Kingsley* and change one of the four fashionable

young ladies into a quiet earnest *holy*-looking one with a book or two and *tracts*? I want *this* put in, for I am much interested in *this* work myself, and know those who are.' Quoted F. M. Hueffer, *Ford Madox Brown: A Record of his Life and Work*, AMS Press, New York, 1972, p. 112. Brown originally intended having a single figure on the right of the picture, an artist. By 1856 he may have decided to make this the figure of Carlyle. Plint's suggestion was to add Kingsley. By early 1857 the second figure was agreed on; not Kingsley but F. D. Maurice. (See also discussion of this case by Janet Wolff in this volume, p. 124.)

4 Entry for 2 June 1840. W. B. Pope, *The Diary of Benjamin Robert Haydon*, Harvard University Press, Cambridge, Mass., 1963, Vol. V.
5 Letter J. Ruskin to E. Heaton, 12 March 1840, in V. Surtees (ed.), *Sublime and Instructive*, Michael Joseph, London, 1972, p. 239.
6 For example, the Third Duke of Bridgewater, who died unmarried in 1803, had to leave his seat and entailed estates to a cousin, John Egerton, but left his personal fortune, and pictures estimated at a value of £50,000, to his sister's son, George Granville, Marquis of Stafford. This case is described by L. Stone, *An Open Elite?*, Clarendon Press, Oxford, 1984, p. 81.
7 Buchanan and Stewart, 2 February 1804: 'Now as works of art are less looked on as a bribe than money.' H. Brigstocke, *William Buchanan and the 19th century Art Trade*, Paul Mellon Centre, London, 1982.
8 *Ibid.*, 13 March 1804, p. 181 and 8 May 1804, p. 305.
9 *Ibid.*, 23 December 1803 and 22 February 1804.
10 W. B. Scott, *Autobiographical Reminiscences* (1892), AMS Press, New York, 1970, Vol. I., p. 210.
11 F. M. Hueffer, *op. cit.*, p. 191, catalogue entry for 1865 exhibition of F. M. Brown's paintings.
12 *Ibid.*, p. 164.
13 William Pole (ed.), *The Life of Sir William Fairbairn* (1877), David and Charles Reprints, Newton Abbot, Devon, 1970.
14 Entry in Fairbairn family Bible, cited in Judith Bronkhurst, 'Fruits of a connoisseur's friendship: Sir Thomas Fairbairn and William Holman Hunt', *Burlington Magazine*, October 1983, No. 967, Vol. CXXV, p. 587, n. 9.
15 See Leonore Davidoff, *The Best Circles: Society, Etiquette and the Season*, Croom Helm, London, 1973.
16 James B. Jefferys, *The Story of the Engineers 1800–1945* (1945), Johnson Reprint Company, London, 1970, pp. 32–48.
17 *The Times*, 15 January 1852.
18 *The Times*, 14 January 1852.
19 *Fortunes Made in Business*, various writers (unspecified), 2 vols., London, Sampson, Low, etc., 1884.
20 *The Times*, 5 January 1852.
21 J. B. Jefferys, *op. cit.*, p. 39; A. E. Musson, *British Trade Unions 1800–1875*, Macmillan, London, 1972, pp. 50–8. I am indebted to Duncan Hallas for discussing this question with me.
22 W. Pole, *op. cit.*, p. 325.
23 J. B. Jefferys, *op. cit.*, p. 41.
24 W. H. Hunt to Thomas Combe, 30 April 1853, quoted J. Bronkhurst, *op. cit.*, p. 588.
25 W. H. Hunt to T. Combe, 21 February 1854, quoted R. Parkinson, 'The Awakening Conscience and the Still Small Voice', *The Tate Gallery 1976–8: Illustrated Biennial Report and Catalogue of Acquisitions*, The Tate Gallery,

London, 1978.
26 A. Egg to T. Combe, 20 March 1854, quoted R. Parkinson, *ibid.*
27 W. H. Hunt, 'Notes on the Life of Augustus Egg', *The Reader*, 1863, II, p. 5.
28 *The Times*, 10 January 1852.
29 *The Times*, 20 January 1852.
30 *The Times*, 27 December 1851.
31 Burton Park in Sussex. J. Bronkhurst, *op. cit.*, p. 593.
32 J. Bronkhurst, *op. cit.*, p. 594.
33 Fairbairn was Chairman of the organising committee of the Manchester Art Treasures Exhibition of 1857. He was responsible for the management of the Fine Art Department in the 1862 International Exhibition. He was commissioner for the International Exhibition of 1851 (elected as commissioner in May 1861), 1862, 1867, and 1871. He had purchased the Soulages Collection of decorative art in 1857 and it was bought from him for the nation in 1859–65. Judith Bronkhurst, *op. cit.*, pp. 588, 592–4.
34 Jeffrey Weeks, *Sex, Politics and Society: The Regulation of Sexuality since 1800*, Longman, London, 1981; M. Foucault, *The History of Sexuality, vol. 1: an introduction*, trans. R. Hurley, Penguin, Harmondsworth, 1979; L. Nead, 'Seduction, prostitution, suicide: *On the Brink* by Alfred Elmore', *Art History*, Vol. 5, No. 3, September 1982, pp. 310–22.
35 *The Times*, 4 May, 25 May 1854.
36 W. H. Hunt, *Pre Raphaelitism and the Pre Raphaelite Brotherhood*, 2 vols., Macmillan, London, 1905. For art historical accounts see: (*i*) *William Holman Hunt*, Exhibition Catalogue by Mary Bennett, Walker Art Gallery, Liverpool, 1969, pp. 35–7 (mainly drawn from Hunt's autobiography, and quotes Ruskin's letter at length); (*ii*) *The Pre Raphaelites*, Exhibition Catalogue, Whitechapel Art Gallery, London, 1972, entry 24 (relies on Ruskin for details discussed and heightened perception of details by the woman, but uses notions alien to Ruskin); (*iii*) *Walpole Society*, Vol. XLIV, 1972–4, 'Letters from William Holman Hunt', p. 76 (cites Millais's statement that Ruskin had misunderstood the picture, but comments 'Millais does not give his own interpretation of the story and Ruskin's is the generally accepted one'); (*iv*) *The Pre-Raphaelites*, Exhibition Catalogue, Tate Gallery, London, 1984, entry pp. 120–1 by Judith Bronkhurst (goes beyond Ruskin in the range of details discussed, but uses some elements from Ruskin, and still sets up a true interpretation versus the bewilderment and misunderstanding of the critics).
37 Andrea Rose, *The Pre-Raphaelites*, Phaidon, Oxford, 1977, no. 15 ('the kept woman . . . is struck with remorse and jumps up to throw off her guilty life and to follow henceforth in the paths of virtue'). Chris Brooks, *Signs for the Times: Symbolic Realism in the Mid Victorian World*, George Allen & Unwin, London, 1984. (He sees a potential for order in the formal organisation of the top of the picture, and the positive decision of the woman to rise up and distance herself from the world where she is an object for sale.) James Thompson, 'Ruskin and Hunt's *Awakening Conscience*', *Victorians Institute Journal*, 1979, Vol. 8, pp. 19–22. (Stresses the left to right reading, and corresponding movement of the girl, towards the patch of sunshine. Also stressed is the pairing with *The Light of the World*: Christ is outside the picture on the right, as he is omitted from the print on the wall. The girl 'appears to be on the verge of release'.)
38 L. Nochlin, 'Lost and Found: Once More the Fallen Woman', *Art Bulletin*, 60, March 1978, pp. 139–53. Reprinted in N. Broude, etc., *Feminism and Art History*, Harper and Row, New York, 1982. (This cites a number of cases where

the repentant fallen woman is represented as returning to a country family. The only English example she gives, however, is an eighteenth-century one, though the French 1830s and 1840s images may have had circulation in England.) L. Nead, 'The Magdalen in modern times: the mythology of the fallen woman in Pre-Raphaelite painting', *Oxford Art Journal*, 1984, Vol. 7, No. 1. (This article makes a clear distinction between the possibility of the soul's salvation and the impossibility of a release from the fallen woman's grim earthly fate.)

39 See L. Nead, as n. 33.
40 *Sun*, 1 May 1854.
41 Letter quoted by Diana Holman Hunt, quoted R. Parkinson, *op. cit.*
42 Letter A. Egg to T. Combe, 27 March 1854, quoted R. Parkinson, *op. cit.*
43 *Athenaeum*, 6 May 1854, p. 561.
44 *Illustrated London News*, 13 May 1854, p. 438.
45 *Art Journal*, 1854.
46 *Morning Chronicle*, 29 April 1854.
47 *Art Journal*, September 1854.
48 *Art Union*, 1842.
49 *Art Union*, 1843.
50 *Blackwood's Edinburgh Magazine*, September 1841.
51 Ruskin, *Modern Painters*, Vol. 1., Pt. 1, Sect. 1, Ch. 4, Library Edition, Vol. III, George Allen, London, 1903, p. 102.
52 *Blackwood's Edinburgh Magazine*, September 1841.
53 S. Freud, Pelican Freud Library, ed. A. Richards, Penguin, Harmondsworth, 1973–, Vol. I, *Introductory Lectures on Psychoanalysis*, p. 370.
54 S. Freud, *ibid.*, pp. 258, 263.
55 S. Freud, *ibid.*, Vol. 7, *On Sexuality*, p. 198.
56 S. Freud, *ibid.*, Vol. 9, *Case Histories II.*, p. 267.
57 *Art Journal*, 1854.
58 See L. Mulvey, 'Visual pleasure and narrative cinema', *Screen*, Vol. 16, No. 3, 1975, for a theorisation of the pleasure derived from viewing cinema, the threat of castration this pleasure seems to entail for the masculine viewer, and the narrative and iconic defence mechanisms adopted.
59 W. H. Hunt, 'Notes on the life of Augustus Egg', *The Reader*, Vol. II, 1863, pp. 42–3.
60 *Aris's Birmingham Gazette*, 6 October 1856.
61 The identification of the woman in the picture with the siren is further confirmed by the common use of the metaphor of the siren for a prostitute in the nineteenth century. Prostitutes were thought to lure young men into sin just as sirens lured their victims. See L. Nead, 'Woman as temptress: the siren and the mermaid in Victorian painting', *Leeds Arts Calendar*, No. 91, 1982, pp. 5–20.
62 F. G. Stephens, *William Holman Hunt and his Works*, 1860.
63 *Punch*, 1854, Vol. 26, p. 229.
64 For examples of this emerging discussion see C. Bronte, *Jane Eyre*, 1847 (novel); D. G. Rossetti, *Jenny*, 1847–8 (poem); E. Gaskell, *Ruth*, 1853 (novel); and W. R. Greg, 'False morality of lady novelists', 1859 (review article). These literary works are discussed at greater length in my forthcoming Ph.D. thesis.

7   CAROLINE ARSCOTT
and GRISELDA POLLOCK
with JANET WOLFF

The partial view:
the visual representation of the early nineteenth-century city

Introduction: picturing the city: the art-historical context

This chapter is an attempt to analyse a collection of paintings, watercolours and prints depicting scenes in and around industrial cities, notably Manchester and Leeds, in the first half of the nineteenth century. The received wisdom is that few artists, especially major ones, were attracted to these subjects, or were able to find appropriate means to represent new industrial towns and cities. In 1980, Ira Bruce Nadel and F. S. Schwarzbach edited a collection of essays, entitled *Victorian Artists and the City*.[1] As literary historians, they were surprised at the paucity of material available on this topic, and offered their book as a catalyst to encourage future interest in what they discerned as a relatively undeveloped subject. 'Scant attention', they claim, has been paid by art historians to 'the city as subject, setting or social environment' (Nadel and Schwarzbach, 1980, p. xiv). Moreover, the editors claim that major Victorian artists themselves consciously or unconsciously avoided dealing with urban subject-matter.[2] Their introduction aims to explore the possible explanations for what is taken to be artists' reticence in confronting the city.

    The first argument they present is that traditional conventions of art strongly favoured subjects which stressed order, sentiment, domestic morality and piety; urban subject-matter might be not only unruly, dirty and unpleasant but also sordid and discomforting. A broader explanation is advanced encompassing literature too (since few major writers looked at the city) for a general Victorian anxiety about the dangerous and threatening social knowledge of the city. This rests on an analogy with (conventional) notions of the Victorian (repressed but fascinated) attitudes to sex. They also explore the possibility that the rapidity of social change and the novelty of the social environment produced by urbanisation 'exceeded the capacity of human consciousness to make sense of the process' (p. xv). This idea derives in part from sociological studies of city life, notably Georg Simmel's seminal analysis, 'The Metropolis and Mental Life'.[3] Nadel and Schwarzbach move from the effects of city life as social experience to the social relations characteristic of modern towns and cities, and consider whether class issues may have made urban themes difficult to handle: looking at pictures of urban subjects might have involved predominantly middle-class consumers of art in 'polluting contact with social inferiors' (p. xv).

While most of these explanations of the negative response to the city are seen by these editors to have some value, they also recognise that more research would be required to support them. They abandon the project of an analysis of the absence of treatments of the city in favour of consideration of those artists who, as exceptions to the general rule, are 'all the greater for their confrontation with the city' (p. xv). What follows is a book which favours the conventional art historical monographic form, with chapters devoted to named artists such as George Scharf, George Cruikshank, William Mulready, F. M. Brown and Gustave Doré. These are supplemented with studies of a more pronounced social and historical character, which are, however, reserved for journalism and illustration, where the editors are obliged to admit that urban themes did proliferate. Thus a clear distinction is erected between high culture and its few 'greatest artists', and low, or even sub-culture, with its second-rate producers (p. xv) and apparently anonymous artisans, engravers and publishers. This radically disfigures the historical material. Those cultural practices which had the broadest impact through widespread daily circulation and consumption in many sections of the population are downgraded in favour of the highly selective indices of responses to the city offered by individuals, canonised by art history, practising in limited arenas. The danger lies in losing sight of the fact that the intelligibility and indeed the recognition of the specificity of meaning in paintings or high-class engravings made by exhibiting professional artists would have necessarily depended, especially when broaching new and so-called 'modern life' subjects, on the mass of imagery of the city – literary and theatrical, as well as visual – which circulated through posters, theatre bills, advertising, popular songs, daily and weekly papers, illustrated magazines, and so forth.[4] The supposed lacuna in images of the city is, therefore, perhaps an art–historical delusion, and a product of a blindness to the necessary historical relations between many different forms of cultural production and its varied sites of consumption. Thus we shall suggest that genuinely to assess the engagements with the city in visual representations, a broad field of representations must be considered in their historical interdependence. There will be, we hope to show, no lack of material for such an enterprise.[5]

In the influential collection of essays, *The Victorian City*, edited by H. J. Dyos and Michael Wolff (1973), E. D. H. Johnson provides the only substantive study to date of Victorian artists and the urban milieu. It is clear that Johnson's argument is a reference point for the previous writers' conclusions about both the restraining effect of artistic conventions and the general reluctance of artists to engage with the city. Yet the evidence Johnson actually offers indicates a considerable range of pictorial representations of many aspects of city life, including topographical scenes, images of the poor and destitute, and of the etiquette of polite society, scenes of urban sexual temptations, and new sites such as railways, banks, omnibuses and crowds on public holidays.[6] Paintings of these topics can be categorised as treatments of 'modern life'. Eighteenth-century genre painting, though largely rural in its subject matter, did provide models for the treatment of modern urban life. Didactic and satirical series by William Hogarth (1697–1764) such as *Marriage à la Mode* (1743–5) were examples that nineteenth-century artists could draw on. Johnson argues that these conventions were available and used by artists like William Powell Frith (1817–1909), George Elgar Hicks (1824–1914) or the *Punch* cartoonists, but were modified by, for example, a toning-down or voiding of the satirical elements.

The other major tradition in art which Johnson considers was that branch of landscape known as 'topography', which traditionally meant detailed, often architectural, depictions of towns, major public buildings, attractive views, country houses and their estates. The visits of the Italian painter known as Canaletto (1697–1768) to London in 1746–55 had stimulated amongst British artists the representation of London as a majestic city, full of stately edifices and noble vistas, especially up and down the Thames. In the nineteenth century, several fine publications of engravings continued this celebration of the capital's architectural splendours.

The majority of examples in both Johnson's work and that of the Nadel and Schwarzbach collection are of London. The latter writers apologise for this limitation, but argue that it is historically reasonable, given the status of London in the nineteenth century, as 'the embodiment of the spirit and consciousness of all great modern cities' (p. xvi). What can be said of London, they suggest, has general implications. To a lesser extent, Johnson sustains this idea of the pre-eminence of London by marking a typical distinction between metropolitan (leading) and provincial (following). 'A rewarding field of investigation awaits the art historian who undertakes to explore the work of nineteenth-century provincial painters of the urban scene, especially those from the midlands and the north, for whom the new manufacturing centers were an integral part of the English landscape.' (p. 464) There is a conflict here. Johnson's essay opens with the very interesting question of why the manufacturing centres which sprang up in the wake of the Industrial Revolution did not (apparently) attract Georgian and Victorian artists. Johnson rightly admits the novelty and difference of the towns and cities based on manufacture, but for the body of the essay this distinction is lost in the cataloguing of the representations of London.[7] It would be foolish to pretend that many aspects of the social life of the capital did not correspond with what was experienced in Liverpool or Newcastle – dirt, disease, poverty, overcrowding, shops, railway stations, public works, as well as a consciousness of change, speed, congestion, and so on. Nonetheless, London was atypical of the new nineteenth-century towns and cities, which were the focus of so much debate and controversy in the middle years of the century.[8] London was never a major industrial centre, and its patterns of work, growth, consumption and population were radically different from the market towns and the collections of small rural or manufacturing villages which rapidly congealed to form the incorporated towns and cities, like Birmingham, Manchester and Leeds.[9] As B. I. Coleman has pointed out, there is a shift around 1800. Before that date, controversies about the city referred mainly to London and its parasitism on the countryside. Thereafter, London was rivalled and then replaced as the major preoccupation in debates about towns and cities by the new industrial centres of the Midlands and the North.

In those sections of the essay where this difference is recognised, Johnson is clearly arguing that the reticence about the city on the part of Victorian artists is a reluctance to engage with industrial sites. Despite the fact that late eighteenth-century artists had integrated into romantic and sublime landscapes some of the mechanical marvels of the new iron foundries, lime-kilns and coke ovens, which were still isolated installations in the countryside (for example, de Loutherbourg's *Coalbrookdale by Night* (1801, coll. Science Museum)), Johnson argues that the modern metropolis produced by the railway system after 1830 found few celebrants,[10] and that artists avoided what were deemed the uglier aspects. Views such as that by William Wyld of *Manchester from Kersal Moor,* 1851 (Figure 7) push the city and its factories into the far distance, while a pastoral scene unfolds in a foreground virtually separated as another world from its misty urban background. Johnson's article explains the emphases of the Nadel and Schwarzbach collection. There are many pictures of London, genre scenes of its population and topographies of its major sites, new and old. But the ugliness and strangeness of 'a new and alien social environment' of the modern manufacturing metropolis inhibited artistic engagement (Johnson, in Dyos and Wolff, 1973, p. 450).

Much of our article will contest this received wisdom by looking at a selection from a multitude of images we have found, portraying two of these new industrial centres, Leeds and Manchester. However, it is important first to examine another strand of the argument, namely the view that the inherited conventions of landscape and townscape painting would not be appropriate or easily modifiable to the new kinds of scene associated with towns and cities of the Midlands and the North.

Johnson mentions topography, but this, as Louis Hawes shows in an exhibition catalogue, *Presences of Nature, British Landscape Painting 1780–1830* (Yale Centre for British Art, New Haven 1982), is only one of a number of ways of representing the town which he lists in a chapter on townscapes (pp. 84–112). Hawes first describes the mid-eighteenth-century models of British landscape, such as those provided by Canaletto, as well as paintings of London's commercial life, especially its markets at Covent Garden and Smithfield. There were in addition close-up portrayals of crowded streets in poorer districts, which were anything but tidy or pleasant. Examples of these were Hogarth's (1697–1764) *Beer Street* and *Gin Lane* (1751). Hawes does point out, however, that such pictures of the seamier side of London life did not in general find favour in the later, Georgian, period. These varied types of townscape were used and expanded by late eighteenth and early nineteenth-century painters, watercolourists and engravers. Scenes such as Thomas Rowlandson's (1756–1827) *Covent Garden* (1810) explored the busy street life of the commercial districts, and Rowlandson also pictured elegant places of leisure, though not without a marked tendency to humour and satire. Work on London's docksides and wharves was also a common theme, as were broader views of London's busy waterways and bridges. Topographical depictions of famous buildings and squares, especially documenting improvements of the Regency period, also formed a substantial category, but the major innovation was the panorama: the vast circular view of the capital seen from a central high point, exhibited for long periods in specially constructed buildings. Finally, Hawes itemises what he calls 'distant prospects of the metropolis', the most popular of which was the view of London from Greenwich Hill. In this format, the city lies in the lowered, middle and far distance, bathed in light which only allows major landmarks to stand out. An entirely separate foreground, if not actually rural, then certainly pastoral, is dotted with strolling fashionable couples, or game animals, in a rustic but regulated parkland. One of the best known of these, *London* (Tate Gallery), by Joseph Mallord William Turner (1775–1851) was painted in 1809 and engraved for the *Liber Studiorum* in 1811. It would, as a result, have had a wide circulation and been available as a model for artists outside London.

London was not the only town or city to feature in Georgian townscape painting, according to Hawes, who includes drawings, paintings and water-colours of Edinburgh, Bath, Oxford, Cambridge, Monmouth and York, for example. The industrial cities and towns of the Midlands and the North receive some attention, Hawes argues, but mostly from what he calls minor artists. Turner, however, made paintings of Nottingham and New-castle, but it was only in his 1816 painting of Leeds, a 'superb panoramic view' (Hawes, p. 112), that industrial aspects were featured. Hawes calls this last work 'one of the richest images in British art of a sprawling industrial town in full operation' (p. 112). At this point, Hawes falls back upon canonical art history, positioning Turner as the exception and con-cluding: 'As observed previously, few major works by major artists of the Romantic era deal with specifically industrial scenes in the modern sense (i.e., factories, machinery, etc.), a subject largely left to lesser artists, and generally handled in the medium of prints' (p. 112). Subscribing to this evaluation, Hawes cannot go on to consider that wealth of material which alone can provide access to the degree of response to, and interest in, the emergent towns and cities of the industrialising North.

Nonetheless, Hawes's paper does confirm that there was a variety of models for representing towns and cities in the early nineteenth century, and that these formats could and did handle commercial activity and the bustle of work, as well as celebrating the architectural splendours and noble prospects of urban spaces. In this chapter, we argue against the con-tention that inherited artistic conventions placed a restraint upon the representation of northern industrial towns and cities. We shall consider instead the ways in which these modalities were reworked in specific con-ditions, and to what effect. Our major purpose will be to explore what the resulting representations were about, and what meanings were produced with and for them at the time of their initial production. We shall ask why and for whom they were made, what effects they had in shaping under-standing of the new forms of social life and work associated with these places, and what political and ideological contests determined the range of meanings and effects of the images. To examine this, it is necessary to criticise the simplistic sense in which most previous writers in art history have considered the city as merely a place, a location, a set of buildings, and at best a collection of representative types. It is also necessary to interrogate what is only chaotically expressed by the term 'industrial city'.

The discursive city: urbanisation and capitalism in contemporary debates

The issue of the city in the nineteenth century was a question of the meanings of new forms of social life, and these were bitterly contested. A mass of written and visual texts was produced, which constituted what the city or town life meant to those whose lives and social relations, habits and ideologies were being shaped by the new forms of production, exchange and consumption characteristic of the new social and economic order we know as industrial capitalism. Debates about the city were debates about capitalism, political economy, social regulation and, of course, class relations. Representations of the city or town were indelibly ideological in the sense of struggling to define an historical process from partial and interested points of view, stressing some aspects, evading others, and employing varying and incompatible rhetorics about 'great wens' (Cobbett) or the advance of modern civilisation (Kay) and individual liberty (Macaulay). The city was the subject of a raging controversy which shifted over the century, as the social system which produced it became more and more entrenched and resistance less imaginable.[11] There emerged a complex pattern of discourses – Tory, Whig, Anglican, Nonconformist. The debate was not about a place, but about a process – urbanisation – which brought in its wake massive and highly visible social problems. It also generated new kinds of analysis of the cities, from statistical enquiries to impressionistic investigative journalism. Urbanisation under capitalism was a process punctuated by dramatic economic fluctuations, which were damaging to the progress of bourgeois groups and devastating for the working populations congregated in the industrial towns. The proletariat and the bourgeoisie had come into existence in an antagonistic relation with one another, and both in opposition to traditional political and economic authority. In that complex class formation, intensified, though not occasioned, by urbanisation, the city became the object of bitter debate about new forms of social regulation, government, social control and political power. Furthermore, the rapid increase in the population of cities incited widespread concern with newly formulated social problems, such as vice, disease, mortality, disorder, irreligion and, crucially, pauperism.[12] These debates were also complicated by the new gender relations which were in process of construction, and which produced an acute preoccupation with sexuality. The much used conception of morality in these discourses must be seen to articulate capitalist demands for a disciplined work-force. It can also be seen in relation to the regulation and positioning of women. Commentary on these issues came not so much from politicians and economists as from the newly specialised professionals, made prominent by the emergence of this new domain of public concern, 'the social', as Donzelot has termed it.[13]

It may be useful to identify some of these discourses in which the city signified the historically shifting debate about capitalism, in order to recognise the field of meanings in which the visual representations we shall analyse may also have functioned, and to which they may have contributed. At one end of the spectrum, the city was represented as a modern-day hell – for instance, in the writings of the Tory poet, Robert Southey (1774–1843). In *Letters from England,* he stigmatised Birmingham as a place of infernal noise and infernal sights, occupying people in infernal employments, which so deracinated them that there was a fearful danger of social disorder and sexual demoralisation. The country is implied as an opposing heaven of paternalistic and hierarchial social harmony. 'It may be well for England when her cities decrease and her villages multiply and grow; and there shall be fewer streets and more cottages.'[14] In opposing Southey, the Whig historian and politician, Thomas Babington Macaulay (1800–59) offered his support of the factory system in terms of its creating a city wherein liberty, freedom and progress flourished and were embodied. His rhetoric dismissed Southey's doom-laden imagery as 'myth', by arguing that the 'facts' (for example, comparative mortality statistics) were evidence of the better life led in the towns.[15]

The growth of conurbations spawned new social problems related to congestion and increasing population, and these were increasingly subject to such statistical and investigative analysis. Some writers, such as Sir James Kay (later Kay-Shuttleworth) (1804–77), argued, like Macaulay, that civilisation was promoted by the unfettered development of commerce and the factory system, but nonetheless recognised 'evils affecting the working classes' associated with its development. These were represented, however, as merely pathological, 'evidence of a disease' whose solution lay in sanitary regulation.[16] By the later 1840s, there was a significant shift in opinion. As the capitalist system became more entrenched, its problems were subject to more extensive investigation. But liberals such as Edwin Chadwick (1800–90), author of *Report on the Sanitary Condition of the Labouring Population of Great Britain* (1842), represented what Kay saw as incidental disease as a more deadly disorder (the term signifying both a pathological and a social dysfunction), threatening the manufacturing system as a whole. In Chadwick's text therefore, there is an ideological conflation of sanitary, moral and political concerns, which displaces the debate about capitalism itself to the necessity to ameliorate its destructive effects and its tendency to foster sexual degeneration and physical weakness in a disaffected working class.

In *The Condition of the English Working Class in 1844* (1845), Friedrich Engels (1820–95) produced a powerful indictment of the social system generated by industrial capitalism,[17] and an image of the modern industrial city in terms of a vicious class war. In his chapter, 'The Great Towns', he describes how the commercial centre of Manchester, with its offices and warehouses linked by the new roads to the pleasant suburban homes of the upper and middle classes, functioned so that the belts of often adjacent working-class slums were hidden from the view of those upper and middle classes. To overcome this lack of visibility and therefore of awareness, the writer entered these screened-off districts and penetrated the courtyards and back alleys. Thus the text offers a reading of the social geography and spatial relations of the great towns which exposes the endemic conflict and exploitation of their social relations, while noting how the very same processes worked to mask the conflict and segregate the classes.

The writer repeatedly expresses a need to defend himself against accusations of exaggeration; he exclaims that words fail to convey the filth, the stench, the dilapidation of districts and houses unfit for human habitation. The text thus acutely exposes the difficulties of finding adequate linguistic forms through which to represent the horror the writer experienced at close quarters, while being able at the same time to relate that horror to its social causes in the modern industrial system and in class conflict.

One notable device used in this text is the artistic convention which hitherto governed the perception and the understanding of the great city as site of labour and wealth. The chapter on the great towns opens with the rhetorical device of approaching London up the Thames, verbally recreating the distant prospect which we have discussed above.[18] The text imagines a traveller filled with wonder at the sight of London's docks and busy waterways, but once the traveller is drawn closer and has tramped the pavements and mingled with the populace, he or she realises the human cost on which the commercial or industrial greatness is secured for the few. Thence, using the habits and language of investigative enquiry and statistical analysis, the text breaks the illusion created by distance to force the reader to confront what both the class-divided geography and traditional artistic conventions struggle to 'keep out of sight'.[19]

The meanings produced in and for diverse representational strategies articulated not only the interests of competing classes, but also the competing power positions within the dominant social groups and fractions. This was further fragmented by political conflicts and religious differences, which divided the traditional and emergent power blocs internally. For example, in an article on the agitation for factory reform in the early 1830s, with regard especially to the employment of children, J. T. Ward reports a Tory meeting at which a banner was prominently displayed. According to the *Leeds Intelligencer* for 13 December 1832, the banner showed 'a view of Messrs. Marshall's mill in Water Lane in a snow-storm on a winter's morning, with several poor decrepit and half-naked factory children trudging in a shivering attitude through the snow; on the picture were painted the words, "A Scene in Water Lane at five o'clock in the morning".'[20] In ignorance of the specific conditions of its production and use, such an image could easily be cited as yet one more historically unplaced genre scene exhibiting some social concern in the manner of Johnson or the Nadel and Schwarzbach collection. On the other hand, it could be appropriated politically, and read as a radical working-class or socialist protest against factory conditions and exploiting capitalists. The evidence indicates its use in the momentary Tory–Radical alliance for factory legislation, which was rigorously opposed by prominent manufacturers such as John Marshall, and the Whig Liberal campaign with the Macaulayan rhetoric of 'real facts and figures'.[21]

Edward Baines, a leading Leeds figure in the 'let-alone' policy, and author of the *History of the Cotton Manufacture in Great Britain* (1835), cites a weighing and measuring exercise used to refute the allegations that factory life was inimical to the health of factory children, who were said to be stunted and weakly. A sample of factory boys was weighed and measured, and the results compared with those from children not thus employed, to prove a slight difference, often in the factory children's favour. After a display of such statistics to counter the foolish and unfounded complaints of the meddlers, Baines concludes:

> These obvious truths, so nearly approaching truisms, would not have been presented to my readers, if they had not been absolutely forgotten by many of the declaimers on factory labour, who have thought it sufficient to collect a few instances of deformity and injury out of nearly half a million work people . . . and have leaped to the conclusion that their labour was dreadfully pernicious.[22]

This contest offers a view of two distinct rhetorics at work, one utilising the pathos of the child in the cold, evoked pictorially through a tradition of genre scenes of the rural poor, and the other disdaining emotional address in favour of the political economist's faith in the evidence of statistical tables. Baines's text is itself illustrated, and the scenes of factory work suggest the deployment of a pictorial form appropriate to that clear faith in the factory system. But the methods used and the manner of representation are clearly recognisable as representation and as rhetoric. In an engraving of power loom weaving, for instance (Figure 8), clean, linear steel-engraving techniques give precision to the major elements – the machinery which appears to work quietly and cleanly, the lack of atmospheric shading allowing the impression of light, open, airy spaces, clear of dust or pollution. The interior is punctuated by a careful disposition of graceful, healthy, well-dressed and coiffured and pleasantly active workers, properly supervised. They are neither toiling nor slacking, but are comfortably engaged in undemanding but skilled tasks.

The banner and these engravings indicate the highly politicised sites of representation of the industrial scene in terms of both localised and national political battles at specific historical moments. By the later 1830s and the 1840s, the debates about factory conditions, fuelled by liberals like Chadwick, by critics like Engels and by the official factory commissions, had transformed the common territory so that reform was accepted as necessary. The rhetoric of statistical evidence and objective research was used by every side in the shifting arguments about political economy and the factory system.

Visions of old Manchester and the Improvement Act, 1821

Even images which seem to fall directly into traditional categories, such as topographical scenes of gracious buildings, can be shown to inhabit this complex ideological space. Hugh Broadbent has drawn attention to several major publications of views of Manchester in the 1820s, for example J. H. James's *Views in Lithography of Old Halls etc. in Manchester and the Vicinity* (thirty plates; 1821–5) and Roger's and Fowler's *Manchester Edifices* (fifteen copperplate engravings; 1818–25). Broadbent is responsible for a facsimile reprint of the prestigious publication by Messrs. D. and P. Jackson, *Views of the Ancient Buildings in Manchester* by John Ralston, of 1823–5. These plates are dedicated to the Boroughreeve, Constables and Commissioners acting under the Manchester Streets Improvement Act. This was an Act of Parliament of July 1821, which had empowered seventy-two commissioners under the chairmanship of Thomas Fleming to widen Market Street in the main commercial district of Manchester. According to the Preamble to the Act, Market Street, 'the principal thoroughfare of the town, is very narrow and inconvenient, and is in its present state dangerous for the persons and carriages passing through the same, and the trade and commerce of the said town have been much obstructed and injured'.[23] There was intense competitiveness between the new towns and cities of the North, and the development of adequate trading, marketing and commercial facilities were increasingly demanded by the business and industrial communities. The job of widening Market Street was a massive undertaking, which took twelve years to complete and cost the vast sum of £232,925 14s 0d.

The large prints effectively celebrate the small and intimate trading community of an earlier era of town life. Even Plate 2 (Figure 9), showing Market Day, depicts a well-disciplined crowd, keeping close to well-spaced stalls, while the large open space of the street is carefully dotted with select groups of traders, shoppers, even a mother and child. Plate 4 (Figure 10), a view down Market Street to its narrowest point (admittedly only five yards across) does give a distant view of a packed and crowded scene, but so sketchily that its interest is displaced by the detailed and spacious foreground, where vehicles could easily pass without danger to pedestrians. The plates show the street as a place where many different social groups encounter one another without disturbance. Elegant ladies chat to top-hatted gentlemen, well-dressed working women with shawls, bonnets and large baskets clutch children's hands, and some ladies walk alone. There are also traders, barrow-boys, the odd urchin throwing stones at a dog, and carts making deliveries at shops whose names and advertising enhance the aura of the place with its intriguing links with far-off countries. One plate shows the beginning of the demolition, but even that is tidied away into a corner and seems unnaturally restrained and unobtrusive. Thus, despite the necessity for progress, to facilitate commerce, nostalgia for an earlier stage of economic, social and urban life could be gratified by the pictorial transformation of what was represented by the Act as a noisome, inconvenient and overcrowded thoroughfare into an ordered and picturesquely attractive vision of old Manchester, where men and women of different classes mingled as they went about their business and their pleasure. The subscribers' list indicates a varied audience, but it is significant that the newly emergent social and economic figures of the Manchester bourgeoisie are amongst those who consume images of the very sites for the demolition of which they are actively responsible. The Boroughreeve and Constables head the list of subscribers to the Ralston plates, and there are at least twenty commissioners listed amongst them. This indicates the need for caution against the crude expectation of pictures hoped for and not found by the authors discussed at the beginning of this chapter, who privilege the artists' sensibilities as an index of social attitudes, but ignore the conditions of cultural production. Vital information about these conditions can be obtained through an assessment of the consumption of images.

Improvement and respectability in Leeds in the 1820s

Although there was no clearance in Leeds on the scale of Market Street in Manchester, a similar impulse led to a massive building boom in the commercial districts in the 1820s. Briggate was one of the major arteries of Leeds trading, but passage was restricted by the Middle Row, composed of a Market Cross (1619), the Old Shambles (*c.* 1615) and the Moot Hall, built in 1710–11 at a cost of £210. Two paintings, one by Thomas Taylor, known through an engraving by Charles Heath (Figure 11), and the other by Joseph Rhodes (1782–1855) (Figure 12) take the scene before the Moot Hall as their subject. They invite comparison with Ralston's views, apparently capturing in picturesque mode the lively interest in Georgian town life. The Moot Hall was a major landmark, with its statue of Queen Anne by Carpenter and a prominent clock. The upper storeys housed a courthouse for judicial sessions and corporation business, while the lower parts were occupied by butchers' shops. In Taylor's painting, the lighting and the angle from which the building is presented emphasise the pleasing but well-worn Palladian façade, and allow the building to rise above the mundane activities of traders such as the fishmongers and butchers congregating on its forecourt. This viewpoint creates a vista up the side of the building, which, although the street appears congested, sweeps away to a distant point and creates a grand impression of space. The food markets on the right of the picture are contrasted with the elegant patrons of the shops on the left. Two women in high fashion converse, prominently occupying the broad pavement. They seem unthreatened by the mingling crowds higher up the street. The picture produces an image of a town centre both functional and elegant, where varied activities are presided over by the monarch in the niche of a building which does not reveal much of the bloody trade carried on within.

Joseph Rhodes's image is by contrast a more troubled and ambiguous view of the same scene. Painted from below and to the right of the Moot Hall, the narrow alley of butchers' shambles becomes highly visible, advertised by an array of bloody carcasses. The perspective of this alley is not a spacious vista, but gives instead the effect of a narrow defile between high and uninteresting cliffs of masonry. Scaffolding and building workers are prominent, producing a sense not so much of improvement as of disorder.

In the forecourt, cattle are herded towards the butchers' shops, and there is no escape for the viewer from the thought that these kine are destined for slaughter, soon to join the other lurid carcasses. The Moot Hall is much defaced by bills and posters stuck to its pillars, and the perspective prevents it from soaring above its surroundings as in Taylor's painting. Here it houses a print shop, at which a woman and a boy are peering. The shops on the left are more detailed and appear mundane and rather curious. A giant knife and fork advertises an ironmonger's premises. Some fashionable women pass down this street, but they cannot be said to occupy it authoritatively. Faceless and attenuated, the figures in this region of the painting are not picturesque, nor are they sufficiently detailed to offer anecdotal or humorous incident illustrative of the scene. The mixture of activities and personnel seems haphazard and is disconcerting. Far from giving a complacent pleasure to the viewer contemplating such a scene of town life, the Rhodes painting creates considerable unease in the viewer about the order and legibility of the place, and about the desirability of belonging to it.

Pressure to improve traffic and moves to reorganise marketing facilities, as well as the erection in 1813 of a Court House, led to the demolition of Middle Row and with it the Moot Hall in 1825. Briggate was opened up, and a new focus for the area was built in the form of the Corn Exchange at the top of Briggate on the corner of the Headrow, at the cost of £12,500. This Corn Exchange and the later building by Cuthbert Broderick (1861) is evidence of the continuing and important role of Leeds as a centre for agricultural goods and commerce. In its colonnaded quadrangle, the Exchange provided space for the sale of corn by sample. In addition, there were warehouses and offices for dealers, a hotel, a tavern and four large shops. All these services are indicative of the range of activities then developing in the new towns and cities, activities which would reshape the character of modern urban centres, and to some extent redefine the city. It was not only the novelty of massive populations congregating to work in factories which marked off the nineteenth-century towns and cities as different from their predecessors. The function of the town as a centre for regular interaction between merchants, traders, dealers and bankers was greatly increased, while the professions, including lawyers and accountants, servicing these business dealings expanded substantially. The buildings erected and celebrated in paintings or prestige engravings were the outward and visible signs of these social processes, which daily constructed and related the emergent groups within the bourgeoisie. Expanding trade and consumership, as well as industry, were important features of the nineteenth-century capitalist economy and its social relations.

The Corn Exchange appears in a range of engravings in this period, including N. Whittock's engraving in a series on new Leeds buildings (Figure 13) published in 1829, J. Greig's painting of 1851 (Figure 14), an undated engraving by Lee (Figure 15) and several woodcuts advertising the neighbouring premises of J. W. Bean, engraver, bookseller and stationer. There is considerable variety in the modes of representation, which exhibit a good deal of licence with perspective and scale. Briggate yawns before the stern, linear presence of the Exchange in the Lee and the Whittock prints. These offer a piazza-like space in which a fashionable array of couples, gentlemen, soldiers and families promenade.[24] The effect is exclusive and elegant, precisely the opposite of that uneasy social mixture and shabbiness which appeared in the Rhodes painting of an older Briggate. Guidebooks of the period attest not to the actual elegance of this new shopping area, however, but to the anxiety of the bourgeoisie about the tone of shops and the commercial districts in Leeds. For example, in *An Historical Guide to Leeds*, published in 1858, the author proudly describes the improvements in the town in recent years, and is pleased to report that the style of shops has improved, yet adds that 'it must be admitted that Leeds is far behind many towns of less importance in the style and order of its retail establishments; and we have fewer streets appropriated for respectable shops'.[25] Briggate, we are told, presents a noble appearance, with its commanding width containing some noble and effective shops, 'but it is much to be regretted that it should be disfigured by so many ugly and insignificant buildings which are a disgrace to the town'.[26] It is certain that shopping areas and thoroughfares were an important aspect of the public image of the town with regard to the pride of its leading citizens, and in competition with other towns and cities. In the 1860s another major street was to be improved, and the plans for Boar Lane elicited intense criticism in the pages of the *Leeds Mercury* of 16 October 1866. The author complained that false economy would deprive the town of the 'only opportunity ever likely to present itself of making the principal thoroughfare of the town a wide and handsome and imposing street, worthy of the wealth of the inhabitants, of the metropolitan character of the borough and of the public spirit which ought to distinguish and in some respects has distinguished our local administration'.[27]

While improvements were usually encouraged, as a means to foster trade, this passage shows how the development of public buildings and spaces advertised, or was thought to advertise, the wealth and taste of leading citizens. Quality meant a new division of types of shops, moving abattoirs and daily food shops out of sight and introducing into the public sphere shops selling goods increasingly required as part of the lifestyle of the enriched bourgeoisie. Women would frequent this part of the public realm of luxury consumership. The stress on respectability is indicative of new anxieties surrounding the appearance of women in a changing public domain.[28] The engravings of Briggate and the Corn Exchange construct the location as respectable, with wide pavements, restrained shops, a select population, claiming the spot as a suitable place for middle-class families and their daughters.

The water-colour by J. Greig, dated 1851 (Figure 14), however, represents Briggate in a different light. Less grandoise, if not bustling, it is certainly a place for more mixed kinds of business and varied social groups. The detailing of the shop-fronts is more clearly picturesque and the figures are almost Hogarthian types. Two well-dressed women chat in the street, but near a tavern entrance, in circumstances that are certainly ambiguous, while more obviously respectable middle-class couples are just visible in the distance, in the light area in front of the Corn Exchange beneath Queen Anne's benevolent gaze.

The presence of the Corn Exchange in the advertisements for J. W. Bean's services as engraver, stationer and bookseller serves to remind us of another site for the production of images of the city – local trade directories and advertisements (Figure 16). Here the stress is on Bean's premises, which remarkably grow in stature beside a diminished Corn Exchange. (Bean's shop appears in the other engravings, but much recessed and slight in scale.) The Corn Exchange serves here as landmark, and as a way to locate an individual trader's shop. But it is interesting to note that even in these advertising images the select quality of those who pass by this site is clearly emphasised, and deemed desirable for the promotion of Bean's business.

Commercial expansion in the public sphere: speculation and identity

One of the forces behind the boom in commercial building in the 1820s in Leeds was the demand to improve the trading and marketing facilties.[29] The pressure for such schemes and the willingness of locals to invest came from a sense of acute competition with rival towns in the district and the aim was to ensure the pre-eminence of Leeds. Many contemporary guidebooks were anxious to stress the advantages of Leeds over nearby towns, with its abundant supply of coal, water, transport and other resources.[30] The majority of projects of this sort in the 1830s were built by private enterprise, with finance being easily and quickly raised from local sources, mostly, according to Kevin Grady's research, from sources classifiable as middle-class (i.e. from merchants and manufacturers, with some contributions from professional and *rentier* groups).[31] The new array of buildings thus erected can be taken as evidence of a burgeoning class-consciousness, an awareness of a community of interests among the diverse and potentially antagonistic fractions of the manufacturing, finance and trading bourgeoisie, a community of interests which could be articulated as well as served by these new buildings. They maintained and improved the commercial interests of the city and its leading economic classes, while advertising through public symbols their wealth and taste.[32] The buildings were therefore aspects of the making of a public culture through which the diverse socio-economic fractions could be incorporated.

Prominent as the frontispiece of *The Stranger's Guide Through Leeds and Its Environs* of 1842 is a picture of the *Commercial Buildings* (drawn by W. Nelson, engraved by H. Cullingworth and Sons of Leeds) (Figure 17). The guide itself claims that the buildings may justly be called 'one of the greatest ornaments of the town and their situation is central and convenient for business'.[33] The first stone was laid on 18 May 1826 by Lupton Dobson, chairman of the subscribers to the unincorporated joint stock company which financed the project, and it was opened on 1 May 1829. It was a venture which became the focal point for commercial activity, yet it was situated at the corner of Park Row and Boar Lane. A large circular vestibule provided a merchants' exchange and regular meeting place for businessmen. In addition, there was a commercial newsroom, a coffee house and restaurant, a concert and meeting hall, offices for solicitors and brokers, a committee room and a fourteen-bedroom hotel. This list illustrates the range of supporting facilities demanded for a growing commercial and trading centre. But when such facilities are housed and used in this central way, they contribute to the practical consolidation of the division of the public world of men and business from the domestic and private spheres, and thus mark the division between an earlier more mixed social, economic and familial system of production and the institutionalised divisions which characterised the nineteenth-century bourgeoisie.[34] An engraving by Rogers after a drawing by N. Whittock, dated 1829, represents the *Commercial Buildings* (Figure 18) in a way which confirms what was still at this date only a general ideological tendency. The space is represented as a masculine domain. The focus of the drawing is the Buildings, in which merchants meet and do business, and this interior purpose is expressed by filling the exterior spaces with well-dressed men, chatting in groups of twos and threes. There are in addition a rider on horseback, a carriage bearing a smart couple, and another strolling down the street. The Buildings stand out in magnificent isolation, proferring a vision of the orderly public business places of bourgeois men. It is useful to compare this kind of image with an engraving by Harwood and M. J. Starling, published in Baines's *History of the Cotton Manufacture of Great Britain* (1835), which represents the Exchange of Manchester (Figure 19). The circular end of the building advances to establish the dominance of the edifice over its surroundings, while in its presence a considerable crowd of formally dressed men of business meet to consult. The scene is somewhat busier than Whittock's view of the Leeds Commercial Buildings, but the tropes are similar. In *Notes of a Tour of the Manufacturing Districts of Lancashire* (1842), W. Cooke Taylor advises the visitor who wishes to form a notion of the character of Manchester to visit the Exchange. 'It is the parliament of the lords of cotton – their legislative assembly – which enacts laws as immutable as those of the Medes and Persians . . .',[35] a particularly striking set of images to celebrate the political and economic significance of this group of men.

The above discussion suggests ways in which drawings or prints, which may appear at first sight as mere topographical records of architectural novelties, function on a more substantial axis of historical meaning. These representations also need to be seen as containing many further layers of meaning for their contemporaries. In addition to the hope of a quick and substantial profit, these buildings represented the civic identity of Leeds to its dominant social groups, who were not only in local rivalry with neighbouring bourgeoisies but who competed with such major industrial towns and cities as Liverpool and Manchester.[36] Civic pride was also served by constructing images of more elaborated views of town centres with a range of new and imposing buildings. The Commercial Buildings function in such a scene engraved by E. Roberts, dated 11 August 1842, by which time the success of the buildings was in some doubt (Figure 20). (By 1849 the place had become shabby and the hotel was closed.) The Commercial Buildings are part of a scene which includes in the foreground the rounded frontage of the Yorkshire District Bank on Bishopgate Street, from where we look up Park Row to the rotunda of the Mixed Cloth Hall (1756–8), and beyond to the Police Office and Court House (1813, built under an Improvement Act of 1809). The print is an attempt at townscape in the tradition of seventeenth-century painting. It is not simple topography. By means of chiaroscuro, the buildings are blended into a unity, and the eye is moved gradually up to the lightest area of the Court House façade. Careful comparison of the scene portrayed with an 1846 Ordnance Survey map of the area throws this view into serious doubt, and reminds us of the constructed character of these representations. The effect is somewhat austere. The imposing and somewhat giantised buildings loom over the groups, which are scattered to fill the empty spaces as so many signs of the town's life. There is no sense of noise or bustle, and the figures form a curious collection of fine ladies and gentlemen strolling by the Commercial Buildings, juxtaposed with humbler folk of a rural type – for example, the man leading the donkey laden with panniers. Recently set down travellers with many trunks talk to a hotel boy, while the stage-coach passes up Park Row. Despite the attempt to integrate the architecture and figures into a townscape scene, the viewer retains a sense of discomfort and disconnectedness; there is a noticeable gulf between the characters in the foreground and the urban bourgeoisie who stay close to their domain. They are those to whom the city belongs, while the other figures, some in fact itinerant, all seem rather provisional elements of what is trying to impress as the elegant city centre of Leeds.[37]

Anxiety, exchange and the Central Markets

The Court House is also represented in the series of engravings drawn by N. Whittock in 1829 (Figure 21). Careful detailing of the architectual appearance of the building, and minimal attention to its setting, suggest a topographical mode, but this format is curiously altered by the inclusion of Rowlandsonesque figures which at points verge on caricature – for instance, the large woman, hands on hips, arguing with a threatening woman in an outsized bonnet. Such incidents would have proliferated in the work of Rowlandson, offering a many-sided and humorous view of town life. What is puzzling in this instance is the sparseness of this population: a family or two, a dandy or two, a carriage and one hand-cart which engages the labours of two faceless men. The attempt to deploy different formats for street scenes which also celebrate major civic improvements, such as the proper housing of judicial officials, leads to an unresolved product. Whittock also drew the *Central Market* (Figure 22), in Duncan Street (built between 1824 and 1827), which was, like the Commercial Buildings, one of the economic and municipal improvements of the 1820s. It offered facilities for butchers and fishmongers in shops around its market hall, which also had stalls for fruit, vegetables and dairy goods. There was also a balcony for a fancy goods bazaar. In all, sixty-seven shops, fifty-six stalls, six offices and a hotel were thus housed. The Whittock image is more pronouncedly reminiscent of Rowlandson's drawings, and equal emphasis falls on the building and the bustle of shoppers outside. Deliveries are made, two soldiers arrest or press-gang a man, while his agitated woman companion is restrained by a third;

respectable ladies window-shop and men meet and shake hands. As a scene of modern life, it provides a bridge between the Georgian humour of Rowlandson and the more anthropological studies later made famous by William Powell Frith in such scenes of modern urban life as *The Railway Station*.[38] Nonetheless, the viewer is kept at a discrete distance from this motley crowd by the band of empty street in the foreground, and the containment of the figures on the pavements in an easily deciphered display of types. The scene bears some comparison with Ralston's sanitised views of Manchester's old Market Street, where pictorially constructed order makes acceptable the greater mixing of the social classes.

Joseph Rhodes drew a scene of Duncan Street, known through an engraving by S. Staers published in J. Heaton's *Walks Through Leeds* (1835) (Figure 23). Here the viewer is placed as a pedestrian with the *Central Market* looming up on the right. It is daytime, and the figures throw clear shadows, but the effect is somewhat eerie. There are few people – a maid with a basket, two older women wrapped in shawls, two gentlemen on foot, and a horse rider, and some other ghostly figures in the distance. The building becomes silent and brooding, and the isolation of the figures gives rise to speculation relating to the anxiety that the confrontation with strangers in the public street generated in the dwellers in expanding towns and cities.

These few examples indicate a range of effects produced by the use of the different conventions available for picturing urban sites. It is hard to locate the purposes of many of the engravings with the precision possible in relation to the Ralston lithograph publication. But there are certain general conditions here too. The combination of high ideas and commercial functions is expressed in J. D. Heaton's lecture to the Leeds Philosophical and Literary Society on 6 January 1854, on the building of Town Halls.

> The municipal buildings about to be erected by the burgesses of Leeds, besides the primary object of furnishing convenient accommodation to their officers in the transaction of public business, are intended to present an appearance worthy of the wealth and property of the town, to show that in the ardour of mercantile pursuits the inhabitants of Leeds have not omitted to cultivate the perception of the beautiful and a taste for the fine arts, and to serve as a lasting monument of their public and generous pride in the possession of their municipal privileges.[39]

It has, however, also been possible to identify from analysis of the images a certain ambivalence surrounding the new public spaces, of which the buildings are the sign and occasion. Shaping what can and cannot be shown, and how figures relate to each other and to the public space there are underlying doubts. Who should be pictured in these spaces and how? To whom do such spaces belong? Anxiety is also registered about the public mingling of social classes – an anxiety which would grow as the developing political language of class forced a new kind of recognition of people on the streets as members of different, and even antagonistic classes, and not just as representative types of particular trades or districts. Was it possible in the 1830s and the 1840s to sustain against the growing economic and political conflicts a sense of a working community, which could be built around joint experiences such as shopping, when that very activity was in the process of being stratified? What are the implications when the community imagined pictorially is constructed in relation to vast commercial enterprises and investments, or expanding consumerism fed by new shopping centres, bazaars and arcades, full of luxury goods? It is striking that apart from the limited number of men delivering or portering, the class mix that is visible in these pictures rarely includes the male working class. Men of business and men of leisure can be seen in the streets, chaperoned bourgeois ladies, and working women (often working for the former as maids) and traders provide a highly selective section of the economically active population of the industrial town or city. Exchange, not production, is the visible activity, and the images of the city confirm Marx's analysis of fetishism of the market under capitalism.[40]

Factory production and the sublime

More problematic is the investigation of images of industrial places – the factory and the foundry. In some examples we have found, the factories are represented primarily as buildings of architectural interest, rather than places of production. In 1840, Marshall's of Leeds opened a new flax mill, Temple Mills, in Marshall Street. Built by Ignatius Bonomi, the building formed a massive pile, and was in a style which was a bizarre imitation of Egyptian temple architecture. In a print from c. 1850, the building is seen from the south, and appears as an isolated edifice in an empty street (Figure 24). Another print, also of c. 1850, looking north, offers a different perspective, locating the Marshall mill in a busy street scene with smoking chimneys, massive warehouses, wagons laden with stock, and a few bourgeois in conversation near to a flower-seller or beggar woman, seated by the railings of the factory (Figure 25). But there is little sense of the factory's own activities. One of the wonders of the building was its vast interior, lit by sixty-six glass domes across a vast floor space, while the ceiling was held up on hollow columns through which the compartmentalised roof was drained. An engraving of this interior, dated 1843, creates an impression of airiness and spaciousness and the orderly attention to efficient machinery by well-fed and tidy women workers. Such an emphasis must be read in the context of bitter arguments about the conditions of factory work and its effect on the health and welfare of factory workers, in which issues of ventilation, space and physical health were constant points of contention. The battles over the reform of the factory system provide one ideological field in which such representations of factories existed.

In a guide to *Manchester As It Is* (1839), B. Love informs the visitor of the difficulties of gaining access to the interiors of great factories in the town, and advises the reader who wants to behold the wonders of the factory system to 'content himself with viewing the exterior of these immense hives of industry'.[41] Love identifies an interesting cluster of mills, situated in Chorlton-upon-Medlock, leading out of Oxford Street, which includes a large pile known as Oxford Road Twist Co. Mill. This was part of a huge complex of factories, which included the cotton mills of Messrs. Birley & Co., and Love provides a detailed description – not of the exterior appearance or interior layout, but of the capital which is invested in it.

> The number of hands employed by this firm is 1,600, whose wages annually amount to the sum of £40,000. The amount of moving power is equivalent to the labour of 397 horses. The number of spindles in the mill is about 80,000. The annual consumption of raw cotton is about 4,000,000 lbs weight! The annual consumption of coal is 8,000 tons. It will perhaps excite surprise in someone unacquainted with the nature of machinery when informed that the annual consumption of oil, for the purpose of oiling the machinery is about 5,000 gallons; and the consumption of tallow, for the same purpose, is 50 cwt.[42]

These figures are not just facts by means of which to describe the factory. Their impact derives from their magnitude, a term which, as Nicholas Taylor has pointed out in his article, 'The Awful Sublimity of the Victorian City', reminds us of the aesthetic category of the Sublime.[43] The 'Sublime' was defined by the eighteenth-century philosopher Edmund Burke[44] as the category by which aesthetic emotion is stirred though an encounter with pain, danger or terror. The qualities which incite such reactions and constitute the Sublime are listed as astonishment, terror, obscurity, power, vastness, infinity, succession, uniformity, magnitude in building, and difficulty. It is easy to see why Taylor argues that the Sublime must be recognised as one of the major categories of nineteenth-century architecture, particularly in relation to the major projects of the age: warehouses, factories, viaducts, gasworks, lunatic asylums, county gaols, railway termini and tunnels. Two engravings of Manchester factories can be looked at in the light of this contention: the Oxford Road Twist Co. and the Cotton Factories on Union Street (drawn by Harwood and Austen respectively, both engraved by McGahey (Figures 26 and 27)). The code of the pictorial

Sublime is deployed to construct a visual representation of the factories to match the numerical ecstasy of the guidebook. In both cases, the factory buildings are monumental. Exaggerated contrast in scale is created by the inclusion of dwarfed examples of traditional building, the rows of shops, including a pawnbroker's in the former and the old factory complex in the latter. Contrast of dark and light also heightens the awe and terror associated with the massive blocks of the factories, with their rows of regular windows, uniform and apparently infinite. There are a few figures in the landscape, but none obviously associated with the enterprises. Indeed, in the former, their appearance and transport seems quite rural, while there is a pointed contrast between the steam-powered factory and the wind-powered or horse-drawn barges on the canal in the picture of the Union Street mills. What goes on behind the windows is not pictured or reflected by an exterior sign. This absence can be heightened by contrasting such depictions of factories with those of warehouses. Another N. Whittock print celebrates the Aire and Calder warehouse in Leeds (1829) (Figure 28), in the manner of the Thames-side scenes of late eighteenth-century London. Workers are visibly working. Trade is there to be seen as the goods are handled, and the rigging of ships with their active seamen provides a sense of energy and activity for the scene, a sign of commercial movement and wealth. In *Walks through Leeds,* published by J. Heaton in 1835, attention is drawn to the picturesque qualities of this scene:

> ... a little below the bridge are the WAREHOUSES of the Aire and Calder company. Those erected in the years 1827–8, on the Northern Bank of the river, by their immense size, command the attention of every stranger, and before the completion of this perambulation, we shall have the pleasure of suggesting to the sketcher a station from which we think they have a very striking effect (p. 98).

Pictorial conventions did not inhibit the depiction of factories, but the meanings of factories are not easily represented within the available repertory. Places such as Marshall's Egyptian Temple Mills and certain warehouses, such as that by Alfred Waterhouse for Binyon and Fryer, Chester Street, Manchester (1855) (City of Manchester Art Galleries) were of sufficient architectural curiosity to invite topographical record. However, the factory could only be treated as a building. The Sublime here offered some means to transcend the topographical in the treatment of architecture. But with its repertoire of vastness and awe, striking contrasts of human frailty and stony permanence, its dramatic use of chiaroscuro, it could hardly convey what the proponents of the factory system saw as its glorious contribution to wealth, trade, progress and civilisation, without introducing a sinister element of threat and inhumanity. This does not suggest unwillingness to handle the subject. It indicates that the field of meanings of which the factory was a sign could only with difficulty find adequate forms of representation – adequate judged by the varying criteria of conflicting ideological positions towards industrial capitalism.

The industrial presence and the agricultural scene

One engraving by J. Tingle after a drawing by T. Allom, which is published in Baines's *History of the Cotton Manufacture in Great Britain*, shows the premises of Swainson, Birley and Co., near Preston, Lancashire (Figure 29). The factory, lying in sunshine, is situated in the most distant plane. Between the spectator and the industrial site is agricultural land, through which a cowherd moves his cows; two smaller buildings, deeply shadowed, add interest to the middle ground. One seems to be some sort of factory, the other perhaps a farm or cottage. Smoke rises from the chimneys of both these industrial and domestic centres of production. The factories are almost set into the landscape, as if they were a harmonious part of the country, or on a continuum with it. It is a surprising image in one sense, since the contrast between city and country formed a major trope within the political debates of the early nineteenth century about the factory system and the social life brought in the wake of industrial capitalism.

Indeed, the couplet 'city and country' formed one of the major axes across which meanings were articulated about the social, economic and political developments of the early nineteenth century. The polarity has, as Raymond Williams has shown, a long and varied history. It was a critical formula in the negotiation of the new industrial city, and in the associated changes in the agricultural sector in the context of the new mode of production.[45] Representations of towns and cities, or such urban features as factories, require to be read across a complex map of historical shifts, new economic relations and unsettled meanings. It is crucial to remember, of course, that many industrial installations were built in rural areas, dependent as many initially were on water power and transport. Areas such as Lancashire therefore offered visitors a complex combination of industrial, urban and rural possibilities, which generated tension in their representation within existing formats. In his volume of letters reporting *Notes on a Tour in the Manufacturing Districts of Lancashire*, 1841, W. Cooke Taylor wrote:

> How a painter would have enjoyed the sight which broke upon my waking eyes this morning! To my right is one of the tributaries of the Irwell, winding through the depths of a richly wooded and precipitous valley, or rather ravine; . . . Before

me, on the extreme level on which I stand, and which I may describe as a promontory of the table-land surrounded by valleys, is the Hall in the Wood, memorable for having been the residence of Crompton, inventor of the spinning jenny, and to me scarcely less interesting as one of the most perfect specimens remaining of the domestic architecture of our Saxon ancestors, and of their descendents the Franklins or old gentlemen of England. . . . Beyond is the hill on which a great part of the busy town of Bolton is built. The intervening valley is studded with factories and bleach-works. Thank God, smoke is rising from the lofty chimneys of most of them! for I have not travelled thus far without learning by many a painful illustration that the absence of smoke from a factory chimney indicates the quenching of the fire on many a domestic hearth, want of employment to many a willing labourer, and want of bread to many an honest family.[46]

The passage, quoted at length, is an important combination of many distinct threads. To convey what he sees, Cooke Taylor conjures up a painter, thus preparing his readers for a picturesque view, complete with wooded ravines. Yet that prospect looks across to a distant industrial town, over a landscape which is not agricultural but industrial, and which is in turn conjoined to the site of the residence of the old English gentry – the English 'who never bowed their heads to the Norman yoke, and who refused to adopt customs imported from the Continent'.[47] The smoking chimneys are decipherable signs within a highly specific context of economic fluctuations and social unrest, resulting from economic depression.

The countryside could be viewed, as in this case, in multiple registers – historical, pictorial, political, economic. There was no clear-cut division for Cooke Taylor between agricultural and industrial aspects, because of the presence of factories in the fields and towns as part of a landscape prospect. There were, however, other crucial ways in which a shift in the interdependence between the rural and the urban in this period undermined or at least revised the meanings and purposes of the traditional antinomy 'city and country'. In 1830, William Cobbett, the journalist and political radical, published a collected edition of tours of inspection of the English country, called *Rural Rides*. He looked for and found signs of the erosion of the traditional economic and social life of the agricultural population by the ever-growing and devouring presence of the Wens, chief amongst which was London, the Great Wen. One of his major complaints was the way in which the towns, and especially the growing industrial centres, absorbed the resources of the countryside. 'Thus it is, every good thing is literally driven or carried away out of the country'.[48] People starve, he claims, while the fatted animals in the fields are sent to keep the growing populations of the towns and cities. 'How long will these people starve in the midst of plenty?'[49]

Cobbett's findings relate to the process whereby the traditionally fairly stable relationship between town and country was disturbed, as industrial towns grew massively in size and population. Cobbett was observing the cost to the rural population of the extraction from the countryside of the raw materials out of which the new cities were built. In this period the towns encroached spatially on rural areas, but also caused disruption of patterns of rural production and settlement. In the first place, the country provided human materials for the towns. People were drawn in from the surrounding villages, or from further afield, particularly from Ireland, to work in the cities' industries. Living conditions were so poor and insanitary, working conditions so hazardous and hard, that in the city mortality outstripped the ability of the population to reproduce itself. Along with the population shift caused by the absolute growth of the cities, yet more people were drawn into the city to make up the shortfall in reproduction. A member of the medical profession in Leeds, Robert Baker (1804–80) conducted surveys and collected evidence of the life-sapping power of the industrial city and its mills and campaigned for improved sanitation and housing and limitation of hours for factory workers. According to his figures in 1858, the chances of living to the age of seventy varied in Leeds between occupations, from one in nine for gardeners or one in thirty-one for saddlers to one in 698 for mill workers.[50] The unprecedented concentration of population that the cities represented demanded a secondary extraction of resources from the countryside. Food was needed to feed the city dwellers. Foodstuffs were brought in to be marketed directly, or for individual retailers to process and sell, or, increasingly, for large-scale processing in industrial concerns. Beer, for example, was being made on an industrial scale in Leeds from the 1820s, when Tetley's breweries were set up in Hunslet.[51]

The countryside was also the source of raw materials for the physical expansion of cities. Building stone from streets and walls, clay for brickmaking, drainage and sanitary pipes, and chimney pots, iron ore for iron structures such as bridges and iron-framed factory buildings, and timber for floors, rafters, doors and windows are just some of the materials that would be hewn from nearby sites to produce the sheer bulk of the buildings that made the city. Wherever possible local materials would be used to minimise transport costs.[52] This was a continuing process as the city spread.[53] Fields at the edges of the city were bought up and used as building plots – the pattern of new streets following old agricultural boundaries, and the sequence of development depending partly on what estates came on to the market.[54] The city, finally, demanded raw materials, not just for construction but for industrial activity. Again local sources of clays, coal, iron, minerals for dyeing and agricultural products such as skins, fat and wool were vital.

The economic relationship between city and country was not one of opposition as the traditional dichotomy had it but of interdependence. It was not however a balanced nor a stable interdependence. The industrial city continued to play the marketing function for agriculture that the pre-industrial town had done. But added to this were new demands on and disruptions of the rural economy. Political struggles developed between sections of the urban bourgeoisie and different groups of country gentry and rural clothiers. The period saw worsening rural poverty. There was an increase in industrial activity in country areas for the purposes of mineral extraction, and a fluctuating relationship between the urban and rural stages of textile manufacture. Those stages carried out by the small masters in the villages round Leeds and Manchester were driven now into increased production and now into a declining and subsidiary role by the dynamic and organisation of industry in the city.

During the course of this transformation, any image using the format of the distant prospect of a city had necessarily to deal with a combination of changed rural and urban elements, as does the engraving after Allom of the Swainson, Birley and Co. factory (Figure 29). Cobbett's writings alert us to the fact that the countryside was not invariably seen as the undisturbed repository of the good, the agreeable and the natural. Cooke Taylor's pious gratitude for the smoke emitted by factory chimneys, and the range of images we have surveyed of streets and buildings, often articulating pride and satisfaction in the grandeur and prosperity of the modern city, demonstrate that the city was by no means always considered or represented as a sphere of vice, dirt and disruption in opposition to the country. Nonetheless the city/country dichotomy was a persistent and powerful construct. In various ways it acted as a major structuring device for the prospects and overall views of Manchester and Leeds that we will go on to consider. In analysing a selection of visual representations in which city and country elements are juxtaposed, it is possible to map several distinctive approaches and their effects.

A distant prospect: assimilation or marginalisation

There are images in which the city is almost totally assimilated into the countryside, and in this case it is presented within the conventions of landscape painting. Here, at one extreme of the range of images available, the presence of the city is scarcely registered as non-rural. Such images could be construed as entailing the suppression of the negative connotations of the city, and the substitution of the positive qualities attributed to the country. An example of such a picture is the engraving by John Landseer after William Marshall Craig's *Manchester From Mount Pleasant* (1802) (Figure 30). The city's presence is rendered no more disruptive than a village and its church over the brow of the hill, or a cottage whose smoking chimney signals habitation and comfort. The interlocking curves of the hillside, trees and clouds confine the prospect of Manchester into a small area in the centre of the picture. The uniformity of the ranks of chimneys is identified with the natural uniformity of the closely-packed ranks of trees immediately in front of them, and these partially mask the beginnings of the town. Throughout the picture rhymes are set up between the man-made and the natural. The wooden fence in the middle distance consists of a series of man-made verticals, but it follows the curve of the landscape, and the vertical fence is resolved in the foreground into a slanting stile that echoes the graceful angle of the tree. The picture maintains an ambiguity between fence-post and sprouting tree stump. What we do see of the city is not identifiably industrial. The chimneys are those of dwellings, not of factories, and are construed as a multiplication of the cosy farmstead in the middle ground. The sunshine illuminates hillside, cloud and city alike. It dissolves the forms of the buildings into the distant glow of a classical vista. Such a picture could be taken as evidence of the Nadel and Schwarzbach thesis that artists avoided the city as a subject, or Johnson's argument that artists were reluctant to engage with industrial sites, but we will see that the same landscape formula, where rows of buildings or ranks of chimneys and steeples are substituted for distant fields or hills in a landscape, and the same structuring divide between town and country, can be used to acknowledge the city's presence and to offer various kinds of access to it.

Containing the industrial in a rural frame

In an engraving after Henry Burn's *View of Leeds from near the Halifax New Road* (1846) (Figure 31) the industrial nature of the city is not denied. In the centre of the picture, the many-storeyed warehouses and factories are shown closely packed together. The forms of the factory chimneys are distinct, and clearly attached to individual premises. The pattern of light and shade in this section of the picture places an area of shadow over the central group of factories, so that these buildings, which rise on a slight hill, appear blackened and almost blot out a church tower which can be made out on the lower ground behind them. The disturbing potential of this part of the picture is neutralised when the whole scene is taken into account. The viewer is situated in a pleasant rural vantage point. A calm group of cows on the left, a smocked farm-hand leaning contemplatively on his stick, a woman carrying a tub of water on her head in a balanced statuesque pose, a plump child accompanying her, and slightly further away, a group of farm labourers passing the final forkfuls of hay onto a heavy-laden cart, all impart an atmosphere of restfulness and well-being to the scene. From this vantage point the city is distanced and takes on a quality of fantasy. The darkened mound of factories could as well be a medieval castle on the hill. It serves to install the rustic figures in a feudal framework. They take on the character of a loyal and happy peasantry. A factory-owning viewer could position himself in the picture as lord of the castle in his surrounding lands. A Whig landlord devoted to improvements in agriculture and campaigning for the repeal of the corn laws could see the town as the seat of a neighbouring ally. A Tory landlord could see it as a mercantile centre guaranteeing the sale of his produce, or alternatively as a slightly menacing but distant rival landowner's castle. Extrapolating in this way from features of the picture that would not have been explicitly recognised, we can arrive at a range of positions from which such an image of the city could make satisfactory sense. All these hypothetical viewpoints have in common a historical transposition which makes economic relationships seem permanent and which posits a fixed boundary and relationship between the rural and the non-rural.

The Burn *View of Leeds* can be grouped together with other views of Leeds and Manchester that similarly employ a notion of rural peace and permanence, and a clear and settled distinction between town and country, to make possible an unthreatening view of the city. Joseph Rhodes's *Leeds from the Meadows* (n.d.) is one example (Figure 32). This oil painting has a clearly painted foreground of flanking trees and bushes, fields, cows and two rustic figures in strong greens, ochres and russets. The view of Leeds occupies the horizon and is reduced to a narrow strip of hazy pinks and greys. The city is contained within a familiar landscape convention. But for one small portion of the picture the painting could be a landscape by an artist specialising in cattle, such as John Dearman (fl. 1824–56). That portion which does represent the city is kept distinct, by being in a different colour register, and subordinate to the landscape. The aspect of Leeds that is shown is one where church towers and spires rather than smoking chimneys occupy the skyline. The tower of St Paul's Church, Park Square, is the largest and tallest, left of centre of the picture. Further to the left the tower of St John's Church can be distinguished, and to the right, the spire of Holy Trinity Church. Nonetheless, it is not the case that all signs of industrialisation are suppressed, because the other notable feature of the skyline is the square bulk of a factory building. This, from its position east of Wellington Bridge, on the River Aire, is part of Benjamin Gott's Park Mills woollen factory. What we can see is the four-storey main mill. The factory had occupied the site since 1792 and the main mill, which was for scribbling (processing raw wool) and fulling (cleaning and finishing woven cloth) had been in existence since 1802.[55] Gott's factory was at the forefront of industrial development in Leeds. The application of steam power to various stages of the manufacturing process, the bringing together on one premises of all the manufacturing stages, and the combining of the functions of merchant and manufacturer, were crucial innovations. The presence of Gott's 1802 scribbling and fulling mill in a picture probably painted in the 1820s did not signify the most modern development in industrial building, but it did give prominence to the most innovative and thoroughgoing industrial concern in Leeds. Wellington Bridge, in front of the woollen mill, can also be perceived as an industrial feature of the cityscape, and in this case it was a strikingly modern feature. It was built in 1818–19 on the initiative of Benjamin Gott, and he headed the list of subscribers.[56] It was important for facilitating and encouraging industrial development in the west of Leeds as well as around the existing Leeds bridge further east. Industrial features therefore are not omitted entirely either in the Burn *View of Leeds*, or in the Rhodes *Leeds from the Meadows*. Each in a different way displays the industrial character of the city, but at the same time existing landscape conventions contain and neutralise the city, keeping it as a minor figure to the major trope of the country.

A water-colour of *Manchester from Chester Road* (early nineteenth-century) again divides off the city along the skyline from the spreading fields, trees and canal of the middleground and foreground (Figure 33). The forms of the chimneys and church spires are all dissolved in light and have only a shadowy presence in comparison with the other elements of the picture: the stiff-limbed cows in the fields, the hedges and fences dividing the fields, the canal boats on the water, the horse and its rider towing a boat, and the farm labourer leaning against a fence in the foreground with his alert dog beside him. Together these two survey the scene, and their function, like that of the rustic figures in the Burn *View of Leeds*, is to impart an air of country peace to the subject. Not only the city itself, but also the role of the canal as a transport route for industrial raw materials and products, are subordinated to the rustic connotations of the scene. The city is almost expunged, the canal is amalgamated. It takes on the character of a river with its loosely painted surface and indefinite margins, overhung on the right by trees and bushes.

Transfiguring the city

The transformation of the city by brilliant illumination is, similarly, a strategy of the *View of Manchester* by William Wyld (1851) (Figure 7). The effect of this picture, however, is not to excise the city but to make it sacred. Rather than a placid country figure in the foreground, Wyld's painting has a family group – perhaps country folk – man, woman, child and dog in a triangular group beneath the trees on the left, suggesting a Holy Family, or a Flight to Egypt subject. The view is vast is scope, taken from a high vantage point on Kersal Moor. The low sun is behind the city. At the central point on the horizon the sun seems to burst through and partially obliterate the buildings of the city, but on the left the square shape of Manchester Cathedral stands out, as do a number of spindly chimneys, and a second church tower. On the right is a range of taller and smokier chimneys, one in particular rising twice as high as the cathedral and dwarfing the churches dotted among the factories. There is, then, a contrast between the character of the city shown on the left and right of the picture, but the effect of the sunlight is to equate the two sides, and draw the whole picture into a symmetrical composition. Trees, distant churches and distant factories alike are the verticals through which the sunlight filters, fanning out across the meadows and moorland.[57] Town and country are transformed by the grandeur of the sun. The city is mediated not through a comforting image of productive agriculture and timeless rustics, but through the sublimity of nature, which here has religious overtones. The *Art Journal* reproduced E. Goodall's engraving after this picture in 1857, and commented on the success of the picture in dealing with a difficult subject: 'His view of Manchester has a Turner-like character, and considering the materials of the composition is most agreeable'.[58] The critic does not offer any explanation of how Wyld managed to achieve this success, but he touches on a religious frame of reference in a line of poetry that he quotes when describing the factory chimneys of Manchester: 'From whatever side the spectator contemplates the city he sees long ranges of factories with their innumerable chimneys, which point "their tapering spires to heaven" but recalling to mind other associations than those to which the poet's line has reference – thoughts of active enterprise, industry and accumulating wealth.' The reference to spires pointing to heaven is qualified as soon as it is made but it nonetheless indicates that it was possible momentarily to hold both a devotional and economic response to the imaged city.

The city in focus: problems of access

The idea mooted in the *Art Journal* review, that the industrial city was a difficult subject, recurs in a pamphlet of 1839 in which a *View of Leeds* by Thomas Burras was reviewed. It is described as 'a very cleverly painted picture of a locality difficult to manage'.[59] This stock critical response to cityscape should not be taken as evidence that the city was rarely represented. It does show that there was an attitude among critics that the city was a problematic subject for artists. Nevertheless there was a steady demand for pictures of the city. The output of Thomas Burras (1790–1870) gives some indication of this. He was a Leeds artist, and was a pupil of Joseph Rhodes, the painter of *Leeds from the Meadows*.[60] A *View of Leeds* dated 1844 by Thomas Burras (Figure 34) is his only surviving painting of the town, but the subject is one that he painted repeatedly over more than thirty years of his career. Five out of seven paintings shown by him at the Leeds Exhibition of the Northern Society in 1822 were of local scenes, though not specifically of city subjects. Two pictures were sold at 35*s* each. In the following year he exhibited three views, one of which was titled *View of Leeds* and priced at ten guineas. It was not sold during the course of the exhibition.[61] The *View of Leeds* reviewed in 1839 was shown at the Leeds Public Exhibition of that year. It does not appear in the catalogue of the exhibition and so we cannot ascertain whether it was being shown by the owner, or was being exhibited and offered for sale by the artist. The same title recurs in the 1843 second Public Exhibition in Leeds. This time the *View of Leeds* by Burras was lent to the exhibition by its owner, a Mr George Morton.[62] According to the local directories, he was a paper stainer and hanger, and dealer in oilcloth or floor cloths.[63] Conceivably these three occurrences of a *View of Leeds* could refer to the same picture, but the existence of a different, 1844, *View of Leeds,* and the showing, in 1854, of two *Views of Leeds* at the Leeds Academy of Arts suggest that such views were standards in Burras's repertoire. The 1844 *View of Leeds* was owned at one point by William Binns, presumed in an article by Terry Friedman to have been a member of the banking and bookselling Binns family.[64] He could well have been the William Binns who exhibited four pictures in the 1839 Leeds Public Exhibition, who can be identified as a cloth dresser in the family firm of James Binns and Sons with mills at New Park Street and Grace Street.[65] Burras's prices for the *View of Leeds from*

Armley Old Hall and *View of Leeds from Richmond Hill* in 1854 were £210 each, far higher than the £63 he asked for a Scottish landscape in 1853.[66] The general impression is of an artist catering for a demand among commercial and industrial local patrons, and able to command substantial and rising prices over the period for paintings of the city: indeed, for oil paintings – a fact which discounts Louis Hawes's suggestion (p. 196 above) that this subject was generally restricted to prints.

The surviving *View of Leeds* by Burras (1844) fits into the pattern of pictures using an archaic rural foreground to qualify the view of the city (Figure 34). The foreground consists of rough stone walls, tangled bushes and low trees, a track with horse and cart, some rustic figures, a substantial farm with a tidy haystack in the enclosed yard, and groups of sheep and cows in the fields. The exaggerated scale of the stile, and the uneven weedy path leading from it (the stile seems nearly as large as the horse or the cart), serves to suppress any idea of the track as a busy thoroughfare or transport route to the city. The wagon takes its place as an element of the pastoral alongside the courtship of the milkmaid and swain who lean on a gate and converse. But in this picture the distant city is not faint or hazy, or compressed into a narrow strip. It spreads in equal detail and equal density all across the horizon, and occupies about a third of the canvas not devoted to sky. The fairly even south-east lighting on the scene brings into relief not just every factory chimney and every factory building or warehouse, but also every gable-end in the staggered rows of terraced housing, and so the recession is established by a dozen or twenty distinct planes. The buildings of the city are not a dark undifferentiated mass with some silhouettes of spires or chimneys giving clues as to its composition. The picture undertakes to show every window, chimney and roof angle of every church, house, factory or public bulding alike. The effect is one where the competing faces of the new town are evened out. The picture does not offer a city identified by its ecclesiastical monuments, nor by monuments of industry, nor by the image of corporate or group commercial edifices, nor by its new housing developments. All are presented in orderly coexistence. Smoke from chimneys is reduced to tiny puffs, so that the factories do not blot out other features of the scene. No one manufacturing establishment is allowed to stand for industry. Gott's Park Mills are shown even more clearly than in Rhodes's *Leeds from the Meadows* (Figure 35). Not just the main mill but the long building forming the frontage to Wellington Street, with its characteristic belfry, the drying houses along the river, the spinning and weaving shops, and the domed gasometer house in the mill yard are all shown. But this is just one identifiable establishment among dozens. Obviously there is a political difference between a painting where industry is represented exclusively by the establishment of a singularly successful Tory Anglican industrialist, who was an employer on a very large scale, and who was accepted socially and politically by the Tory merchant community which had a virtual monopoly of local political influence in the early years of the nineteenth century, and a painting like the Burras *View of Leeds*, where the notion of industry includes every establishment large or small, Whig or Tory, Anglican or Dissenting, and where large and small-scale trading concerns could be identified too.

Comparable precision is displayed in a view of *Leeds taken from Beeston Hill* (1833), etched by J. W. Cook and engraved by R. C. Reeve after a painting by Robert Buttery (Figure 36). Here, too, buildings are individually delineated. The picture separates them out to such an extent that they seem exaggeratedly isolated from each other, and the city seems extensive but not densely packed. The sharp angles, smooth surfaces and uniform lighting on the town make it resemble a collection of wooden models; everything seems miniaturised.

The structuring device (seen in the Burras and other views) of splitting the picture into pastoral and urban sections is scarcely evident in this picture. As a consequence, it offers a different kind of access to the image of the city for the viewer. In the Burras *View of Leeds* there was a contradiction for the viewer between the kind of attention invited by the two halves of the picture. From the pastoral foreground the city is distant and alien. If the viewer skims over the foreground and attends to the details of the city itself, he or she is offered the delight of recognition and participation. The industrialist can locate his factory, his house, the church where he worships and the market where he trades. The picture employs a dichotomy between town and country but does not use it in a synthesising or coherent way. The dichotomy is not used to envelop the urban in a reassuring rustic context because the separation between the two is so complete. There is no blurring and no rhyming between town and country. *Leeds taken from Beeston Hill* by Buttery moves away from that dichotomy, formulating instead a notion of the countryside as, primarily, an area of recreation for the city, using the country-city axis to oppose leisure and industry – a phenomenon of the modern industrial social system. There are rustic figures in the picture and peaceful-looking cattle and sheep in the fields. We see a farmer and his man busy in a field and a woman milking a cow, but these are not the principal figures. The principal figures are seen in the foreground, where the lane and the margin of a field are populated with townsfolk out for a walk, displaying themselves and enjoying the view. These people occupy and identify the space in much the same way as the ladies and gentlemen shown in some of the street views of Leeds and

Manchester discussed above. A single woman wearing a bonnet and pelisse and holding a rolled parasol stands on the extreme right. Her stance suggests that she is, without any suggestion of impropriety, courting male admiration. Her rolled parasol, contrasted with the matronly spread parasol of the wife in the adjacent figure group, recalls the remark made in a provincial paper of the early 1820s: 'It is the fashion now not to hold up the parasol for it only prevents the men getting a glimpse at us, but merely to carry it dangling in the hand to show that you've got one.'[67] Ranged along the fence are a smartly-dressed family group, a young man in beaver hat and tail-coat, and finally a man in shirtsleeves with his dog on a lead, perhaps a city artisan out for the afternoon with his dog. On the path another elegantly dressed woman with her two children, the boy holding a hoop, has stopped to exchange a few words with a traveller. These mainly bourgeois figures, with the harmonious admixture of a worker at rest, are town dwellers. The traveller with his broad hat, backpack and staff is on his way towards the town, as are the man, woman and child, the woman bearing a small bundle. These last could be approaching Leeds from a neighbouring farm or village. Like the travellers in the E. Roberts engraving of the Commercial Buildings, they show that Leeds is worth visiting. Their humble, though respectable dress, shows up by contrast the wealth and sophistication of Leeds. The multiple planes of the Burras *View of Leeds* are found in the Buttery view too, but here they extend beyond the city, throughout the landscape. The fences and hedges of the field divisions, and the gradually diminishing figures dotted over the landscape, establish a series of grounds, each with its identifiable activity. Beyond the woman milking, five men can be seen stretching cloth on to tenter frames to dry. Beyond this field is another, where mounds of hay are arranged. The industrial premises of the city, potteries, flax works and woollen mills, and the tiny railway wagons, visibly carrying coal into the heart of the city, are further instances of productive activity, directly continuous with the agricultural activities of the fields. Although this picture does not show the rural mills, it is the closest of all the views discussed to the landscape evoked by W. Cooke Taylor (p. 215 above), where the presence of factories in the fields made for a continuity between the agricultural and the industrial rather than a rupture between city and country. The picture is organised around a division between leisure and work. The spectator is at leisure, and he or she stands with the bourgeois family group, looking over the first fence. The productive labour of the town and countryside alike is the satisfactory object of their gaze. Moreover it is the precondition of their well-being. The pleasant spectacle of the industrious town enables them to promenade as a secondary spectacle, in their fashionable attire. This dual

226 *The culture of capital*

focus is expressed by the alternating fronts and backs of the figures along the fence: looking and being looked at.

The advancing city: dismantling the prospect

A different sort of departure from an oppositional use of city and country is seen in two final works included in this discussion. These are both water-colours. One has already been mentioned (p. 196 above), a view of *Leeds* by J. M. W. Turner (1816), probably painted as one of many Yorkshire views and intended for use as an illustration to the *History of Richmondshire* (Figure 38). The other is a water-colour, *Leeds from Rope Hill* (1827–31), by a French artist, Alphonse Dousseau, who spent many years in Leeds and the north of England (Figure 37). Dousseau is stated to have painted more than a hundred views of Yorkshire, Lancashire, Cheshire, Cumberland and Westmorland between 1823 and 1869.[68] In the view by Turner, the countryside is formulated neither as rural idyll nor as recreational space, but rather as industrialised countryside. A large field stretches from the foreground into the middle ground of the picture, but it is not a neat enclosure for sheep or cattle, nor for tenter frames. It is an irregular space, uneven in level. Its margins are not all visible and it is the site of a variety of disparate activities. On the left two men are lifting cloth on to a tenter frame. This is not the rhythmic, almost balletic activity of the team in the picture by Buttery, but a slow job with heavy swathes of cloth. A man and woman in the centre of the picture are gathering something, probably mushrooms.[69] This is not a traditional pastoral image, but it is necessarily a country activity. On the right of the field two labourers are building a stone wall along the road edge. The physical effort of this job is emphasised even more as they strain to lift a massive stone block. This process of building the wall is one that effects a transformation from the scrubby ground on the left of the picture, via a pile of unshaped stone and the heap of mortar, to the regularity of the wall and pavement on the right. In this activity the relatively empty field is being transmuted into the throng of the street on the right, where tradesmen and women make their way up the hill. The strange and indeterminate space of the rural margins of the town is being made into the town proper: earth and stone become an urban thoroughfare. The image of the city presented by this picture is not really embodied in the hazy background, where a few mills and the church towers of Leeds emerge faintly from illuminated smoke. Rather, it is one where the city invades the foreground. The progress up the hill of people with milk churns and baskets, one with a sheep carcass wrapped in cloth over his shoulders, represents the advance and expansion of the city. The sharp perspective produced by the second vanishing point on this side of the picture places the figures one on top of another as if they are hard on each other's heels. These figures drive the viewer back. There is no mythically permanent rural position from which to view the picture because the identity of the countryside is rendered so uncertain. Nor is there the access offered by the view by Buttery of *Leeds taken from Beeston Hill.* There is no area of leisure in the picture from which the well-ordered labour of the city can be viewed with complacency and proprietory satisfaction and pride. In this sense, the Turner view of Leeds is exceptional. It is not exceptional in representing the industrial features of the view as might be concluded from Hawes's account (p. 196 above). It uses compositional elements found in a large body of other visual material, but it is exceptional in that it does not resolve the elements in the standard ways available.

The water-colour by Alphonse Dousseau, *Leeds from Rope Hill,* makes an interesting comparison with the Turner painting. Like Turner's *Leeds,* it gives us no picturesque rustic farm buildings, haystacks or winding lanes. A featureless square brick building stands on the right beside the gates of the Middleton Railway line, which forms the central feature of the foreground. The Middleton Railway line, connecting coal-workings a few miles outside Leeds to its industrial centre and transport systems, was one of the first railways to be built. It was in operation from 1812 and was renowned for its use of a steam locomotive – indeed, it was the first steam railway. On the left of Dousseau's picture is a low rectangular house, with a garden prosaically divided into a dozen vegetable plots. High hedges give the impression of access barred rather than vistas opened in this landscape. Small trees interrupt the view of fields rather than framing it. The view of the city beyond is unusually smoky. The glassworks in particular, with its tall conical chimneys, dominates the view, belching out smoke. The mound of houses on the right of the town shows them piled up with very little illusion of recession, and with factory chimneys punctuating the edge of the slope all the way up.

Notes attached to the water-colour identify the churches, pottery, china and glass factories. Nonetheless the buildings are not represented so as to invite the viewer into the picture to lay claim to his or her town – or part of it. Yet the overall effect is one at the extreme other end of the spectrum from Marshall Craig's *Manchester from Mount Pleasant* (Figure 30). We are confronted with the city of Leeds as a highly specific and knowable centre of a diversity of industrial activities. Leeds viewers could recognise it, while others would be forced to acknowledge the specificity of Leeds. Thus, although viewed from a distance from slightly outside the city, the city/country opposition is less relevant. This is not only because it details a specific worked landscape and specific industrial processes, but also because the viewer is not given a secure position outside the processes. The city therefore is not represented as a series of architectural features, whose purposes sunlight or mist can efface, but as a site of human labour, activity, and production. This quality pervades its surroundings and the distant prospect now ensures a sufficient scale from which to comprehend the vastness of this enterprise.

Conclusion

In this chapter we have challenged the existing arguments about the representation – or lack of representation – of the industrial city in the nineteenth century. There is a considerable amount of visual material in which Leeds and Manchester are figured. It has been necessary to go beyond the over-simplified art–historical criteria of what constitutes an image of an industrial city. Manchester and Leeds were not merely collections of factories or foundries. The city of industrial capitalism has to be broached in terms of its multiple social relations, processes and class formations. We have therefore offered readings of images of new buildings and public spaces in the commercial centres of exchange and consumption, as well as analysing the views taken from outside the cities' centres. The purpose has not been to produce definitive interpretations of meanings contained within paintings or prints, but rather to specify the potential functions and effects of such images upon an historical and ideological field of social practices and meanings. It has been part of our purpose to show how cultural products, in this case images, provide a specific kind of access to historical analysis of social life and social experience. The works discussed are not documents, reflecting an historical situation or the interests of a class. As the case of the factory reform banner or the plates of old Manchester made by John Ralston indicate, the greatest caution needs to be used to discover the exact and local meanings images may have had in their immediate, highly partisan and tendentious context of production and use.

We have also challenged the idea that standard representational formats inhibited artists in dealing with new kinds of city and their social processes. That is not to say that we ignore the landscape and topographical conventions. These were the starting-point for those both making and viewing the representations of urban subjects. Nonetheless, in the range of works discussed we have stressed the manipulations and manoeuvrings within and between conventions. In the resulting images those conventions, such as the distant prospect or the grand view of public splendour, have been radically transformed by the attempt to use them to deal with a shifting territory of new social relations and economic purposes. In the tensions between the inherited modalities of townscape or landscape and the modern industrial city being represented, we suggest that it is possible to read the inscription of the historical and ideological preoccupations of those inhabiting, meeting and trading in, and commenting on the city. Thus in views of Leeds Central Market, the model of Rowlandson's Covent Garden is useful to recall as a means to sharpen recognition of the unease and ambiguity that pervades the nineteenth-century representation of the shopping street. In the introduction we referred to the distant prospect taken from a viewpoint outside the city. We discuss a number of views of Leeds and Manchester which employ such a framework, while showing how different are their applications and how diversely – and uneasily – the spectator is positioned. In the example of the view of Leeds by Turner, the distant prospect convention is invoked but eroded, as the activities of the city threaten to engulf the spectator who is thus dispaced from his or her controlling viewpoint. The invasion of the surrounding territory by urban, industrial and commercial activities, from work to leisure, becomes visible precisely through the erosion of the typical boundaries which the artistic conventions signified.

The images which we have analysed used the modes and rhetorics which constituted artistic practice at the time, but they were inherited from and formed by an older social formation. Applied to new materials, in an emergent social formation with its developing social geographies, they were redefined, while the meanings generated for that novel scene and social life, the industrial city, were qualified in the act of being thus represented. We are arguing therefore that such images were both structured – by the conventions and their interaction with the historical conditions of the production of the images in the themes to which the conventions were applied – and structuring. These visual representations of the city, in conjunction with related discourses (literary, medical, legal, political, and so on), contributed to the perception of social life in the cities. In this preliminary study of the image of the industrial city in nineteenth-century English bourgeois culture, we suggest that the city was as central a preoccupation in visual representation as it was in those other discourses and practices which, collectively but heterogeneously, constituted the culture of the emergent urban bourgeoisie.

Notes

We would like to acknowledge valuable assistance given by Professor Maurice Beresford; Mrs Forster of the Thoresby Society; Mrs Heap and the staff of Leeds City Libraries, Department of Local History; Mr P. C. D. Brears of Leeds City Museum; Sandra Martin of City of Manchester Art Galleries.

1. I. B. Nadel and F. S. Schwarzbach (eds.), *Victorian Artists and the City*, Pergamon Press, Oxford, 1980.

    Throughout the text we use the terms 'towns' and 'cities' collectively to underscore the ambiguity of the word 'city'. 'City' is a legal entity, either as the seat of a bishopric or in terms of legal incorporation. However, in the nineteenth century, 'city' came to be used of any large towns or populous districts (for instance in the 1851 Census) and 'city' became the term in which the debates about urbanisation were couched. For full discussion see B. I. Coleman, *The Idea of the City in Nineteenth-Century Britain*, Routledge & Kegan Paul, London, 1973.

2. For a different view, see J. P. Hulin and P. Coustillas, *Victorian Writers and the City*, Publications de l'Université de Lille, 1979.

3. G. Simmel, 'The Metropolis and Mental Life', reprinted in R. Sennett (ed.), *Classic Essays in the Culture of Cities*, Appleton-Century-Crofts, New York, 1969.

4. For example, in 1858 Augustus Egg exhibited a trilogy of paintings which are now known as *Past and Present*. The theme is the discovery of a middle-class wife's adultery, the destruction of her family and her subsequent degradation and possible death. The *Art Journal* was disturbed by the treatment of such a subject in the Royal Academy and commented: 'Although the domestic wreck illustrated in these pictures . . . may be in real life of daily occurrence, it is a subject too poignant for a series of paintings. We are saturated by the public prints with the details of such incidents, and would rather fall back upon the consoling influences of Art.' *Art Journal*, June 1858, pp. 167–8. The passage indicates both the exchange between different kinds of representation and the threat that the line that divided art from its competitors would be dissolved.

5. Extended research on this topic, the image of the city in nineteenth-century culture, is being funded by the University of Leeds and undertaken by Caroline Arscott and Griselda Pollock.

6. Examples include W. P. Frith's *Derby Day* (1858) and *The Railway Station* (1862), William Maw Egley, *Omnibus Life in London* (1859), George Elgar Hicks, *The General Post Office: One Minute to Six* (1860) and George Frederic Watts, *Found Drowned* (*c.* 1850).

7. Johnson reproduces William Wyld's *View of Manchester* (1851) (Coll. H. M. Queen) and Eyre Crowe's *Dinner Hour, Wigan* (1874) (City of Manchester Art Galleries).

8. See Coleman, *op. cit.*, pp. 3–4.

9. G. Stedman Jones, *Outcast London* Oxford University Press, London, 1971, and A. Briggs, *Victorian Cities* (1963), Pelican Books, London, 1968.

10. See F. D. Klingender, *Art and the Industrial Revolution* (1947), Paladin Books, London, 1972.

11. Coleman, *op. cit.*, pp. 2–3.

12. Giovanna Procacci, 'Social economy and the government of poverty', *Ideology and Consciousness*, 1978, No. 4.

13. J. Donzelot, *The Policing of Families*, trans. R. Hirley, London, 1979, esp. Gilles

Deleuze, Foreword, 'The Rise of the Social'.
14 Robert Southey, *Letters from England* (1807), ed. and intr. J. Simmons, Sutton, Gloucester, 1984, Letter 61.
15 [T. B. Macaulay], 'Southey's colloquies on society', *Edinburgh Review*, January 1830, Vol. 50, p. 528, cited in Coleman, *op. cit.*, p. 63.
16 J. P. Kay, *The Moral and Physical Condition of the Working Classes Employed in the Cotton Manufacture in Manchester*, London, 1832.
17 F. Engels, *The Condition of the Working Class in England in 1844* (1845) trans. and ed. W. O. Henderson and W. H. Chaloner, Blackwell, Oxford, 1971.
18 'I know of nothing more imposing than the view one obtains of the river when sailing from the sea up to London Bridge . . . The traveller has good reason to marvel at England's greatness even before he steps on English soil.' *Ibid.*, p. 30.
19 Cf Letter XVII on Leeds, in the *Morning Chronicle*, 1850, 'A short walk from the Briggate, in the direction in which Kirkgate branches off from the main entry, will conduct the visitor into a perfect wilderness of foulness.' Reprinted in J. Ginswick, *Labour and the Poor in England and Wales 1849–51*, Vol. 1, Frank Cass & Co., London and Totowa, New Jersey, 1983, p. 195.
20 J. T. Ward, 'Leeds and the factory reform movement', *Publications of the Thoresby Society*, Vol. 46, 1963, p. 95.
21 Cf. W. Cooke Taylor, *Notes of a Tour in the Manufacturing Districts of Lancashire* (1841), reprinted Frank Cass and Co., London, 1968. His investigation was sponsored by the Anti-Corn Law League and his advocacy of the Factory System utilised this notion: 'I set out with a determination to see and judge for myself; I repeated my visits to the manufacturing districts for the purpose of testing the accuracy of my former observations' (Preface, n.p.).
22 E. Baines, *History of the Cotton Manufacture in Great Britain*, Fisher, Son & Co., London, 1835, p. 455.
23 Cited in H. Broadbent (ed.), *Views of the Ancient Buildings in Manchester* (1823–5), Oldham, 1975, n.p.
24 For an interesting discussion of the social history of the promenade see Meyer Schapiro, 'The Social Bases of Art' [1936], in D. Shapiro (ed.), *Social Realism: Art as a Weapon*, Frederick Ungar, New York, 1973, pp. 118–27.
25 *An Historical Guide to Leeds and Its Environs*, T. Fenteman & Sons, Leeds, 1858, p. 5.
26 *Ibid.*, pp. 5–6.
27 It is interesting to note that in this same article the commentator refers to the most notable civic improvements organised by Baron Haussman for Napoleon III in Paris. 'Any street of the character we have named ought to be built like the great streets of Paris, on some uniform plan.'
28 See R. Sennett, *The Fall of Public Man*, Cambridge University Press, 1977. See also Janet Wolff, 'The invisible flâneuse: women and the literature of modernity', *Theory, Culture and Society*, Vol. 2, No. 3, 1985.
29 K. Grady, 'Commercial, Marketing and Retail Amenities 1700–1914', in D. Fraser (ed.), *A History of Modern Leeds*, Manchester University Press, 1980. See also 'The provision of markets in Leeds 1822–9' in *Publications of the Thoresby Society*, 1976, Vol. LIV, Pt. 3.
30 e.g. *The Stranger's Guide through Leeds and its Environs*, H. Cullingworth, Leeds, 1831.
31 K. Grady, *The Provision of Public Buildings in the West Riding of Yorkshire 1600–1840*, unpublished Leeds Ph.D., 1980, pp. 170ff.
32 It is notable that a neo-Greek classical style was favoured for most public

buildings during the early part of century. Edward Baines wrote in the *Leeds Mercury*, 18 September 1823, that 'This is an age of combined effort for public purposes.'
33 *The Strangers' Guide Through Leeds and its Environs*, H. Cullingworth, Leeds, 1842, p. 15.
34 L. Davidoff and C. Hall, 'The Architecture of Public and Private Life: English Middle-Class Society in a Provincial Town 1780–1850', in D. Fraser and A. Sutcliffe (eds.), *The Pursuit of Urban History*, Edward Arnold, London, 1983.
35 W. Cooke Taylor, *op. cit.*, p. 10.
36 Grady provides figures of a prospective return on investment of twenty per cent offered as opposed to four per cent interest on government consols (*op. cit.*).
37 M. Beresford dicusses the various projects for a city centre in 'The Face of Leeds', in D. Fraser (ed.), *A History of Modern Leeds*, Manchester University Press, 1980.
38 See M. Cowling, 'The artist as anthropologist', *Art History*, Vol. 6, No. 4, December 1983.
39 T. Wemyss Reid, *Memoir of J. D. Heaton*, Longmans Green & Co., London, 1883, p. 147.
40 K. Marx, *Capital*, Vol. 1, Ch. 1, 'The Commodity'.
41 B. Love, *Manchester As It Is* (1939), reprinted E. J. Morton, Manchester 1971, pp. 202–3. Restriction of entry to factories was often caused by intense competitiveness and fear of industrial espionage.
42 *Ibid.*, pp. 203–4.
43 N. Taylor, 'The Awful Sublimity of the Victorian City', in H. J. Dyos and M. Wolff (eds.), *The Victorian City*, Routledge & Kegan Paul, London, 1973, Vol. 2, pp. 431–48.
44 E. Burke, *A Philosophical Enquiry into the Origin of Our Ideas of the Sublime and Beautiful* (1757), reprinted Routledge & Kegan Paul, London, 1958.
45 R. Williams, *The Country and the City*, Chatto & Windus, Glasgow, 1973.
46 W. Cooke Taylor, *op. cit.*, Letter II, p. 21.
47 *Ibid.*
48 W. Cobbett, *Rural Rides* (1830), Vol. 2, Everyman Edition, n.d., p. 253.
49 *Ibid.*, p. 257.
50 Robert Baker, 'On the industrial and sanitary economy of the Borough of Leeds in 1858', *Journal of the Statistical Society of London*, Vol. XXI, 1858.
51 E. J. Connell and M. Ward, 'Industrial Development 1780–1914', in D. Fraser (ed.), *A History of Modern Leeds*, p. 168.
52 Some examples of local building materials for Leeds are millstone grit, found in Bramley Fall Quarries, brickmaking clay in East Leeds, Holbeck and Farnley, clay for sanitary pipes, blast furnaces, etc., in Wortley, Farnley and Barwick, and slate quarried at Thorner. E. J. Connell and M. Ward, *op. cit.*
53 Studies of building activity nationally, based on statistics of brick production, have shown peaks in 1815 and roughly every ten years until 1849, with large expansion in the 1830s, and twin peaks in 1836 and 1840. E. W. Cooney, 'Long waves in building in the British economy of the nineteenth century', *The Economic History Review*, SS., 13, 2, 1960, pp. 257–62.
54 E. J. Connell and M. Ward, *op. cit.*, p. 172, and Maurice Beresford, 'The Face of Leeds 1780–1914' in D. Fraser (ed.), *op. cit.*, pp. 72–112.
55 The painting does not make clear the exact disposition of buildings in the Park Mills complex, so it is not possible to date it by comparing the buildings shown with the ground plan of the Mills in 1815 and information about alterations

made in 1825–30. See W. B. Crump, 'The History of Gott's Mills', in W. B. Crump (ed.), 'The Leeds woollen industry', *Publications of the Thoresby Society*, Vol. XXXII, 1929.
56 Wellington Bridge, 1818–19, built by John Rennie, cost £7,000. R. Unwin, 'Leeds Becomes A Transport Centre', in D. Fraser (ed.), *op. cit.*, p. 137, and W. B. Crump, *op. cit.*, p. 264.
57 It is interesting to compare the painting with the engraving of it by E. Goodall which makes many minor changes in the composition. The particularly tall factory chimney is omitted. Chimneys are made generally more even in height and far less smoky. The dark mass of the cathedral is made correspondingly less prominent. The buildings where the sun breaks through are darkened, so that the whole skyline is more unified, making the picture work in rather a different way.
58 *Art Journal*, 1857, p. 204.
59 Edward Baines, jun., and William West, *A Description of Some of the Principal Paintings, Machinery, Models, Apparatus and other Curiosities at the Leeds Public Exhibition, 1839*, Edward Baines & Sons, Leeds, 1839.
60 W. Thorp, *John N. Rhodes, A Yorkshire Painter, 1809–1842*, Richard Jackson, Leeds and Bemrose & Sons Ltd, London, 1904, p. 27; Terry F. Friedman, 'Leeds in 1844', *Leeds Arts Calendar*, No. 79, 1976, pp. 27–32.
61 Northern Society Catalogues, with manuscript additions, in Leeds City Reference Library. *View of Leeds*, NS 1823, No. 114.
62 *Catalogue of the Second Public Exhibition of Paintings, Sculpture, Curiosities, etc*, Leeds, 1843, p. 21. *View of Leeds*, Picture Gallery, no. 18.
63 1839, house at 12 Warwick Place; by 1843 at 2 Springfield Mount. Shop in Commercial Street. Votes for Liberal candidates registered in 1837.
64 Terry F. Friedman, *op. cit.*
65 Address in 1837, Park Lane; 1839, Springfield Place; 1841, Little Woodhouse; 1843 and 1845, 35 New Park Street. Votes for the Liberal candidates in the 1841 election.
66 Catalogues of the first and second Annual Exhibition of the Academy of Arts, Leeds, 1853 and 1854.
67 *The Lewes and Brighthelmston Journal*, 1823, quoted in C. W. and P. Cunnington, *Handbook of English Costume in the Nineteenth Century*, Faber & Faber, London, 1959, p. 399.
68 Notes transcribed from the back of the picture, Thoresby Society Library, Leeds.
69 This would fit in with the autumn date of composition – probably early September 1816. David Hill, *In Turner's Footsteps*, John Murray, 1984. Thanks to David Hill for discussing this picture with us.

INDEX

Agnew, Thomas 53, 54–5
Aikin, John 47
Aire and Calder Warehouse, Leeds 213
Allen, Joseph 58
Amicus 164, 167, 171, 177, 187
Anderson, Perry 2–3, 4, 5, 18, 19
Armstrong, Thomas 57
Arnold, Matthew 46
Art Treasures Exhibition of 1857, Manchester 38, 39, 71–2, 147
Art Union Journal, Art Journal 51, 54, 55, 56, 176, 177, 221, 222
Ashtons of Hyde 33
Athenaeum 129, 130, 176
Awakening Conscience, The (Hunt) 12, 159–87

Babylonian Marriage Market, The (Long) 130
Baines, Edward 33, 141, 200–1
Baines, Edward, Jr. 101
Baker, Robert 216
Bamford, Samuel 47
Barrit, Thomas 49
Bartolomé, M. M. de 92, 105–6, 108
Bates, Edmund 147
Bell, Quentin 135
Bergier, J. F. 4
Borzello, Frances 125
Bradley, William 57–8, 59
Bright, John 7, 18
Broken Vows, (Calderon) 183
Brown, Ford Madox 73, 124, 160, 162
Brown, Mather 59
Browning, Elizabeth Barrett 138
Buchanan, William 161
Burke, Peter 8
Burn, Henry (*View of Leeds from near the Halifax New Road*) 218–19, 220
Burras, Thomas (*View of Leeds*) 222–4, 225
Buttery, Robert (*Leeds taken from Beeston Hill*) 224–6, 227

Carlisle, Earl of 96
Carlyle, Jane 123

Carlyle, Thomas 120–1
Chadwick, Edwin 198–9, 201
Chartism 5, 153, 165
Checkland, Sydney 5
Chetham Society 7, 56
Children's Holiday, The (Hunt) 166, 168–71, 177
Chorley, Katherine 63, 121
Clark, T. J. 9
Claudio and Isabella (Hunt) 166–7
Claxton, Marshall 145–6
Cobbett, William 215–16, 217
Cobden, Richard 7, 18, 31, 72
Craig, William Marshall (*Manchester from Mount Pleasant*) 218, 227
Cummins, Charles 145

Davidoff, Leonore 118, 119
Dodd, Thomas 52
Dousseau, Alphonse (*Leeds from Rope Hill*) 226, 227–8
Duval, Charles 60

Egg, Augustus 129, 165–6, 175
Ellison, Michael 100
Engels, Friedrich 199, 201

Fairbairn, Peter 160, 162, 164, 165
Fairbairn, Thomas 12, 162–71, 185, 187
Farington, Joseph 48, 50
Faulkner, B. R. 58
Field, John 17
Fiennes, Celia 46
First Class – The Meeting (Soloman) 184
Ford, John 54
Ford, William 47, 51, 53, 64
Freud, Sigmund 182–3

Gaskell, Elizabeth 9, 123, 128
Gatrell, V. A. C. 23
Gibbs, Henry 54
Girouard, Mark 119–20
Glasgow School of Design 127
Going to Service (Redgrave) 180

Index

Gott, Benjamin 155, 220
Gott, Joseph 145
Great Exhibition of 1851 25
Green, William 48–9
Greig, J. 205, 206
Grundy, John Clowes 53–4

Hadjinicolaou, Nicos 9, 159
Halèvy, E. 5
Hall, Catherine 118, 119, 120
Hardman, William 49, 50, 64
Hawes, Louis 195–6
Hawthorne, Nathaniel 60
Haydon, B. R. 138, 144, 160, 165
Heaton, Ellen 136, 160
Heaton, John 143, 210
Heywood, Abel 39
Heywood family 29, 33
Heywood, George 68
Holberry, Samuel 86
Houldsworth, Thomas 6
Hudson, J. W. 117
Hunt, William Holman 12, 160, 162, 165, 166, 173, 183, 184, 185

Illidge, Thomas Henry 58
Industrial Revolution 4–5, 25, 26, 118, 194

Jackson, George 70
Jewsbury, Geraldine 120–1, 123, 128
Johnson, E. D. H. 193, 194, 195, 218
Joynes, Sara E. 108, 109

Kay-Shuttleworth, James 69, 198
Kershaw, James 119
Kusamitsu, Toshio 139–40

Lee, engraver 205
Leeds 191, 195, 203–10, 211, 213, 216, 217, 218–20, 222–8
Leigh, Roger Holt 144–5
London 20, 21, 22, 23, 33, 49–50, 193–5, 196, 199, 215
Love, B. 212
Loyd, Edward 51, 64
Lyceum Club, Sheffield 99–100

Macauley, Thomas Babington 198
McConnel, Henry 64, 123
Manchester 6, 22, 23, 31, 45–73, 191, 195, 199, 201–3, 212, 217, 218, 220–2, 228

Manchester Academy of Fine Arts 62
Manchester Athenaeum 88, 94
Manchester from Chester Road 220–1
Manchester School 7, 32
Manchester Statistical Society 127
Marx 1, 10, 19, 211
Mayer, Arno 27
Mechanics' Institution, Leeds 143–4, 153
Mechanics' Institution, Manchester 69–70, 71, 117
Mechanics' Institute, Sheffield 88, 89, 91, 95, 97–8, 100, 102, 105
Merriman, John 8
Moers, Ellen 128
Morley, John 18
Morris, R. J. 140
Mudie's circulating library 122
Mulready, William 123–4, 127, 130

Nadel, I. B. and Schwarzbach, F. S. 191–2, 193, 195, 218
Nairn, Tom, 18, 19
Nasmyth, James 69, 70
Nelson, W. (*Commercial Buildings, Leeds*) 207
Northern Society, Leeds 147, 155, 222
Nunneley, Thomas 147–8

Orme, Daniel 58
Oxford Road Twist Co. mill 212–13

Parker, Hugh 86
Passavant, J. D. 50–1
Past and Present (Egg) 129
Pay for Peeping (Horsley) 183
Philips, John Leigh 49, 50, 64
Phillips, Sir Richard 86
Plint, Thomas 123, 124, 135–6, 155, 160, 161, 162, 171
Polytechnic Exhibitions, Leeds 12, 135–55
Potter, Edmund 61, 65
Potter, Richard 50
Pre-Raphaelites 135, 185
Prince Albert 38, 39
Proctor, Richard 52

Queen Victoria 39, 125, 139

Ralston, John (*Views of the Ancient Buildings in Manchester*) 201–3, 210, 228
Rhodes, Joseph (*The Central Market, &c,*

Leeds) 210
Rhodes, Joseph (*Leeds from the Meadows*) 219–20
Rhodes, Joseph (*The Old Moot Hall*) 203–4, 205
Roberts, E. J. 208–9, 225
Robinson, Revd J. 101–2
Rogerson, Joseph 137
Romney, Peter 48
Royal Academy 50, 51, 163, 165, 171, 176
Royal Academy Schools 127
Royal Manchester Institution 51, 52, 55–6, 64, 65–8, 70, 71
Rubinstein, W. D. 18, 19, 20–4, 25, 30, 31, 32, 34
Ruskin, John 120, 121, 122, 136, 160, 171–8, 180, 181, 184, 186, 187

Sadler, Michael Thomas 147
School of Design, Manchester 56, 70, 71
Select Committee on Arts and Manufactures 1835–6 69, 70
Shaw, Joshua, 48, 49
Sheffield 83–109
Sheffield Athenaeums 12, 83–109
Sheffield Club 104–5, 106
Smiles, Samuel 23
Smith, Dennis 105–6, 108
Smith, W., Jr. 92–3
Southey, R. 67, 198
Stephens, F. G. 186
Stone, Frank 57
Stone, L. and J. C. F. 28
Stubbs, Patricia 129
Sutherland, J. A. 122–3
Swainson, Birley & Co. factory 214, 217

Symons, Jelinger C. 83, 87

Taylor, Thomas 203
Taylor, W. Cooke 208, 214–15, 217, 225
Temple Mills, Leeds 211
Thompson, E. P. 3, 19
Turner, J. M. W. 10, 123, 149–50, 196, 226–7

Union Street mills, Manchester 212–13

Victoria Park, Manchester 119

Ward, H. G. 83, 87, 89
Watts, James, 28, 38–9
Webb, Igor 3, 4
Weber, Max 10
Whitechapel Art Gallery 125–6
Whittock, N. (*The Aire and Calder, at Leeds*) 213
Whittock, N. (*Central Market, Leeds*) 209
Whittock, N. (*Commercial Buildings, Leeds*) 207–8
Whittock, N. (*Corn Exchange, Leeds*) 205
Whittock, N. (*Court House, Leeds*) 209
Wiener, Martin 3–4, 5, 18, 19, 20, 25–30, 31, 32
Williams, Raymond 2, 129, 214
Winning Gloves (Horsley) 179
Wood, G. W. 66–7
Work (Brown) 124, 160, 161–2, 171
Wyld, William (*Manchester from Kersal Moor*) 194, 221–2

Zanetti, Vittore 52, 54